COMPUTERIZED TESTING SUPPLEMENT FOR INSTRUMENT RATING

1996

U.S. DEPARTMENT OF TRANSPORTATION
FEDERAL AVIATION ADMINISTRATION
Flight Standards Service

PREFACE

This computerized testing supplement is designed for use by the Federal Aviation Administration (FAA) for testing centers and computer testing designees (CTD's) in conjunction with administration of the following computer-assisted tests:

    Instrument Rating - Airplane (IRA)
    Instrument Rating - Rotorcraft/Helicopter (IRH)
    Instrument Rating - Airplane (added rating) (IAS)
    Instrument Rating - Rotorcraft/Helicopter (added rating) - (IHS)
    Instrument Rating - Foreign Pilot (IFP)
    Instrument Flight Instructor - Airplane (FII)
    Instrument Flight Instructor - Rotorcraft/Helicopter - (FIH)
    Instrument Flight Instructor - Airplane (added rating) (AIF)
    Instrument Flight Instructor - Rotorcraft/Helicopter (added rating) (HIF)
    Ground Instructor - Instrument (IGI)

Applicants for Instrument Rating Certificates will be required to use FAA-CT-8080-3B, Computerized Testing Supplement for Instrument Rating, to answer those computer-assisted airman knowledge test questions which reference figures.

Comments regarding FAA-CT-8080-3B should be directed to:

    Federal Aviation Administration
    Operations Standards Development Section, AFS-631
    P.O. Box 25082
    Oklahoma City, OK 73125

CONTENTS

	Page
Preface	iii
Contents	v

APPENDIX 2

LEGEND 1.—Abbreviations	1
LEGEND 2.—Airport/Facility Directory	2
LEGEND 3.—Airport/Facility Directory	3
LEGEND 4.—Airport/Facility Directory	4
LEGEND 5.—Airport/Facility Directory	5
LEGEND 6.—Airport/Facility Directory	6
LEGEND 7.—Airport/Facility Directory	7
LEGEND 8.—Airport/Facility Directory	8
LEGEND 9.—Standard Instrument Departure Chart (SID)	9
LEGEND 10.—General Information, Standard Terminal Arrival (STAR)	10
LEGEND 11.—Profile Descent Procedures	11
LEGEND 12.—Standard Terminal Arrival Chart (STAR)	12
LEGEND 13.—Instrument Approach Procedures Explanation of Terms	13
LEGEND 14.—General Information and Abbreviations	14
LEGEND 15.—Instrument Approach Procedures (Planview)	15
LEGEND 16.—Instrument Approach Procedures (Profile)	16
LEGEND 17.—Instrument Approach Procedures (Airport Diagram/Sketch)	17
LEGEND 18.—Instrument Takeoff Procedure Charts, Rate-of-Climb Table	18
LEGEND 19.—Instrument Approach Procedure Charts, Rate-of-Descent Table	19
LEGEND 20.—Inoperative Components or Visual Aids Table	20
LEGEND 21.—Approach Lighting Systems (U.S.)	21
LEGEND 22.—En Route Low Altitude Charts	22
LEGEND 23.—En Route Altitude Charts	23
LEGEND 24.—En Route Low Altitude Charts	24
LEGEND 25.—Aircraft Equipment Codes	25
LEGEND 26.—Air Navigation Radio Aids	26
LEGEND 27.—(Withdrawn) PAGE INTENTIONALLY LEFT BLANK	27
LEGEND 28.—ILS Standard Characteristics and Terminology	28
LEGEND 29.—Temperature Conversion Chart	29

APPENDIX 3

FIGURE 1.—Flight Plan	1
FIGURE 2.—Winds and Temperatures Aloft Forecast	1
FIGURE 3.—Standard Conversion Chart	2
FIGURE 4.—Weather Depiction Chart	3
FIGURE 5.—Symbol Used on Low-Level Significant Weather Prognostic Chart	4
FIGURE 6.—(Withdrawn) PAGE INTENTIONALLY LEFT BLANK	5
FIGURE 7.—High-Level Significant Weather Prognostic Chart	6
FIGURE 8.—Radar Summary Chart	7
FIGURE 9.—Severe Weather Outlook Charts	8
FIGURE 10.—Tropopause Height/Vertical Wind Shear Prognostic Chart	9
FIGURE 11.—Tropopause Pressure Temperature and Winds	10
FIGURE 12.—Observed Winds Aloft for 34,000 Feet	11
FIGURE 13.—Microburst Section Chart	12
FIGURE 14.—ISA Conversion Chart	13
FIGURE 15.—500 MB Analysis Heights/Temperature Chart	14
FIGURE 16.—300 MB Analysis Heights/Isotachs Chart	15
FIGURE 17.—200 MB Analysis Heights/Isotachs Chart	16
FIGURE 18.—U.S. Low-Level Significant Weather Prognostic Charts	17
FIGURE 19.—Low-Level Significant Weather Prognostic Chart	18
FIGURE 20.—High-Level Significant Weather Prognostic Chart	19

CONTENTS—Continued

	Page
FIGURE 21.—Flight Plan and Aircraft Information	20
FIGURE 21A.—Flight Plan and Aircraft Information	21
FIGURE 22.—Flight Planning Log	22
FIGURE 22A.—Flight Planning Log	23
FIGURE 23.—Grand Junction Nine Departure (JNC9.JNC)	24
FIGURE 23A.—Grand Junction Nine Departure (JNC9.JNC)	25
FIGURE 24.—En Route Low-Altitude Chart Segment	26
FIGURE 25.—ILS/DME RWY 2	27
FIGURE 25A.—ILS/DME RWY 2	28
FIGURE 26.—ILS RWY 11	29
FIGURE 26A.—ILS RWY 11, Grand Junction, Colorado	30
FIGURE 27.—Flight Plan and Aircraft Information	31
FIGURE 28.—Flight Planning Log	32
FIGURE 29.—ILS RWY 16 (EUG) and Excerpt from Airport/Facility Directory	33
FIGURE 29A.—ILS RWY 16 (EUG)	34
FIGURE 30.—GNATS One Departure and Excerpt from Airport/Facility Directory	35
FIGURE 30A.—RMI Indicator	36
FIGURE 31.—En Route Low-Altitude Chart Segment	37
FIGURE 32.—Flight Plan and Aircraft Information	38
FIGURE 33.—Flight Planning Log	39
FIGURE 34.—En Route Chart	40
FIGURE 34A.—Airport/Facility Directory (HOT)	41
FIGURE 35.—En Route Chart Segment and Blue Ridge Three Arrival	42
FIGURE 35A.—Blue Ridge Three Arrival Description	43
FIGURE 36.—Excerpt from Airport/Facility Directory	44
FIGURE 36A.—RNAV RWY 33 (ADS)	45
FIGURE 36B.—RNAV RWY 33 (ADS)	46
FIGURE 37.—CDI and RMI – NAV 1 and NAV 2	47
FIGURE 38.—Flight Plan and Aircraft Information	48
FIGURE 39.—Flight Log and Excerpt from Airport/Facility Directory (21 XS)	49
FIGURE 39A.—Excerpt from Airport/Facility Directory (21 XS)	50
FIGURE 40.—En Route Chart Segment	51
FIGURE 41.—ACTON Two Arrival	52
FIGURE 41A.—ACTON Two Arrival Description	53
FIGURE 42.—ILS-1 RWY 36L, Dallas-Fort Worth Intl	54
FIGURE 42A.—ILS RWY 36L	55
FIGURE 42B.—ILS-1 RWY 36L (DFW)	56
FIGURE 43.—CDI and RMI – NAV 1 and NAV 2	57
FIGURE 44.—Flight Plan and Aircraft Information	58
FIGURE 45.—Flight Planning Log	59
FIGURE 46.—GROMO Two Departure and Excerpt from Airport/Facility Directory	60
FIGURE 47.—En Route Chart Segment	61
FIGURE 48.—CDI – NAV 1	62
FIGURE 49.—LORAN RNAV RWY 10R (PDX)	63
FIGURE 49A.—LORAN RNAV RWY 10R	64
FIGURE 50.—Flight Plan and Aircraft Information	65
FIGURE 51.—Flight Planning Log	66
FIGURE 52.—HABUT One Departure and Excerpt from Airport/Facility Directory	67
FIGURE 53.—En Route Chart Segment	68
FIGURE 54.—RMI and CDI Indicators	69
FIGURE 55.—VOR/DME-B (PRB)	70
FIGURE 55A.—VOR/DME-B (PRB)	71
FIGURE 56.—IFR Flight Plan and Aircraft Information	72
FIGURE 57.—Flight Planning Log	73
FIGURE 58.—Excerpts from Airport/Facility Directory	74
FIGURE 59.—En Route Chart Segment	75
FIGURE 60.—Airport/Facility Directory and En Route Flight Advisory Service (EFAS)	76

CONTENTS—Continued

	Page
FIGURE 60A.—ILS RWY 4 (HOU)	77
FIGURE 60B.—ILS RWY 4 (HOU)	78
FIGURE 61.—RMI and CDI Indicators	79
FIGURE 62.—Flight Plan and Aircraft Information	80
FIGURE 63.—Flight Planning Log	81
FIGURE 64.—Excerpt from Airport/Facility Directory (LFT)	82
FIGURE 65.—En Route Chart Segment	83
FIGURE 66.—CDI and OBS Indicators	84
FIGURE 67.—Localizer Symbol	84
FIGURE 68.—COPTER VOR DME-117 Degrees (HUM)	85
FIGURE 68A.—COPTER VOR DME	86
FIGURE 69.—Flight Plan and Aircraft Information	87
FIGURE 70.—Flight Planning Log	88
FIGURE 71.—En Route Chart Segment	89
FIGURE 71A.—CDI and OBS Indicators	90
FIGURE 72.—JUDDS TWO ARRIVAL	91
FIGURE 72A.—JUDDS TWO ARRIVAL	92
FIGURE 73.—ILS RWY 6 (BDL)	93
FIGURE 73A.—ILS RWY 6 (BDL)	94
FIGURE 74.—Flight Plan and Aircraft Information	95
FIGURE 75.—Flight Planning Log	96
FIGURE 76.—VOR Indications and Excerpts from Airport/Facility Directory (HLN)	97
FIGURE 77.—STAKK TWO DEPARTURE	98
FIGURE 78.—En Route Chart Segment	99
FIGURE 79.—RMI Indicator	100
FIGURE 80.—VOR/DME RWY 27R and Airport/Facility Directory (BIL)	101
FIGURE 81.—Dual VOR System, VOT Check	102
FIGURE 82.—Dual VOR System, Accuracy Check	103
FIGURE 83.—Altimeter/12,000 Feet	104
FIGURE 84.—Altimeter/8,000 Feet	105
FIGURE 85.—WASHOE TWO DEPARTURE	106
FIGURE 86.—CDI and OBS Indicators	107
FIGURE 87.—En Route Chart Segment	108
FIGURE 88.—CDI and OBS Indicators	109
FIGURE 89.—En Route Chart Segment	110
FIGURE 90.—CDI/OBS Indicators	111
FIGURE 91.—En Route Chart Segment	112
FIGURE 92.—Minimum In-Flight Visibility and Distance from Clouds	113
FIGURE 93.—New Airspace Classification	114
FIGURE 94.—Application Examples for Holding Positions	115
FIGURE 95.—No. 1 and No. 2 NAV Presentation	116
FIGURE 96.—Aircraft Position and Direction of Flight	116
FIGURE 97.—HSI Presentation	117
FIGURE 98.—Aircraft Position	118
FIGURE 99.—HSI Presentation	119
FIGURE 100.—RMI Illustrations	120
FIGURE 101.—Directional Gyro and ADF Indicator	121
FIGURE 102.—Directional Gyro and ADF Indicator	121
FIGURE 103.—Directional Gyro and ADF Indicator	121
FIGURE 104.—Radio Magnetic Indicator	122
FIGURE 105.—Aircraft Magnetic Heading and ADF Illustration	123
FIGURE 106.—Aircraft Location Relative to VOR	124
FIGURE 107.—RMI—DME—ARC Illustration Wind Component	124
FIGURE 108.—RMI—DME—ARC Illustration Wind Component	124
FIGURE 109.—CDI Direction from VORTAC	125
FIGURE 110.—CDI Direction from VORTAC	125
FIGURE 111.—CDI Direction from VORTAC	125
FIGURE 112.—Holding Entry Procedure	126

CONTENTS—Continued

Page

FIGURE 113.—Aircraft Course and DME Indicator 126
FIGURE 114.—Aircraft Course and DME Indicator 126
FIGURE 115.—DME Fix with Holding Pattern 127
FIGURE 116.—Holding Entry Procedure 127
FIGURE 117.—Heading and ADF Indicators 127
FIGURE 118.—ILS RWY 12L (DSM) 128
FIGURE 119.—ILS RWY 24R (LAX) 129
FIGURE 120.—ILS RWY 35R (DEN) 130
FIGURE 121.—ILS RWY 30R (DSM) 131
FIGURE 122.—ILS RWY 8L (ATL) 132
FIGURE 123.—VOR/DME-A (7D3) 133
FIGURE 124.—LOC RWY 35, Duncan, Oklahoma 134
FIGURE 124A.—LOC RWY 35, Duncan, Oklahoma 135
FIGURE 125.—ILS RWY 17R, Lincoln, Nebraska 136
FIGURE 125A.—ILS RWY 17R, Lincoln, Nebraska 137
FIGURE 126.—ILS RWY 31, Dothan, Alabama 138
FIGURE 126A.—ILS RWY 31, Dothan, Alabama 139
FIGURE 127.—NDB RWY 28, Lancaster/Fairfield County 140
FIGURE 127A.—NDB RWY 28, Lancaster, Ohio 141
FIGURE 128.—VOR RWY 36 (PUC) 142
FIGURE 128A.—VOR RWY 36 (PUC) 143
FIGURE 129.—RNAV RWY 36 (LIT) 144
FIGURE 129A.—RNAV RWY 36 (LIT) 145
FIGURE 130.—LDA RWY 6 (ROA) 146
FIGURE 130A.—LDA RWY 6 (ROA) 147
FIGURE 131.—LOC RWY 18 (DEN) 148
FIGURE 132.—Terminal Area Chart 149
FIGURE 133.—ILS RWY 9 (RAL) 150
FIGURE 133A.—ILS RWY 9 151
FIGURE 134.—2-BAR VASI 152
FIGURE 135.—3-BAR VASI 152
FIGURE 136.—Precision Approach Path Indicator (PAPI) 152
FIGURE 137.—Precision Instrument Runway 153
FIGURE 138.—Runway Legend 153
FIGURE 139.—Glide Slope and Localizer Illustration 154
FIGURE 140.—OBS, ILS, and GS Displacement 155
FIGURE 141.—OBS, ILS, and GS Displacement 155
FIGURE 142.—OBS, ILS, and GS Displacement 155
FIGURE 143.—Slaved Gyro Illustration 156
FIGURE 144.—Turn-and-Slip Indicator 156
FIGURE 145.—Instrument Sequence (Unusual Attitude) 157
FIGURE 146.—Instrument Sequence (System Failed) 158
FIGURE 147.—Instrument Sequence (Unusual Attitude) 159
FIGURE 148.—Instrument Interpretation (System Malfunction) 160
FIGURE 149.—Instrument Interpretation (System Malfunction) 161
FIGURE 150.—Instrument Interpretation (Instrument Malfunction) 162
FIGURE 151.—Instrument Interpretation (Instrument Malfunction) 163
FIGURE 152.—Instrument Interpretation (System Failed) 164

APPENDIX 2

ABBREVIATIONS

The following abbreviations are those commonly used within this Directory. Other abbreviations may be found in the Legend and are not duplicated below.

AAS	airport advisory service	ldg	landing
acft	aircraft	med	medium
apch	approach	NFCT	non-federal control tower
arpt	airport	ngt	night
avbl	avai able	ntc	notice
bcn	beacon	opr	operate
blo	below	ops	operates operation
byd	beyond	ovrn	overrun
clsd	closed	p-line	power line
ctc	contact	PPR	prior permission required
dalgt	daylight	req	request
dsplc	displace	rqr	requires
dsplcd	displaced	rgt tfc	right traffic
durn	duration	rwy	runway
emerg	emergency	svc	service
extd	extend, extended	tmpry	temporary, temporarily
ftd	field	tkf	take off
FSS	Flight Service Station	tfc	traffic
ints	intensity	thld	threshold
lgtd	lighted	twr	tower
lgts	lights		

LEGEND 1.—Abbreviations.

Appendix 2

SAMPLE

CITY NAME (1)

§ **AIRPORT NAME** (ORL) 4 E GMT 5(4DT) 28°32'43"N 81°20'10"W   JACKSONVILLE
  200 B S4 **FUEL** 100, JET A OX 1, 2, 3 TPA—1000(800) AOE CFR Index A Not insp.   H-4G, L-19C

(2) (9) (10) (11) (12) (13) (14) (15) (16) (17)   (8) IAP

(18) → **RWY 07-25:** H6000X150 (ASPH-PFC)   S-90, D-160, DT-300   HIRL CL
    RWY 07: ALSF1 Trees.   **RWY 25:** REIL Rgt tfc
   RWY 13-31: H4620X100 (ASPH)   HIRL
    RWY 13: VASI(V2L)—GA 3.3 TCH 89' Pole   **RWY 31:** VASI(V2L)—GA 3.1 TCH 36'. Tree. Rgt tfc.
(19) → **AIRPORT REMARKS:** Special Air Traffic Rules—Part 93, see Regulatory Notices Attended 1200-0300Z‡. Parachute
   Jumping. CAUTION cattle and deer on arpt. Acft 100,000 lbs or over ctc Director of Aviation for approval (305)
   894-9831 Fee for all airline charters, travel clubs and certain revenue producing acft. Flight Notification Service
   (ADCUS) available. Control Zone effective 1500-0700Z‡.   ← (5)
(20) → **WEATHER DATA SOURCES:** AWOS-1 120.3 (202) 426-8000. LLWAS.
(21) → **COMMUNICATIONS:** ATIS 127.25   UNICOM 122.95
   NAME FSS (ORL) on fld.   123.65 122.65 122.2   (305) 894-0861   ← (5)
  (R) **NAME APP/DEP CON** 128.35 (1200-0400Z‡)
   TOWER 118.7   **GND CON** 121.7   **CLNC DEL** 125.55   **PRE TAXI CLNC** 125.5
   TCA GROUP II: See VFR Terminal Area Chart.
(22) → **RADIO AIDS TO NAVIGATION:** VHF/DF ctc FSS
   (H) **ABVORTAC** 112.2 ■ ORL Chan 59   28°32'33"N 81°20'07"W   at fld   1110/8E   ← (5)
    TWEB avbl 1300-0100Z‡
    VOR unusable 050-060' beyond 15 NM below 5000'
   HERNY NDB (LOM) 221   OR   28°30'24"N 81°26'03"W   067° 5.4 NM to fld.
   ILS 109.9 I-ORL Rwy 07 LOM HERNY NDB
   ASR/PAR
(23) → **COMM/NAVAID REMARKS:** Emerg frequency 121.5 not available at tower

---

AIRPORT NAME (X30) 7 W GMT 5(4DT) 28°31'50"N 81°32'26"W   JACKSONVILLE
  130 S4 **FUEL** 100 OX 2
  RWY 18-36: 2430X150 (TURF) LIRL
   RWY 18: Thld dsplcd 215' Trees.   **RWY 36:** Thld dsplcd 270' Road.
  AIRPORT REMARKS: Attended dawn-0300Z‡
  COMMUNICATIONS: UNICOM 122.8
   NAME FSS (ORL)

---

§ **D AIRPORT NAME** (MCO) 6.1 SE GMT 5(4DT) 28°25'53"N 81°19'29"W   JACKSONVILLE
  96 B **FUEL** 100 JET A LRA CFR Index D   H-4G, L-19C
  RWY 18R-36L: H12004X300 (CONC-GRVD)   S-100, D-200, DT-400   HIRL   IAP
   RWY 18R: ALSF1 REIL Rgt tfc.   **RWY 36L:** ALSF1
  RWY 18L-36R: H12004X200 (ASPH)   S-165, D-200, DT-400   HIRL
   RWY 18L: LDIN ALSF1 TDZ REIL VASI(V4L)—GA 3° TCH 36' Thld dsplcd 300' Trees. Rgt tfc. Arresting device
  AIRPORT REMARKS: Attended 1200-0300Z‡ ACTIVATE HIRL Rwy 18L/36R—123.0.
  COMMUNICATIONS: CTAF 124.3   ATIS 127.75   UNICOM 122.8
   NAME FSS (ORL) NOTAM FILE MCO
  (R) **APP CON** 124.8 (337°-179°)   120.1 (180°-336°)   **DEP CON** 120.15
   TOWER 124.3 (1200-0400Z‡)   **GND CON** 121.85   **CLNC DEL** 134.7
   STAGE III SVC ctc APP CON
  RADIO AIDS TO NAVIGATION:
   NAME (H) **VORTAC** 112.2   ORL   Chan 59   28°32'33"N 81°20'07"W   173° 5.7 NM to fld 1110/8E
   MLS Chan 514 Rwy 36R

E AIRPORT NAME (See PLYMOUTH)

All Bearings and Radials are Magnetic unless otherwise specified.
All mileages are nautical unless otherwise noted
All times are GMT except as noted

LEGEND 2.—Airport/Facility Directory

This Directory is an alphabetical listing of data on record with the FAA on all airports that are open to the public, associated terminal control facilities, air route traffic control centers and radio aids to navigation within the conterminous United States, Puerto Rico and the Virgin Islands. Airports are listed alphabetically by associated city name and cross referenced by airport name. Facilities associated with an airport, but with a different name, are listed individually under their own name, as well as under the airport with which they are associated.

The listing of an airport in this directory merely indicates the airport operator's willingness to accommodate transient aircraft, and does not represent that the facility conforms with any Federal or local standards, or that it has been approved for use on the part of the general public.

The information on obstructions is taken from reports submitted to the FAA. It has not been verified in all cases. Pilots are cautioned that objects not indicated in this tabulation (or on charts) may exist which can create a hazard to flight operation.

Detailed specifics concerning services and facilities tabulated within this directory are contained in Airman's Information Manual, Basic Flight Information and ATC Procedures.

The legend items that follow explain in detail the contents of this Directory and are keyed to the circled numbers on the sample on the preceding page.

① CITY/AIRPORT NAME
Airports and facilities in this directory are listed alphabetically by associated city and state. Where the city name is different from the airport name the city name will appear on the line above the airport name. Airports with the same associated city name will be listed alphabetically by airport name and will be separated by a dashed rule line. All others will be separated by a solid rule line.

② NOTAM SERVICE
§—NOTAM "D" (Distant teletype dissemination) and NOTAM "L" (Local dissemination) service is provided for airport. Absence of annotation § indicates NOTAM "L" (Local dissemination) only is provided for airport. See AIM, Basic Flight Information and ATC Procedures for detailed description of NOTAM.

③ LOCATION IDENTIFIER
A three or four character code assigned to airports. These identifiers are used by ATC in lieu of the airport name in flight plans, flight strips and other written records and computer operations.

④ AIRPORT LOCATION
Airport location is expressed as distance and direction from the center of the associated city in nautical miles and cardinal points, i.e., 4 NE.

⑤ TIME CONVERSION
Hours of operation of all facilities are expressed in Greenwich Mean Time (GMT) and shown as "Z" time. The directory indicates the number of hours to be subtracted from GMT to obtain local standard time and local daylight saving time GMT −5(−4DT). The symbol ‡ indicates that during periods of Daylight Saving Time effective hours will be one hour earlier than shown. In those areas where daylight saving time is not observed that (−4DT) and ‡ will not be shown. All states observe daylight savings time except Arizona and that portion of Indiana in the Eastern Time Zone and Puerto Rico and the Virgin Islands.

⑥ GEOGRAPHIC POSITION OF AIRPORT

⑦ CHARTS
The Sectional Chart and Low and High Altitude Enroute Chart and panel on which the airport or facility is located.

⑧ INSTRUMENT APPROACH PROCEDURES
IAP indicates an airport for which a prescribed (Public Use) FAA Instrument Approach Procedure has been published.

⑨ ELEVATION
Elevation is given in feet above mean sea level and is the highest point on the landing surface. When elevation is sea level it will be indicated as (00). When elevation is below sea level a minus (−) sign will precede the figure.

⑩ ROTATING LIGHT BEACON
B indicates rotating beacon is available. Rotating beacons operate dusk to dawn unless otherwise indicated in AIRPORT REMARKS.

⑪ SERVICING
S1: Minor airframe repairs.
S2: Minor airframe and minor powerplant repairs.
S3: Major airframe and minor powerplant repairs.
S4: Major airframe and major powerplant repairs.

LEGEND 3.—Airport/Facility Directory

Appendix 2

(12) FUEL

CODE	FUEL
80	Grade 80 gasoline (Red)
100	Grade 100 gasoline (Green)
100LL	Grade 100LL gasoline (low lead) (Blue)
115	Grade 115 gasoline
A	Jet A—Kerosene freeze point – 40° C.
A1	Jet A-1—Kerosene, freeze point – 50° C.
A1+	Jet A-1—Kerosene with icing inhibitor, freeze point – 50° C.
B	Jet B—Wide-cut turbine fuel, freeze point – 50° C.
B+	Jet B—Wide-cut turbine fuel with icing inhibitor, freeze point – 50° C.

(13) OXYGEN

OX 1 High Pressure
OX 2 Low Pressure
OX 3 High Pressure—Replacement Bottles
OX 4 Low Pressure—Replacement Bottles

(14) TRAFFIC PATTERN ALTITUDE

Traffic Pattern Altitude (TPA)—The first figure shown is TPA above mean sea level. The second figure in parentheses is TPA above airport elevation.

(15) AIRPORT OF ENTRY AND LANDING RIGHTS AIRPORTS

AOE—Airport of Entry—A customs Airport of Entry where permission from U.S. Customs is not required, however, at least one hour advance notice of arrival must be furnished.

LRA—Landing Rights Airport—Application for permission to land must be submitted in advance to U.S. Customs. At least one hour advance notice of arrival must be furnished.

NOTE: Advance notice of arrival at both an AOE and LRA airport may be included in the flight plan when filed in Canada or Mexico, where Flight Notification Service (ADCUS) is available the airport remark will indicate this service. This notice will also be treated as an application for permission to land in the case of an LRA. Although advance notice of arrival may be relayed to Customs through Mexico, Canadian, and U.S. Communications facilities by flight plan, the aircraft operator is solely responsible for insuring that Customs receives the notification. (See Customs, Immigration and Naturalization, Public Health and Agriculture Department requirements in the International Flight Information Manual for further details.)

(16) CERTIFICATED AIRPORT (FAR 139)

Airports serving Civil Aeronautics Board certified carriers and certified under FAR, Part 139, are indicated by the CFR index; i.e., CFR Index A, which relates to the availability of crash, fire, rescue equipment.

FAR—PART 139 CERTIFICATED AIRPORTS
INDICES AND FIRE FIGHTING AND RESCUE EQUIPMENT REQUIREMENTS

Airport Index	Required No. Vehicles	Aircraft Length	Scheduled Departures	Agent + Water for Foam
A	1	≤90'	≥1	500#DC or 450#DC + 50 gal H$_2$O
AA	1	>90', ≤126'	<5	300#DC + 500 gal H$_2$O
B	2	>90', ≤126'	≥5	Index A + 1500 gal H$_2$O
		>126', ≤160'	<5	
C	3	>126', ≤160'	≥5	Index A + 3000 gal H$_2$O
		>160', ≤200'	<5	
D	3	>160', ≤200'	≥5	Index A + 4000 gal H$_2$O
		>200'	<5	
E	3	>200'	≥5	Index A + 6000 gal H$_2$O

> Greater Than; < Less Than; ≥ Equal or Greater Than; ≤ Equal or Less Than; H$_2$O–Water; DC–Dry Chemical.

NOTE: If AFFF (Aqueous Film Forming Foam) is used in lieu of Protein Foam, the water quantities listed for Indices AA thru E can be reduced 33 ⅓%. See FAR Part 139.49 for full details. The listing of CFR index does not necessarily assure coverage for non-air carrier operations or at other than prescribed times for air carrier. CFR index Ltd.—indicates CFR coverage may or may not be available, for information contact airport manager prior to flight.

LEGEND 4.—Airport/Facility Directory

Appendix 2

⑰ FAA INSPECTION

All airports not inspected by FAA will be identified by the note: Not insp. This indicates that the airport information has been provided by the owner or operator of the field.

⑱ RUNWAY DATA

Runway information is shown on two lines. That information common to the entire runway is shown on the first line while information concerning the runway ends are shown on the second or following line. Lengthy information will be placed in the Airport Remarks.

Runway direction, surface, length, width, weight bearing capacity, lighting, gradient (when gradient exceeds 0.3 percent) and appropriate remarks are shown for each runway. Direction, length, width, lighting and remarks are shown for sealanes. The full dimensions of helipads are shown, i.e., 50X150.

RUNWAY SURFACE AND LENGTH

Runway lengths prefixed by the letter "H" indicate that the runways are hard surfaced (concrete, asphalt). If the runway length is not prefixed, the surface is sod, clay, etc. The runway surface composition is indicated in parentheses after runway length as follows:

(AFSC)—Aggregate friction seal coat
(ASPH)—Asphalt
(CONC)—Concrete
(DIRT)—Dirt
(GRVD)—Grooved
(GRVL)—Gravel, or cinders
(PFC)—Porous friction courses
(RFSC)—Rubberized friction seal coat
(TURF)—Turf
(TRTD)—Treated
(WC)—Wire combed

RUNWAY WEIGHT BEARING CAPACITY

Runway strength data shown in this publication is derived from available information and is a realistic estimate of capability at an average level of activity. It is not intended as a maximum allowable weight or as an operating limitation. Many airport pavements are capable of supporting limited operations with gross weights of 25-50% in excess of the published figures. Permissible operating weights, insofar as runway strengths are concerned, are a matter of agreement between the owner and user. When desiring to operate into any airport at weights in excess of those published in the publication, users should contact the airport management for permission. Add 000 to figure following S, D, DT, DDT and MAX for gross weight capacity.

S—Runway weight bearing capacity for aircraft with single-wheel type landing gear. (DC-3), etc.
D—Runway weight bearing capacity for aircraft with dual-wheel type landing gear. (DC-6), etc.
DT—Runway weight bearing capacity for aircraft with dual-tandem type landing gear. (707), etc.
DDT—Runway weight bearing capacity for aircraft with double dual-tandem type landing gear. (747), etc.

Quadricycle and dual-tandem are considered virtually equal for runway weight bearing consideration, as are single-tandem and dual-wheel.

Omission of weight bearing capacity indicates information unknown.

RUNWAY LIGHTING

Lights are in operation sunset to sunrise. Lighting available by prior arrangement only or operating part of the night only and/or pilot controlled and with specific operating hours are indicated under airport remarks. Since obstructions are usually lighted, obstruction lighting is not included in this code. Unlighted obstructions on or surrounding an airport will be noted in airport remarks.

Temporary, emergency or limited runway edge lighting such as flares, smudge pots, lanterns or portable runway lights will also be shown in airport remarks.

Types of lighting are shown with the runway or runway end they serve.

LIRL—Low Intensity Runway Lights
MIRL—Medium Intensity Runway Lights
HIRL—High Intensity Runway Lights
REIL—Runway End Identifier Lights
CL—Centerline Lights
TDZ—Touchdown Zone Lights
ODALS—Omni Directional Approach Lighting System.
AF OVRN—Air Force Overrun 1000' Standard Approach Lighting System.
LDIN—Lead-In Lighting System.
MALS—Medium Intensity Approach Lighting System.
MALSF—Medium Intensity Approach Lighting System with Sequenced Flashing Lights.
MALSR—Medium Intensity Approach Lighting System with Runway Alignment Indicator Lights.

SALS—Short Approach Lighting System.
SALSF—Short Approach Lighting System with Sequenced Flashing Lights.
SSALS—Simplified Short Approach Lighting System.
SSALF—Simplified Short Approach Lighting System with Sequenced Flashing Lights.
SSALR—Simplified Short Approach Lighting System with Runway Alignment Indicator Lights.
ALSAF—High Intensity Approach Lighting System with Sequenced Flashing Lights
ALSFI—High Intensity Approach Lighting System with Sequenced Flashing Lights, Category I, Configuration.
ALSF2—High Intensity Approach Lighting System with Sequenced Flashing Lights, Category II, Configuration.
VASI—Visual Approach Slope Indicator System

VISUAL APPROACH SLOPE INDICATOR SYSTEMS

VASI—Visual Approach Slope Indicator
SAVASI—Simplified Abbreviated Visual Approach Slope Indicator

LEGEND 5.—Airport/Facility Directory

Appendix 2

S2L	2-box SAVASI on left side of runway
S2R	2-box SAVASI on right side of runway
V2R	2-box VASI on right side of runway
V2L	2-box VASI on left side of runway
V4R	4-box VASI on right side of runway
V4L	4-box VASI on left side of runway
V6R	6-box VASI on right side of runway
V6L	6-box VASI on left side of runway
V12	12-box VASI on both sides of runway
V16	16-box VASI on both sides of runway
*NSTD	Nonstandard VASI, VAPI, or any other system not listed above

VASI approach slope angle and threshold crossing height will be shown when available; i.e., GA 3.5° TCH 37.0'.

PILOT CONTROL OF AIRPORT LIGHTING

Key Mike	Function
7 times within 5 seconds	Highest intensity available
5 times within 5 seconds	Medium or lower intensity (Lower REIL or REIL-Off)
3 times within 5 seconds	Lowest intensity available (Lower REIL or REIL-Off)

Available systems will be indicated in the Airport Remarks, as follows:

ACTIVATE MALSR Rwy 7, HIRL Rwy 7/25-122.8.
or
ACTIVATE MIRL Rwy 18/36-122.8.
or
ACTIVATE VASI and REIL, Rwy 7-122.8.

Where the airport is not served by an instrument approach procedure and/or has an independent type system of different specification installed by the airport sponsor, descriptions of the type lights, method of control, and operating frequency will be explained in clear text. See AIM, "Basic Flight Information and ATC Procedures," for detailed description of pilot control of airport lighting.

RUNWAY GRADIENT

Runway gradient will be shown only when it is 0.3 percent or more. When available the direction of slope upward will be indicated, i.e., 0.5% up NW.

RUNWAY END DATA

Lighting systems such as VASI, MALSR, REIL; obstructions; displaced thresholds will be shown on the specific runway end. "Rgt tfc"—Right traffic indicates right turns should be made on landing and takeoff for specified runway end.

⑲ AIRPORT REMARKS

Landing Fee indicates landing charges for private or non-revenue producing aircraft. in addition, fees may be charged for planes that remain over a couple of hours and buy no services, or at major airline terminals for all aircraft.
Remarks—Data is confined to operational items affecting the status and usability of the airport.

⑳ WEATHER DATA SOURCES

AWOS—Automated Weather Observation System

AWOS-1—reports altimeter setting, wind data and usually temperature, dewpoint and density altitude.
AWOS-2—reports the same as AWOS-1 plus visibility.
AWOS-3—reports the same as AWOS-1 plus visibility and cloud/ceiling data.
See AIM, Basic Flight Information and ATC Procedures for detailed description of AWOS.

SAWRS—identifies airports that have a Supplemental Aviation Weather Reporting Station available to pilots for current weather information.
LLWAS—indicates a Low Level Wind Shear Alert System consisting of a center field and several field perimeter anemometers.

㉑ COMMUNICATIONS

Communications will be listed in sequence in the order shown below:
Common Traffic Advisory Frequency (CTAF), Automatic Terminal Information Service (ATIS) and Aeronautical Advisory Stations (UNICOM) along with their frequency is shown, where available, on the line following the heading "COMMUNICATIONS." When the CTAF and UNICOM is the same frequency, the frequency will be shown as CTAF/UNICOM freq.
Flight Service Station (FSS) information. The associated FSS will be shown followed by the identifier and information concerning availability of telephone service, e.g. Direct Line (DL), Local Call (LC), etc. Where the airport NOTAM File identifier is different than the associated FSS it will be shown as "NOTAM FILE IAD." Where the FSS is located on the field it will be indicated as "on arpt"

LEGEND 6.—Airport/Facility Directory

Appendix 2

following the identifier. Frequencies available will follow. The FSS telephone number will follow along with any significant operational information. FSS's whose name is not the same as the airport on which located will also be listed in the normal alphabetical name listing for the state in which located. Remote Communications Outlet (RCO) providing service to the airport followed by the frequency and name of the Controlling FSS.

FSS's provide information on airport conditions, radio aids and other facilities, and process flight plans. Airport Advisory Service is provided on the CTAF by FSS's located at non-tower airports or airports where the tower is not in operation.
(See AIM, Par. 157/158 Traffic Advisory Practices at airports where a tower is not in operation or AC 90 - 42C.)
Aviation weather briefing service is provided by FSS specialists. Flight and weather briefing services are also available by calling the telephone numbers listed.

Remote Communications Outlet (RCO)—An unmanned air/ground communications facility, remotely controlled and providing UHF or VHF communications capability to extend the service range of an FSS.

Civil Communications Frequencies—Civil communications frequencies used in the FSS air/ground system are now operated simplex on 122.0, 122.2, 122.3, 122.4, 122.6, 123.6; emergency 121.5, plus receive-only on 122.05, 122.1, 122.15, and 123.6.

    a. 122.0 is assigned as the Enroute Flight Advisory Service channel at selected FSS's.
    b. 122.2 is assigned to all FSS's as a common enroute simplex service.
    c. 123.6 is assigned as the airport advisory channel at non-tower FSS locations, however, it is still in commission at some FSS's collocated with towers to provide part time Airport Advisory Service.
    d. 122.1 is the primary receive-only frequency at VOR's. 122.05, 122.15 and 123.6 are assigned at selected VOR's meeting certain criteria.
    e. Some FSS's are assigned 50 kHz channels for simplex operation in the 122-123 MHz band (e.g. 122.35). Pilots using the FSS A/G system should refer to this directory or appropriate charts to determine frequencies available at the FSS or remoted facility through which they wish to communicate.

Part time FSS hours of operation are shown in remarks under facility name.

    Emergency frequency 121.5 is available at all Flight Service Stations, Towers, Approach Control and RADAR facilities, unless indicated as not available.

Frequencies published followed by the letter "T" or "R", indicate that the facility will only transmit or receive respectively on that frequency. All radio aids to navigation frequencies are transmit only.

TERMINAL SERVICES

CTAF—A program designed to get all vehicles and aircraft at uncontrolled airports on a common frequency.
ATIS—A continuous broadcast of recorded non-control information in selected areas of high activity.
UNICOM—A non-government air/ground radio communications facility utilized to provide general airport advisory service.
APP CON—Approach Control. The symbol ® indicates radar approach control.
TOWER—Control tower
GND CON—Ground Control
DEP CON—Departure Control. The symbol ® indicates radar departure control.
CLNC DEL—Clearance Delivery.
PRE TAXI CLNC—Pre taxi clearance
VFR ADVSY SVC—VFR Advisory Service. Service provided by Non-Radar Approach Control.
    Advisory Service for VFR aircraft (upon a workload basis) ctc APP CON.
STAGE II SVC—Radar Advisory and Sequencing Service for VFR aircraft
STAGE III SVC—Radar Sequencing and Separation Service for participating VFR Aircraft within a Terminal Radar Service Area (TRSA)
ARSA—Airport Radar Service Area
TCA—Radar Sequencing and Separation Service for all aircraft in a Terminal Control Area (TCA)
TOWER, APP CON and DEP CON RADIO CALL will be the same as the airport name unless indicated otherwise.

㉒ RADIO AIDS TO NAVIGATION

The Airport Facility Directory lists by facility name all Radio Aids to Navigation, except Military TACANS, that appear on National Ocean Service Visual or IFR Aeronautical Charts and those upon which the FAA has approved an Instrument Approach Procedure. All VOR, VORTAC ILS and MLS equipment in the National Airspace System has an automatic monitoring and shutdown feature in the event of malfunction. Unmonitored, as used in this publication for any navigational aid, means that FSS or tower personnel cannot observe the malfunction or shutdown signal.

NAVAID information is tabulated as indicated in the following sample:

                TWEB   TACAN/DME Channel   Geographical Position   Site Elevation

NAME (L) ABVORTAC 117.55 ■ ABE Chan 122(Y) 40°43'36"N 75°27'18"W 180° 4.1 NM to fld. 1110/8E

    Class   Frequency Identifier   Bearing and distance   Magnetic Variation
                                    facility to airport

              VOR unusable 020°-060° beyond 26 NM below 3500'

Restriction within the normal altitude/range of the navigational aid (See primary alphabetical listing for restrictions on VORTAC and VOR/DME).

Note: Those DME channel numbers with a (Y) suffix require TACAN to be placed in the "Y" mode to receive distance information.

LEGEND 7.—Airport/Facility Directory

Appendix 2

ASR/PAR—Indicates that Surveillance (ASR) or Precision (PAR) radar instrument approach minimums are published in U.S. Government Instrument Approach Procedures.

RADIO CLASS DESIGNATIONS

Identification of VOR/VORTAC/TACAN Stations by Class (Operational Limitations):

Normal Usable Altitudes and Radius Distances

Class	Altitudes	Distance (miles)
(T)	12,000' and below	25
(L)	Below 18,000'	40
(H)	Below 18,000'	40
(H)	Within the Conterminous 48 States only, between 14,500' and 17,999'	100
(H)	18,000' FL 450	130
(H)	Above FL 450	100

(H) = High   (L) = Low   (T) = Terminal

NOTE: An (H) facility is capable of providing (L) and (T) service volume and an (L) facility additionally provides (T) service volume.

The term VOR is, operationally, a general term covering the VHF omnidirectional bearing type of facility without regard to the fact that the power, the frequency protected service volume, the equipment configuration, and operational requirements may vary between facilities at different locations.

AB	Automatic Weather Broadcast (also shown with ■ following frequency.)
DF	Direction Finding Service.
DME	UHF standard (TACAN compatible) distance measuring equipment.
DME(Y)	UHF standard (TACAN compatible) distance measuring equipment that require TACAN to be placed in the "Y" mode to receive DME.
H	Non-directional radio beacon (homing), power 50 watts to less than 2,000 watts (50 NM at all altitudes).
HH	Non-directional radio beacon (homing), power 2,000 watts or more (75 NM at all altitudes).
H-SAB	Non-directional radio beacons providing automatic transcribed weather service.
ILS	Instrument Landing System (voice, where available, on localizer channel).
ISMLS	Interim Standard Microwave Landing System.
LDA	Localizer Directional Aid.
LMM	Compass locator station when installed at middle marker site (15 NM at all altitudes).
LOM	Compass locator station when installed at outer marker site (15 NM at all altitudes).
MH	Non-directional radio beacon (homing) power less than 50 watts (25 NM at all altitudes).
MLS	Microwave Landing System
S	Simultaneous range homing signal and/or voice.
SABH	Non-directional radio beacon not authorized for IFR or ATC. Provides automatic weather broadcasts.
SDF	Simplified Direction Facility.
TACAN	UHF navigational facility-omnidirectional course and distance information.
VOR	VHF navigational facility-omnidirectional course only.
VOR/DME	Collocated VOR navigational facility and UHF standard distance measuring equipment.
VORTAC	Collocated VOR and TACAN navigational facilities.
W	Without voice on radio facility frequency.
Z	VHF station location marker at a LF radio facility.

LEGEND 8.—Airport/Facility Directory

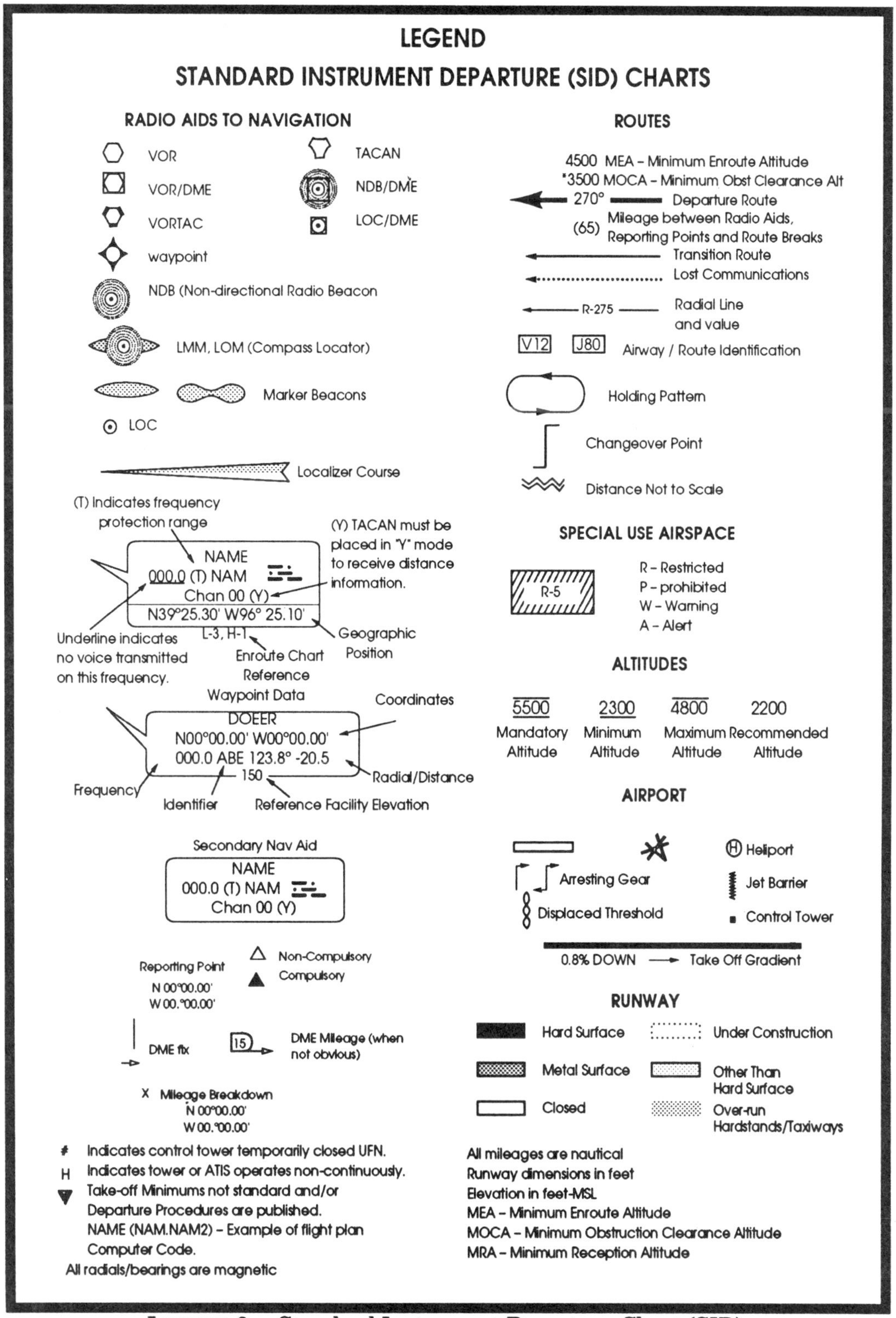

LEGEND
STANDARD INSTRUMENT DEPARTURE (SID) CHARTS

RADIO AIDS TO NAVIGATION

- VOR
- TACAN
- VOR/DME
- NDB/DME
- VORTAC
- LOC/DME
- waypoint
- NDB (Non-directional Radio Beacon)
- LMM, LOM (Compass Locator)
- Marker Beacons
- LOC
- Localizer Course

(T) Indicates frequency protection range
(Y) TACAN must be placed in "Y" mode to receive distance information.

NAME
000.0 (T) NAM
Chan 00 (Y)
N39°25.30' W96°25.10'
L-3, H-1

Underline indicates no voice transmitted on this frequency.
Enroute Chart Reference
Geographic Position

Waypoint Data

DOEER
N00°00.00' W00°00.00'
000.0 ABE 123.8° -20.5
150

Frequency | Identifier | Reference Facility Elevation
Coordinates | Radial/Distance

Secondary Nav Aid
NAME
000.0 (T) NAM
Chan 00 (Y)

Reporting Point
N 00°00.00'
W 00.°00.00'
△ Non-Compulsory
▲ Compulsory

DME fix
15 DME Mileage (when not obvious)

X Mileage Breakdown
N 00°00.00'
W 00.°00.00'

\# Indicates control tower temporarily closed UFN.
H Indicates tower or ATIS operates non-continuously.
▼ Take-off Minimums not standard and/or Departure Procedures are published.
NAME (NAM.NAM2) — Example of flight plan Computer Code.
All radials/bearings are magnetic

ROUTES

4500 MEA – Minimum Enroute Altitude
*3500 MOCA – Minimum Obst Clearance Alt
270° Departure Route
(65) Mileage between Radio Aids, Reporting Points and Route Breaks
Transition Route
Lost Communications
R-275 Radial Line and value
V12 J80 Airway / Route Identification
Holding Pattern
Changeover Point
Distance Not to Scale

SPECIAL USE AIRSPACE

R-5
R – Restricted
P – prohibited
W – Warning
A – Alert

ALTITUDES

5500 Mandatory Altitude
2300 Minimum Altitude
4800 Maximum Altitude
2200 Recommended Altitude

AIRPORT

Arresting Gear
Displaced Threshold
Heliport
Jet Barrier
Control Tower

0.8% DOWN → Take Off Gradient

RUNWAY

- Hard Surface
- Under Construction
- Metal Surface
- Other Than Hard Surface
- Closed
- Over-run Hardstands/Taxiways

All mileages are nautical
Runway dimensions in feet
Elevation in feet-MSL
MEA – Minimum Enroute Altitude
MOCA – Minimum Obstruction Clearance Altitude
MRA – Minimum Reception Altitude

LEGEND 9.—Standard Instrument Departure Chart (SID).

Appendix 2

GENERAL INFORMATION

This publication consists of Standard Terminal Arrivals (STAR) and Profile Descent Procedures for use by both civil and military aviation and is issued every 56 days.

STANDARD TERMINAL ARRIVAL

The use of the associated codified STAR and transition identifiers are requested of users when filing flight plans via teletype and are required for users filing flight plans via computer interface. It must be noted that when filing a STAR with a transition, the first three coded characters of the STAR are replaced by the transition code. Examples: ACTON SIX ARRIVAL, file (AQN.AQN6); ACTON SIX ARRIVAL EDNAS TRANSITION, file (EDNAS.AQN6).

PROFILE DESCENT PROCEDURAL NOTE

A profile descent is an uninterrupted descent (except where level flight is required for speed adjustment, e.g., 250 knots at 10,000 feet MSL) from cruising altitude/level to interception of a glide slope or to a minimum altitude specified for the initial or intermediate approach segment of a non-precision instrument approach. The profile descent normally terminates at the approach gate or where the glide slope or other appropriate minimum altitude is intercepted.

Profile descent clearances are subject to traffic conditions and may be altered by ATC if necessary. Acceptance, by the pilot, of a profile descent clearance; i.e., "cleared for Runway 28 profile descent," requires the pilot to adhere to all depicted procedures on the profile descent chart.

After a profile descent has been issued and accepted:

(1) Any subsequent ATC revision of altitude or route cancels the remaining portion of the charted profile descent procedure. ATC will then assign necessary altitude, route, and speed clearances.

(2) Any subsequent revision of depicted speed restriction voids all charted speed restrictions. Charted route and altitude restrictions are not affected by revision to depicted speed restrictions. If the pilot cannot comply with charted route and/or altitude restrictions because of revised speed, he is expected to so advise ATC.

THE PROFILE DESCENT CLEARANCES DOES NOT CONSTITUTE CLEARANCE TO FLY AN INSTRUMENT APPROACH PROCEDURE (IAP). The last "maintain altitude" specified in the PROFILE DESCENT procedure constitutes that the last ATC assigned altitude and the pilot must maintain such altitude until he is cleared for an approach unless another altitude is assigned by ATC.

PILOTS SHOULD REVIEW RUNWAY PROFILE DESCENT CHARTS BEFORE FLIGHT INTO AIRPORTS WITH CHARTED PROCEDURES.

CORRECTIONS, COMMENTS AND/OR PROCUREMENT

CIVIL

FOR CHARTING ERRORS:	FOR CHANGES, ADDITIONS, OR RECOMMENDATIONS ON PROCEDURAL ASPECTS:	PROCURE FROM:
Contact National Ocean Service NOAA, N/CG31 6010 Executive Blvd. Rockville, MD. 20852 Telephone Toll-Free 800-626-3677	Contact Federal Aviation Administration, ATO-258 800 — Independence Avenue, S.W. Washington, D.C., 20591 Telephone (202) 267-9297	National Ocean Service NOAA, N/CG33 Distribution Branch Riverdale, MD 20737 Telephone (301) 436-6993

MILITARY

For Corrections Information, see Chapter 11 of General Planning (GP). For Procurement refer to DOD Catalog of Aeronautical Charts and Flight Information Publications.

LEGEND 10.—General Information, Standard Terminal Arrival (STAR)

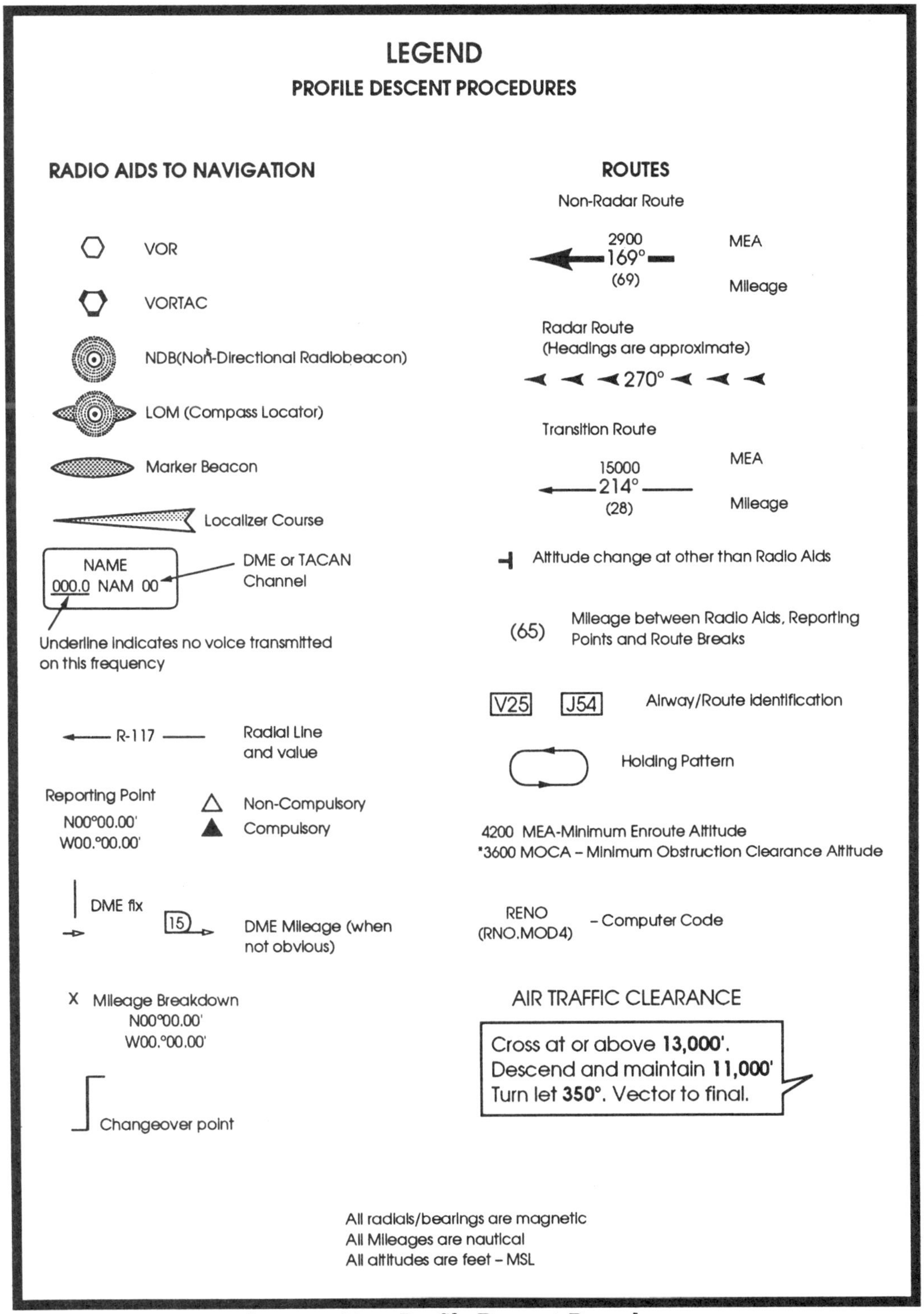

LEGEND
PROFILE DESCENT PROCEDURES

RADIO AIDS TO NAVIGATION

- ⬡ VOR
- ⬡ VORTAC
- NDB (Non-Directional Radiobeacon)
- LOM (Compass Locator)
- Marker Beacon
- Localizer Course
- NAME / 000.0 NAM 00 — DME or TACAN Channel

Underline indicates no voice transmitted on this frequency

- ← R-117 — Radial Line and value

Reporting Point
N00°00.00'
W00.°00.00'
- △ Non-Compulsory
- ▲ Compulsory

- DME fix
- 15 DME Mileage (when not obvious)

- X Mileage Breakdown
  N00°00.00'
  W00.°00.00'

- Changeover point

ROUTES

Non-Radar Route

2900 — MEA
←169°—
(69) — Mileage

Radar Route (Headings are approximate)

◄ ◄ ◄270°◄ ◄ ◄

Transition Route

15000 — MEA
←214°—
(28) — Mileage

⊣ Altitude change at other than Radio Aids

(65) Mileage between Radio Aids, Reporting Points and Route Breaks

V25 J54 Airway/Route identification

⬭ Holding Pattern

4200 MEA–Minimum Enroute Altitude
*3600 MOCA – Minimum Obstruction Clearance Altitude

RENO
(RNO.MOD4) – Computer Code

AIR TRAFFIC CLEARANCE

Cross at or above **13,000'**.
Descend and maintain **11,000'**
Turn let **350°**. Vector to final.

All radials/bearings are magnetic
All Mileages are nautical
All altitudes are feet – MSL

LEGEND 11.— Profile Descent Procedures.

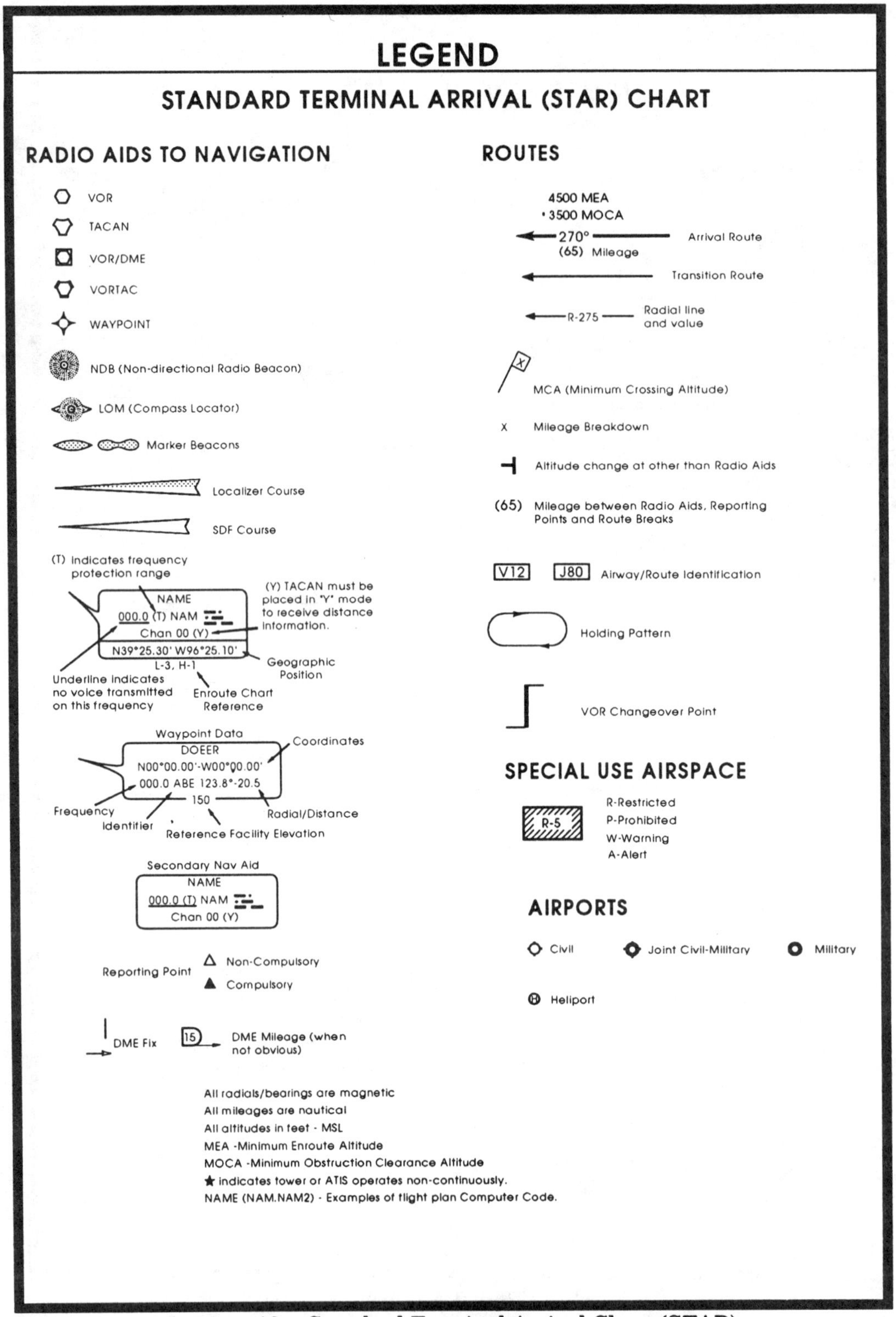

Appendix 2

LEGEND

STANDARD TERMINAL ARRIVAL (STAR) CHART

RADIO AIDS TO NAVIGATION

- VOR
- TACAN
- VOR/DME
- VORTAC
- WAYPOINT
- NDB (Non-directional Radio Beacon)
- LOM (Compass Locator)
- Marker Beacons
- Localizer Course
- SDF Course

(T) indicates frequency protection range

NAME
000.0 (T) NAM
Chan 00 (Y)
N39°25.30' W96°25.10'
L-3, H-1

(Y) TACAN must be placed in "Y" mode to receive distance information.
Geographic Position
Enroute Chart Reference
Underline indicates no voice transmitted on this frequency

Waypoint Data
DOEER
N00°00.00'-W00°00.00'
000.0 ABE 123.8°-20.5
150

Coordinates
Frequency
Identifier
Reference Facility Elevation
Radial/Distance

Secondary Nav Aid
NAME
000.0 (T) NAM
Chan 00 (Y)

Reporting Point
△ Non-Compulsory
▲ Compulsory

DME Fix [15] DME Mileage (when not obvious)

All radials/bearings are magnetic
All mileages are nautical
All altitudes in feet - MSL
MEA - Minimum Enroute Altitude
MOCA - Minimum Obstruction Clearance Altitude
★ indicates tower or ATIS operates non-continuously.
NAME (NAM.NAM2) - Examples of flight plan Computer Code.

ROUTES

4500 MEA
*3500 MOCA
270° (65) — Arrival Route / Mileage
— Transition Route
R-275 — Radial line and value
MCA (Minimum Crossing Altitude)
X Mileage Breakdown
⊣ Altitude change at other than Radio Aids
(65) Mileage between Radio Aids, Reporting Points and Route Breaks

[V12] [J80] Airway/Route Identification

Holding Pattern

VOR Changeover Point

SPECIAL USE AIRSPACE

R-5
R - Restricted
P - Prohibited
W - Warning
A - Alert

AIRPORTS

◇ Civil   ◆ Joint Civil-Military   ● Military
Ⓗ Heliport

LEGEND 12.—Standard Terminal Arrival Chart (STAR).

12

Appendix 2

INSTRUMENT APPROACH PROCEDURES EXPLANATION OF TERMS

The United States Standard for Terminal Instrument Procedures (TERPS) is the approved criteria for formulating instrument approach procedures.

AIRCRAFT APPROACH CATEGORIES

Speeds are based on 1.3 times the stall speed in the landing configuration at maximum gross landing weight. An aircraft shall fit in only one category. If it is necessary to maneuver at speeds in excess of the upper limit of a speed range for a category, the minimums for the next higher category should be used. For example, an aircraft which falls in Category A, but is circling to land at a speed in excess of 91 knots, should use the approach Category B minimums when circling to land. See following category limits:

MANEUVERING TABLE

Approach Category	A	B	C	D	E
Speed (Knots)	0-90	91-120	121-140	141-165	Abv 165

RVR/Meteorological Visibility Comparable Values

The following table shall be used for converting RVR to meteorological visibility when RVR is not reported for the runway of intended operation. Adjustment of landing minima may be required — see Inoperative Components Table.

RVR (feet)	Visibility (statute miles)	RVR (feet)	Visibility (statute miles)
1600	1/4	4500	7/8
2400	1/2	5000	1
3200	5/8	6000	1 1/4
4000	3/4		

LANDING MINIMA FORMAT

In this example airport elevation is 1179, and runway touchdown zone elevation is 1152.

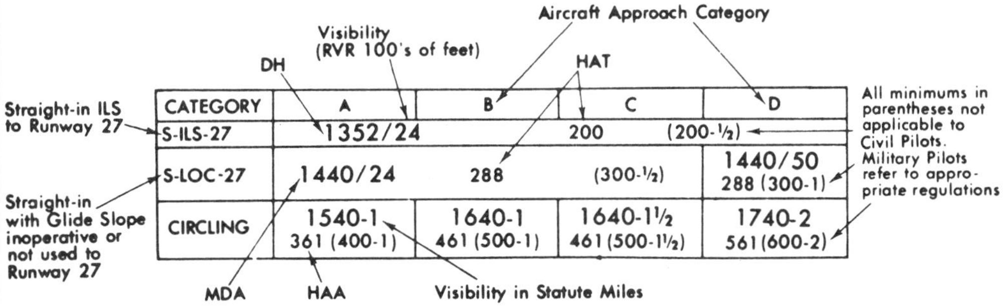

CATEGORY	A	B	C	D
S-ILS-27	1352/24	200		(200-1/2)
S-LOC-27	1440/24	288	(300-1/2)	1440/50 288 (300-1)
CIRCLING	1540-1 361 (400-1)	1640-1 461 (500-1)	1640-1 1/2 461 (500-1 1/2)	1740-2 561 (600-2)

Straight-in ILS to Runway 27
Straight-in with Glide Slope inoperative or not used to Runway 27

Visibility (RVR 100's of feet)
DH
Aircraft Approach Category
HAT
MDA HAA Visibility in Statute Miles

All minimums in parentheses not applicable to Civil Pilots. Military Pilots refer to appropriate regulations

CORRECTIONS, COMMENTS AND/OR PROCUREMENT

FOR CHARTING ERRORS:

Contact National Ocean Service
NOAA, N/CG31
6010 Executive Blvd.
Rockville, MD. 20852
Telephone Toll-Free 800-626-3677

FOR CHANGES, ADDITIONS, OR RECOMMENDATIONS ON PROCEDURAL ASPECTS:

Contact Federal Aviation Administration, ATO-258
800 Independence Avenue, S.W.
Washington, D.C. 20591
Telephone (202) 267-9297

PROCURE FROM:

National Ocean Service
NOAA, N/CG33
Distribution Branch
Riverdale, MD. 20737
Telephone (301) 436-6993

LEGEND 13.—Instrument Approach Procedures Explanation of Terms

Appendix 2

87295 Julian Date of Last Revision **GENERAL INFORMATION & ABBREVIATIONS**

★ Indicates control tower or ATIS operates non-continuously, or non-standard Pilot Controlled Lighting.
Distances in nautical miles (except visibility in statute miles and Runway Visual Range in hundreds of feet).
Runway Dimensions in feet. Elevations in feet Mean Sea Level (MSL). Ceilings in feet above airport elevation.
Radials/bearings/headings/courses are magnetic
\# Indicates control tower temporarily closed UFN.

ADF	Automatic Direction Finder	MALSR	Medium Intensity Approach Light Systems with RAIL
ALS	Approach Light System	MAP	Missed Approach Point
ALSF	Approach Light System with Sequenced Flashing Lights	MDA	Minimum Descent Altitude
APP CON	Approach Control	MIRL	Medium Intensity Runway Lights
ARR	Arrival	MLS	Microwave Landing System
ASR/PAR	Published Radar Minimums at this Airport	MM	Middle Marker
		NA	Not Authorized
ATIS	Automatic Terminal Information Service	NDB	Non-directional Radio Beacon
		NM	Nautical Miles
AWOS	Automated Weather Observing System	NoPT	No Procedure Turn Required (Procedure Turn shall not be executed without ATC clearance)
AZ	Azimuth		
BC	Back Course	ODALS	Omnidirectional Approach Light System
C	Circling		
CAT	Category	OM	Outer Marker
CCW	Counter Clockwise	R	Radial
Chan	Channel	RA	Radio Altimeter setting height
CLNC DEL	Clearance Delivery	Radar Required	Radar vectoring required for this approach
CTAF	Common Traffic Advisory Frequency		
		RAIL	Runway Alignment Indicator Lights
CW	Clockwise		
DH	Decision Heights	RBn	Radio Beacon
DME	Distance Measuring Equipment	RCLS	Runway Centerline Light System
DR	Dead Reckoning	REIL	Runway End Identifier Lights
ELEV	Elevation	RNAV	Area Navigation
FAF	Final Approach Fix	RPI	Runway Point of Intercept(ion)
FM	Fan Marker	RRL	Runway Remaining Lights
GPI	Ground Point of Interception	Runway Touchdown Zone	First 3000' of Runway
GS	Glide Slope	Rwy	Runway
HAA	Height Above Airport	RVR	Runway Visual Range
HAL	Height Above Landing	S	Straight-in
HAT	Height Above Touchdown	SALS	Short Approach Light System
HIRL	High Intensity Runway Lights	SSALR	Simplified Short Approach Light System with RAIL
IAF	Initial Approach Fix		
ICAO	International Civil Aviation Organization	SDF	Simplified Directional Facility
		TA	Transition Altitude
IM	Inner Marker	TAC	TACAN
Intcp	Intercept	TCH	Threshold Crossing Height (height in feet Above Ground Level)
INT	Intersection		
LDA	Localizer Type Directional Aid		
Ldg	Landing	TDZ	Touchdown Zone
LDIN	Lead in Light System	TDZE	Touchdown Zone Elevation
LIRL	Low Intensity Runway Lights	TDZ/CL	Touchdown Zone and Runway Centerline Lighting
LOC	Localizer		
LR	Lead Radial. Provides at least 2 NM (Copter 1 NM) of lead to assist in turning onto the intermediate/final course	TDZL	Touchdown Zone Lights
		Tlv	Transition Level
		VASI	Visual Approach Slope Indicator
		VDP	Visual Descent Point
MALS	Medium Intensity Approach Light System	WPT	Waypoint (RNAV)
		X	Radar Only Frequency

PILOT CONTROLLED AIRPORT LIGHTING SYSTEMS

Available pilot controlled lighting (PCL) systems are indicated as follows:
1. Approach lighting systems that bear a system identification are symbolized using negative symbology, e.g., Ⓐ1, V, ☆
2. Approach lighting systems that do not bear a system identification are indicated with a negative " Ⓛ " beside the name.

A star (★) indicates non-standard PCL, consult Directory/Supplement, e.g., Ⓛ★
To activate lights use frequency indicated in the communication section of the chart with a Ⓛ or the appropriate lighting system identification e.g., UNICOM 122.8 Ⓛ, Ⓐ1, V

KEY MIKE	FUNCTION
7 times within 5 seconds	Highest intensity available
5 times within 5 seconds	Medium or lower intensity (Lower REIL or REIL-off)
3 times within 5 seconds	Lowest intensity available (Lower REIL or REIL-off)

LEGEND 14.—General Information and Abbreviations

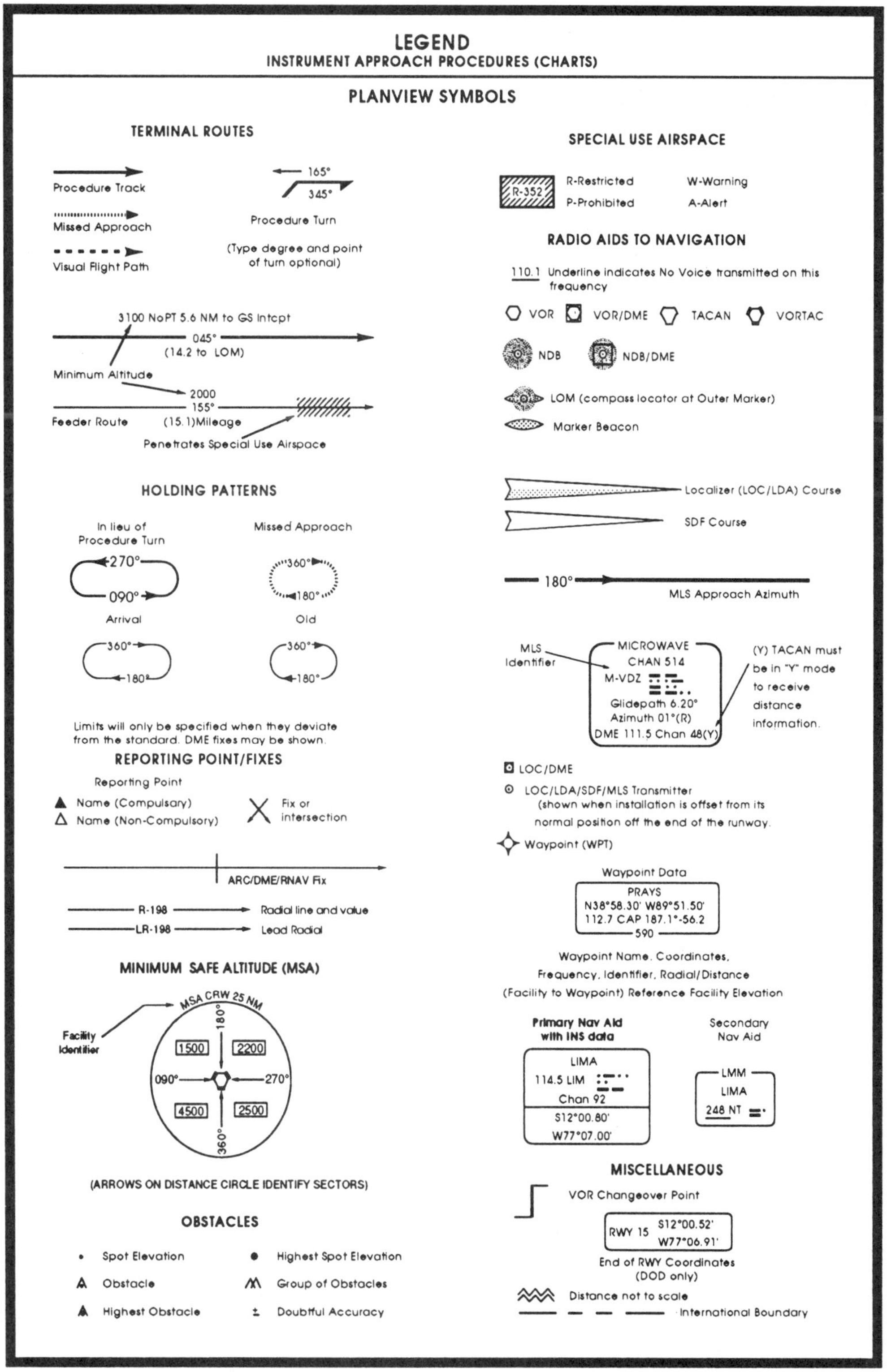

Appendix 2

LEGEND
INSTRUMENT APPROACH PROCEDURES (CHARTS)

PLANVIEW SYMBOLS

TERMINAL ROUTES

- Procedure Track
- Missed Approach
- Visual Flight Path
- Procedure Turn (Type degree and point of turn optional) — 165°/345°

3100 NoPT 5.6 NM to GS Intcpt
045° (14.2 to LOM) — Minimum Altitude
2000
155° (15.1) Mileage — Feeder Route
Penetrates Special Use Airspace

HOLDING PATTERNS

- In lieu of Procedure Turn: 270° / 090°
- Missed Approach: 360° / 180°
- Arrival: 360° / 180°
- Old: 360° / 180°

Limits will only be specified when they deviate from the standard. DME fixes may be shown.

REPORTING POINT/FIXES

- ▲ Name (Compulsory) — Reporting Point
- △ Name (Non-Compulsory)
- ✕ Fix or intersection
- ARC/DME/RNAV Fix
- R-198 — Radial line and value
- LR-198 — Lead Radial

MINIMUM SAFE ALTITUDE (MSA)

MSA CRW 25 NM
- 1500 | 2200
- 090° — 270°
- 4500 | 2500
- Facility Identifier

(ARROWS ON DISTANCE CIRCLE IDENTIFY SECTORS)

OBSTACLES

- • Spot Elevation
- ● Highest Spot Elevation
- ▲ Obstacle
- ⋏ Group of Obstacles
- ▲ Highest Obstacle
- ± Doubtful Accuracy

SPECIAL USE AIRSPACE

- R-352
- R-Restricted   W-Warning
- P-Prohibited   A-Alert

RADIO AIDS TO NAVIGATION

110.1 Underline indicates No Voice transmitted on this frequency

- ⬡ VOR
- ⬡ VOR/DME
- △ TACAN
- ⬡ VORTAC
- ◉ NDB
- ◉ NDB/DME
- LOM (compass locator at Outer Marker)
- Marker Beacon

- Localizer (LOC/LDA) Course
- SDF Course

— 180° — MLS Approach Azimuth

MLS Identifier:
MICROWAVE
CHAN 514
M-VDZ
Glidepath 6.20°
Azimuth 01°(R)
DME 111.5 Chan 48(Y)

(Y) TACAN must be in "Y" mode to receive distance information.

- ▫ LOC/DME
- ⊙ LOC/LDA/SDF/MLS Transmitter (shown when installation is offset from its normal position off the end of the runway.
- ✧ Waypoint (WPT)

Waypoint Data:
PRAYS
N38°58.30' W89°51.50'
112.7 CAP 187.1°-56.2
590

Waypoint Name, Coordinates, Frequency, Identifier, Radial/Distance (Facility to Waypoint) Reference Facility Elevation

Primary Nav Aid with INS data
LIMA
114.5 LIM
Chan 92
S12°00.80'
W77°07.00'

Secondary Nav Aid
LMM
LIMA
248 NT

MISCELLANEOUS

- ⌐ VOR Changeover Point
- RWY 15 S12°00.52' W77°06.91'
  End of RWY Coordinates (DOD only)
- ∿∿∿ Distance not to scale
- — — — International Boundary

LEGEND 15.—Instrument Approach Procedures (Planview).

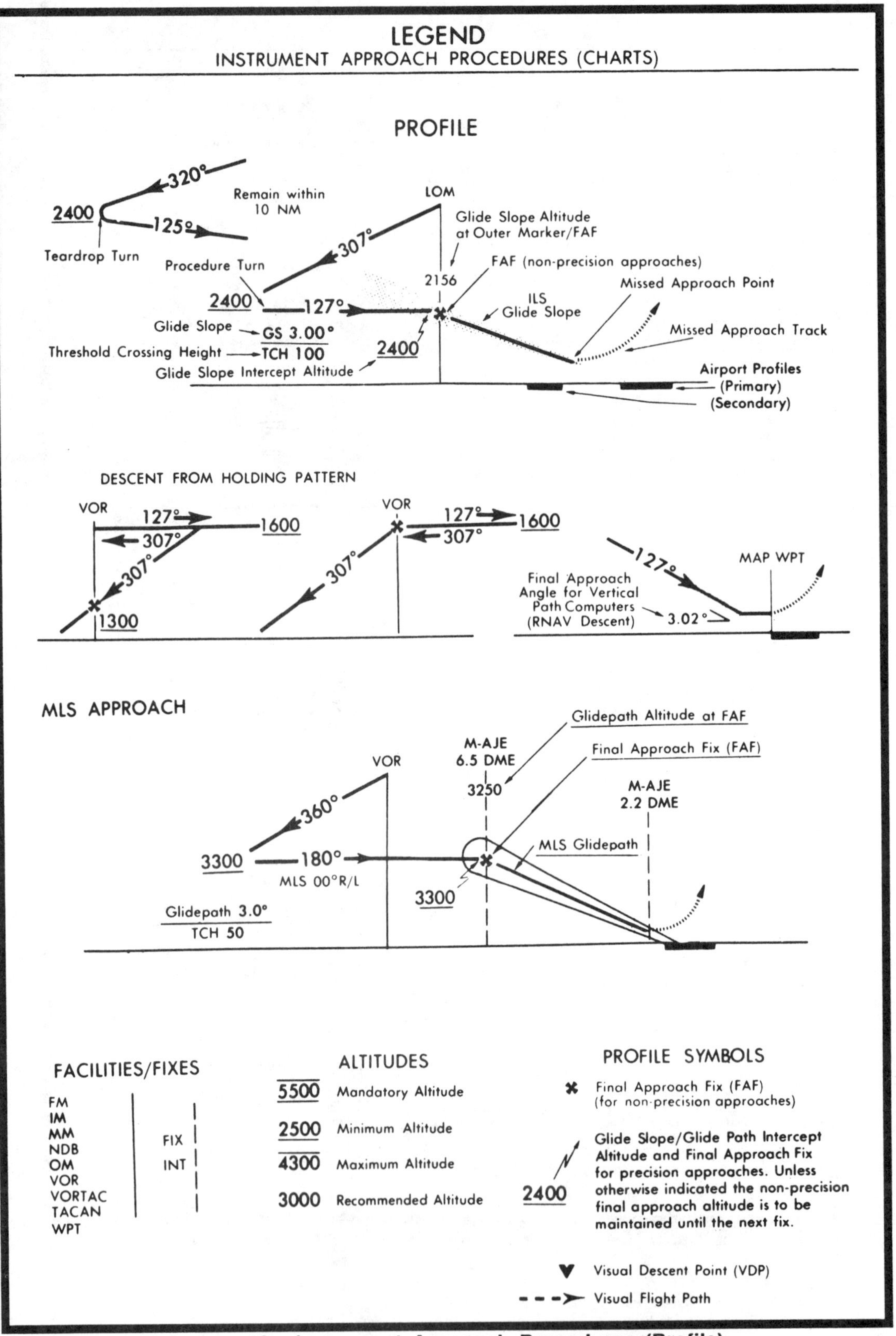

Appendix 2

LEGEND
INSTRUMENT APPROACH PROCEDURES (CHARTS)

PROFILE

- 320° — Remain within 10 NM
- 2400 — Teardrop Turn
- 125°
- LOM
- 307°
- Glide Slope Altitude at Outer Marker/FAF
- 2156 — FAF (non-precision approaches)
- Missed Approach Point
- 2400 — Procedure Turn
- 127°
- ILS Glide Slope
- Missed Approach Track
- Glide Slope — GS 3.00°
- Threshold Crossing Height — TCH 100
- 2400 — Glide Slope Intercept Altitude
- Airport Profiles (Primary) (Secondary)

DESCENT FROM HOLDING PATTERN

- VOR 127° → 1600
- 307°
- 307°
- 1300
- VOR 127° → 1600
- 307°
- 307°
- 127° MAP WPT
- Final Approach Angle for Vertical Path Computers (RNAV Descent) — 3.02°

MLS APPROACH

- VOR
- 360°
- 3300 — 180°
- MLS 00°R/L
- Glidepath 3.0° / TCH 50
- 3300
- M-AJE 6.5 DME — 3250 — Glidepath Altitude at FAF
- Final Approach Fix (FAF)
- M-AJE 2.2 DME
- MLS Glidepath

FACILITIES/FIXES
FM
IM
MM — FIX
NDB
OM — INT
VOR
VORTAC
TACAN
WPT

ALTITUDES
- 5500 Mandatory Altitude
- 2500 Minimum Altitude
- 4300 Maximum Altitude
- 3000 Recommended Altitude

PROFILE SYMBOLS
- ✳ Final Approach Fix (FAF) (for non-precision approaches)
- 2400 Glide Slope/Glide Path Intercept Altitude and Final Approach Fix for precision approaches. Unless otherwise indicated the non-precision final approach altitude is to be maintained until the next fix.
- ▼ Visual Descent Point (VDP)
- - - → Visual Flight Path

LEGEND 16.—Instrument Approach Procedures (Profile)

Appendix 2

LEGEND
INSTRUMENT APPROACH PROCEDURES (CHARTS)

AIRPORT DIAGRAM/AIRPORT SKETCH

Runways

- Hard Surface
- Other Than Hard Surface
- Overruns, Taxiways, Parking Areas
- Displaced Threshold

Helicopter Alighting Areas: (H) ⊞ [H] ⚠ ⊞

Negative Symbols used to identify Copter Procedure landing point .... ● ⊞ H ⚠ ⊞

- Closed Runways
- Closed Taxiways
- Under Construction
- Metal Surface
- Runway Centerline Lighting

Runway TDZ elevation .... TDZE 123

Total Runway Gradient .... 0.8% → UP
(shown when runway gradient exceeds 0.3%)

Arresting Gear

- uni-directional
- bi-directional
- Jet Barrier

■ U.S. Navy Optical Landing System (OLS) "OLS" location is shown because of its height of approximately 7 feet and proximity to edge of runway may create an obstruction for some types of aircraft.

REFERENCE FEATURES

Buildings .... ■

Tanks .... ●

Obstruction .... ∧

Airport Beacon # .... ☆

Runway Radar Reflectors .... ⧖

Control Tower # .... ▪

\# When Control Tower and Rotating Beacon are co-located, Beacon symbol will be used and further identified as TWR.

Approach light symbols are shown on a separate legend.

Airport diagram scales are variable.

True/magnetic North orientation may vary from diagram to diagram.

Coordinate values are shown in 1 or ½ minute increments. They are further broken down into 6 second ticks, within each 1 minute increment.

Positional accuracy within ±600 feet unless otherwise noted on the chart.

NOTE:
Airport diagrams that are referenced to the World Geodetic System (WGS) (noted on appropriate diagram), may not be compatible with local coordinates published in FLIP.

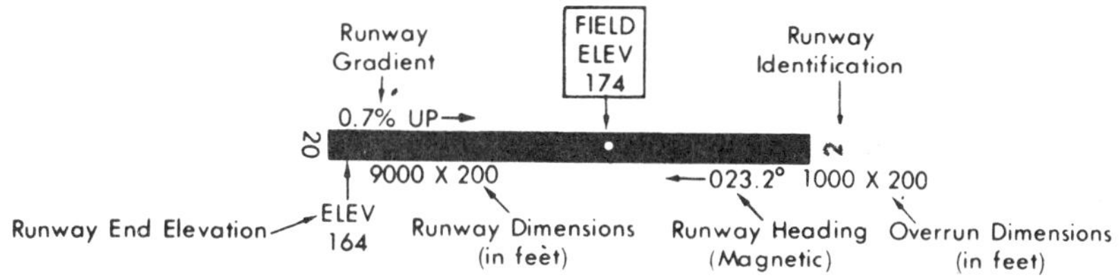

```
           Runway        FIELD         Runway
          Gradient       ELEV       Identification
             ↓            174             ↓
          0.7% UP→
  20 ▬▬▬▬▬▬▬▬▬▬▬▬▬▬▬▬▬▬▬▬▬▬▬▬▬▬▬▬  2
          ↓ 9000 X 200    ←023.2°  1000 X 200
    ELEV   Runway Dimensions  Runway Heading  Overrun Dimensions
Runway End Elevation─164  (in feet)   (Magnetic)       (in feet)
```

GENERAL INFORMATION (NOS)
SCOPE

Airport diagrams are specifically designed to assist in the movement of ground traffic at locations with complex runway/taxiway configurations and provide information for updating Inertial Navigation Systems (INS) aboard aircraft. Airport diagrams are not intended to be used for approach and landing or departure operations. Requisition for the creation of airport diagrams must meet the above criteria and will be approved by the FAA or DOD on a case-by-case

MINIMA DATA

⚠ Alternate Minimums not standard.
Civil users refer to tabulation.
USA/USN/USAF pilots refer to appropriate regulations.

⚠ NA Alternate minimums are Not Authorized due to unmonitored facility or absence of weather reporting service.

▽ Take-off Minimums not standard and/or Departure Procedures are published. Refer to tabulation.

LEGEND 17.—Instrument Approach Procedures (Airport Diagram/Sketch)

Appendix 2

INSTRUMENT TAKEOFF PROCEDURE CHARTS
RATE-OF-CLIMB TABLE
(ft. per min.)

A rate-of-climb table is provided for use in planning and executing takeoff procedures under known or approximate ground speed conditions.

REQUIRED CLIMB RATE (ft. per NM)	GROUND SPEED (KNOTS)						
	30	60	80	90	100	120	140
200	100	200	267	300	333	400	467
250	125	250	333	375	417	500	583
300	150	300	400	450	500	600	700
350	175	350	467	525	583	700	816
400	200	400	533	600	667	800	933
450	225	450	600	675	750	900	1050
500	250	500	667	750	833	1000	1167
550	275	550	733	825	917	1100	1283
600	300	600	800	900	1000	1200	1400
650	325	650	867	975	1083	1300	1516
700	350	700	933	1050	1167	1400	1633

REQUIRED CLIMB RATE (ft. per NM)	GROUND SPEED (KNOTS)					
	150	180	210	240	270	300
200	500	600	700	800	900	1000
250	625	750	875	1000	1125	1250
300	750	900	1050	1200	1350	1500
350	875	1050	1225	1400	1575	1750
400	1000	1200	1400	1600	1700	2000
450	1125	1350	1575	1800	2025	2250
500	1250	1500	1750	2000	2250	2500
550	1375	1650	1925	2200	2475	2750
600	1500	1800	2100	2400	2700	3000
650	1625	1950	2275	2600	2925	3250
700	1750	2100	2450	2800	3150	3500

LEGEND 18.—Instrument Takeoff Procedure Charts, Rate-of-Climb Table.

Appendix 2

INSTRUMENT APPROACH PROCEDURE CHARTS
RATE OF DESCENT TABLE
(ft. per min.)

A rate of descent table is provided for use in planning and executing precision descents under known or approximate ground speed conditions. It will be especially useful for approaches when the localizer only is used for course guidance. A best speed, power, attitude combination can be programmed which will result in a stable glide rate and attitude favorable for executing a landing if minimums exist upon breakout. Care should always be exercised so that the minimum descent altitude and missed approach point are not exceeded.

ANGLE OF DESCENT (degrees and tenths)	\multicolumn{11}{c	}{GROUND SPEED (knots)}
	30	45	60	75	90	105	120	135	150	165	180
2.0	105	160	210	265	320	370	425	475	530	585	635
2.5	130	200	265	330	395	465	530	595	665	730	795
3.0	160	240	320	395	480	555	635	715	795	875	955
3.5	185	280	370	465	555	650	740	835	925	1020	1110
4.0	210	315	425	530	635	740	845	955	1060	1165	1270
4.5	240	355	475	595	715	835	955	1075	1190	1310	1430
5.0	265	395	530	660	795	925	1060	1190	1325	1455	1590
5.5	290	435	580	730	875	1020	1165	1310	1455	1600	1745
6.0	315	475	635	795	955	1110	1270	1430	1590	1745	1905
6.5	345	515	690	860	1030	1205	1375	1550	1720	1890	2065
7.0	370	555	740	925	1110	1295	1480	1665	1850	2035	2220
7.5	395	595	795	990	1190	1390	1585	1785	1985	2180	2380
8.0	425	635	845	1055	1270	1480	1690	1905	2115	2325	2540
8.5	450	675	900	1120	1345	1570	1795	2020	2245	2470	2695
9.0	475	715	950	1190	1425	1665	1900	2140	2375	2615	2855
9.5	500	750	1005	1255	1505	1755	2005	2255	2510	2760	3010
10.0	530	790	1055	1320	1585	1845	2110	2375	2640	2900	3165
10.5	555	830	1105	1385	1660	1940	2215	2490	2770	3045	3320
11.0	580	870	1160	1450	1740	2030	2320	2610	2900	3190	3480
11.5	605	910	1210	1515	1820	2120	2425	2725	3030	3335	3635
12.0	630	945	1260	1575	1890	2205	2520	2835	3150	3465	3780

LEGEND 19.—Instrument Approach Procedure Charts, Rate-of-Descent Table.

Appendix 2

INOPERATIVE COMPONENTS OR VISUAL AIDS TABLE

Landing minimums published on instrument approach procedure charts are based upon full operation of all components and visual aids associated with the particular instrument approach chart being used. Higher minimums are required with inoperative components or visual aids as indicated below. If more than one component is inoperative, each minimum is raised to the highest minimum required by any single component that is inoperative. ILS glide slope inoperative minimums are published on instrument approach charts as localizer minimums. This table may be amended by notes on the approach chart. Such notes apply only to the particular approach category(ies) as stated. See legend page for description of components indicated below.

(1) ILS, MLS, and PAR

Inoperative Component or Aid	Approach Category	Increase Visibility
ALSF 1 & 2, MALSR, & SSALR	ABCD	1/4 mile

(2) ILS with visibility minimum of 1,800 RVR.

ALSF 1 & 2, MALSR, &SSALR	ABCD	To 4000 RVR
TDZI RCLS	ABCD	To 2400 RVR
RVR	ABCD	To 1/2 mile

(3) VOR, VOR/DME, VORTAC, VOR (TAC), VOR/DME (TAC), LOC, LOC/DME, LDA, LDA/DME, SDF, SDF/DME, RNAV, and ASR

Inoperative Visual Aid	Approach Category	Increase Visibility
ALSF 1 & 2, MALSR, & SSALR	ABCD	1/2 mile
SSALS, MALS, & ODALS	ABC	1/4 mile

(4) NDB

ALSF 1 & 2, MALSR & SSALR	C	1/2 mile
	ABD	1/4 mile
MALS, SSALS, ODALS	ABC	1/4 mile

LEGEND 20.—Inoperative Components or Visual Aids Table.

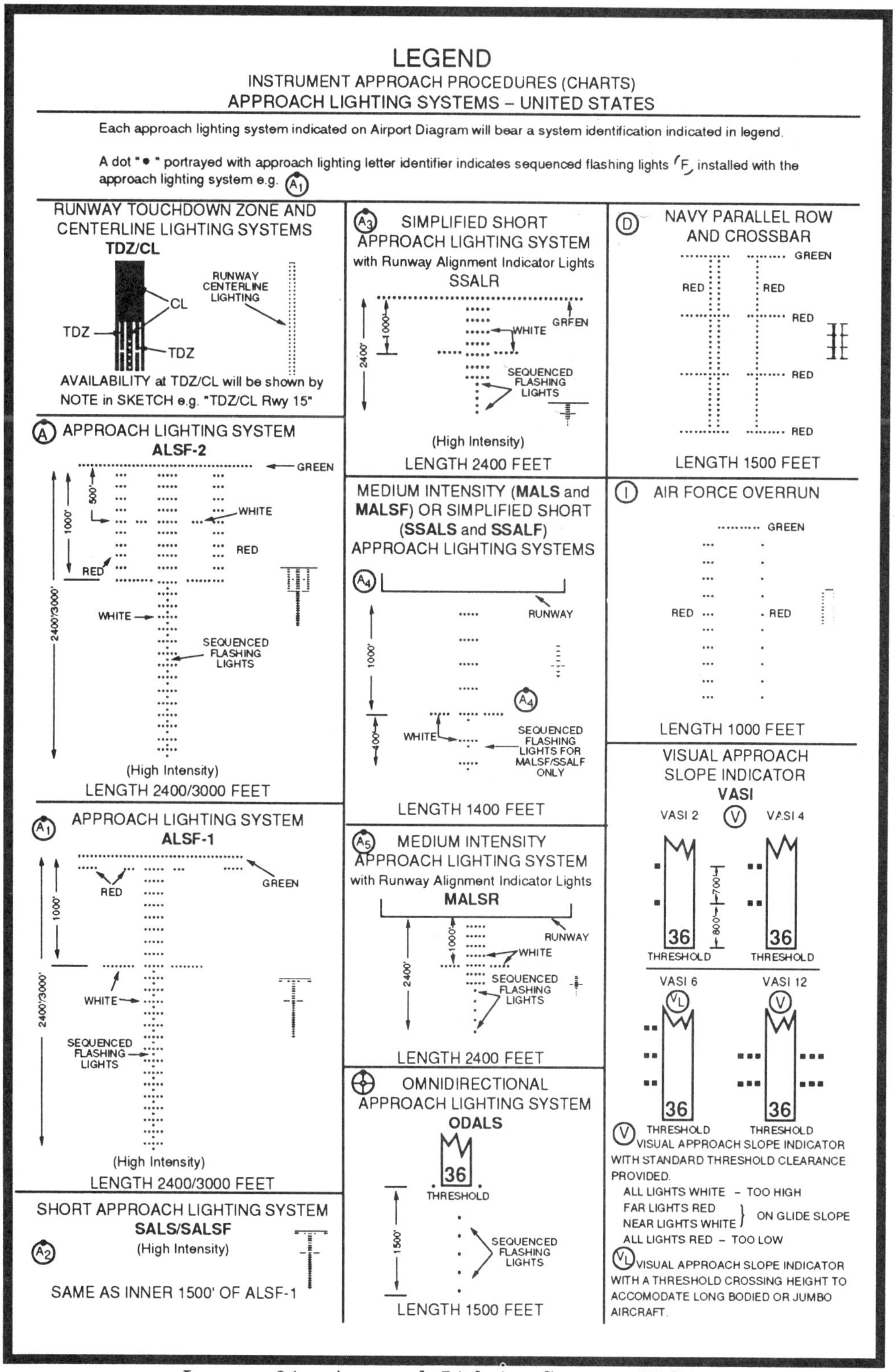

Appendix 2

LEGEND 21.—Approach Lighting Systems (U.S.).

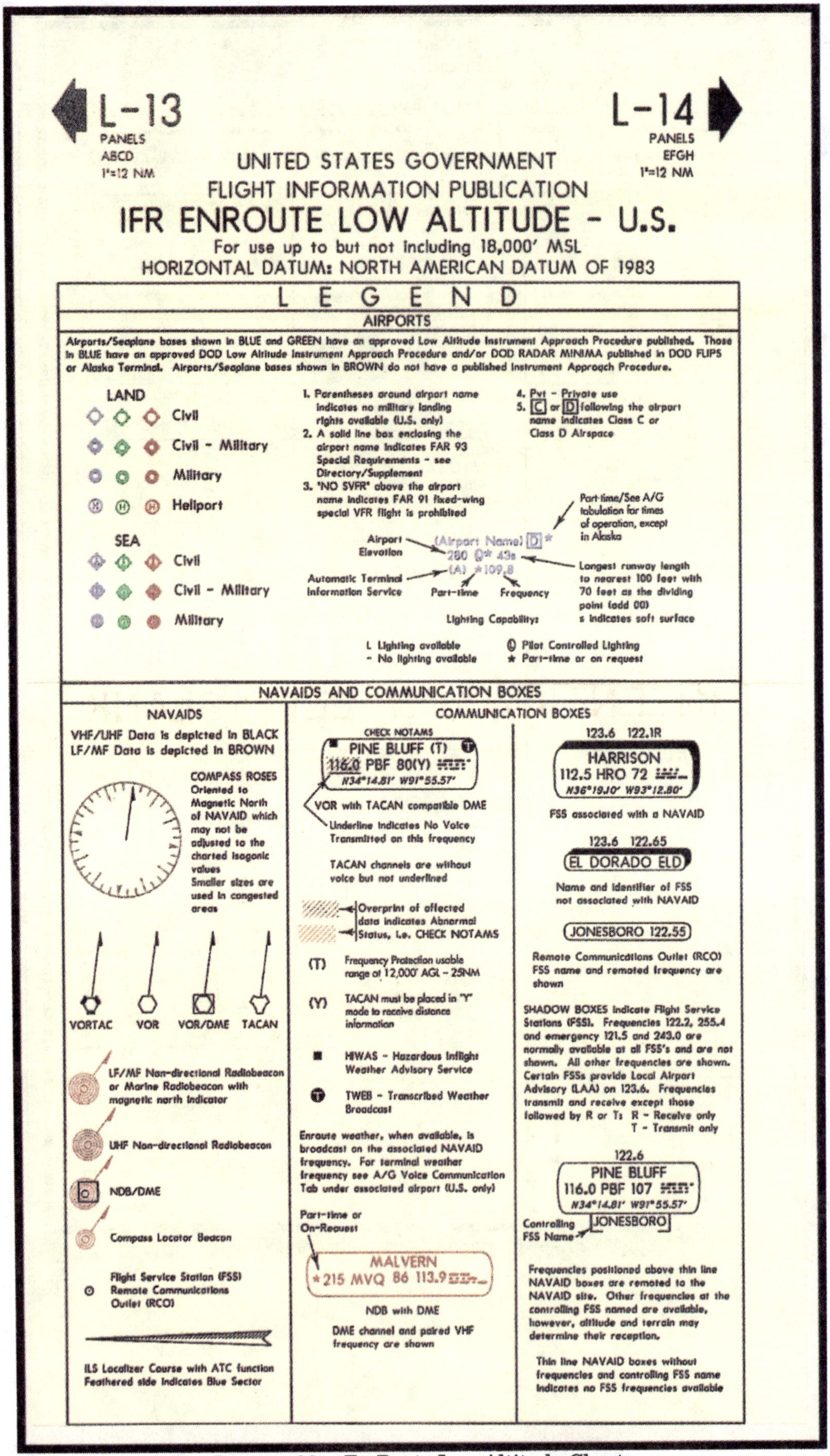

Appendix 2

LEGEND 22.—En Route Low Altitude Charts.

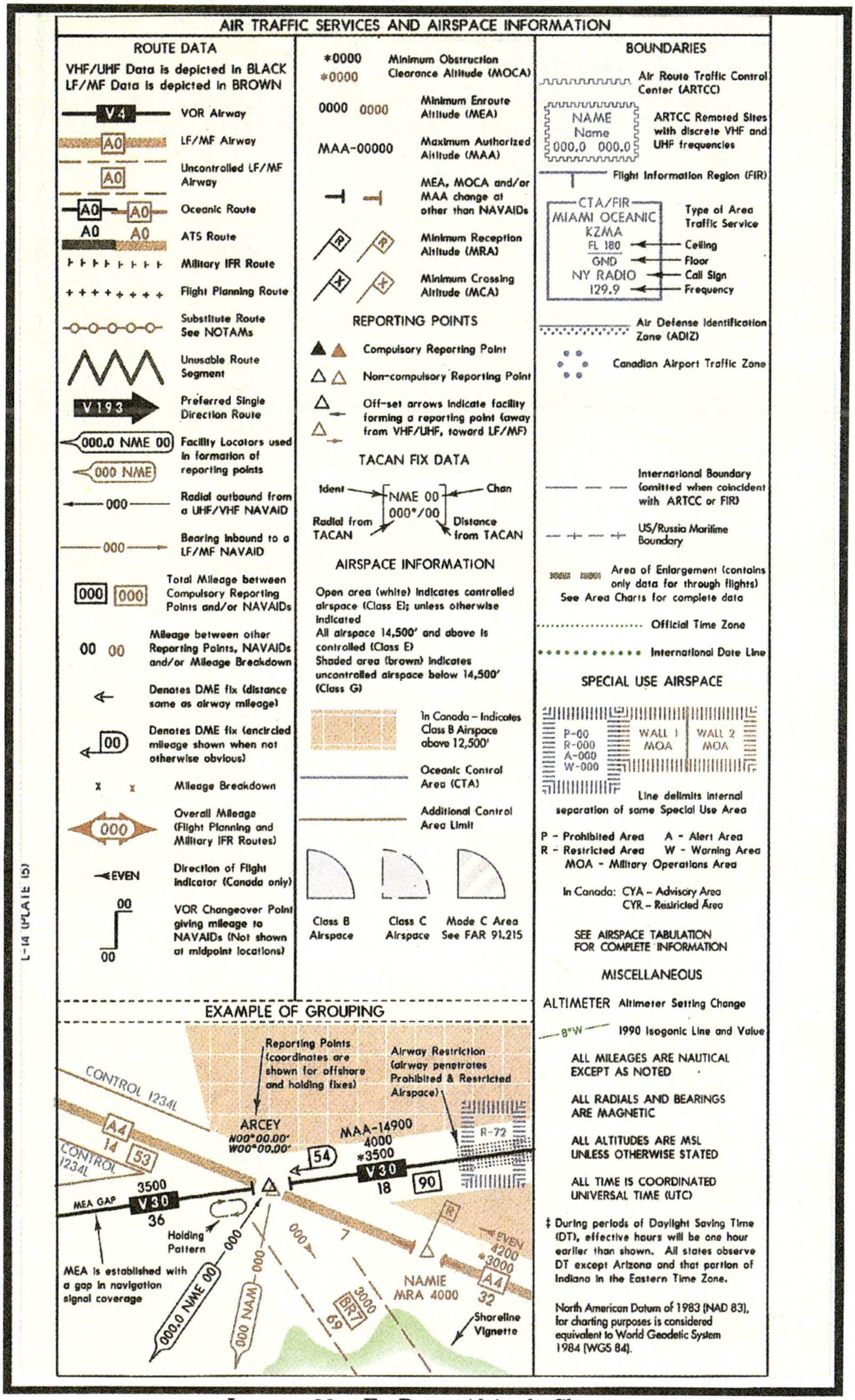

AIR TRAFFIC SERVICES AND AIRSPACE INFORMATION

ROUTE DATA

VHF/UHF Data is depicted in BLACK
LF/MF Data is depicted in BROWN

- VOR Airway
- LF/MF Airway
- Uncontrolled LF/MF Airway
- Oceanic Route
- ATS Route
- Military IFR Route
- Flight Planning Route
- Substitute Route See NOTAMs
- Unusable Route Segment
- Preferred Single Direction Route
- Facility Locators used in formation of reporting points
- Radial outbound from a UHF/VHF NAVAID
- Bearing inbound to a LF/MF NAVAID
- Total Mileage between Compulsory Reporting Points and/or NAVAIDs
- Mileage between other Reporting Points, NAVAIDs and/or Mileage Breakdown
- Denotes DME fix (distance same as airway mileage)
- Denotes DME fix (encircled mileage shown when not otherwise obvious)
- Mileage Breakdown
- Overall Mileage (Flight Planning and Military IFR Routes)
- Direction of Flight Indicator (Canada only)
- VOR Changeover Point giving mileage to NAVAIDs (Not shown at midpoint locations)

*0000 Minimum Obstruction Clearance Altitude (MOCA)
0000 0000 Minimum Enroute Altitude (MEA)
MAA-00000 Maximum Authorized Altitude (MAA)
MEA, MOCA and/or MAA change at other than NAVAIDs
Minimum Reception Altitude (MRA)
Minimum Crossing Altitude (MCA)

REPORTING POINTS

- ▲ Compulsory Reporting Point
- △ Non-compulsory Reporting Point
- Off-set arrows indicate facility forming a reporting point (away from VHF/UHF, toward LF/MF)

TACAN FIX DATA

Ident — NME 00 — Chan
Radial from TACAN 000°/00 Distance from TACAN

AIRSPACE INFORMATION

Open area (white) indicates controlled airspace (Class E); unless otherwise indicated
All airspace 14,500' and above is controlled (Class E)
Shaded area (brown) indicates uncontrolled airspace below 14,500' (Class G)

In Canada — Indicates Class B Airspace above 12,500'

Oceanic Control Area (CTA)
Additional Control Area Limit

Class B Airspace | Class C Airspace | Mode C Area See FAR 91.215

BOUNDARIES

- Air Route Traffic Control Center (ARTCC)
- ARTCC Remoted Sites with discrete VHF and UHF frequencies NAME 000.0 000.0
- Flight Information Region (FIR)
- CTA/FIR MIAMI OCEANIC KZMA — Type of Area Traffic Service
  - FL 180 — Ceiling
  - GND — Floor
  - NY RADIO — Call Sign
  - 129.9 — Frequency
- Air Defense Identification Zone (ADIZ)
- Canadian Airport Traffic Zone
- International Boundary (omitted when coincident with ARTCC or FIR)
- US/Russia Maritime Boundary
- Area of Enlargement (contains only data for through flights) See Area Charts for complete data
- Official Time Zone
- International Date Line

SPECIAL USE AIRSPACE

P-00 | WALL 1 MOA | WALL 2 MOA
R-000
A-000
W-000

Line delimits internal separation of same Special Use Area

P - Prohibited Area   A - Alert Area
R - Restricted Area   W - Warning Area
MOA - Military Operations Area

In Canada: CYA - Advisory Area
CYR - Restricted Area

SEE AIRSPACE TABULATION FOR COMPLETE INFORMATION

MISCELLANEOUS

ALTIMETER Altimeter Setting Change

8°W 1990 Isogonic Line and Value

ALL MILEAGES ARE NAUTICAL EXCEPT AS NOTED

ALL RADIALS AND BEARINGS ARE MAGNETIC

ALL ALTITUDES ARE MSL UNLESS OTHERWISE STATED

ALL TIME IS COORDINATED UNIVERSAL TIME (UTC)

‡ During periods of Daylight Saving Time (DT), effective hours will be one hour earlier than shown. All states observe DT except Arizona and that portion of Indiana in the Eastern Time Zone.

North American Datum of 1983 (NAD 83), for charting purposes is considered equivalent to World Geodetic System 1984 (WGS 84).

EXAMPLE OF GROUPING

Reporting Points (coordinates are shown for offshore and holding fixes)
Airway Restriction (airway penetrates Prohibited & Restricted Airspace)

CONTROL 1234L
ARCEY N00°00.00' W00°00.00'
MAA-14900
4000
*3500
V30
R-72
CONTROL 1234L
14 53
54
90
3500
MEA GAP V30
36
18
Holding Pattern
000
000
000.0 NME 00
000 NAM
EVEN 4200
*3000
A4
32
BR7 3000
69
NAMIE MRA 4000
Shoreline Vignette
MEA is established with a gap in navigation signal coverage

LEGEND 23.—En Route Altitude Charts.

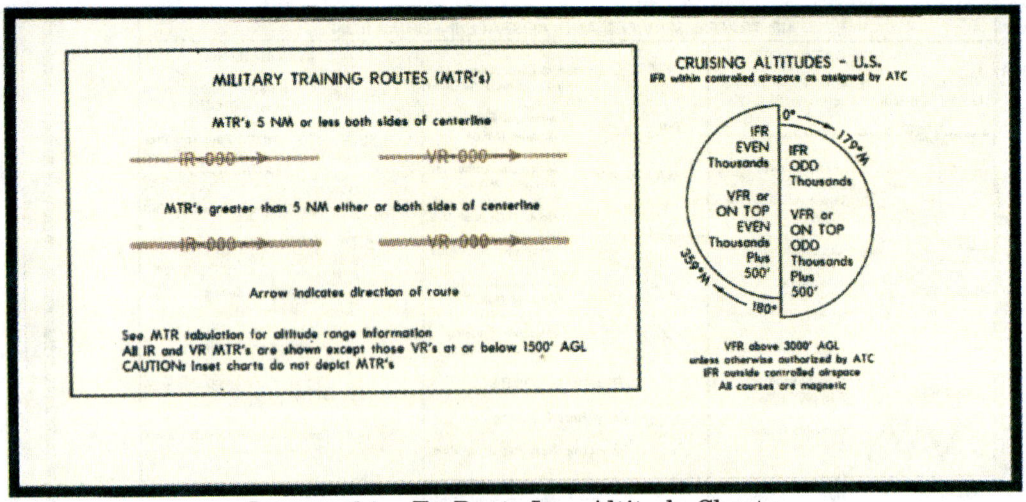

Appendix 2

LEGEND 24.—En Route Low Altitude Charts.

Appendix 2

AIRCRAFT EQUIPMENT CODE

/X—NO TRANSPONDER
/T—TRANSPONDER WITH NO ALTITUDE ENCODING CAPABILITY
/U—TRANSPONDER WITH ALTITUDE ENCODING CAPABILITY
/D—DME, BUT NO TRANSPONDER
/B—DME AND TRANSPONDER, BUT NO ALTITUDE ENCODING CAPABILITY
/A—DME AND TRANSPONDER WITH ALTITUDE ENCODING CAPABILITY
/M—TACAN ONLY, BUT NO TRANSPONDER
/N—TACAN ONLY AND TRANSPONDER, BUT WITH NO ALTITUDE ENCODING CAPABILITY
/P—TACAN ONLY AND TRANSPONDER WITH ALTITUDE ENCODING CAPABILITY
/C—RNAV AND TRANSPONDER, BUT WITH NO ALTITUDE ENCODING CAPABILITY
/R—RNAV AND TRANSPONDER WITH ALTITUDE ENCODING CAPABILITY
/W—RNAV BUT NO TRANSPONDER
/G—FLIGHT MANAGEMENT SYSTEM (FMS) AND ELECTRONIC FLIGHT INSTRUMENT SYSTEM (EFIS) EQUIPPED AIRCRAFT WITH /R CAPABILITY HAVING A "SPECIAL AIRCRAFT AND AIRCREW AUTHORIZATION" ISSUED BY THE FAA.

LEGEND 25.—Aircraft Equipment Codes.

Appendix 2

AIR NAVIGATION RADIO AIDS

STANDARD HIGH ALTITUDE SERVICE VOLUME

- 60,000 ft. — 100 nmi
- 45,000 ft. — 130 nmi
- 18,000 ft.
- 14,500 ft.
- 1,000 ft. — 40 nmi

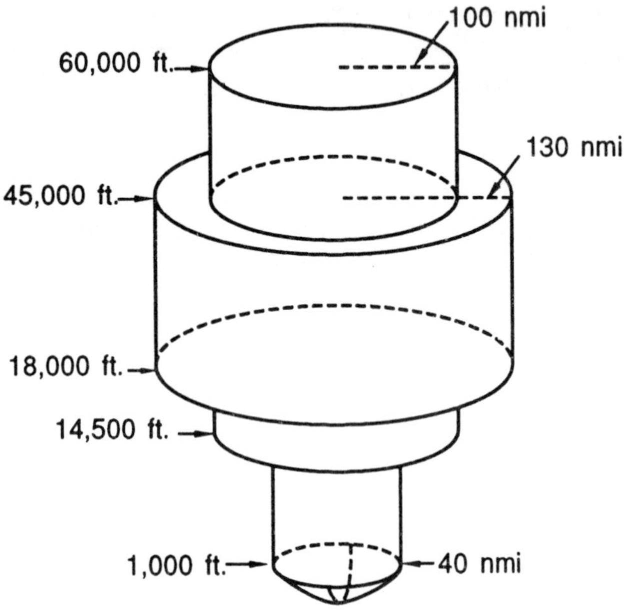

STANDARD LOW ALTITUDE SERVICE VOLUME

- 40 nmi — 18,000 ft.
- 1,000 ft.

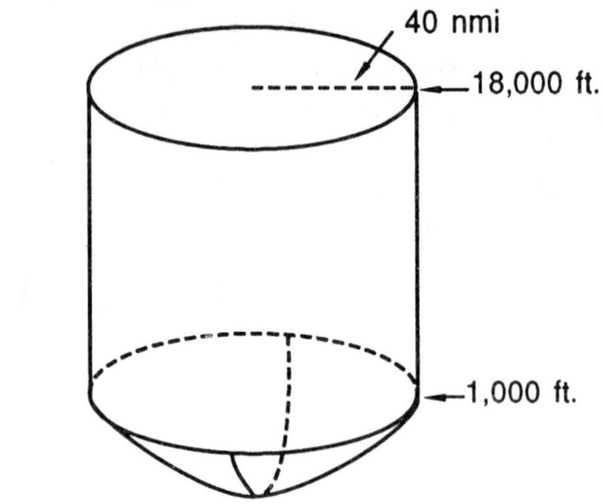

NOTE: All elevations shown are with respect to the station's site elevation (AGL). Coverage is not available in a cone of airspace directly above the facility.

STANDARD TERMINAL SERVICE VOLUME

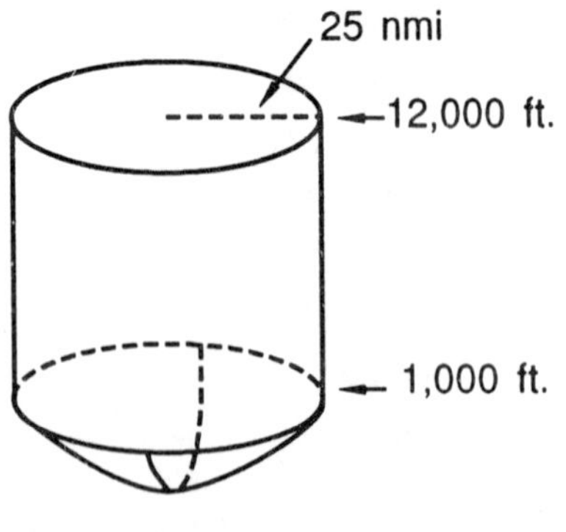

- 25 nmi — 12,000 ft.
- 1,000 ft.

LEGEND 26.—Air Navigation Radio Aids.

Appendix 2

THIS PAGE INTENTIONALLY LEFT BLANK

Appendix 2

LEGEND 28.—ILS Standard Characteristics and Terminology.

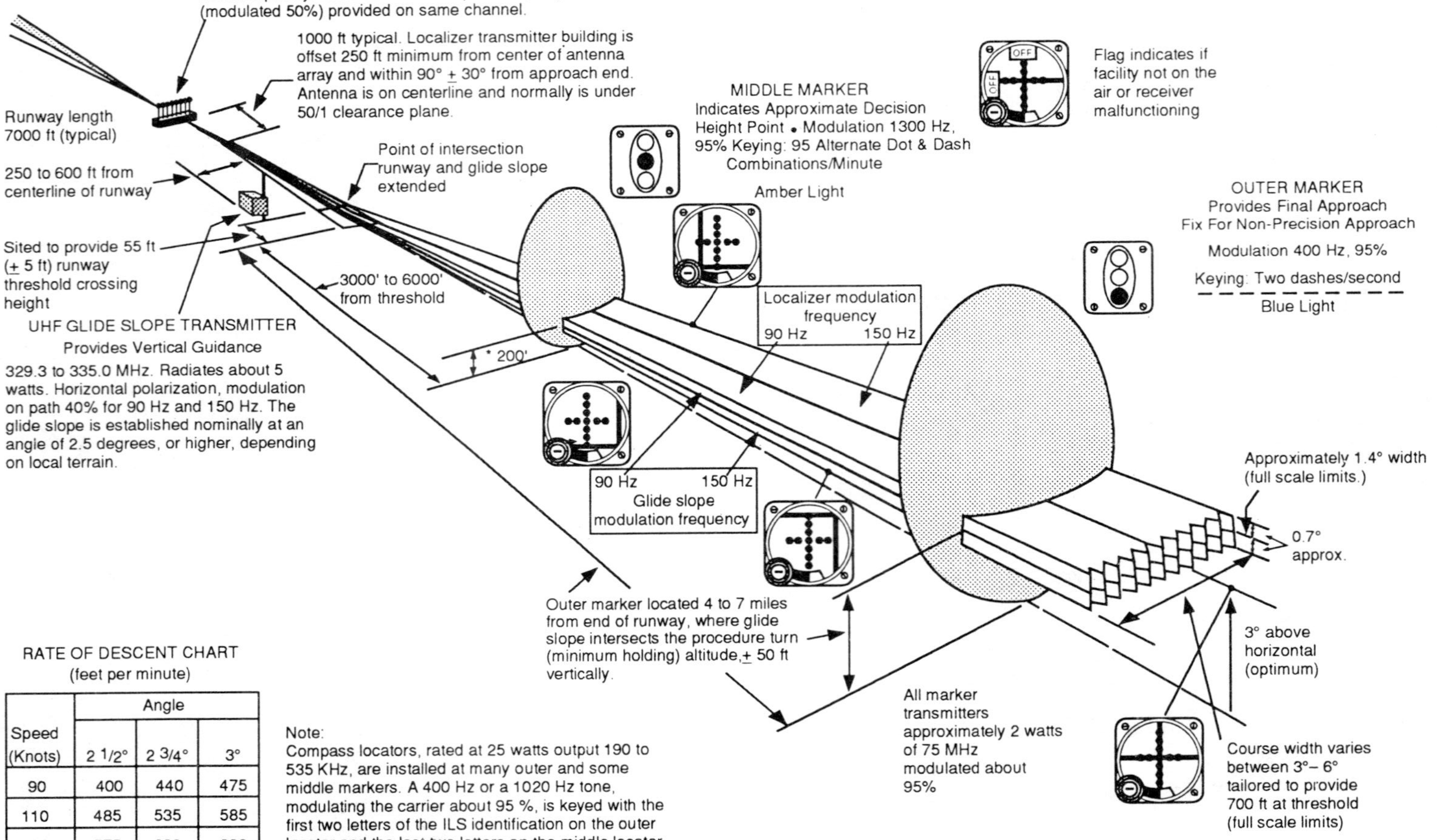

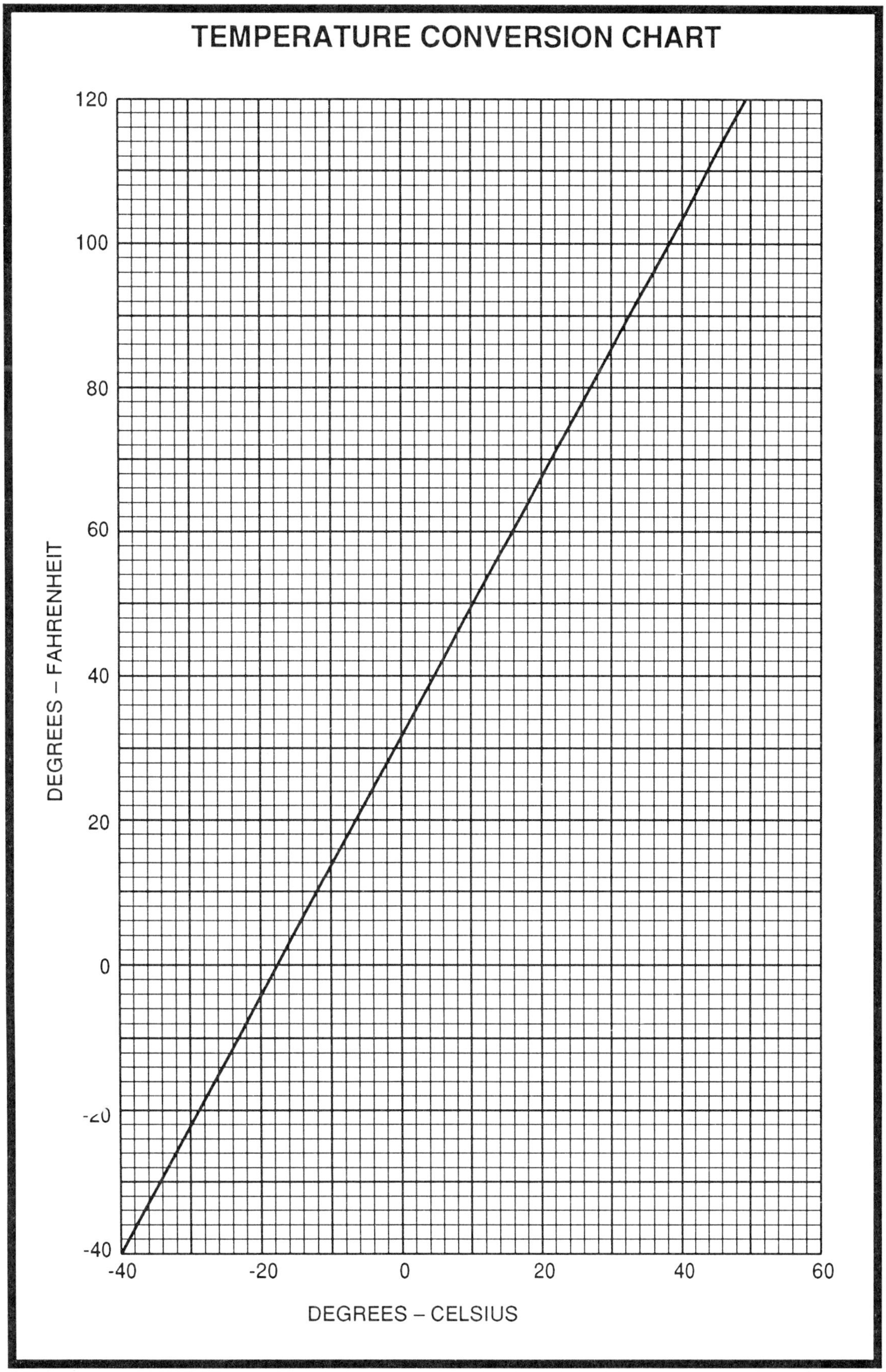

Appendix 2

LEGEND 29.—Temperature Conversion Chart.

APPENDIX 3

Appendix 3

U.S. DEPARTMENT OF TRANSPORTATION FEDERAL AVIATION ADMINISTRATION **FLIGHT PLAN**	(FAA USE ONLY)	☐ PILOT BRIEFING ☐ STOPOVER	☐ VNR	TIME STARTED		SPECIALIST INITIALS
1. TYPE ☐ VFR ☒ IFR ☐ DVFR	2. AIRCRAFT IDENTIFICATION	3. AIRCRAFT TYPE/ SPECIAL EQUIPMENT	4. TRUE AIRSPEED KTS	5. DEPARTURE POINT	6. DEPARTURE TIME PROPOSED (Z) | ACTUAL (Z)	7. CRUISING ALTITUDE
8. ROUTE OF FLIGHT							
9. DESTINATION (Name of airport and city)	10. EST. TIME ENROUTE HOURS | MINUTES	11. REMARKS				
12. FUEL ON BOARD HOURS | MINUTES	13. ALTERNATE AIRPORT(S)	14. PILOT'S NAME, ADDRESS & TELEPHONE NUMBER & AIRCRAFT HOME BASE 17. DESTINATION CONTACT/TELEPHONE (OPTIONAL)			15. NUMBER ABOARD	
16. COLOR OF AIRCRAFT	CIVIL AIRCRAFT PILOTS. FAR Part 91 requires you file an IFR flight plan to operate under instrument flight rules in controlled airspace. Failure to file could result in a civil penalty not to exceed $1,000 for each violation (Section 901 of the Federal Aviation Act of 1958, as amended). Filing of a VFR flight plan is recommended as a good operating practice. See also Part 99 for requirements concerning DVFR flight plans.					

FAA Form 7233-1 (8-82)   CLOSE VFR FLIGHT PLAN WITH _____ FSS ON ARRIVAL

FIGURE 1.—Flight Plan.


```
              VALID 141200Z FOR USE 0900-1500Z. TEMPS NEG ABV 24000

FT      3000    6000     9000     12000    18000    24000    30000   34000   39000

EMI     2807    2715-07  2728-10  2842-13  2867-21  2891-30  751041  771150  780855
ALB     0210    9900-07  2714-09  2728-12  2656-19  2777-28  781842  760150  269658
PSB             1509+04  2119+01  2233-04  2262-14  2368-26  781939  760850  780456
STL     2308    2613+02  2422-03  2431-08  2446-19  2461-30  760142  782650  760559
```

FIGURE 2.—Winds and Temperatures Aloft Forecast.

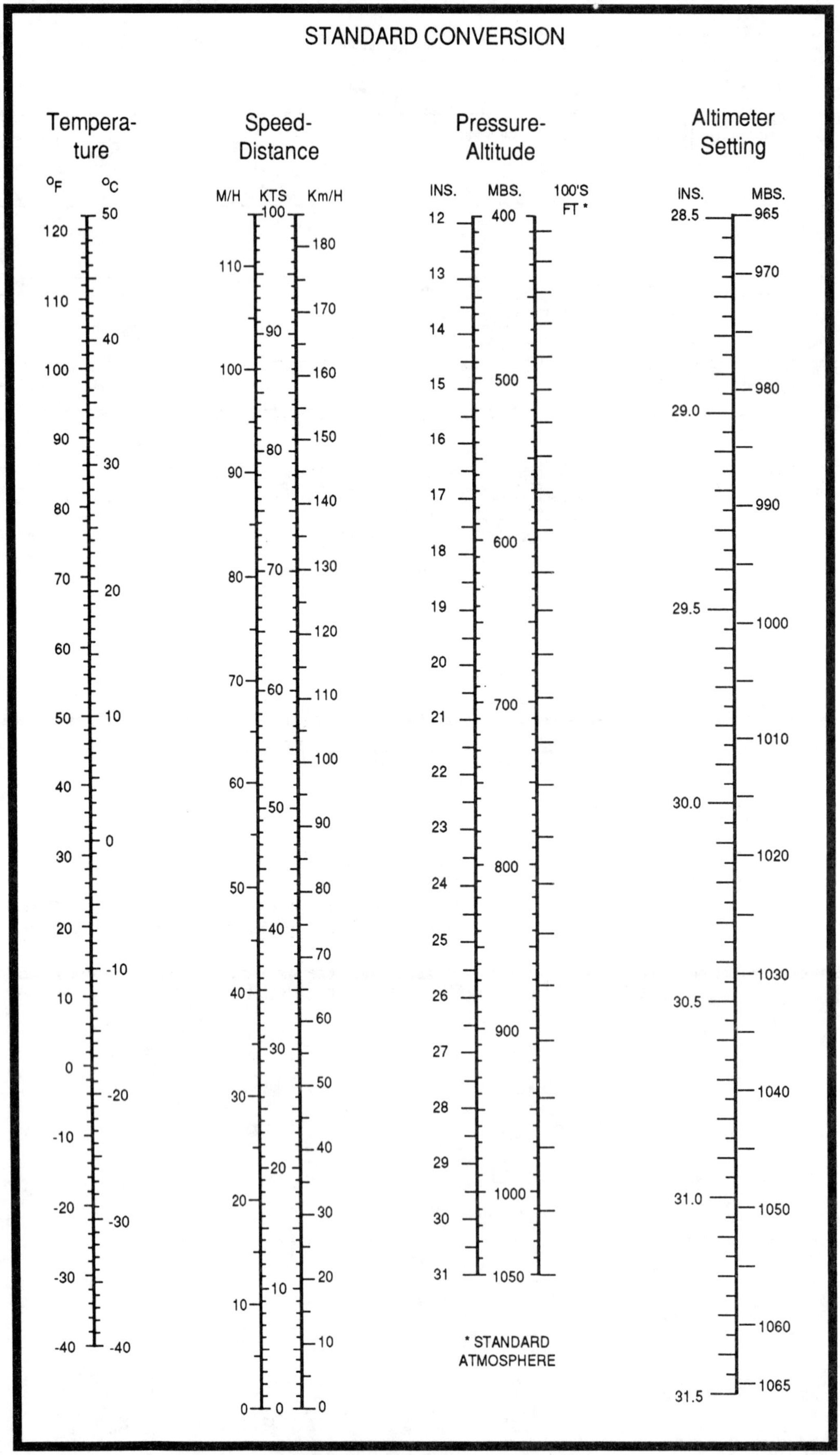

Appendix 3

FIGURE 3.—Standard Conversion Chart.

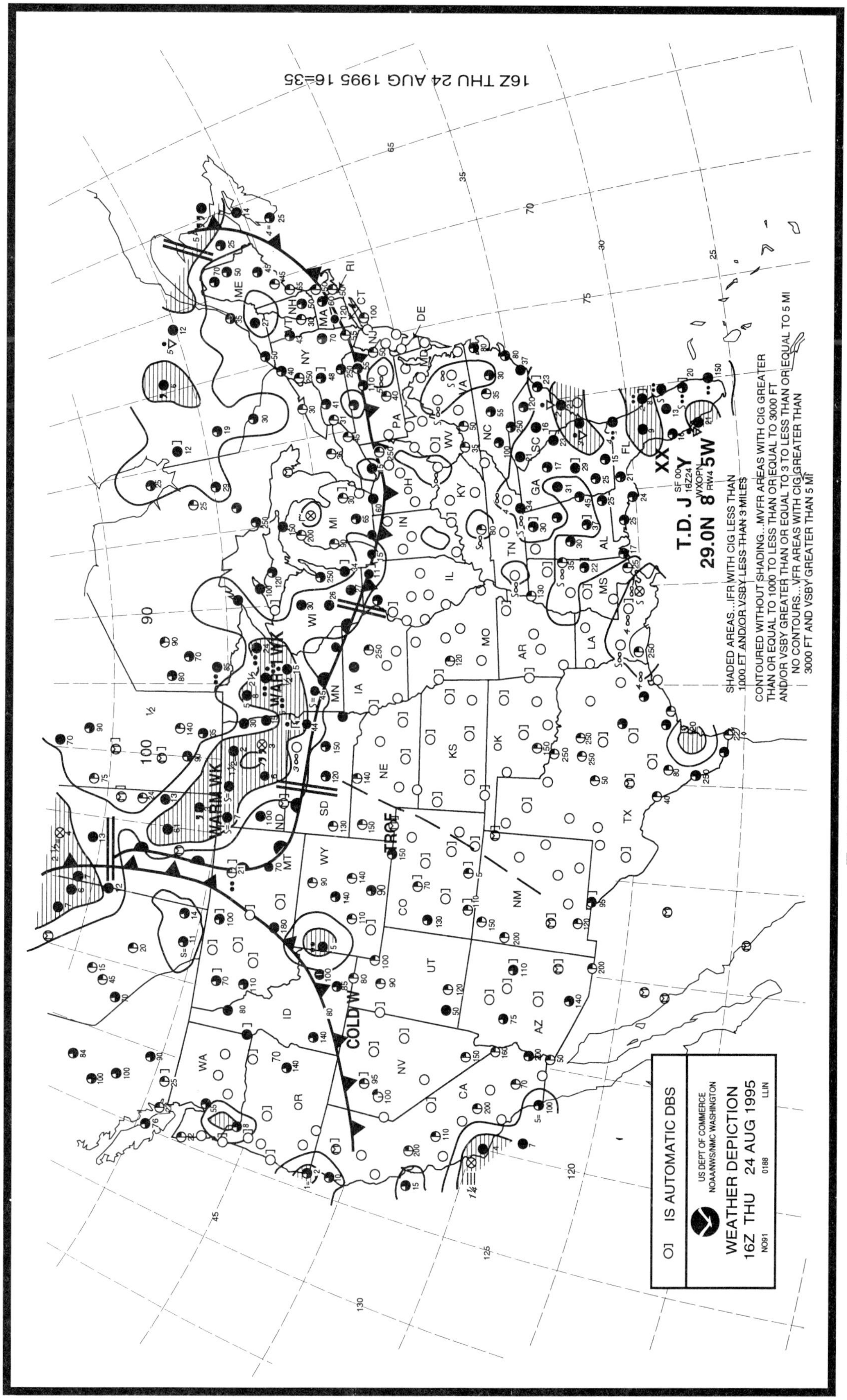

Appendix 3
Change 1

FIGURE 4.—Weather Depiction Chart.

FAA-CT-8080-3B

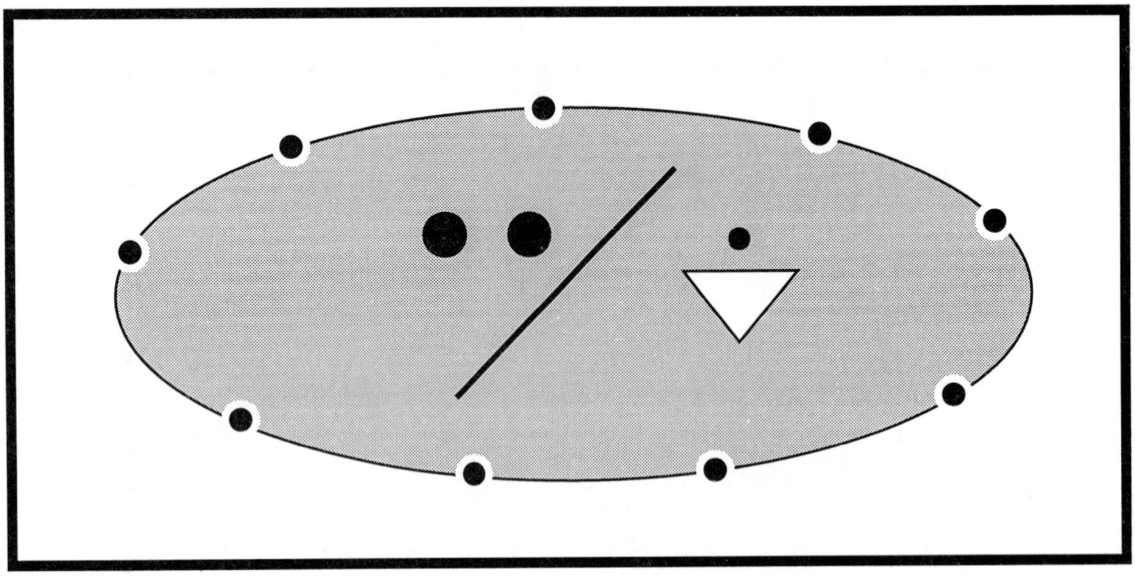

Appendix 3

FIGURE 5.—Symbol Used on Low-Level Significant Weather Prognostic Chart.

Appendix 3

THIS PAGE INTENTIONALLY LEFT BLANK

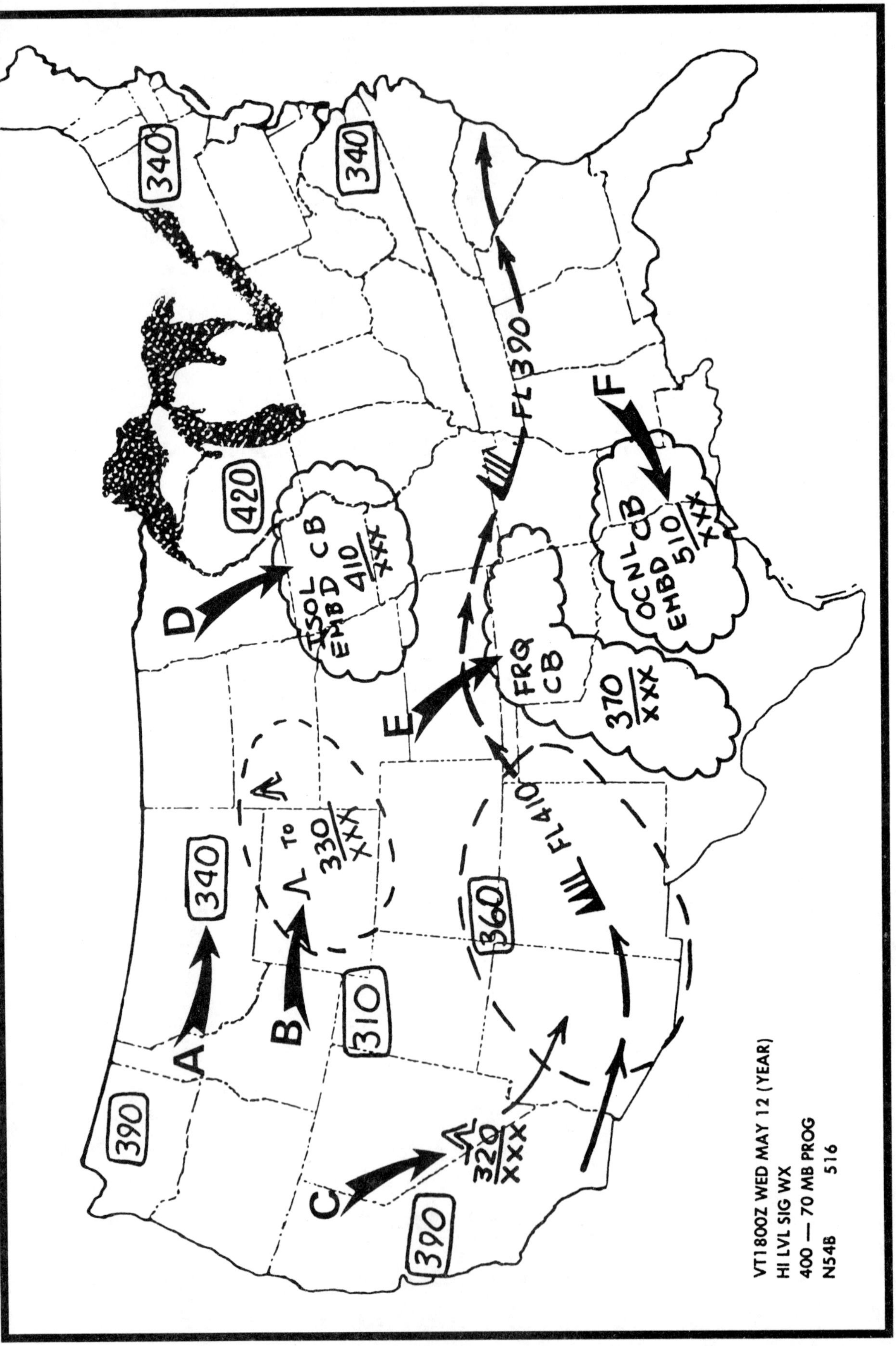

Appendix 3

FIGURE 7.—High-Level Significant Weather Prognostic Chart.

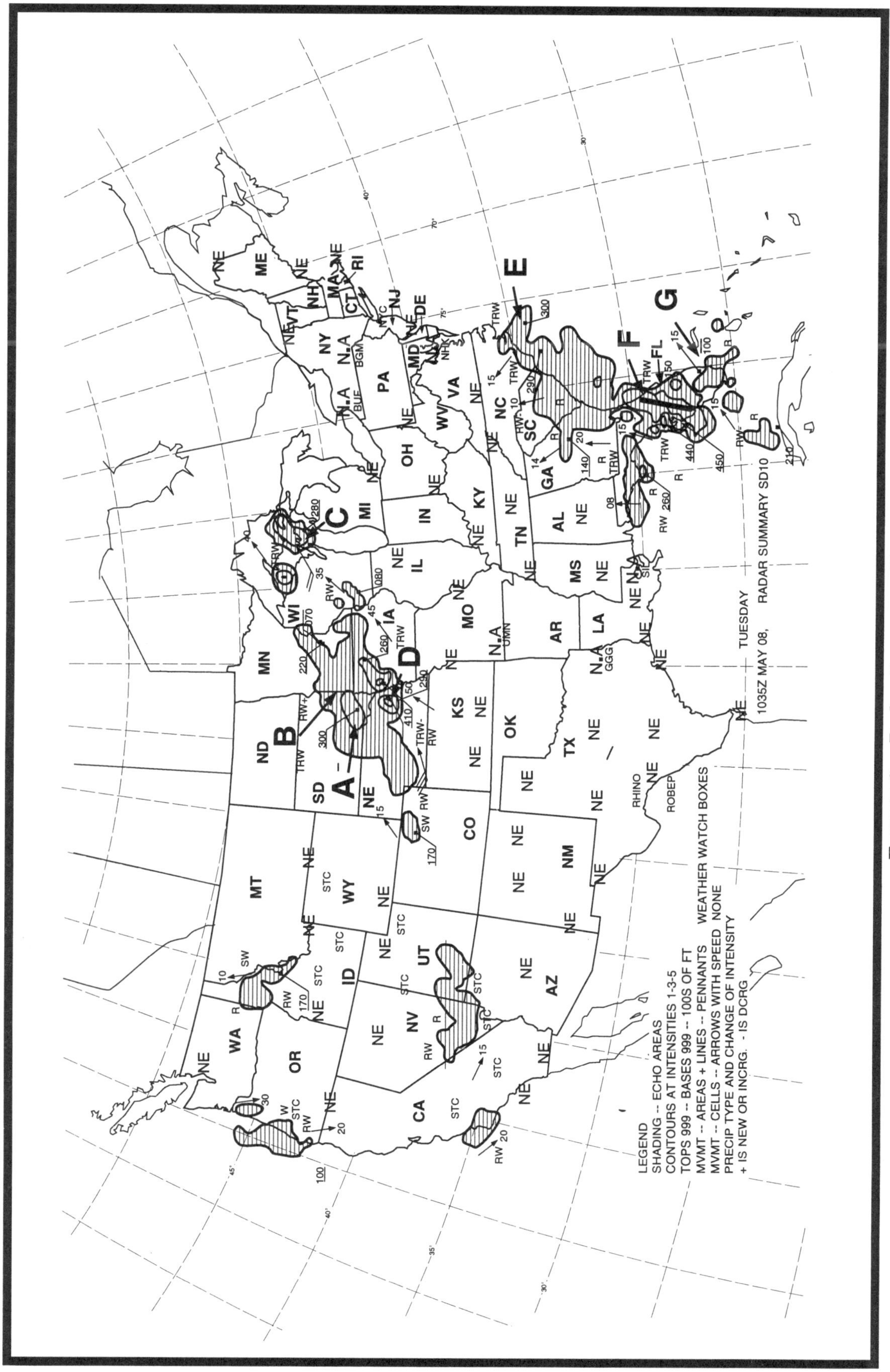

Appendix 3

FIGURE 8.—Radar Summary Chart.

FAA-CT-8080-3B

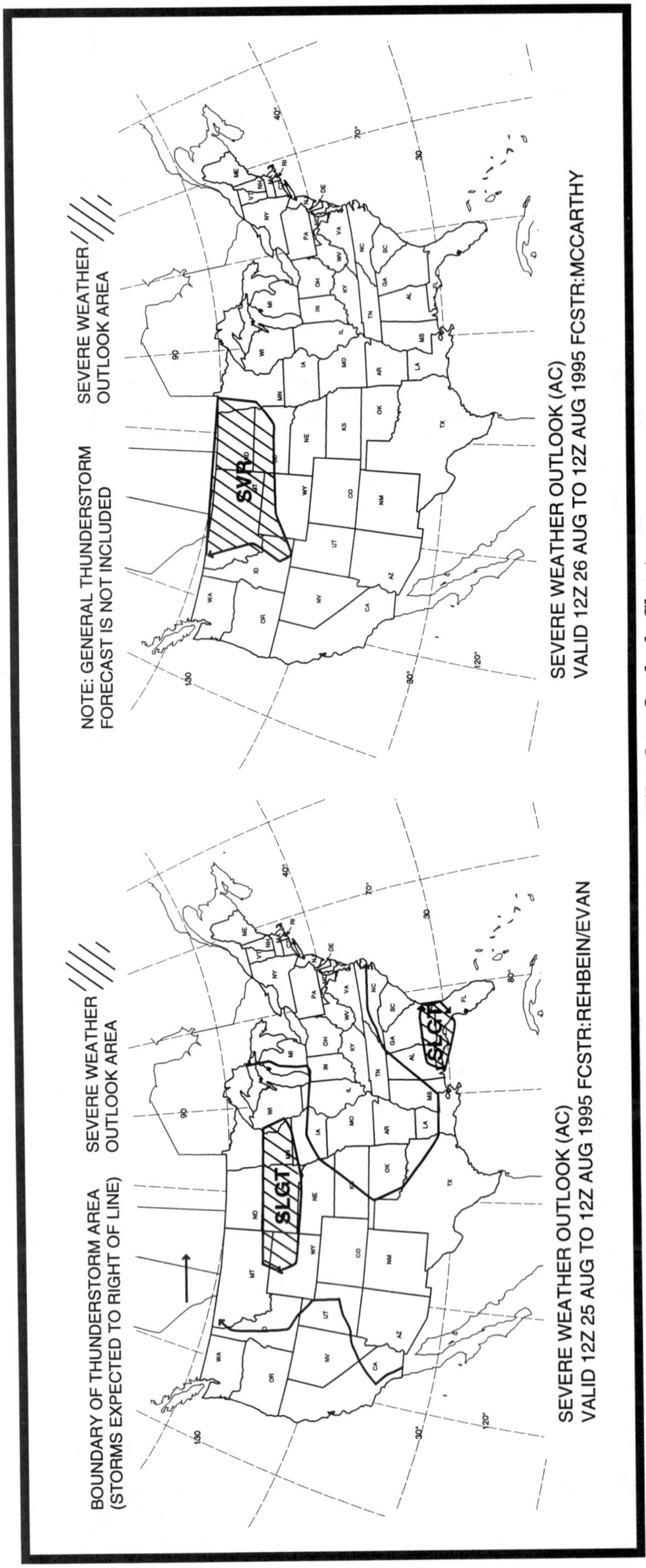

Appendix 3
Change 1

FIGURE 9.—Severe Weather Outlook Charts.

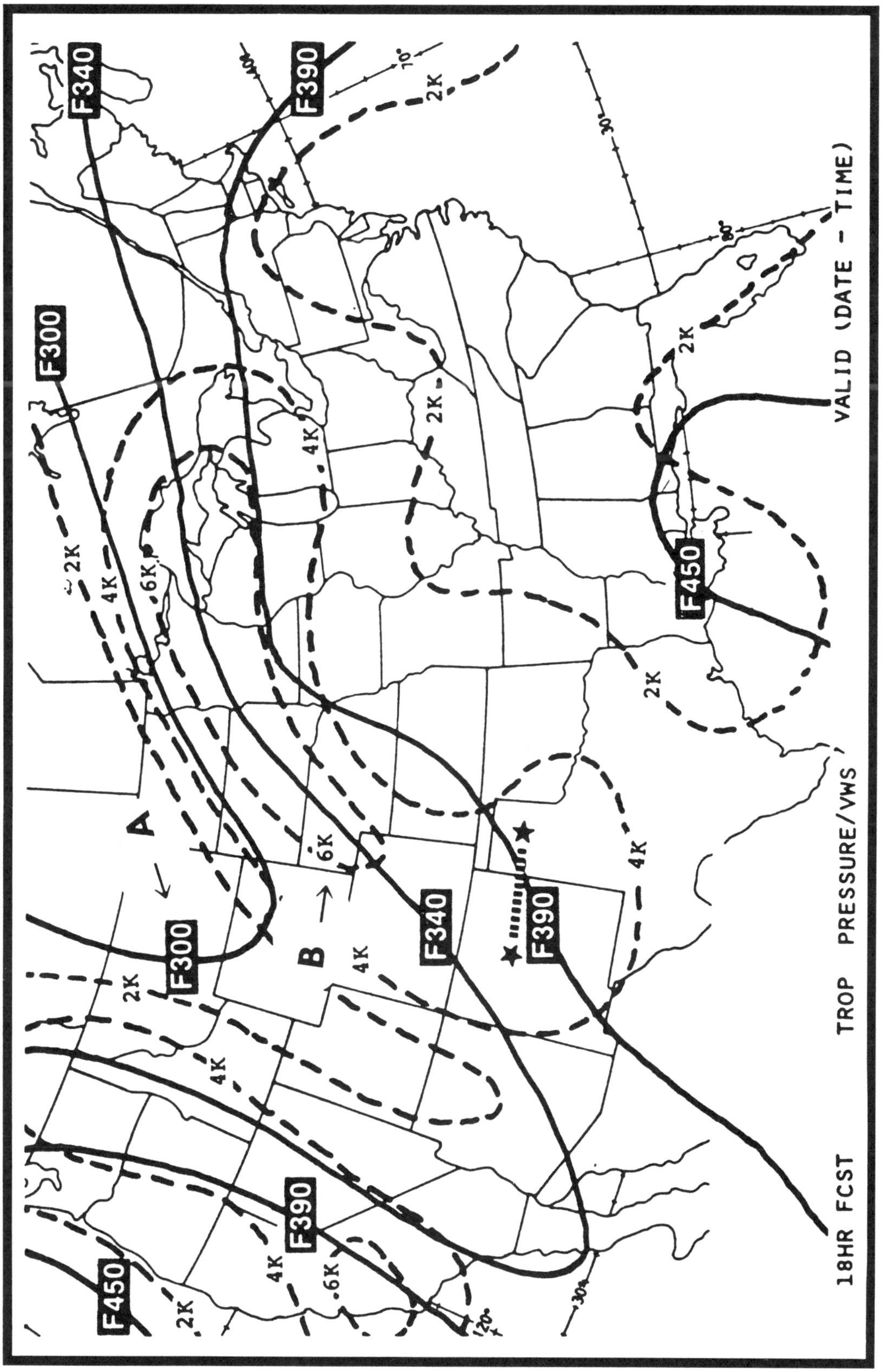

FIGURE 10.—Tropopause Height/Vertical Wind Shear Prognostic Chart.

Appendix 3

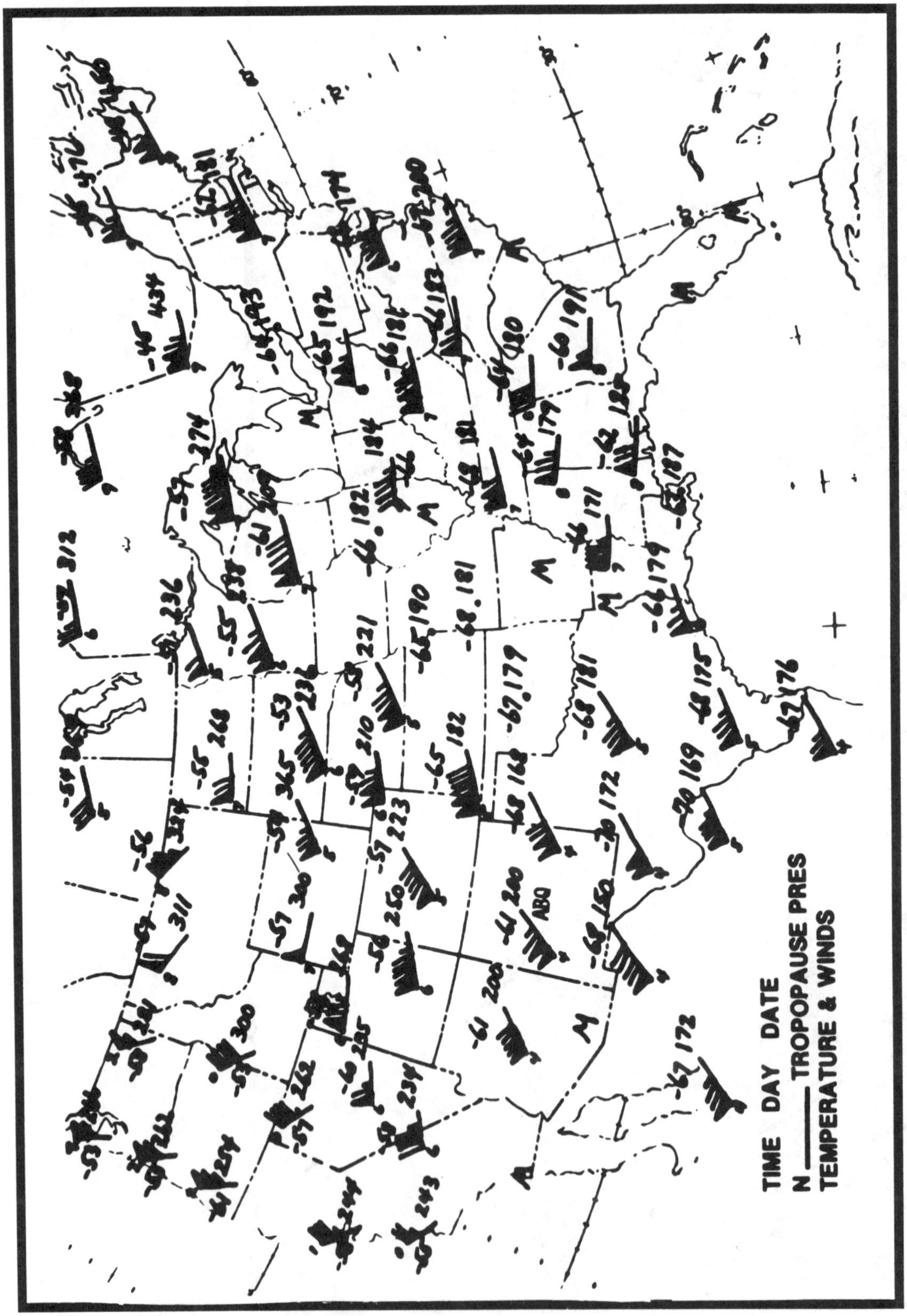

Appendix 3

FIGURE 11.—Tropopause Pressure Temperature and Winds.

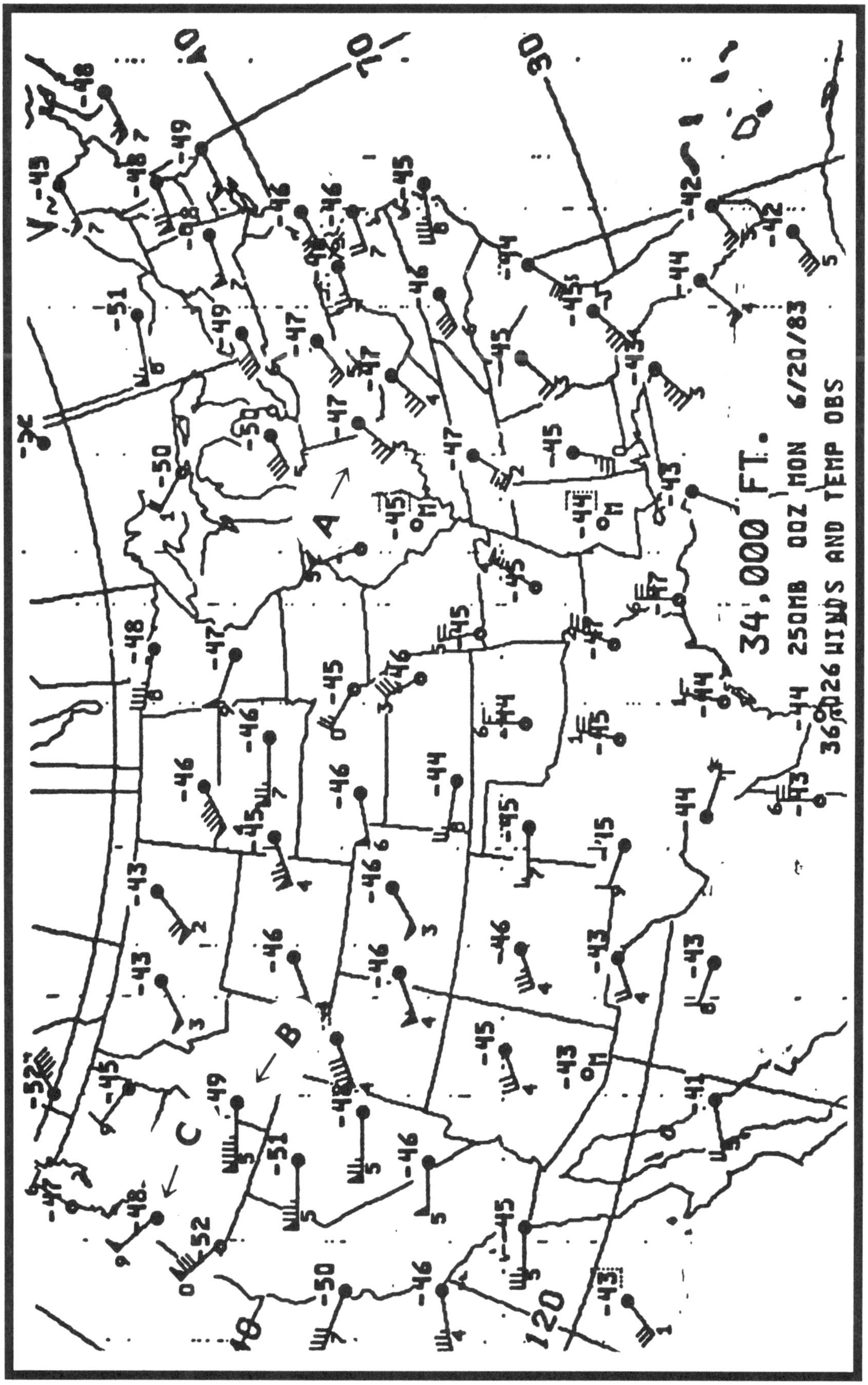

Appendix 3

FIGURE 12.—Observed Winds Aloft for 34,000 Feet.

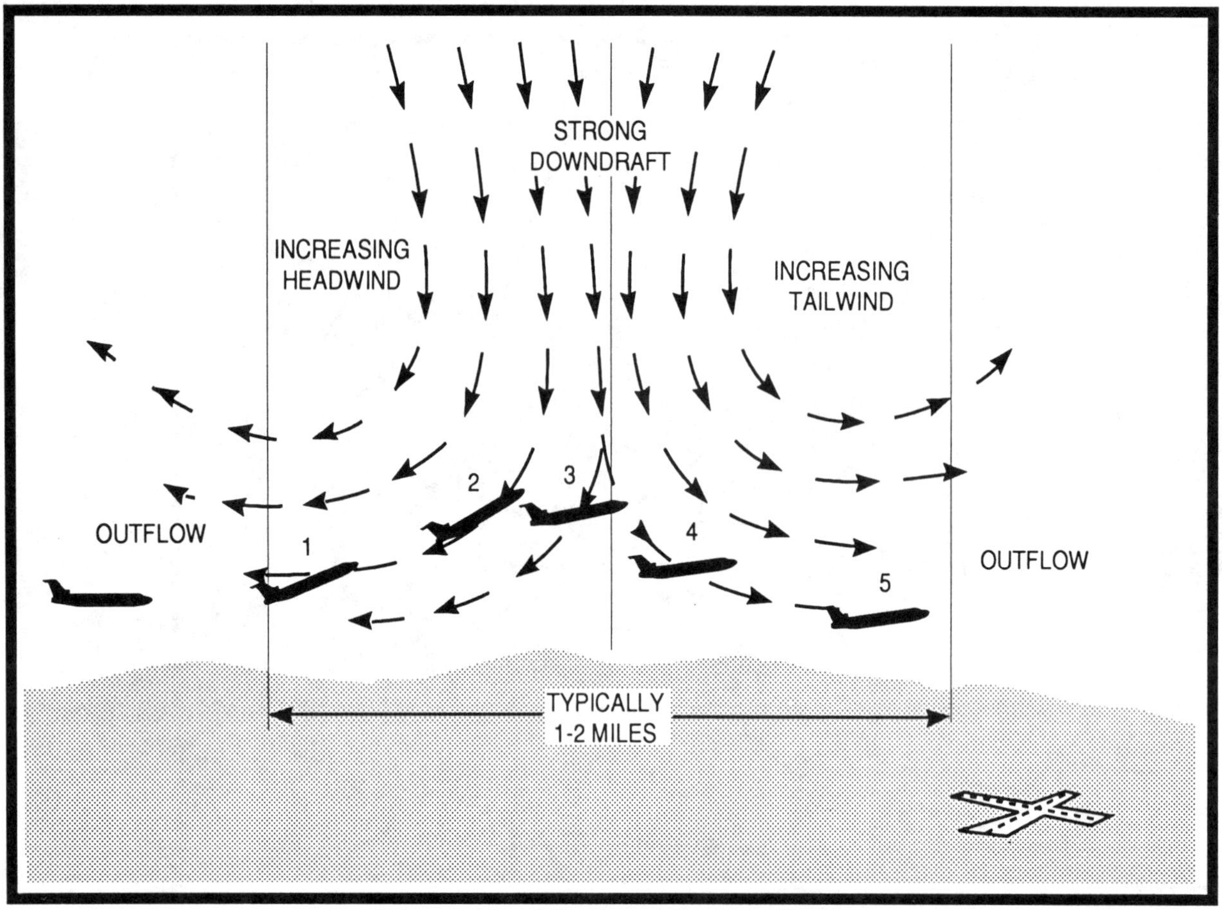

Appendix 3

FIGURE 13.—Microburst Section Chart.

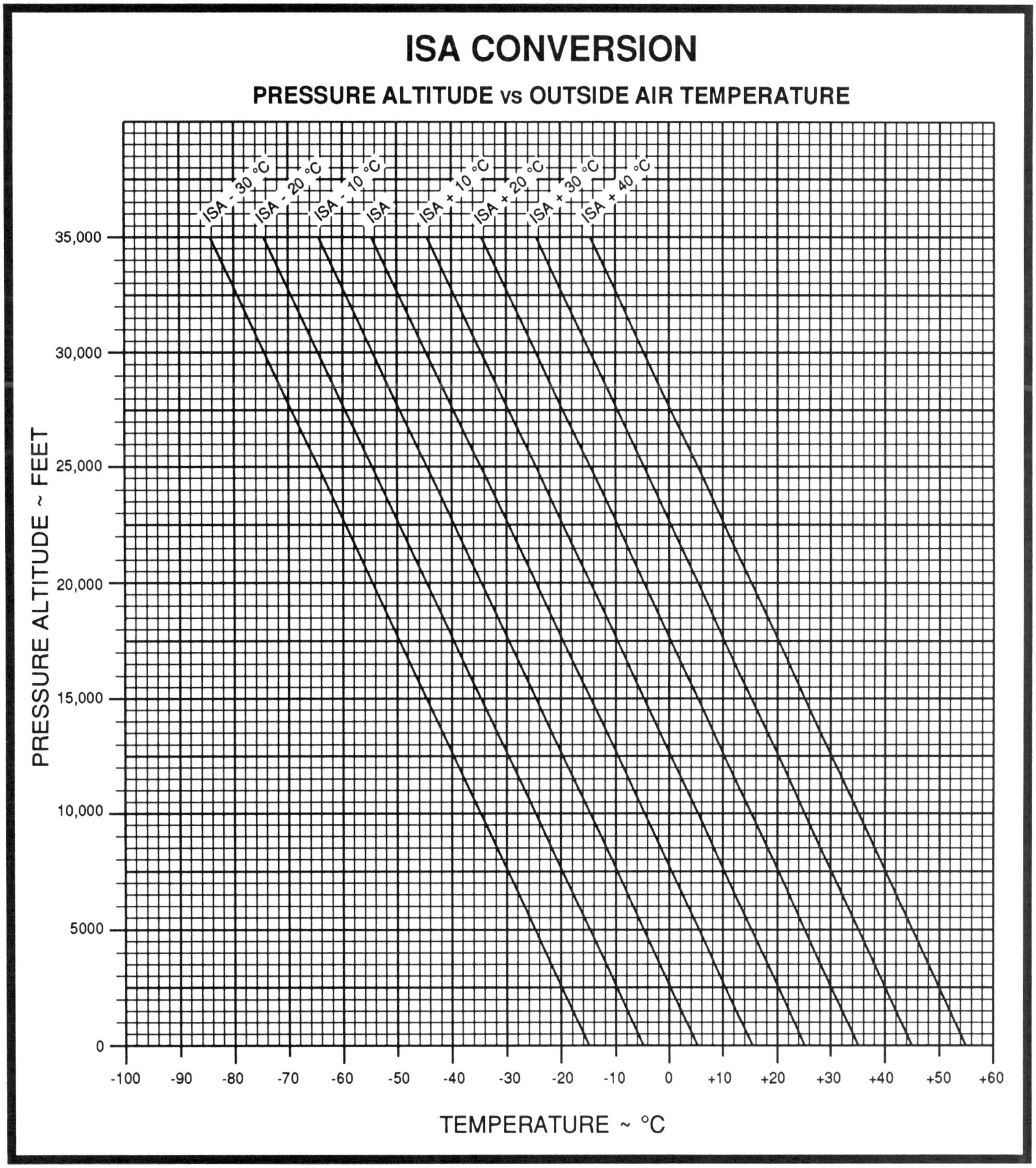

Appendix 3

FIGURE 14.—ISA Conversion Chart.

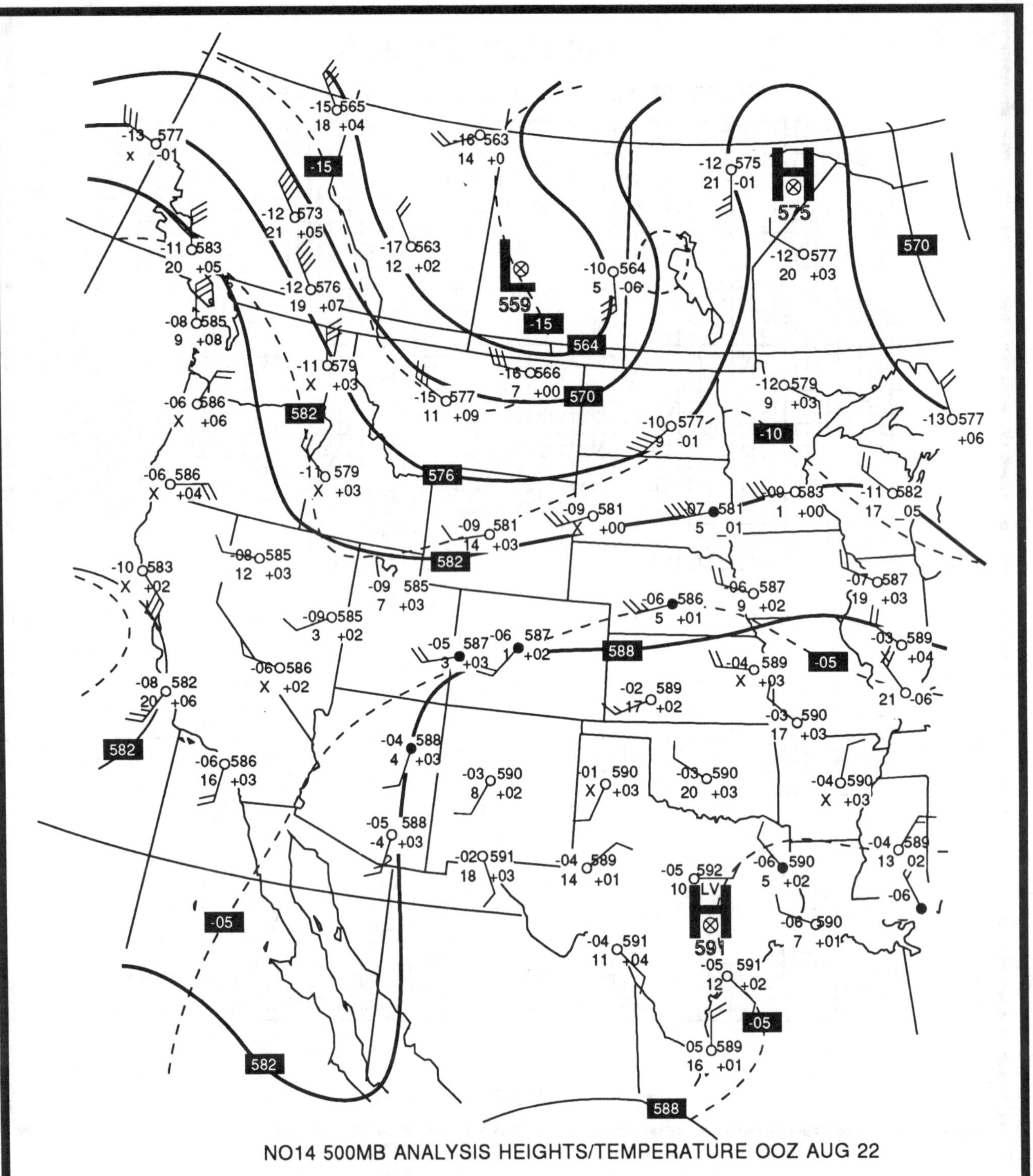

Appendix 3

FIGURE 15.—500 MB Analysis Heights/Temperature Chart.

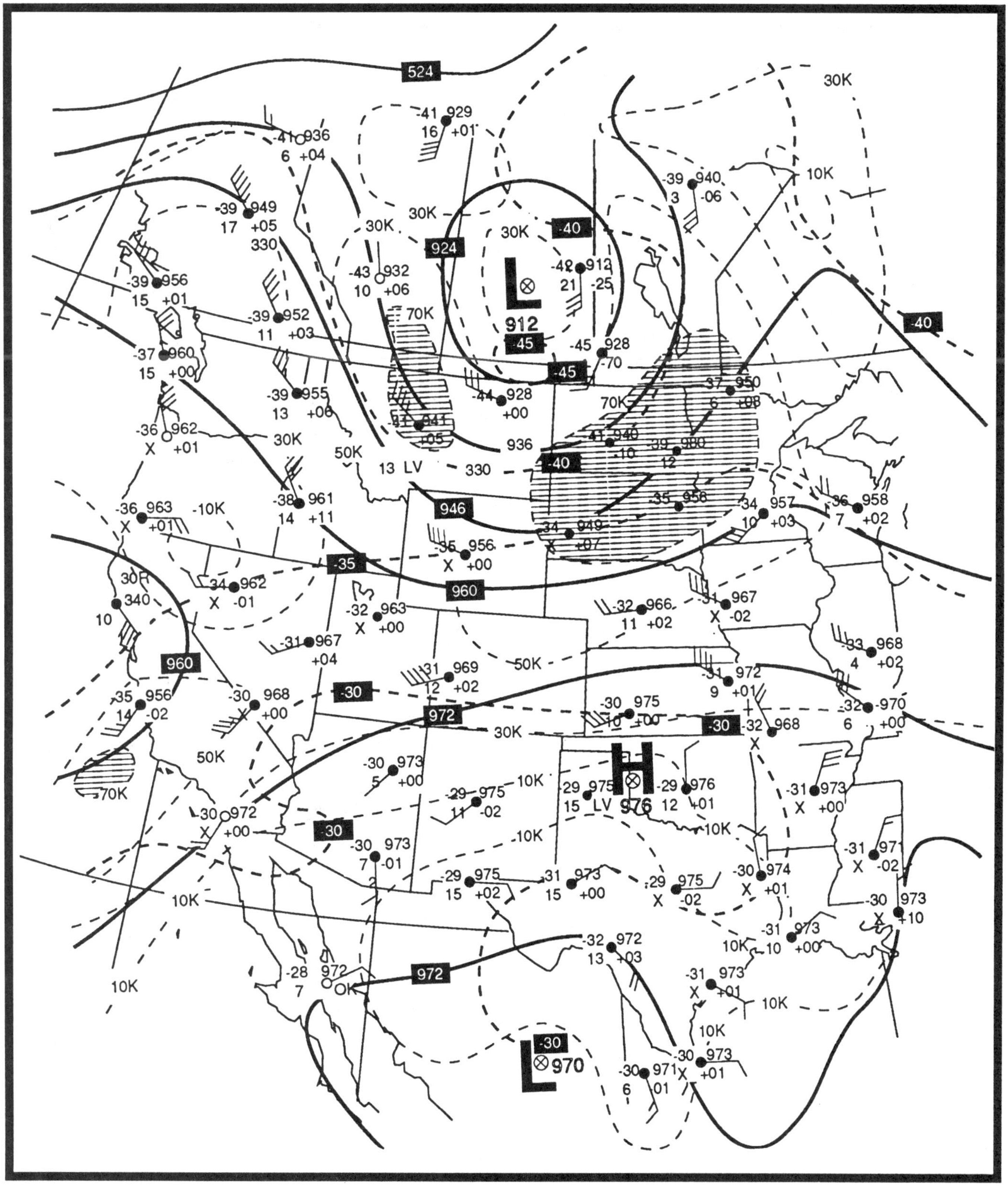

Appendix 3

FIGURE 16.—300 MB Analysis Heights/Isotachs Chart.

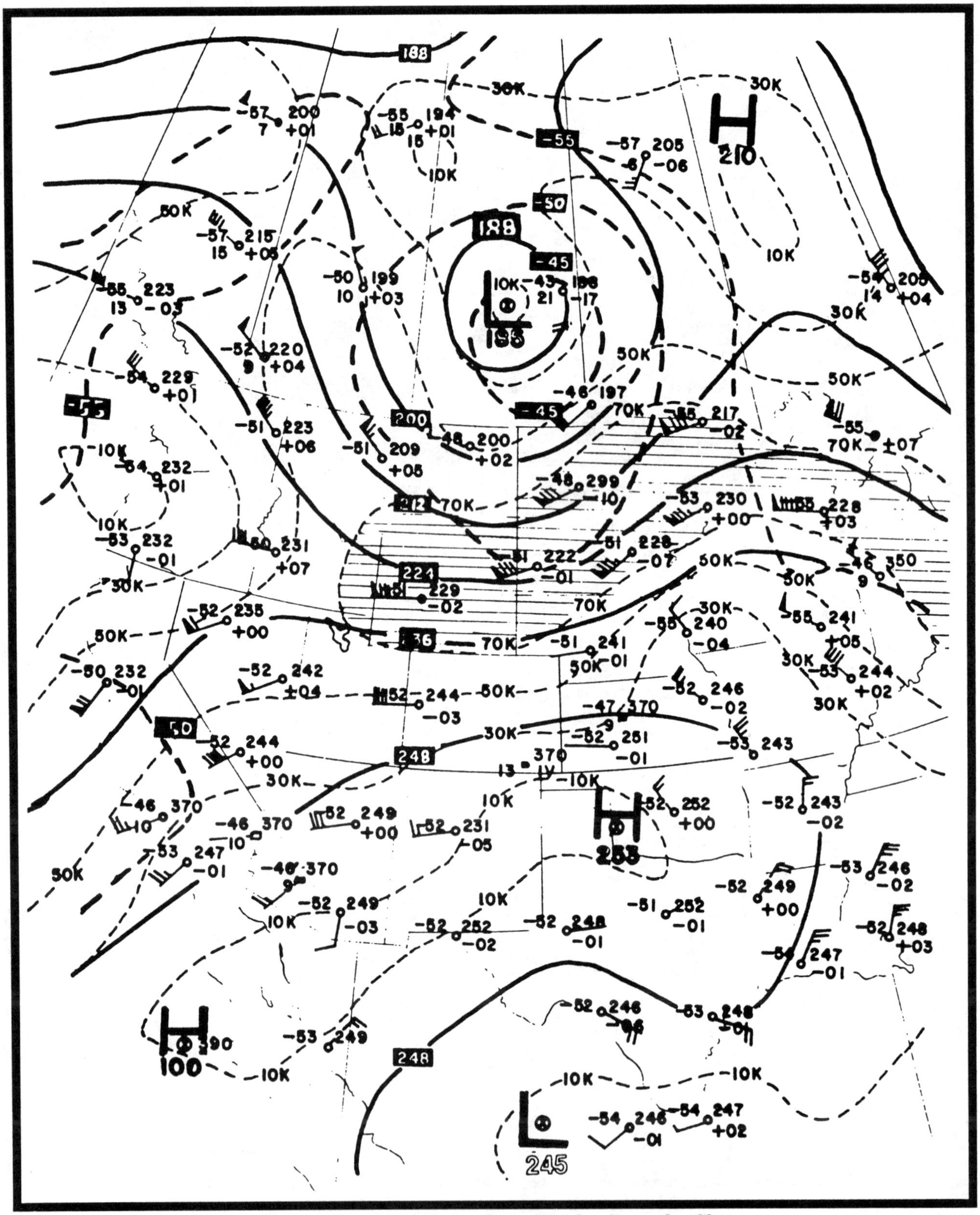

Appendix 3

FIGURE 17.—200 MB Analysis Heights/Isotachs Chart.

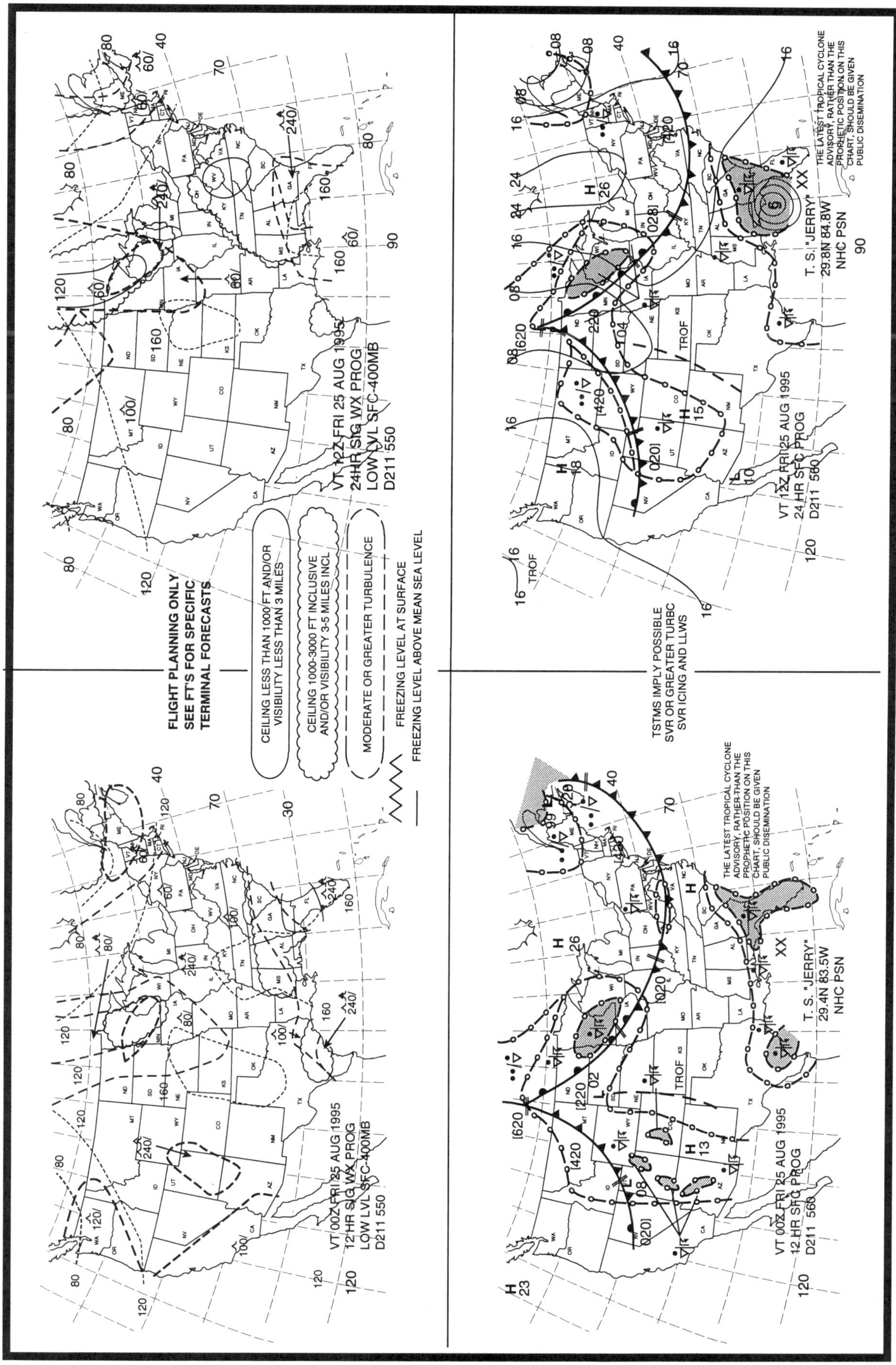

FIGURE 18.—U.S. Low-Level Significant Weather Prognostic Charts.

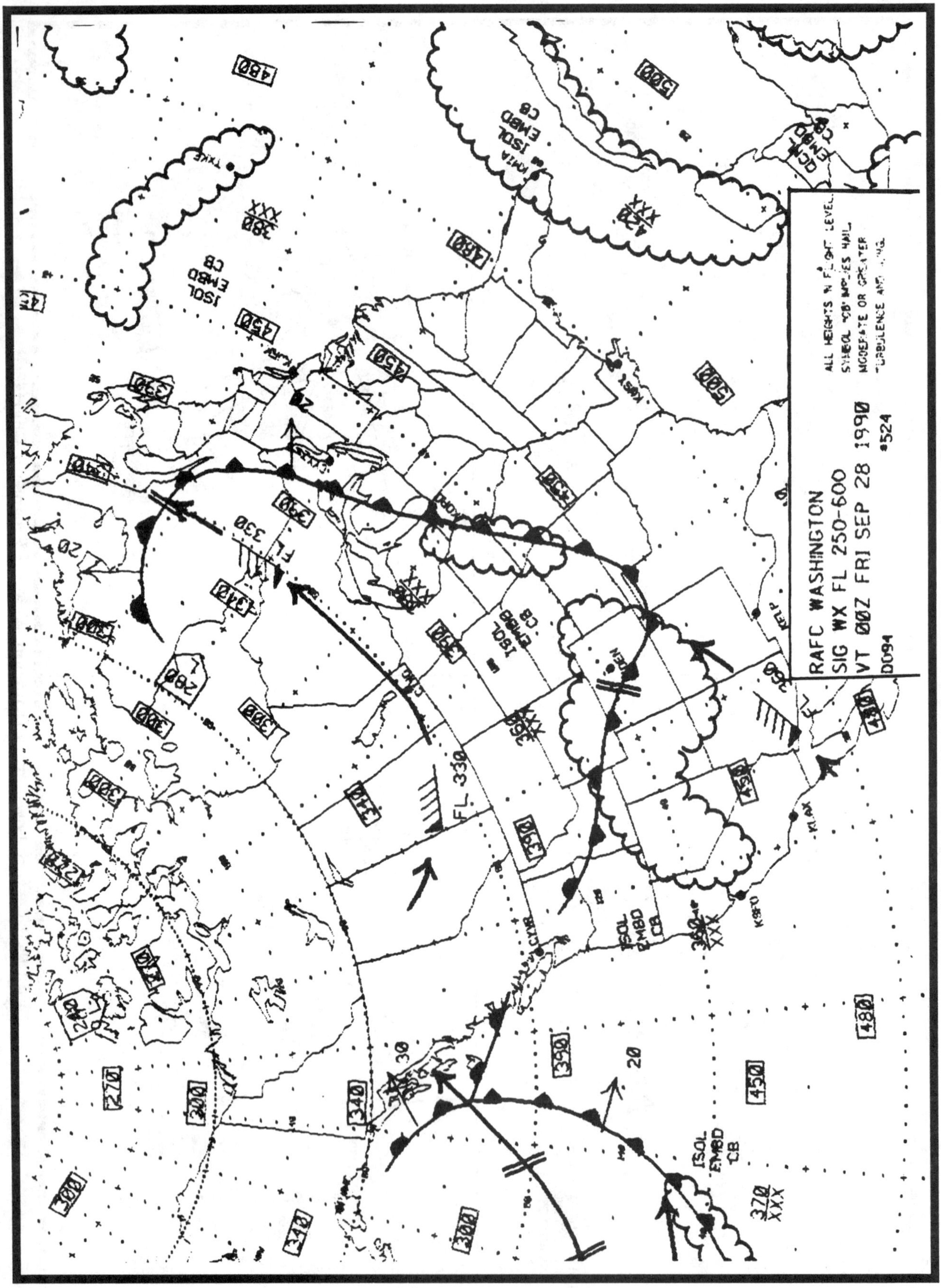

Appendix 3

FIGURE 19.—Low-Level Significant Weather Prognostic Chart.

FAA-CT-8080-3B

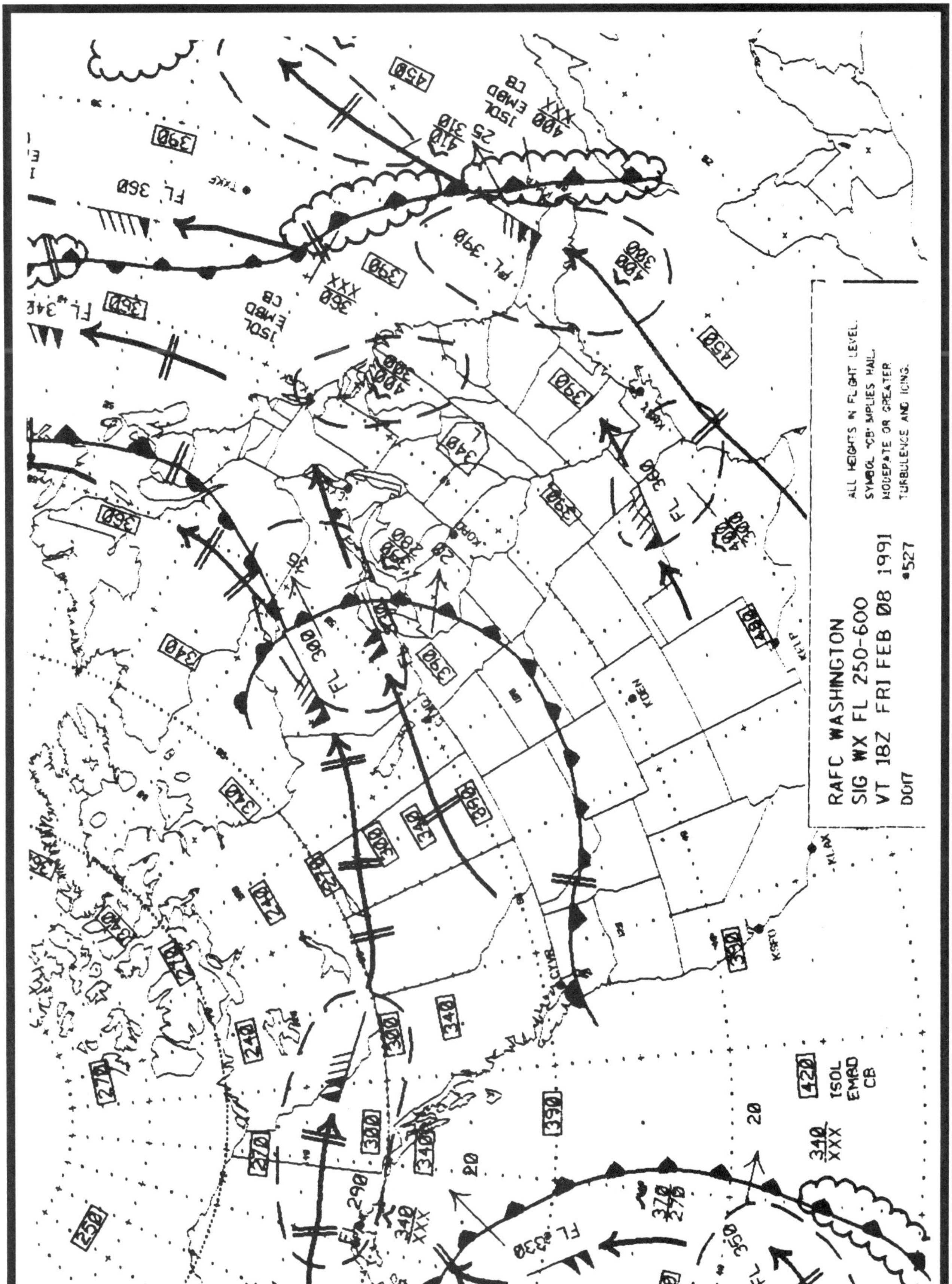

Appendix 3

FIGURE 20.—High-Level Significant Weather Prognostic Chart.

Appendix 3

							Form Approved: OMB No. 2120-0034

U.S. DEPARTMENT OF TRANSPORTATION
FEDERAL AVIATION ADMINISTRATION
FLIGHT PLAN

(FAA USE ONLY) ☐ PILOT BRIEFING ☐ VNR TIME STARTED SPECIALIST INITIALS
☐ STOPOVER

1. TYPE	2. AIRCRAFT IDENTIFICATION	3. AIRCRAFT TYPE/ SPECIAL EQUIPMENT	4. TRUE AIRSPEED	5. DEPARTURE POINT	6. DEPARTURE TIME		7. CRUISING ALTITUDE
☐ VFR X IFR ☐ DVFR	N 123RC	T210N/	175 KTS	GJT	PROPOSED (Z)	ACTUAL (Z)	15,000

8. ROUTE OF FLIGHT
JNC9, JNC, V187, MANCA, V211

9. DESTINATION (Name of airport and city)	10. EST. TIME ENROUTE HOURS MINUTES	11. REMARKS
DRO		

12. FUEL ON BOARD HOURS MINUTES	13. ALTERNATE AIRPORT(S)	14. PILOT'S NAME, ADDRESS & TELEPHONE NUMBER & AIRCRAFT HOME BASE	15. NUMBER ABOARD
4 30	GJT	17. DESTINATION CONTACT/TELEPHONE (OPTIONAL)	2

16. COLOR OF AIRCRAFT
RED/WHITE/BLUE

CIVIL AIRCRAFT PILOTS. FAR Part 91 requires you file an IFR flight plan to operate under instrument flight rules in controlled airspace. Failure to file could result in a civil penalty not to exceed $1,000 for each violation (Section 901 of the Federal Aviation Act of 1958, as amended). Filing of a VFR flight plan is recommended as a good operating practice. See also Part 99 for requirements concerning DVFR flight plans.

FAA Form 7233-1 (8-82)   CLOSE VFR FLIGHT PLAN WITH _____ FSS ON ARRIVAL

AIRCRAFT INFORMATION

MAKE   Cessna   MODEL   T210N

N 123RC   Vso 58 ___

AIRCRAFT EQUIPMENT/STATUS**

**NOTE: X= OPERATIVE   INOP= INOPERATIVE   N/A= NOT APPLICABLE
TRANSPONDER: X (MODE C) X ILS: (LOCALIZER) X (GLIDE SLOPE) X
VOR NO. 1 X (NO. 2) X ADF: X RNAV: X
VERTICAL PATH COMPUTER: N/A DME: X
MARKER BEACON: X (AUDIO) X (VISUAL) X

FIGURE 21.—Flight Plan and Aircraft Information.

Appendix 3

FLIGHT PLAN

U.S. DEPARTMENT OF TRANSPORTATION — FEDERAL AVIATION ADMINISTRATION

Form Approved: OMB No. 2120-0034

(FAA USE ONLY) ☐ PILOT BRIEFING ☐ VNR ☐ STOPOVER   TIME STARTED ____   SPECIALIST INITIALS ____

1. TYPE	2. AIRCRAFT IDENTIFICATION	3. AIRCRAFT TYPE/ SPECIAL EQUIPMENT	4. TRUE AIRSPEED	5. DEPARTURE POINT	6. DEPARTURE TIME (PROPOSED Z / ACTUAL Z)	7. CRUISING ALTITUDE
☐ VFR ☒ IFR ☐ DVFR	N 123RC	T210N/	175 KTS	DRO		16,000

8. ROUTE OF FLIGHT: V211, MANCA, V187, HERRM, V187, JNC

9. DESTINATION (Name of airport and city): GJT

10. EST. TIME ENROUTE — HOURS ____ MINUTES ____

11. REMARKS:

12. FUEL ON BOARD — HOURS ____ MINUTES ____

13. ALTERNATE AIRPORT(S):

14. PILOT'S NAME, ADDRESS & TELEPHONE NUMBER & AIRCRAFT HOME BASE

17. DESTINATION CONTACT/TELEPHONE (OPTIONAL)

15. NUMBER ABOARD: 2

16. COLOR OF AIRCRAFT: RED/WHITE/BLUE

CIVIL AIRCRAFT PILOTS. FAR Part 91 requires you file an IFR flight plan to operate under instrument flight rules in controlled airspace. Failure to file could result in a civil penalty not to exceed $1,000 for each violation (Section 901 of the Federal Aviation Act of 1958, as amended). Filing of a VFR flight plan is recommended as a good operating practice. See also Part 99 for requirements concerning DVFR flight plans.

FAA Form 7233-1 (8-82)   CLOSE VFR FLIGHT PLAN WITH _____ FSS ON ARRIVAL

AIRCRAFT INFORMATION

MAKE Cessna   MODEL T210N

N 123RC   Vso 58 ___

AIRCRAFT EQUIPMENT/STATUS**

NOTE: X= OPERATIVE   INOP= INOPERATIVE   N/A= NOT APPLICABLE

TRANSPONDER: X (MODE C) X   ILS: (LOCALIZER) X   (GLIDE SLOPE) X
VOR NO. 1 X (NO. 2) X   ADF: X   RNAV: X
VERTICAL PATH COMPUTER: N/A   DME: X
MARKER BEACON: X (AUDIO) X (VISUAL) X

FIGURE 21A.—Flight Plan and Aircraft Information.

Appendix 3

FLIGHT LOG
GRAND JUNCTION (GJT) TO DURANGO (DRO)

CHECK POINTS		ROUTE	COURSE	WIND	SPEED-KTS		DIST	TIME		FUEL	
FROM	TO	ALTITUDE		TEMP	TAS	GS	NM	LEG	TOT	LEG	TOT
GJT	JNC	JNC9JNC CLIMB		230 08				✕			
	HERRM	V187 15,000	151°		175			:24:0			
	MANCA	V187	151°								
APPROACH & LANDING		V211 DESCENT	092°					:18:30			
	DRO										

OTHER DATA:
NOTE: TAKEOFF RUNWAY 29.
MAG VAR, 14° E.

FLIGHT SUMMARY

TIME	FUEL (LB)	
		EN ROUTE
		RESERVE
		MISSED APPR.
		TOTAL

FIGURE 22.—Flight Planning Log.

Appendix 3

FLIGHT LOG
DURANGO (DRO) TO GRAND JUNCTION, WALKER FIELD (GJT)

| CHECK POINTS || ROUTE | COURSE | WIND | SPEED-KTS || DIST | TIME || FUEL ||
FROM	TO	ALTITUDE		TEMP	TAS	GS	NM	LEG	TOT	LEG	TOT
DRO	MANCA	V211 CLIMB	272°	230 08				:14:30			
	HERRM	V187 16,000	333°		174						
	JNC	V187	331°								
APPROACH & LANDING		DESCENT						:12:00			
	GJT										

OTHER DATA:
NOTE: MAG. VAR. 14° E.

FLIGHT SUMMARY

TIME	FUEL (LB)	
		EN ROUTE
		RESERVE
		MISSED APPR.
		TOTAL

FIGURE 22A.—Flight Planning Log.

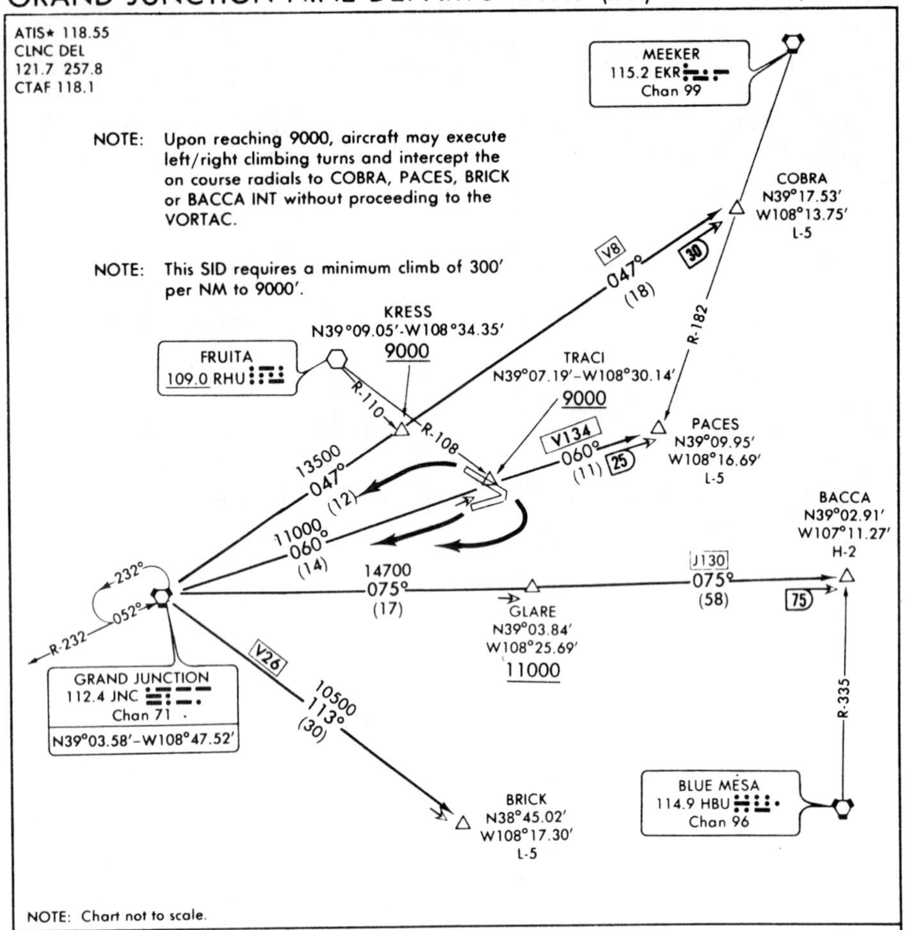

DEPARTURE ROUTE DESCRIPTION

TAKE-OFF RUNWAYS 11 and 22: Right turn direct to JNC VORTAC. Then via (transition) or (assigned route).

TAKE-OFF RUNWAY 29: Left turn direct to JNC VORTAC. Then via (transition) or (assigned route).

BACCA TRANSITION (JNC9.BACCA): From over JNC VORTAC via JNC R-075 to BACCA INT.

BRICK TRANSITION (JNC9.BRICK): From over JNC VORTAC via JNC R-113 to BRICK DME Fix.

COBRA TRANSITION(JNC9.COBRA): From over JNC VORTAC via JNC R-047 to COBRA INT.

PACES TRANSITION (JNC9.PACES): From over JNC VORTAC via JNC R-060 to PACES INT.

GRAND JUNCTION NINE DEPARTURE
(PILOT NAV) (JNC9.JNC)

GRAND JUNCTION, COLORADO
GRAND JUNCTION/WALKER FIELD

FIGURE 23.— Grand Junction Nine Departure (JNC9.JNC).

FIGURE 23A.—Grand Junction Nine Departure (JNC9.JNC).

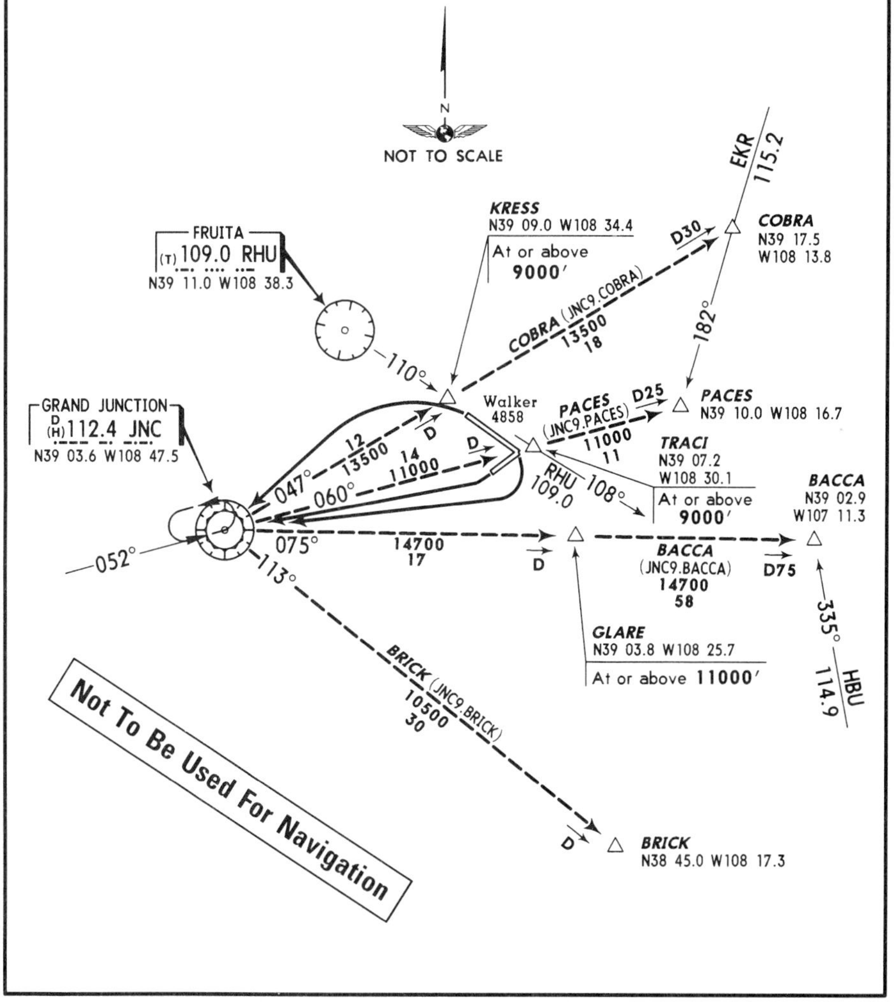

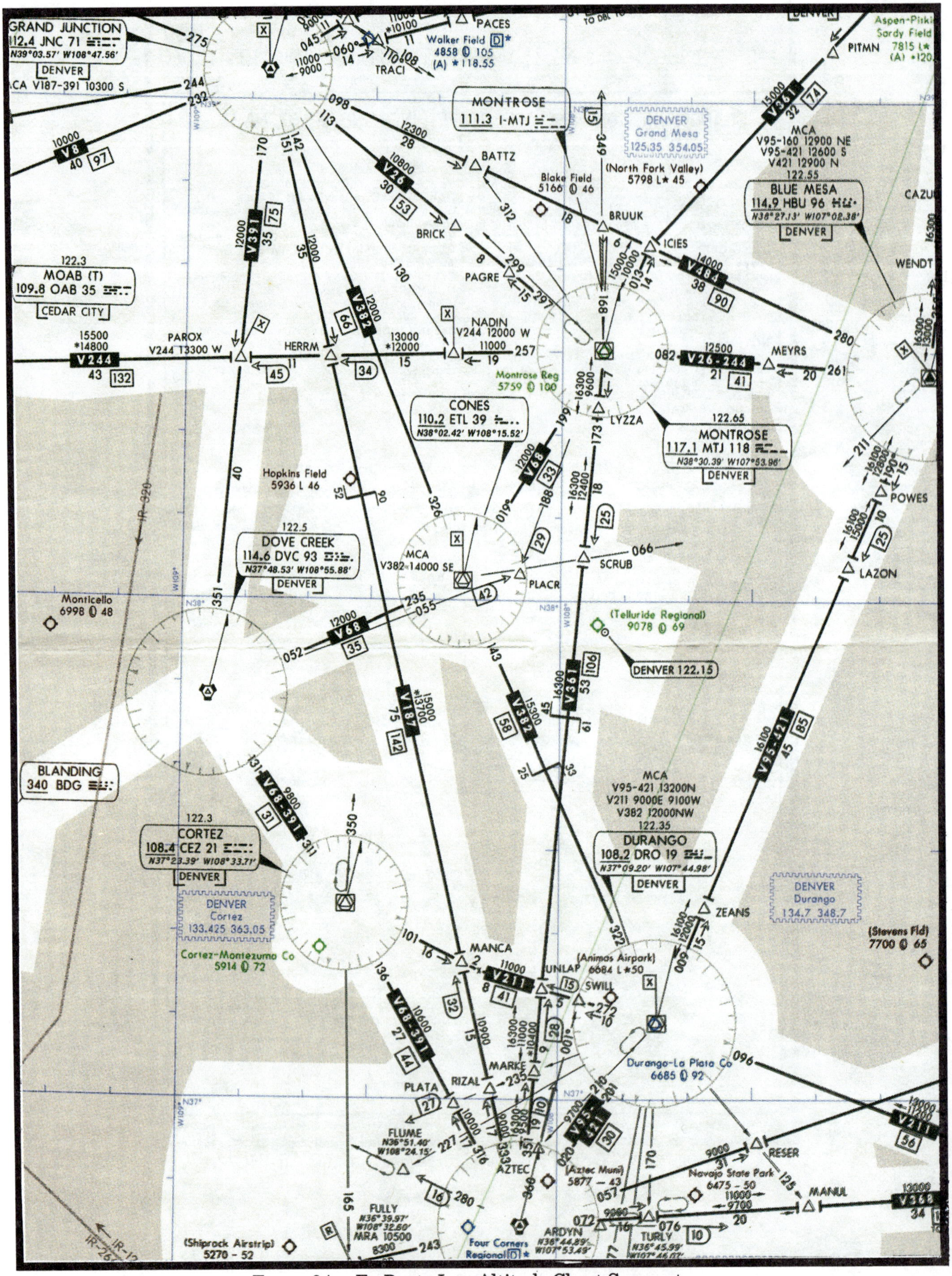

Appendix 3

FIGURE 24.—En Route Low-Altitude Chart Segment.

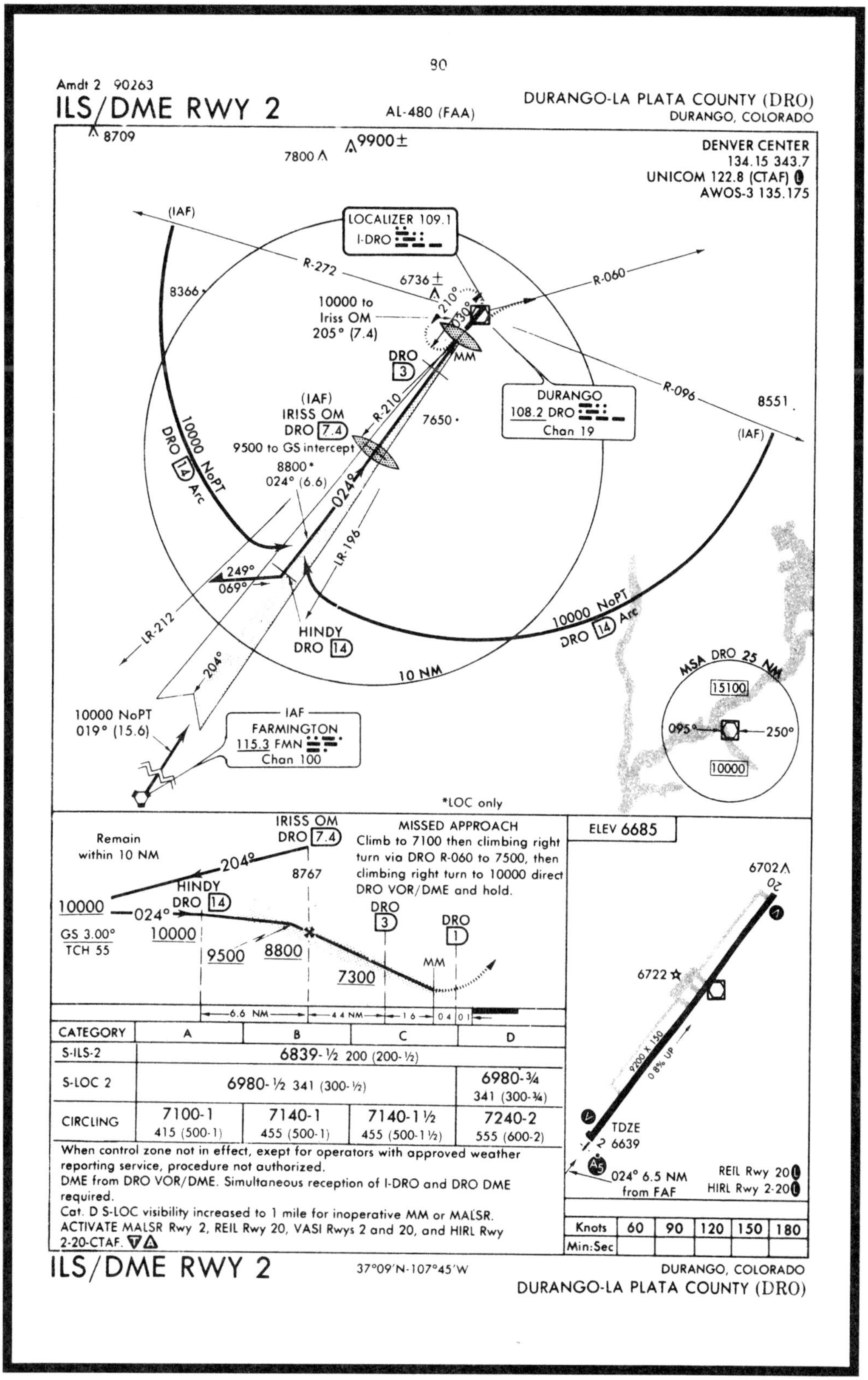

FIGURE 25.—ILS/DME RWY 2.

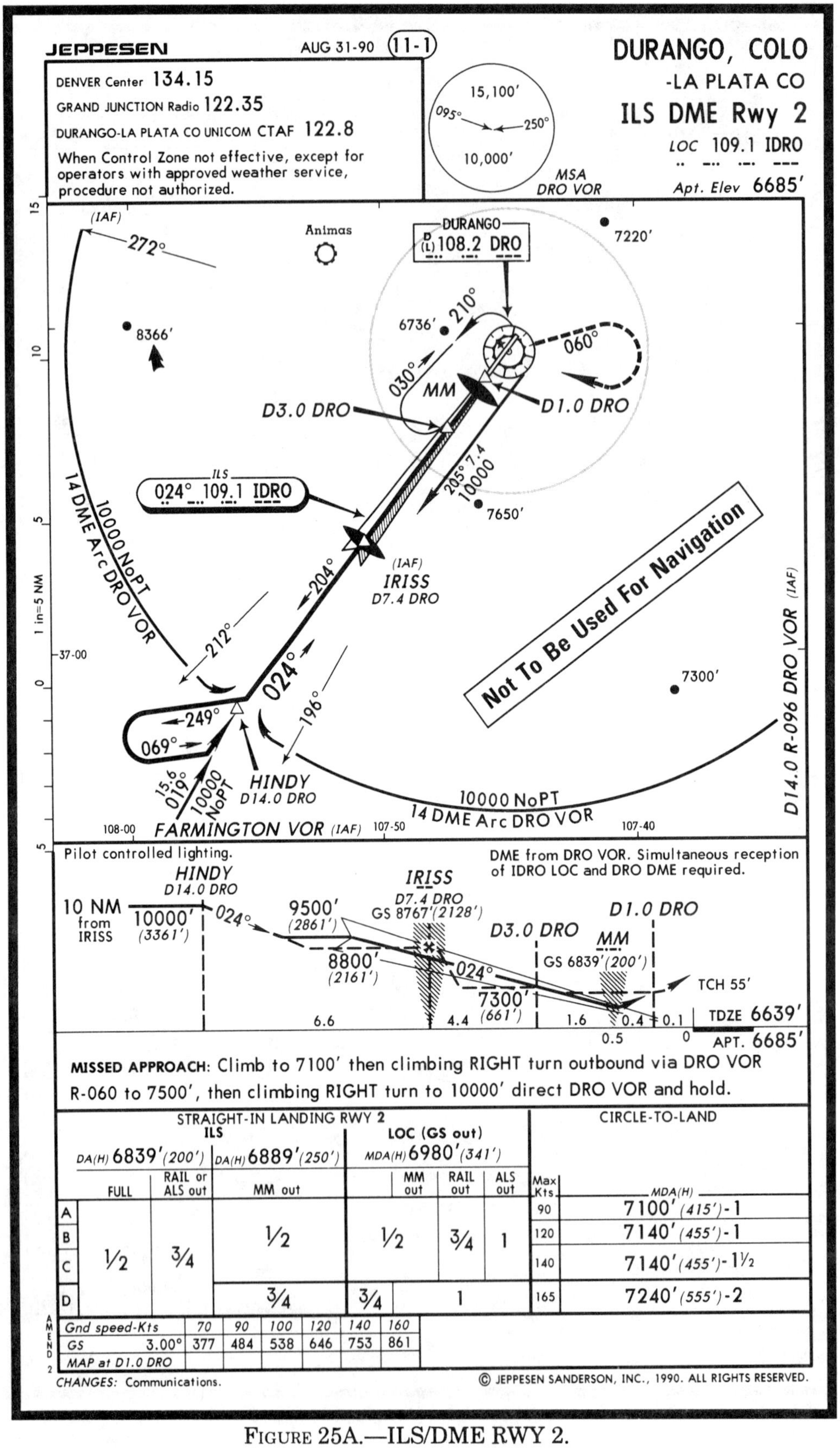

FIGURE 25A.—ILS/DME RWY 2.

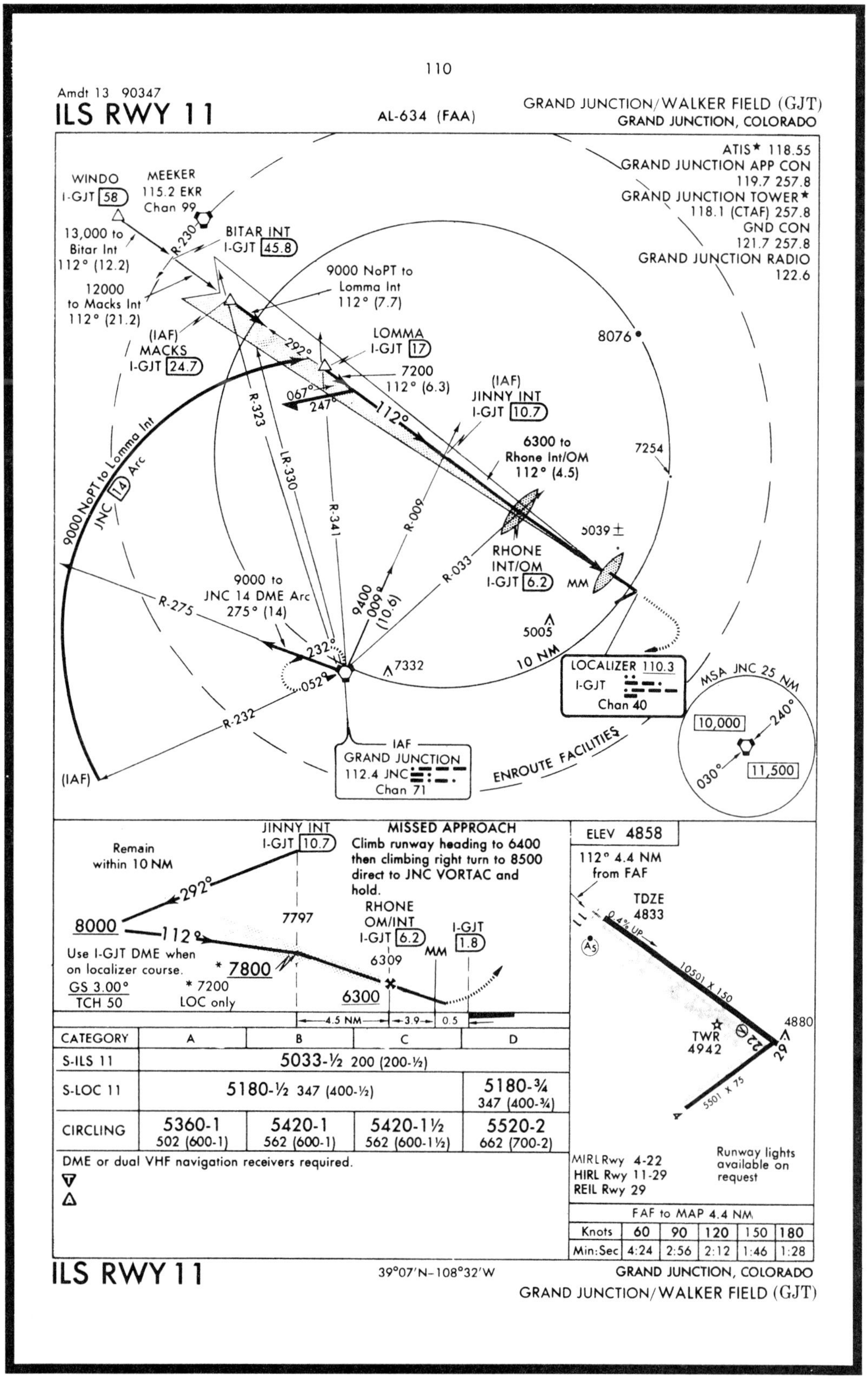

FIGURE 26.— ILS RWY 11.

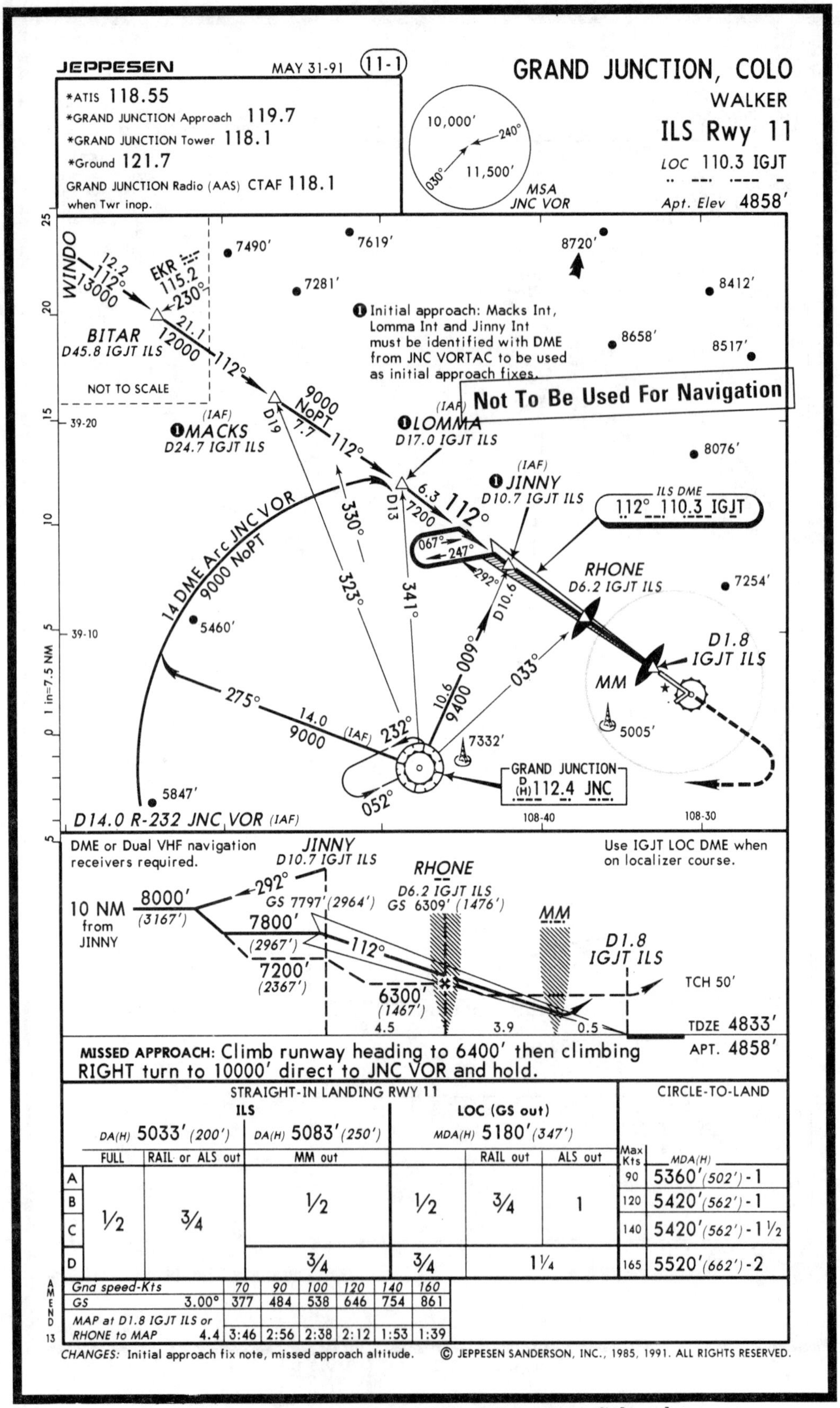

Appendix 3

FIGURE 26A.—ILS RWY 11, Grand Junction, Colorado.

Appendix 3

U.S. DEPARTMENT OF TRANSPORTATION FEDERAL AVIATION ADMINSTRANTION **FLIGHT PLAN**	(FAA USE ONLY)	☐ PILOT BRIEFING ☐ STOPOVER	☐ VNR	TIME STARTED	SPECIALIST INITIALS		

Form Approved: OMB No.2120-0034

1 TYPE	2 AIRCRAFT IDENTIFICATION	3 AIRCRAFT TYPE/ SPECIAL EQUIPMENT	4 TRUE AIRSPEED	5 DEPARTURE POINT	6 DEPARTURE TIME PROPOSED (Z) / ACTUAL (Z)	7 CRUISING ALTITUDE
☐ VFR X IFR ☐ DVFR	N132SM	C 182/	155	MFR		8,000

8 ROUTE OF FLIGHT

GNATS 1, MOURN, V121 EUG

9 DESTINATION (Name of airport and city): MAHLON/SWEET FIELD, EUGENE, OR.

10 EST TIME ENROUTE — HOURS / MINUTES

11 REMARKS: INSTRUMENT TRAINING FLIGHT

12 FUEL ON BOARD — HOURS / MINUTES

13 ALTERNATE AIRPORT(S): N/R

14 PILOTS NAME, ADDRESS & TELEPHONE NUMBER & AIRCRAFT HOME BASE

15 NUMBER ABOARD

17 DESTINATION CONTACT/TELEPHONE (OPTIONAL)

16 COLOR OF AIRCRAFT

CIVIL AIRCRAFT PILOTS. FAR Part 91 requires you file an IFR flight plan to operate under instrument flight rules in controlled airspace. Failure to file could result in a civil penalty not to exceed $1,000 for each violation (Section 901 of the Federal Aviation Act of 1958, as amended; Filing of a VFR flight plan is recommended as a good operating practice. See also Part 99 for requirements concerning DVFR flight plans.

FAA Form 7233-1 (8-82) CLOSE VFR FLIGHT PLAN WITH _____ FSS ON ARRIVAL

AIRCRAFT INFORMATION

MAKE CESSNA   MODEL 182

N 132SM   Vso 57

AIRCRAFT EQUIPMENT/STATUS**

**NOTE: X= OPERATIVE   INOP= INOPERATIVE   N/A= NOT APPLICABLE
TRANSPONDER: X (MODE C) X ILS: (LOCALIZER) X (GLIDE SLOPE) N/A
VOR NO.1 X (NO 2) X ADF: X RNAV: N/A
VERTICAL PATH COMPUTER: NA   DME: X
MARKER BEACON: (AUDIO) Inop. (VISUAL) Inop.

FIGURE 27.—Flight Plan and Aircraft Information.

Appendix 3

FLIGHT LOG

MEDFORD - JACKSON CO. AIRPORT TO HAHLON/SWEET FIELD, EUGENE, OR.

CHECK POINTS		ROUTE	COURSE	WIND	SPEED-KTS		DIST	TIME		FUEL	
FROM	TO	ALTITUDE		TEMP	TAS	GS	NM	LEG	TOT	LEG	TOT
MFR	MERLI	GNATS 1 CLIMB	270°		155			:11:0			
	MOURN	V121 8000	333°			AVER. 135					
	RBG	V121 8000	287°								
	OTH	V121 8000	272°								
	EUG	APPROACH DESCENT	026°								
APPROACH & LANDING								:10:0			
	SWEET FIELD										

OTHER DATA:
NOTE:

MAG. VAR. 20° E.
AVERAGE G.S. 135 KTS. FOR GNATS 1
DEPARTURE CLIMB.

FLIGHT SUMMARY

TIME	FUEL (LB)	
		EN ROUTE
		RESERVE
		MISSED APPR.
		TOTAL

FIGURE 28.—Flight Planning Log.

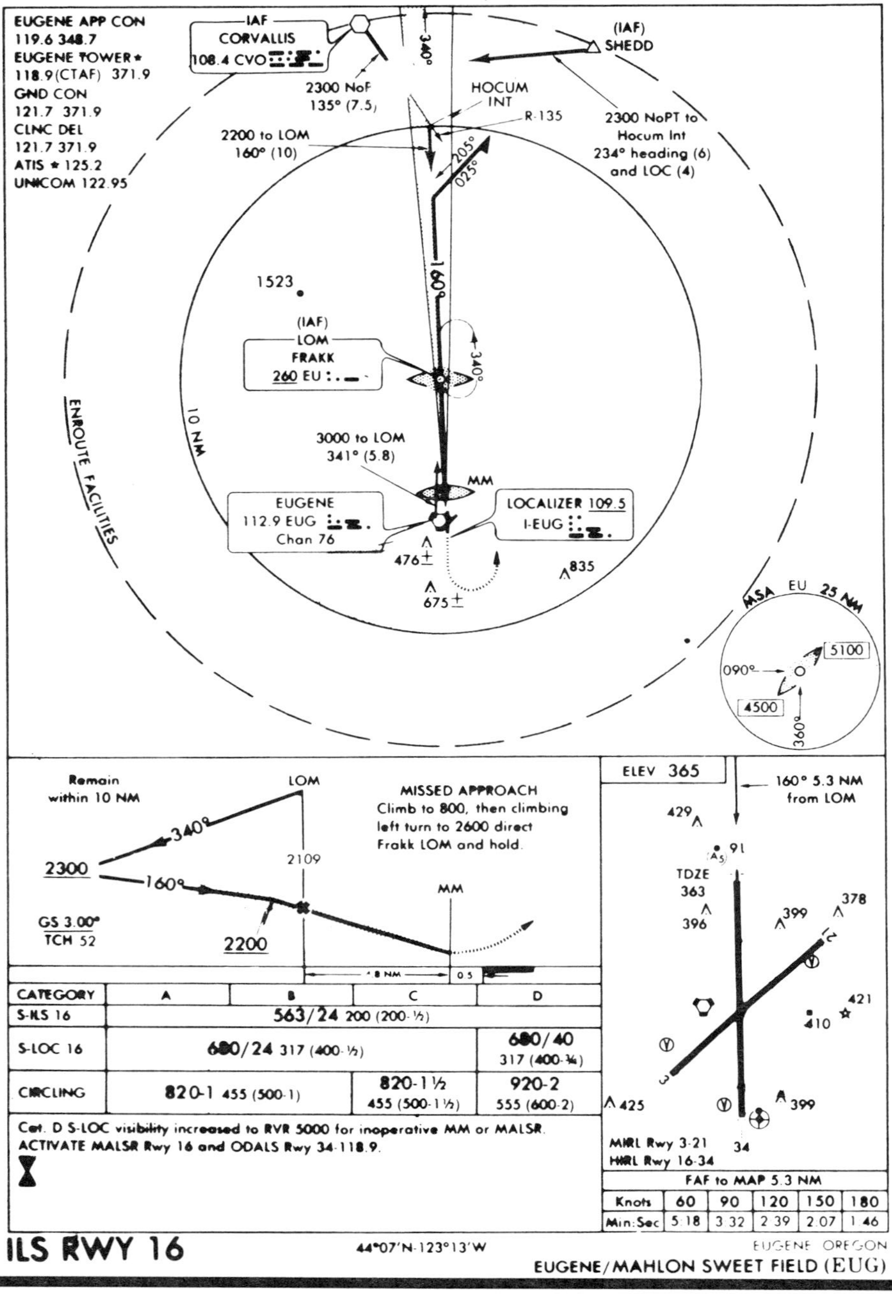

EUGENE

§ **MAHLON SWEET FLD** (EUG) 7 NW GMT-8(-7DT) 44°07'19"N 123°13'03"W — KLAMATH FALLS H-1A, L-1B IAP

365 B S4 **FUEL** 100LL, JET A OX 1, 2, 3, 4 TPA—1165(800) CFR Index B

RWY 16-34: H6202X150 (ASPH-PFC) S-155, D-190, DT-300 HIRL

RWY 16: MALSR. **RWY 34:** ODALS. VASI(V4L)—GA 3.0°TCH 54'

RWY 03-21: H5221X150 (ASPH) S-60, D-68, DT-105 MIRL

RWY 03: VASI(V4L)—GA 3.0°TCH 50.4'. Trees. **RWY 21:** VASI(V4L)—GA 3.0°TCH 53.2'. Trees

AIRPORT REMARKS: Attended continuously, phone 503-687-5431 between 0100-1600Z‡. CAUTION—migratory waterfowl and other birds in vicinity. ACTIVATE MALSR Rwy 16 and ODALS Rwy 34—118.9. MIRL Rwy 03-21 unavailable when twr clsd. CLOSED to unscheduled air carrier operations with more than 30 passenger seats during twr closure except PPR call arpt manager 503-687-5430. Taxiways F and G closed to Part 121 opns. Terminal apron available to scheduled air carriers and flights with prior permission. Control Zone effective continuously.

COMMUNICATIONS: CTAF 118.9 **ATIS** 125.2 (1400-0800Z‡) **UNICOM** 122.95

PORTLAND FSS (PDX) LC 688-8411. NOTAM FILE EUG

EUGENE RCO 122.3 122.1R 112.9T (PORTLAND FSS)

Ⓡ **EUGENE APP/DEP CON** 119.6 (280°-090°) 120.2 (091°-279°) (1400-0800Z‡)

Ⓡ **SEATTLE CENTER APP/DEP CON** 125.8 (0800-1400Z‡)

EUGENE TOWER 118.9 (1400-0800Z‡) **GND CON/CLNC DEL** 121.7

STAGE II SVC ctc **APP CON** within 25 NM

RADIO AIDS TO NAVIGATION: NOTAM FILE EUG

EUGENE (H) ABVORTAC 112.9 ■ EUG Chan 76 44°07'16"N 123°13'18"W at fld. 360/20E

General outlook on TWEB 0600-1300Z‡.

FRAKK NDB (LOM) 260 EU 44°12'47"N 123°13'10"W 179° 5.5 NM to fld.

NDB unusable 190°-270° beyond 11 NM

ILS 109.5 I-EUG RWY 16 LOM FRAKK NDB

ILS unmonitored when tower closed.

FIGURE 29.—ILS RWY 16 (EUG) and Excerpt from Airport/Facility Directory.

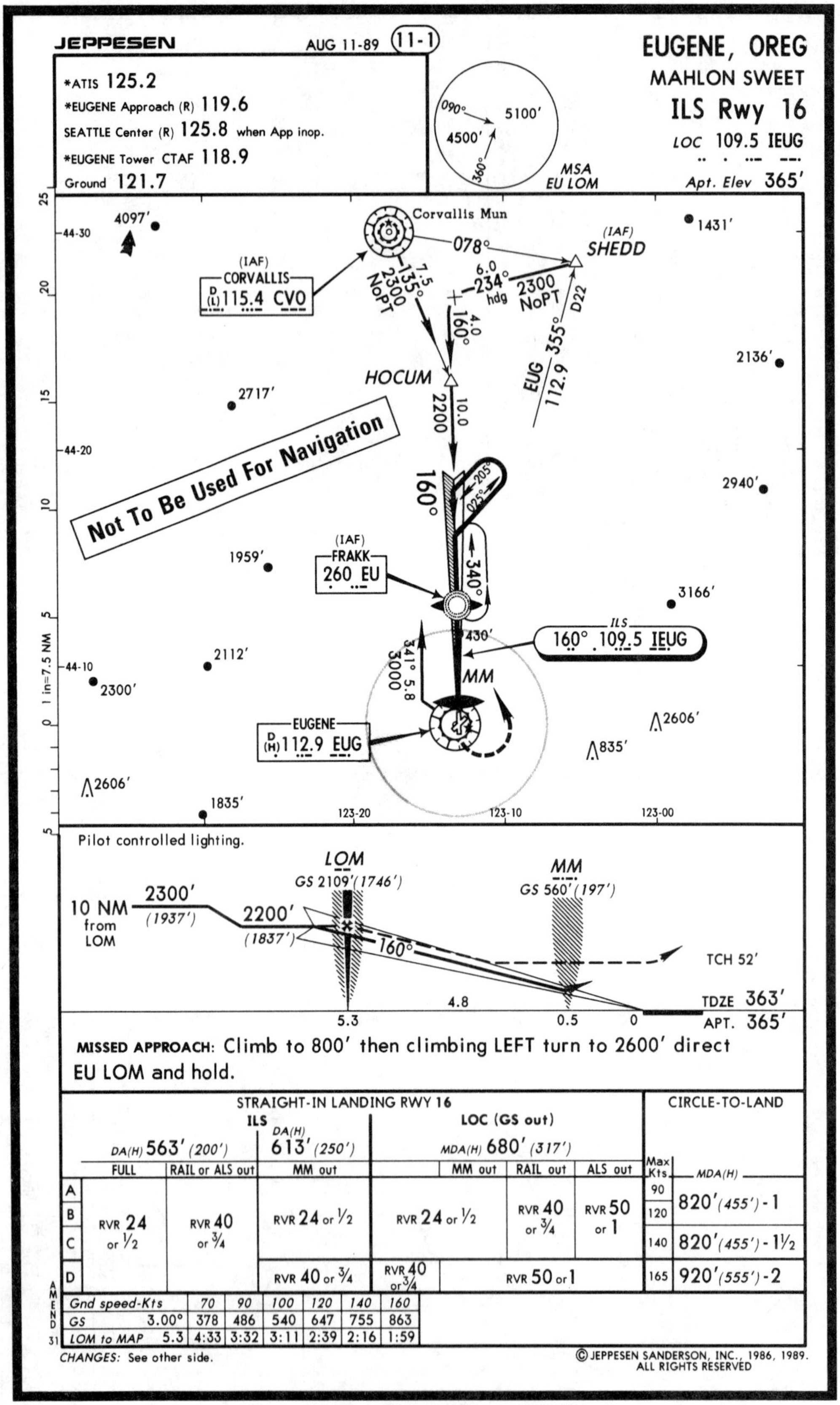

Appendix 3

FIGURE 29A.—ILS RWY 16 (EUG).

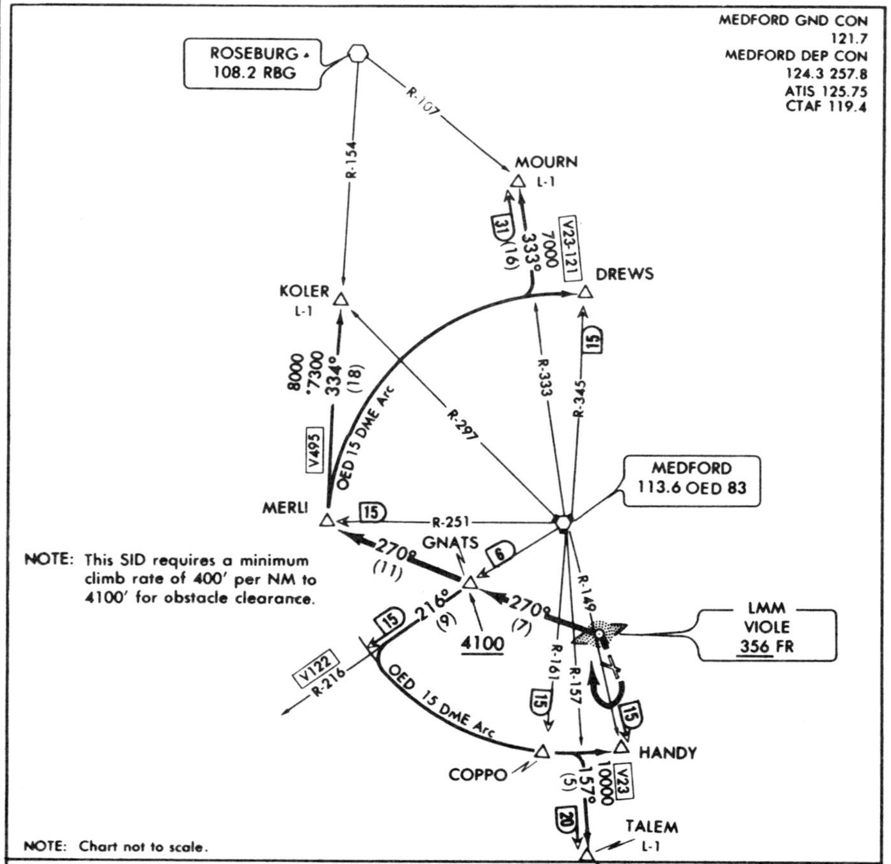

GNATS ONE DEPARTURE (GNATS1.GNATS)

DEPARTURE ROUTE DESCRIPTION
(Continued)

MOURN TRANSITION (GNATS1.MOURN): Continue via 270° magnetic bearing from the LMM to MERLI INT, turn right via MEDFORD 15 DME ARC to intercept V23-121 to MOURN INT.

DREWS TRANSITION (GNATS1.DREWS): Continue via 270° magnetic bearing from the LMM to MERLI INT, turn right via MEDFORD 15 DME ARC to DREWS INT.

TALEM TRANSITION (GNATS1.TALEM): Turn left via MEDFORD R-216 to 15 DME Fix thence turn left via MEDFORD 15 DME ARC to Intercept V23 to TALEM INT.

HANDY TRANSITION (GNATS1.HANDY): Turn left via MEDFORD R-216 to 15 DME Fix, thence turn left via MEDFORD 15 DME Arc to HANDY DME Fix.

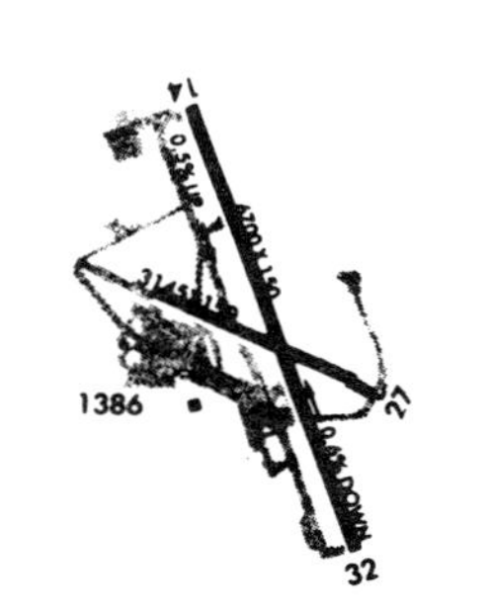

GNATS ONE DEPARTURE (GNATS1.GNATS)   MEDFORD-JACKSON CO
                                      MEDFORD, OREGON

§ MEDFORD-JACKSON CO (MFR) 3 N GMT-8(-7DT) 42°22'21"N 122°52'17"W   KLAMATH FALLS
  1331 B S4 FUEL 80, 100, 100LL, JET A1 + OX 1.3 CFR Index B   H-1A, L-1A
  RWY 14-32: H6700X150 (ASPH-PFC) S-200, D-200, DT-400 HIRL .5% up S   IAP
  RWY 14: MALSR. Trees. RWY 32: REIL. VASI(V4L)—GA 3.0°TCH 49'. Road.
  RWY 09-27: H3145X150 (ASPH) S-50, D-70, DT-108 MIRL
  RWY 27: Road.
  AIRPORT REMARKS: Attended continuously. CLOSED to unscheduled Part 121 air carriers operation, without prior
   approval, call 503-776-7222. Night refueling delay sunset-1500Z‡, ctc TOWER. Rwy 09-27 clsd to acft over 12,500
   lbs GWT. Rwy 09/27 CLOSED when tower clsd. Rwy lgts 14/32 operate med ints when tower closed. ACTIVATE
   MALSR 14—119.4. Flocks of large waterfowl in vicinity Nov-May
  COMMUNICATIONS: CTAF 119.4 ATIS 125.75 UNICOM 122.95
   NORTH BEND FSS (OTH) LC 773-3256. NOTAM FILE MFR.
   RCO 122.65 122.1R 113.6T (NORTH BEND FSS)
   APP CON 124.3 (1400-0800Z‡) DEP CON 125.3 (0800-1400Z‡)
   SEATTLE CENTER APP/DEP CON 125.3 (1400-0800Z‡)
   TOWER 119.4 (1400-0800Z‡) ctc TOWER   GND CON 121.7
   VFR ADVSY SVC ctc TOWER
  RADIO AIDS TO NAVIGATION: NOTAM FILE OTH. VHF/DF ctc Medford TOWER
   (H) ADVORTAC 113.6   ■OED Chan 83 42°28'47"N 122°54'43"W 146° 6.1 NM to fld. 2080'/19E
    VORTAC unusable:
     160°-165° beyond 35 NM below 8900'   280°-345° beyond 30 NM below 6500'
     198°-205° beyond 35 NM below 8500'   345°-360° beyond 35 NM below 6800'
     250°-280° beyond 25 NM below 6100'
   PUMIE NDB (LOM) 373   MF 42°27'04"N 122°54'44"W 140° 4.5 NM to fld. NOTAM FILE MFR
    LOM unusable 150°-165° and 260°-265° beyond 5 miles.
   VIOLE NDB (LMM) 356   FR 42°23'22"N 122°52'47"W 140° 0.5 NM to fld. NOTAM FILE MFR
    LMM unusable 305°-335° beyond 10 NM, all altitudes
   ILS/DME 110.3 I-MFR Chan 40 Rwy 14 LOM PUMIE NDB. LMM VIOLE NDB. ILS unmonitored when tower closed.
    Localizer unusable inside threshold.

MEDFORD GND CON 121.7
MEDFORD DEP CON 124.3 257.8
ATIS 125.75
CTAF 119.4

NOTE: This SID requires a minimum climb rate of 400' per NM to 4100' for obstacle clearance.

NOTE: Chart not to scale.

DEPARTURE ROUTE DESCRIPTION

Climb direct to the VIOLE ILS Middle Compass Locator (south take-off turn right), then climb on the 270° magnetic bearing from the LMM to GNATS INT, cross GNATS INT at or above 4100; thence via (transition) or (route).

COPPO TRANSITION (GNATS1.COPPO): Turn left via R-216 to 15 DME Fix, thence turn left via MEDFORD 15 DME Arc to COPPO DME Fix.

KOLER TRANSITION (GNATS1.KOLER): Continue via 270° magnetic bearing from the LMM to MERLI INT, turn right via ROSEBURG R-154 to KOLER INT.

(Continued on next page)

GNATS ONE DEPARTURE (GNATS1.GNATS)

FIGURE 30.—GNATS One Departure and Excerpt from Airport/Facility Directory.

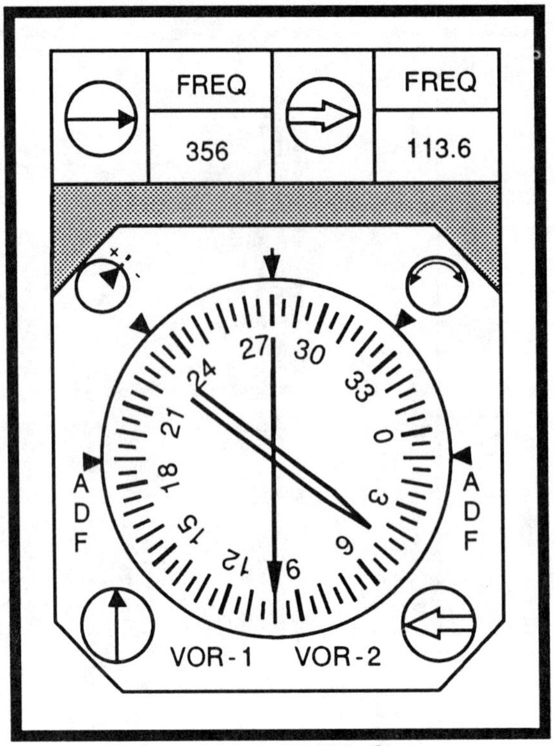

Appendix 3

FIGURE 30A.—RMI Indicator.

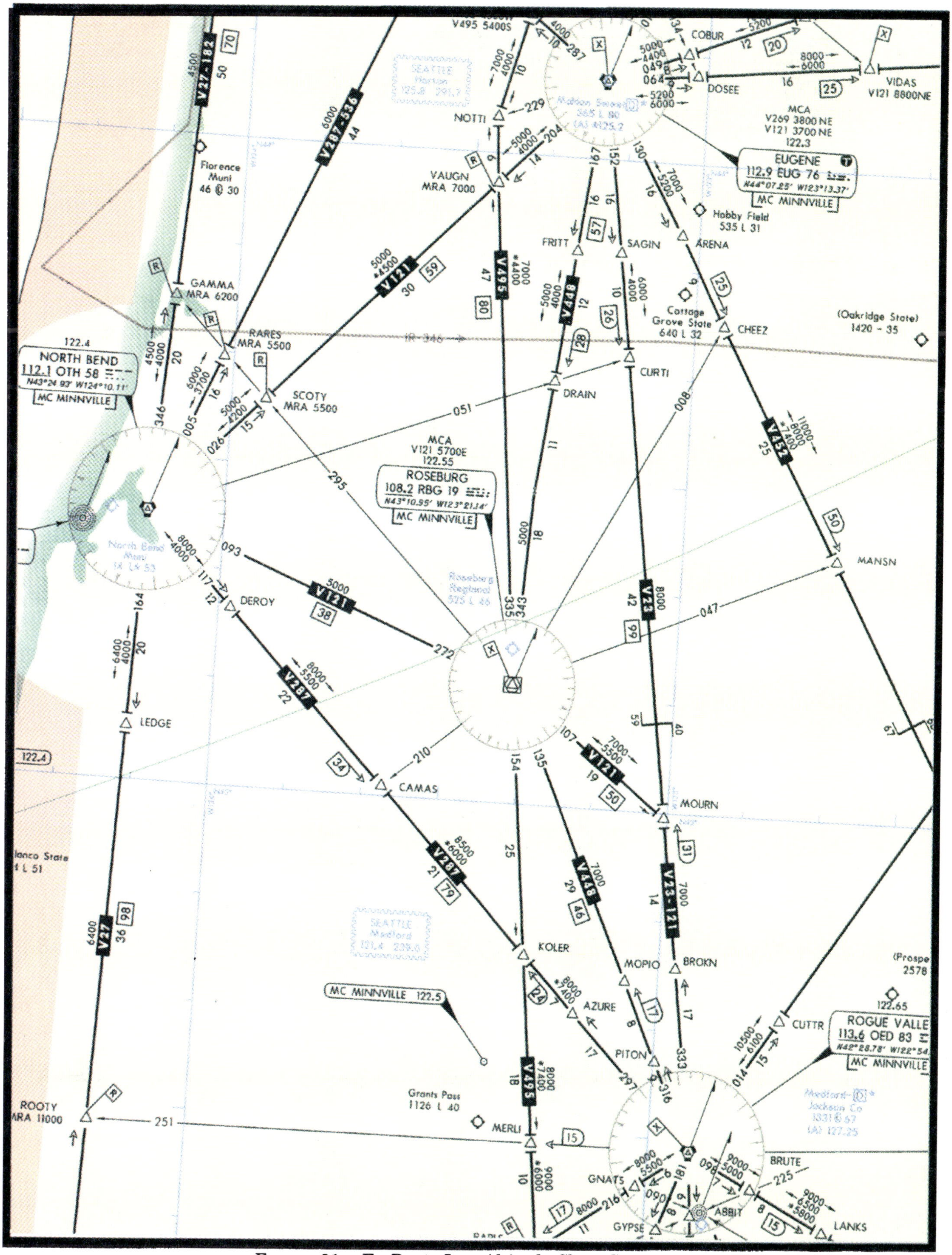

Appendix 3

FIGURE 31.—En Route Low-Altitude Chart Segment.

Appendix 3

	U.S. DEPARTMENT OF TRANSPORTATION FEDERAL AVIATION ADMINISTRATION **FLIGHT PLAN**	(FAA USE ONLY)	☐ PILOT BRIEFING ☐ STOPOVER	☐ VNR	TIME STARTED		SPECIALIST INITIALS
1. TYPE ☐ VFR X IFR ☐ DVFR	2. AIRCRAFT IDENTIFICATION N4078A	3. AIRCRAFT TYPE/ SPECIAL EQUIPMENT PA 31/	4. TRUE AIRSPEED 180 KTS	5. DEPARTURE POINT HOT	6. DEPARTURE TIME PROPOSED (Z) / ACTUAL (Z)		7. CRUISING ALTITUDE 8,000

8. ROUTE OF FLIGHT
HOT V573, TXK, TXK.BUJ3

9. DESTINATION (Name of airport and city)
DALLAS ADDISON AIRPORT DALLAS, TX

10. EST. TIME ENROUTE HOURS / MINUTES

11. REMARKS

12. FUEL ON BOARD HOURS / MINUTES

13. ALTERNATE AIRPORT(S)

14. PILOT'S NAME, ADDRESS & TELEPHONE NUMBER & AIRCRAFT HOME BASE

17. DESTINATION CONTACT/TELEPHONE (OPTIONAL)
N/A

15. NUMBER ABOARD
2

16. COLOR OF AIRCRAFT
TAN/WHITE

CIVIL AIRCRAFT PILOTS. FAR Part 91 requires you file an IFR flight plan to operate under instrument flight rules in controlled airspace. Failure to file could result in a civil penalty not to exceed $1,000 for each violation (Section 901 of the Federal Aviation Act of 1958, as amended). Filing of a VFR flight plan is recommended as a good operating practice. See also Part 99 for requirements concerning DVFR flight plans.

FAA Form 7233-1 (8-82)   CLOSE VFR FLIGHT PLAN WITH _____ FSS ON ARRIVAL

AIRCRAFT INFORMATION

MAKE Piper   MODEL PA-31

N 4078A   Vso 74

AIRCRAFT EQUIPMENT/STATUS**

**NOTE: X= OPERATIVE   INOP= INOPERATIVE   N/A= NOT APPLICABLE
TRANSPONDER: X (MODE C) X ILS: (LOCALIZER) X (GLIDE SLOPE) X
VOR NO. 1 X (NO. 2) X ADF: X RNAV: X
VERTICAL PATH COMPUTER: N/A DME: X
MARKER BEACON: X (AUDIO) X (VISUAL) X

FIGURE 32.—Flight Plan and Aircraft Information.

Appendix 3

FLIGHT LOG

HOT SPRINGS, MEMORIAL FIELD TO DALLAS, ADDISON, TX.

CHECK POINTS		ROUTE	COURSE	WIND	SPEED-KTS		DIST	TIME		FUEL	
FROM	TO	ALTITUDE		TEMP	TAS	GS	NM	LEG	TOT	LEG	TOT
HOT	MARKI	V573 CLIMB	221°					:12:00			
	TXK	V573 8000	210°		180						
	TXK BUJ3	BUJ3 8000	272°								
	BUJ3	BUJ3 DESCENT	239°								
APPROACH & LANDING								:10:00			
	DALLAS ADDISON										

OTHER DATA:
NOTE: MAG. VAR. 4° E.

FLIGHT SUMMARY

TIME	FUEL (LB)	
		EN ROUTE
		RESERVE
		MISSED APPR.
		TOTAL

FIGURE 33.—Flight Planning Log.

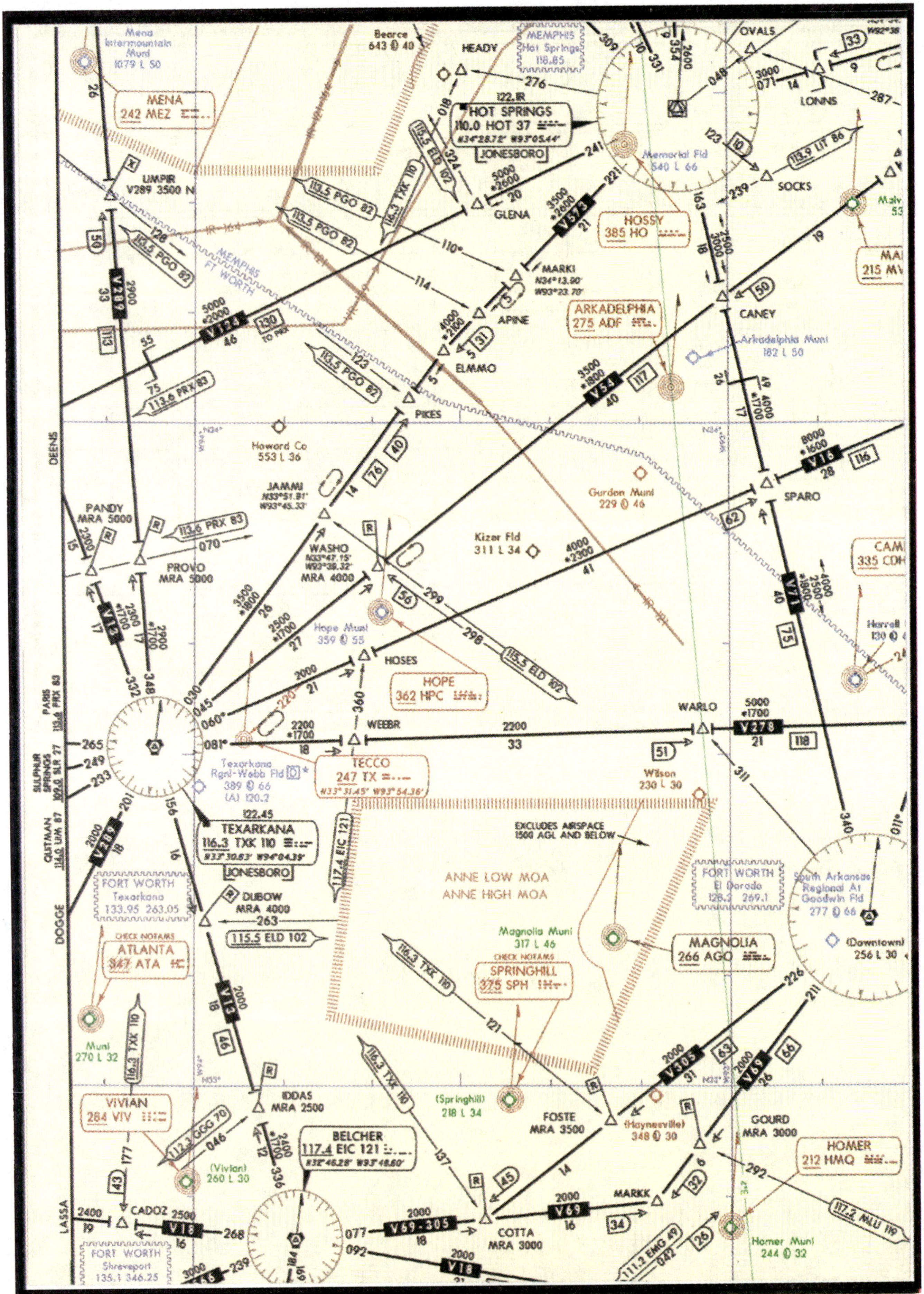

Appendix 3

FIGURE 34.—En Route Chart.

Appendix 3

ARKANSAS

HOT SPRINGS
 MEMORIAL FLD (HOT) 3 SW UTC−6(−5DT) 34°28'41"N 93°05'46"W MEMPHIS
  540 B S4 FUEL 100LL, JET A ARFF Index Ltd. H-4G, L-14E
  RWY 05-23: H6595X150 (ASPH-GRVD) S-75, D-125, DT-210, DDT-400. HIRL 0.6% up NE IAP
   RWY 05: MALSR. Tree. RWY 23: REIL. Thld dsplcd 490'. Tree.
  RWY 13-31: H4099X150 (ASPH) S-28, D-36, DT-63 MIRL
   RWY 13: REIL. Road/Trees. RWY 31: Pole.
  AIRPORT REMARKS: Attended 1130-0400Z‡. CLOSED to unscheduled air carrier ops with more than 30 passenger seats except PPR, call arpt manager 501-624-3306. Last 500' Rwy 05 CLOSED to takeoffs. Rwy 13-31 fair with extensive loose grvl-pavement debris. ACTIVATE HIRL Rwy 05-23 and MALSR Rwy 05—CTAF. Rwy 23 REIL out of svc indefinitely. Control Zone effective 1200-0400Z‡.
  COMMUNICATIONS: CTAF/UNICOM 123.0
   JONESBORO FSS (JBR) TF 1-800-WX-BRIEF. NOTAM FILE HOT.
   HOT SPRINGS RCO 122.1R 110.0T (LITTLE ROCK FSS)
   MEMPHIS CENTER APP/DEP CON: 118.85
  RADIO AIDS TO NAVIGATION: NOTAM FILE HOT.
   HOT SPRINGS (L) VOR/DME 110.0 HOT Chan 37 34°28'43"N 93°05'26"W at fld. 530/4E.
   HOSSY NDB (HW/LOM) 385 HO 34°25'21"N 93°11'22"W 050° 5.7 NM to fld.
   ILS/DME 111.5 I-HOT Chan 52 Rwy 05 LOM HOSSY NDB. Unmonitored.

FIGURE 34A.—Airport/Facility Directory (HOT).

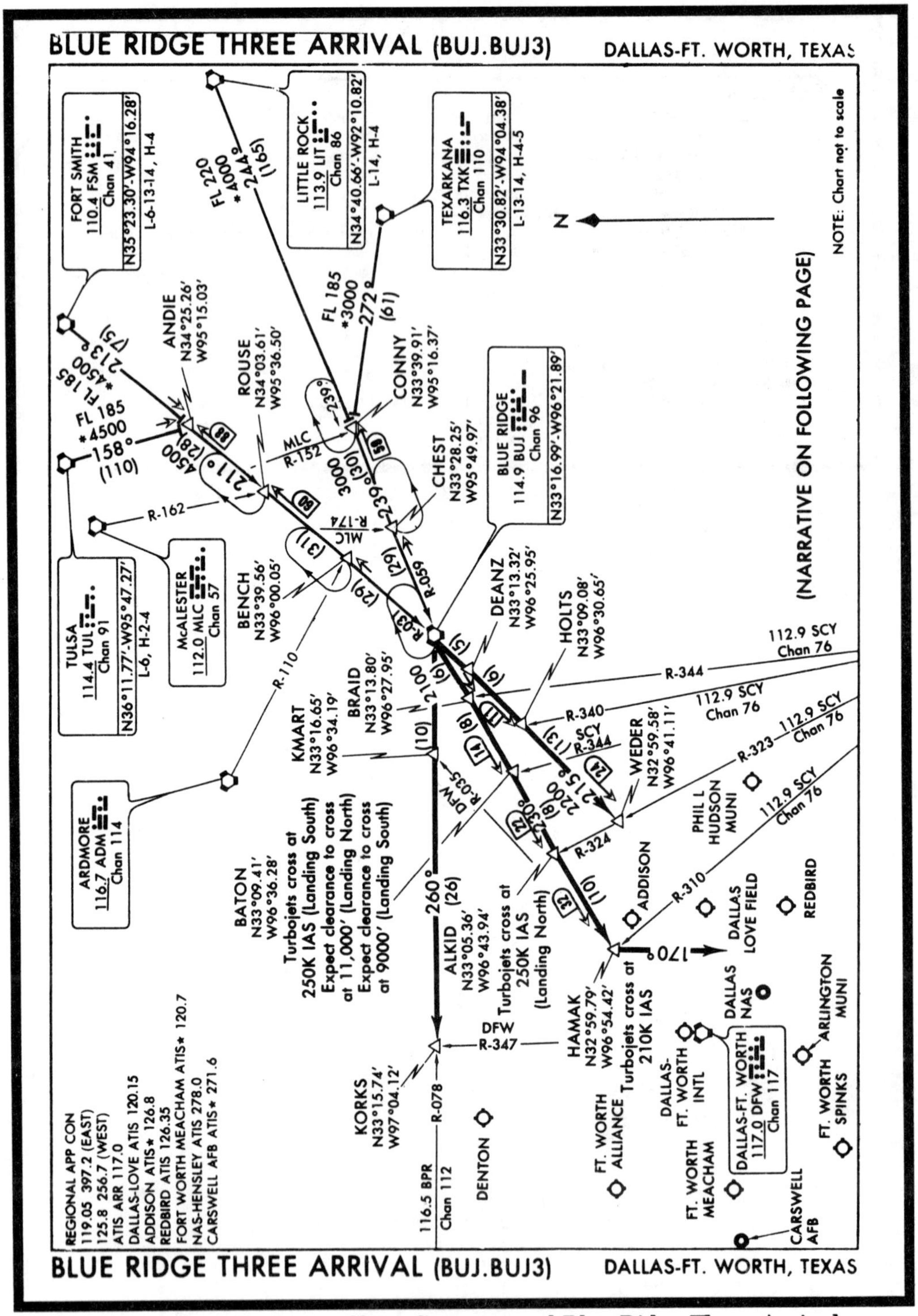

Appendix 3

FIGURE 35.—En Route Chart Segment and Blue Ridge Three Arrival.

Appendix 3

> 91094   SL-6039 (FAA)
> **BLUE RIDGE THREE ARRIVAL (BUJ.BUJ3)**   DALLAS-FT. WORTH, TEXAS
>
> ARRIVAL DESCRIPTION
>
> <u>FORT SMITH TRANSITION (FSM.BUJ3)</u>: From over FSM VORTAC via FSM R-213 and BUJ R-031 to BUJ VORTAC. Thence . . . .
> <u>LITTLE ROCK TRANSITION (LIT.BUJ3)</u>: From over LIT VORTAC via LIT R-244 and BUJ R-059 to BUJ VORTAC. Thence . . . .
> <u>TEXARKANA TRANSITION (TXK.BUJ3)</u>: From over TXK VORTAC via TXK R-272 and BUJ R-059 to BUJ VORTAC. Thence . . . .
> <u>TULSA TRANSITION (TUL.BUJ3)</u>: From over TUL VORTAC via TUL R-158 and BUJ R-031 to BUJ VORTAC. Thence . . . .
> <u>TURBOJETS LANDING DALLAS-FT WORTH INTL</u>: (Landing South): From over BUJ VORTAC via BUJ R-230 to HAMAK INT. Expect vectors at BATON INT. (Landing North): From over BUJ VORTAC via BUJ R-230 to HAMAK INT, thence heading 170° for vector to final approach course.
> <u>NON-TURBOJETS LANDING DALLAS-FT WORTH INTL</u>: (Landing South): From over BUJ VORTAC via BUJ R-230 to HAMAK INT. Expect vectors at BATON INT. (Landing North): From over BUJ VORTAC via BUJ R-215 to WEDER INT. Expect vectors to final approach course.
> <u>ALL AIRCRAFT LANDING DALLAS-LOVE FIELD, ADDISON, REDBIRD, NAS DALLAS, and PHIL L. HUDSON</u>: (Landing South/North): From over BUJ VORTAC via BUJ R-215 to WEDER INT. Expect vectors to final approach course.
> <u>ALL AIRCRAFT LANDING MEACHAM, CARSWELL AFB, ALLIANCE, ARLINGTON, DENTON and FT. WORTH SPINKS</u>: (Landing South/North): From over BUJ VORTAC via BUJ R-260 to KORKS INT. Expect vectors to final approach course.

FIGURE 35A.—Blue Ridge Three Arrival Description.

Appendix 3

| TEXAS | 145 |

DALLAS
  ADDISON   (ADS)   9 N   UTC–6(–5DT)   32°58'06"N 96°50'10"W   DALLAS-FT. WORTH
   643   B   S4   FUEL 100LL, JET A   H-2K, 4F, 5B, L-13C, A
   RWY 15-33: H7201X100 (ASPH)   S-80, D-100, DT-160   MIRL   IAP
    RWY 15: MALSR. VASI(V4R)—GA 3.0°TCH 51'. Thld dsplcd 980'. Ground.
    RWY 33: REIL. Thld dsplcd 468'. Road.
   AIRPORT REMARKS: Attended continuously. Numerous flocks of birds on and in vicinity of arpt. Use extreme care:
    numerous 200' AGL buildings within 1 mile East, and South of arpt, transmission towers and water tanks West of
    arpt. Rwy 33 REIL out of svc indefinitely. ACTIVATE MALSR Rwy 15—CTAF. Rwy limited to maximum gross
    weight 120,000 pounds. Control Zone effective 1200-0400Z‡.
   WEATHER DATA SOURCES: LAWRS
   COMMUNICATIONS: CTAF 121.1   ATIS 126.8 (1200-0400Z‡)   UNICOM 122.95
    FORT WORTH FSS (FTW) TF 1–800–WX–BRIEF. NOTAM FILE ADS.
   ®**REGIONAL APP CON** 123.9   ® **REGIONAL DEP CON** 124.3
    TOWER 121.1 (1200-0400Z‡)   **GND CON** 121.6   **CLNC DEL** 119.55
   RADIO AIDS TO NAVIGATION: NOTAM FILE DAL.
    LOVE (L) VORW/DME 114.3   LUE   Chan 90   32°50'51"N 96°51'42"W   002° 7.4 NM to fld. 490/08E.
    BRONS NDB (LOM) 407   AD   33°02'40"N 96°52'13"W   153° 4.9 NM to fld.
    ILS/DME 110.1 I-ADS Chan 38 Rwy 15. LOM BRONS NDB. Unmonitored when tower closed.
    ILS 110.1 I-TBQ Rwy 33 LOC only. Unmonitored when twr clsd.

FIGURE 36.—Excerpt from Airport/Facility Directory.

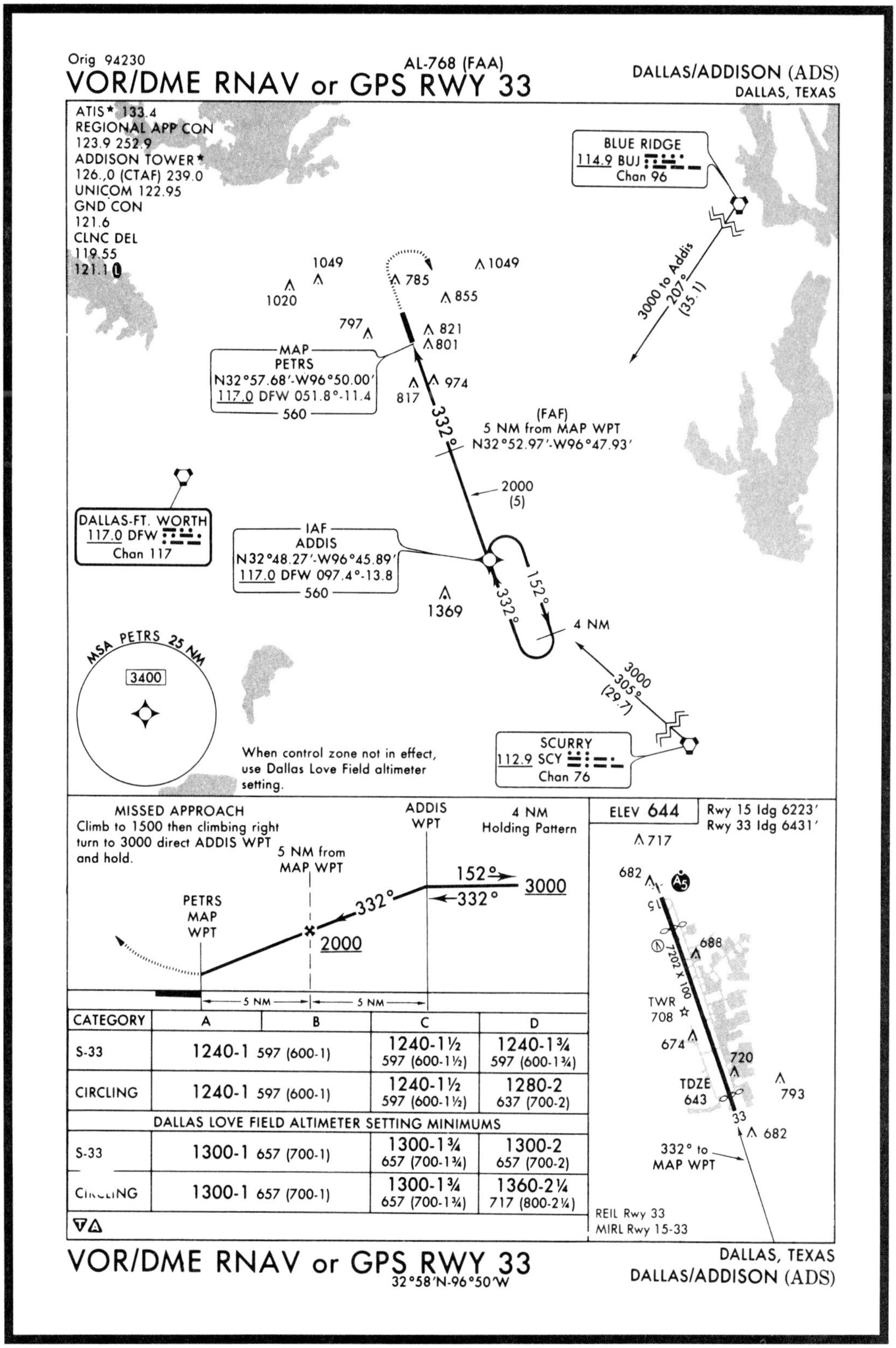

FIGURE 36A.—RNAV RWY 33 (ADS).

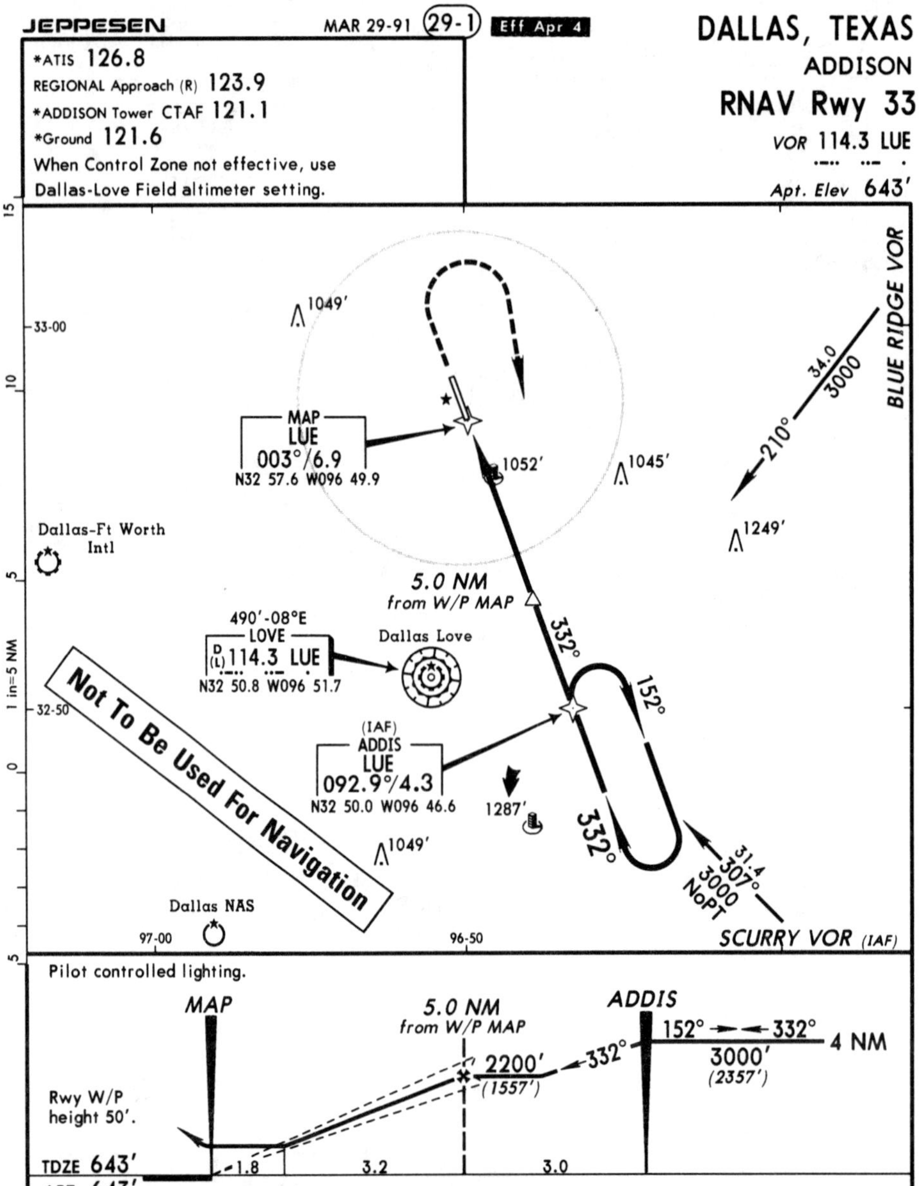

MISSED APPROACH: Climb to 1500' then climbing RIGHT turn to 3000' direct W/P ADDIS and hold.

	STRAIGHT-IN LANDING RWY 33 MDA(H) 1240' (597')	Max Kts	CIRCLE-TO-LAND MDA(H)
A	1	90	1240'(597')-1
B	1	120	1240'(597')-1
C	1½	140	1240'(597')-1½
D	1¾	165	1280'(637')-2

Gnd speed-Kts	70	90	100	120	140	160
GS Setting 2.85°	359	461	512	615	717	820

AMEND 1

CHANGES: W P Addis bearing.

FIGURE 36B.— RNAV RWY 33 (ADS).

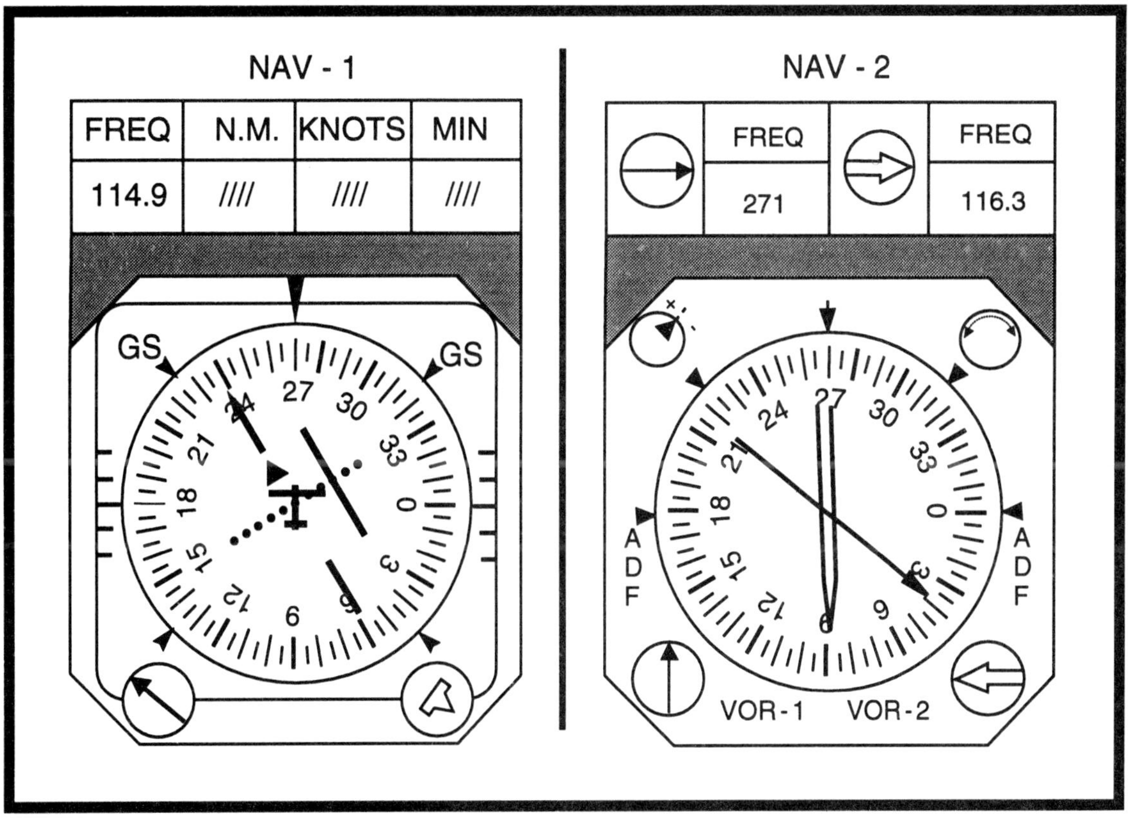

Appendix 3

FIGURE 37.—CDI and RMI — NAV 1 and NAV 2.

Appendix 3

					Form Approved: OMB No. 2120-0034
U.S. DEPARTMENT OF TRANSPORTATION FEDERAL AVIATION ADMINISTRATION **FLIGHT PLAN**	(FAA USE ONLY)	☐ PILOT BRIEFING ☐ STOPOVER	☐ VNR	TIME STARTED	SPECIALIST INITIALS

1. TYPE	2. AIRCRAFT IDENTIFICATION	3. AIRCRAFT TYPE/ SPECIAL EQUIPMENT	4. TRUE AIRSPEED	5. DEPARTURE POINT	6. DEPARTURE TIME		7. CRUISING ALTITUDE
					PROPOSED (Z)	ACTUAL (Z)	
VFR / X IFR / DVFR	N4321P	C402/	156 KTS	BGS			11000

8. ROUTE OF FLIGHT
DIRECT BGS, V16 ABI, ABI.AQN2

9. DESTINATION (Name of airport and city)	10. EST. TIME ENROUTE		11. REMARKS
	HOURS	MINUTES	
DALLAS FT. WORTH DFW			

12. FUEL ON BOARD		13. ALTERNATE AIRPORT(S)	14. PILOT'S NAME, ADDRESS & TELEPHONE NUMBER & AIRCRAFT HOME BASE	15. NUMBER ABOARD
HOURS	MINUTES			
		N/A	17. DESTINATION CONTACT/TELEPHONE (OPTIONAL)	2

16. COLOR OF AIRCRAFT	CIVIL AIRCRAFT PILOTS. FAR Part 91 requires you file an IFR flight plan to operate under instrument flight rules in controlled airspace. Failure to file could result in a civil penalty not to exceed $1,000 for each violation (Section 901 of the Federal Aviation Act of 1958, as amended). Filing of a VFR flight plan is recommended as a good operating practice. See also Part 99 for requirements concerning DVFR flight plans.
RED/BLUE/WHITE	

FAA Form 7233-1 (8-82)   CLOSE VFR FLIGHT PLAN WITH _____ FSS ON ARRIVAL

AIRCRAFT INFORMATION

MAKE Cessna   MODEL 402C

N 4321P   Vso 71

AIRCRAFT EQUIPMENT/STATUS**

**NOTE: X= OPERATIVE   INOP= INOPERATIVE   N/A= NOT APPLICABLE
TRANSPONDER: X (MODE C) X ILS: (LOCALIZER) X (GLIDE SLOPE) X
VOR NO. 1 X (NO. 2) X ADF: X RNAV: X
VERTICAL PATH COMPUTER: N/A DME: X
MARKER BEACON: X (AUDIO) X (VISUAL) X

FIGURE 38.—Flight Plan and Aircraft Information.

Appendix 3

FLIGHT LOG
BIG SPRING McMAHON-WRINKLE TO DALLAS FT. WORTH (DFW)

CHECK POINTS		ROUTE		WIND	SPEED-KTS		DIST	TIME		FUEL	
FROM	TO	ALTITUDE	COURSE	TEMP	TAS	GS	NM	LEG	TOT	LEG	TOT
21XS	BGS	DIRECT CLIMB	DIRECT					:06:0			
	LORAN	V16 11,000	075°								
	ABI	V16 11,000	076°		156						
	COTTN	DIRECT 11,000	087°								
	AQN	AQN2	075°								
	CREEK	AQN2	040°								
APPROACH & LANDING		RADAR VEC-DESCENT						:08:0			
	DFW AIRPORT										

OTHER DATA:
NOTE: MAG. VAR. 11° E.
(STAR) ACTON TWO ARRIVAL (AQN2)

FLIGHT SUMMARY

TIME	FUEL (LB)	
		EN ROUTE
		RESERVE
		MISSED APPR.
		TOTAL

BIG SPRING McMAHON-WRINKLE (21XS) 2SW UTC-6(-5DT). DALLAS-FT. WORTH
32°12'45"N 101°31'17"W   H-21, 5A, L-13A, 15B
2572 B S4 FUEL 100LL, JET A   IAP
RWY 17-35: H8803X100 (ASPH-CONC) S-44, D-62, DDT-101 MIRL
  RWY 17:SSALS.PVASI(ASPH)-GA3.0°TCH 41'.
RWY 06-24:H4600X75(ASPH) MIRL
  RWY 24:PVASI(PSIL)-GA3.55°TCH31'. P-line.
AIRPORT REMARKS: Attended 1400-2300Z . For fuel after hours call 915-263-3958. ACTIVATE MIRL Rwy 06-24
  and Rwy 17-35, SSALS Rwy 17 and PVASI Rwy 17 and 24-CTAF.
COMMUNICATIONS:CTAF/UNICOM 122.8
  SAN ANGELOSFSS (SJT) TF 1-800-WX-BRIEF. NOTAM FILE SJT.
  RCO 122.4(SAN ANGELOFSS)
  FORT WORTH CENTER APP/DEP CON 133.7
RADIO AIDS TO NAVIGATION: NOTAM FILE SJT.
  (L) VORTACW 144.3 BGS Chan 90 32°23'08"N 101°10.5NM to fld. 2670/11E.

EXCERPT FROM AIRPORT/FACILITY DIRECTORY (21 XS)

FIGURE 39.—Flight Log and Excerpt from Airport/Facility Directory (21 XS).

Appendix 3

```
HELENA REGIONAL    (HLN)   2 NE   UTC-7(-6DT)   46°36'25"N 111°58'55"W              GREAT FALLS
  3873   B   S4   FUEL 100LL, JET A   OX 1,3   AOE   ARFF Index B                    H-1C, L-9B
  RWY 09-27: H9000X150 (ASPH-PFC)   S-100, D-160, DT-250   HIRL                       IAP
  RWY 09: VASI(V4L)—GA 3.0°TCH 45'. Ground.      RWY 27: MALSR. VASI(V4L)—GA 3.0°TCH 55'. Rgt tfc.
  RWY 05-23: H4599X75 (ASPH-PFC)   S-21, D-30
  RWY 05: Road.         RWY 23: Fence. Rgt tfc.
  RWY 16-34: H2979X75 (ASPH)   S-21, D-30   MIRL
  RWY 34: Ground. Rgt tfc.
  AIRPORT REMARKS: Attended 1200-0800Z‡. East 2400' Taxiway C and first 900' Rwy 27 not visible from tower.
    Prior permission for unscheduled FAR 121 operations, Call 406-442-2821. AOE, 1 hour prior notice required,
    phone 449-1569 1500-0000Z‡, 0000-1500Z‡ 449-1024. Twys A;B; high speed and C (between A and D)
    not available for air carrier use by acft with greater than 30 passenger seats. Rwy 16-34 and Rwy 05-23 (except
    between Rwy 09-27 and Twy D) not available for air carrier use by acft with greater than 30 passenger seats.
    When tower closed, ACTIVATE HIRL Rwy 09-27 and MALSR Rwy 27—CTAF, when twr closed MIRL Rwy 16-34
    are off. Ldg fee for all acft over 12,500 lbs. NOTE: See SPECIAL NOTICE—Simultaneous Operations on
    Intersecting Runways.
  COMMUNICATIONS: CTAF 118.3       ATIS 120.4 (Mon-Fri 1300-0700Z‡, Sat-Sun 1300-0500Z‡)
    UNICOM 122.95
    GREAT FALLS FSS (GTF) TF 1-800-WX-BRIEF. NOTAM FILE HLN.
    RCO 122.2 122.1R 117.7T (GREAT FALLS FSS)
    APP/DEP CON 119.5 (Mon-Fri 1300-0700Z‡, Sat-Sun 1300-0500Z‡)
    SALT LAKE CENTER APP/DEP CON 133.4 (Mon-Fri 0700-1300Z‡, Sat-Sun 0500-1300Z‡)
    TOWER 118.3 (Mon-Fri 1300-0700Z‡, Sat-Sun 1300-0500Z‡)   GND CON 121.9
  RADIO AIDS TO NAVIGATION: NOTAM FILE HLN.
    (H) VORTAC 117.7   HLN   Chan 124   46°36'25"N 111°57'10"W   254° 1.2 NM to fld. 3810/16E.
      VORTAC unusable:
        006°-090° beyond 25 NM below 11,000'         091°-120° beyond 20 NM below 16,000'
        121°-240° beyond 25 NM below 10,000'         355°-006° beyond 15 NM below 17,500'
        241°-320° beyond 25 NM below 10,000'
    CAPITOL NDB (HW) 317   CVP   46°36'24"N 111°56'11"W   254° 1.9 NM to fld.
      NDB unmonitored when tower closed.
    HAUSER NDB (MHW) 386   HAU   46°34'08"N 111°45'26"W   268° 9.6 NM to fld.
    ILS 110.1 I-HLN Rwy 27 ILS unmonitored when tower closed.


                        Excerpt from Airport/Facility
                             Directory (21 XS)

BIG SPRING McMAHON-WRINKLE    (21XS)   2 SW   UTC-6(-5DT).                      DALLAS-FT WORTH
    32°12'45"N 101°31'17"W                                                       H-21, 5A, L-13A, 15B
  2572   B   S4   FUEL 100LL, JET A                                               IAP
  RWY 17-35: H8803X100 (ASPH-CONC)   S-44, D-62, DDT-101   MIRL
  RWY 17: SSALS. PVASI (PSIL)—GA 3.0° TCH 41'.
  RWY 06-24: H4600X75 (ASPH)   MIRL
  RWY 24: PVASI (PSIL)—GA 3.55°TCH 31'. P-line.
  AIRPORT REMARKS: Attended 1400-2300Z‡. For fuel after hours call 915-263-3958. ACTIVATE MIRL Rwy 06-24
    and Rwy 17-35, SSALS Rwy 17 and PVASI Rwy 17 and 24—CTAF.
  COMMUNICATIONS: CTAF/UNICOM 122.8
    SAN ANGELO FSS (SJT) TF 1-800-WX-BRIEF. NOTAM FILE SJT.
    RCO 122.4 (SAN ANGELO FSS)
    FORT WORTH CENTER APP/DEP CON 133.7
  RADIO AIDS TO NAVIGATION: NOTAM FILE SJT.
    (L) VORTACW 114.3   BGS   Chan 90   32°23'08"N 101°29'00"W   180° 10.5 NM to fld. 2670/11E.
```

FIGURE 39A.—Excerpt from Airport/Facility Directory (21 XS).

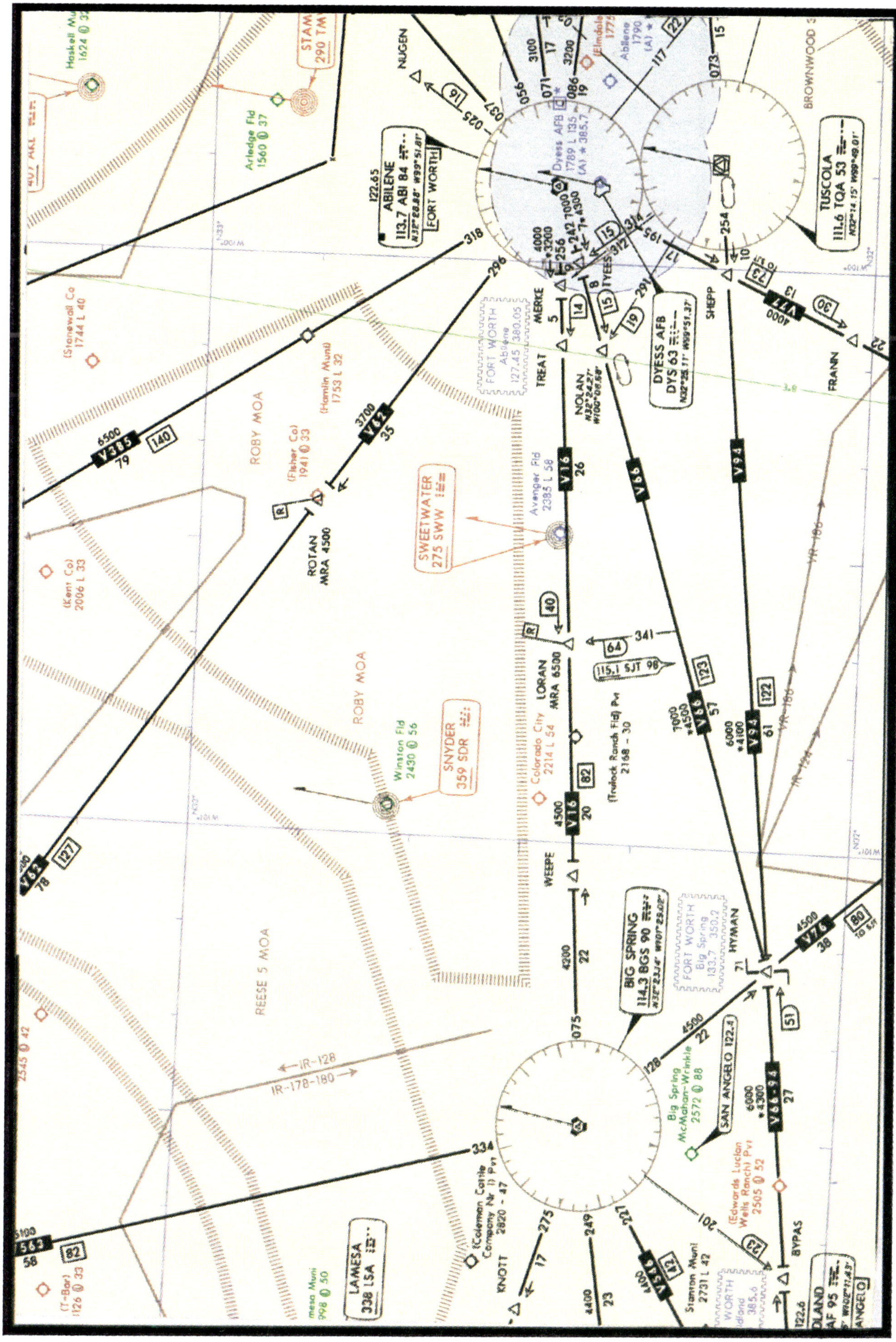

Appendix 3

FIGURE 40.—En Route Chart Segment.

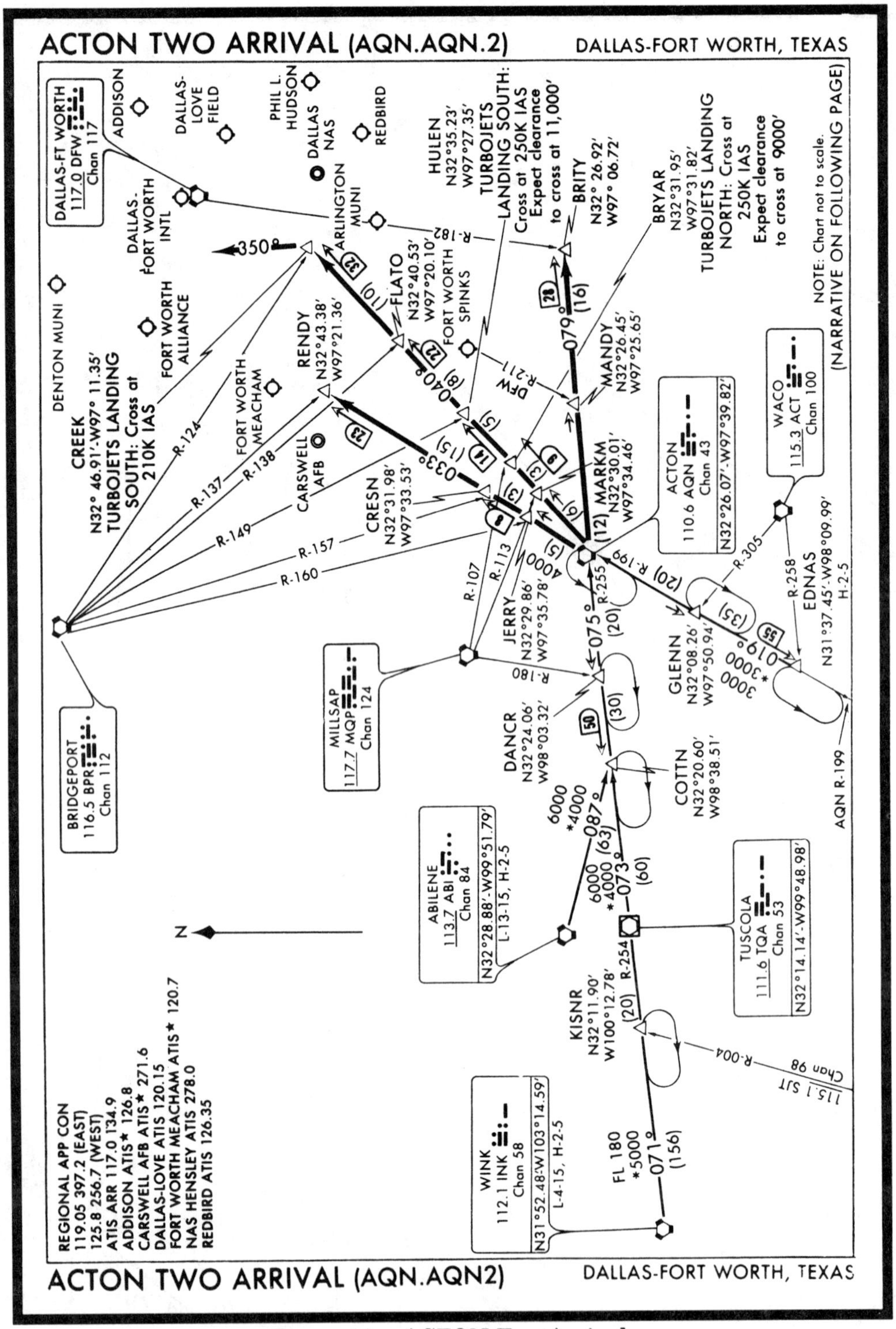

Appendix 3

Figure 41.—ACTON Two Arrival.

Appendix 3

ACTON TWO ARRIVAL (AQN.AQN2)
DALLAS-FORT WORTH, TEXAS

ARRIVAL DESCRIPTION

ABILENE TRANSITION (ABI.AQN2): From over ABI VORTAC via ABI R-087 and AQN R-255 to AQN VORTAC. Thence . . . .
EDNAS TRANSITION (EDNAS.AQN2): From over EDNAS INT via AQN R-199 to AQN VORTAC. Thence . . . .
WINK TRANSITION (INK.AQN2): From over INK VORTAC via INK R-071, TQA R-254, TQA R-073 and AQN R-255 to AQN VORTAC. Thence . . . .
TURBOJETS LANDING DALLAS-FT. WORTH INTL, MEACHAM, CARSWELL AFB, DENTON, ALLIANCE: (Landing South): From over AQN VORTAC via AQN R-040 to CREEK INT, thence heading 350° for vector to final approach course. (Landing North): From over AQN VORTAC via AQN R-040 to CREEK INT. Expect vectors at BRYAR INT.
NON-TURBOJETS LANDING DALLAS-FT. WORTH INTL, MEACHAM, CARSWELL AFB, DENTON, ALLIANCE: (Landing South): From over AQN VORTAC via AQN R-033 to RENDY INT. Expect vectors to final approach course. (Landing North): From over AQN VORTAC via AQN R-040 to CREEK INT. Expect vector at BRYAR INT.
TURBOJETS LANDING DALLAS-LOVE FIELD and ADDISON: (Landing South): From over AQN VORTAC via AQN R-040 to CREEK INT, thence heading 350° for vector to final approach course. (Landing North): From over AQN VORTAC via AQN R-079 to BRITY INT. Expect vector to final approach course.
NON-TURBOJETS LANDING DALLAS-LOVE FIELD and ADDISON: (Landing South/North): From over AQN VORTAC via AQN R-079 to BRITY INT. Expect vector to final approach course.
ALL AIRCRAFT LANDING FORT WORTH SPINKS, ARLINGTON, NAS DALLAS, REDBIRD, and PHIL L. HUDSON: (Landing South/North): From over AQN VORTAC via AQN R-079 to BRITY INT. Expect vectors to final approach course.

FIGURE 41A.—ACTON Two Arrival Description.

TEXAS

DALLAS-FORT WORTH INTL (DFW) 12 NW UTC-6(-5DT) 32°53'47"N 97°02'28"W DALLAS-FT. WORTH
603 B FUEL 100LL, JET A OX 1, 3 LRA ARFF Index E H-2K, 4F, 5B, L-13C, A
    RWY 17L-35R: H11,388X150 (CONC-GRVD) S-120, D-200, DT-600, DDT-850 HIRL CL IAP
      RWY 17L: ALSF2. TDZ. RWY 35R: MALSR. TDZ.
    RWY 17R-35L: H11,388X200 (CONC-GRVD) S-120, D-200, DT-600, DDT-850 HIRL CL
      RWY 17R: MALSR. TDZ. RWY 35L: TDZ. VASI(V6L).
    RWY 18R-36L: H11,388X150(CONC-GRVD) S-120, D-200, DT-600, DDT-850 HIRL CL
      RWY 18R: ALSF2. TDZ RWY 36L: MALSR. TDZ
    RWY 18L-36R: H11,387X200 (CONC-GRVD) S-120, D-200, DT-600, DDT-850 HIRL CL
      RWY 18L: MALSR. TDZ. RWY 36R: TDZ. VASI(V6L).
    RWY 13R-31L: H9300X150(CONC-GRVD) S-120, D-220, DT-600, DDT-850 HIRL CL
      RWY 13R: MALSR. TDZ. RWY 31L: TDZ.
    RWY 13L-31R: H9000X200 (CONC-GRVD) S-120, D-200, DT-600, DDT-850 HIRL CL 0.5% up NW
      RWY 13L: TDZ. VASI(V6L)—Upper GA 3.25° TCH 93'. Lower GA 3.0° TCH 47'. RWY 31R: MALSR. TDZ.
    RWY 18S-36S: H4000X100 (CONC)
    AIRPORT REMARKS: Attended continuously. Rwy 18S-36S CLOSED indefinitely. Arpt under construction, men and equipment in movement areas. Partial outages of arpt lgt circuits will occur daily. Prior Permission Required from arpt ops for General Aviation acft to proceed to airline terminal gate except to General Aviation Facility. Rwy 18S-36S located on taxiway G, 4000' long 100' wide restricted to prop acft 12,500 lbs. & below and stol acft daylight VFR plus IFR departures. Prior permission required from the primary tenant airlines to operate within central terminal area, CAUTION: proper minimum clearance may not be maintained within the central terminal area. Landing fee. Helipad H1 on apt 104X104 (CONC) Heliport located at Twy G and Twy 24 intersection, daylight VFR. Clearways 500X1000 each end Rwy 17L-35R, Rwy 17R-35L, Rwy 18L-36R and Rwy 18R-36L. Flight Notification Service (ADCUS) available.
    WEATHER DATA SOURCES: LLWAS.
    COMMUNICATIONS: ATIS 117.0 134.9 (ARR) 135.5 (DEP) UNICOM 122.95
      FORT WORTH FSS (FTW) LC 429-6434, TF 1-800-WX-BRIEF. NOTAM FILE DFW
    ®REGIONAL APP CON 119.05(E) 119.4(E) 125.8(W) 132.1(W)
      REGIONAL TOWER 126.55 (E) 124.15 (W) GND CON 121.65 133.15(E) 121.8 (W) CLNC DEL 128.25 127.5
    ®REGIONAL DEP CON 118.55 (E) 124.25 (WEST) 127.75 (NORTH-SOUTH)
    TCA: See VFR Terminal Area chart.
    RADIO AIDS TO NAVIGATION: NOTAM FILE DFW.
      (H) VORTACW 117.0 DFW Chan 117 32°51'57"N 97°01'40"W at fld. 560/08E.
        VOR Portion unusable 045°-050° all altitudes and distances, 350-100° beyond 30 NM below 2100'.
      ISSUE NDB (LOM) 233 PK 32°47'35"N 97°01'49"W 348° 6.2 NM to fld.
      JIFFY NDB (LOM) 219 FL 32°59'44"N 97°01'46"W 179° 6.0 NM to fld.
      ILS/DME 109.5 I-LWN Chan 32 Rwy 13R.
      ILS/DME 109.1 I-FLQ Chan 28 Rwy 17L. LOM JIFFY NDB.
      ILS 111.5 I-JHZ Rwy 17R. LOM JIFFY NDB.
      ILS 111.3 I-CIX Rwy 18L.
      ILS/DME 111.9 I-VYN Chan 56 Rwy 18R.
      ILS 110.9 I-RRA Rwy 31R.
      ILS/DME 109.1 I-PKQ Chan 28 Rwy 35R. LOM ISSUE NDB.
      ILS/DME 111.9 I-BXN Chan 56 Rwy 36L.

FIGURE 42.—ILS-1 RWY 36L, Dallas-Fort Worth Intl.

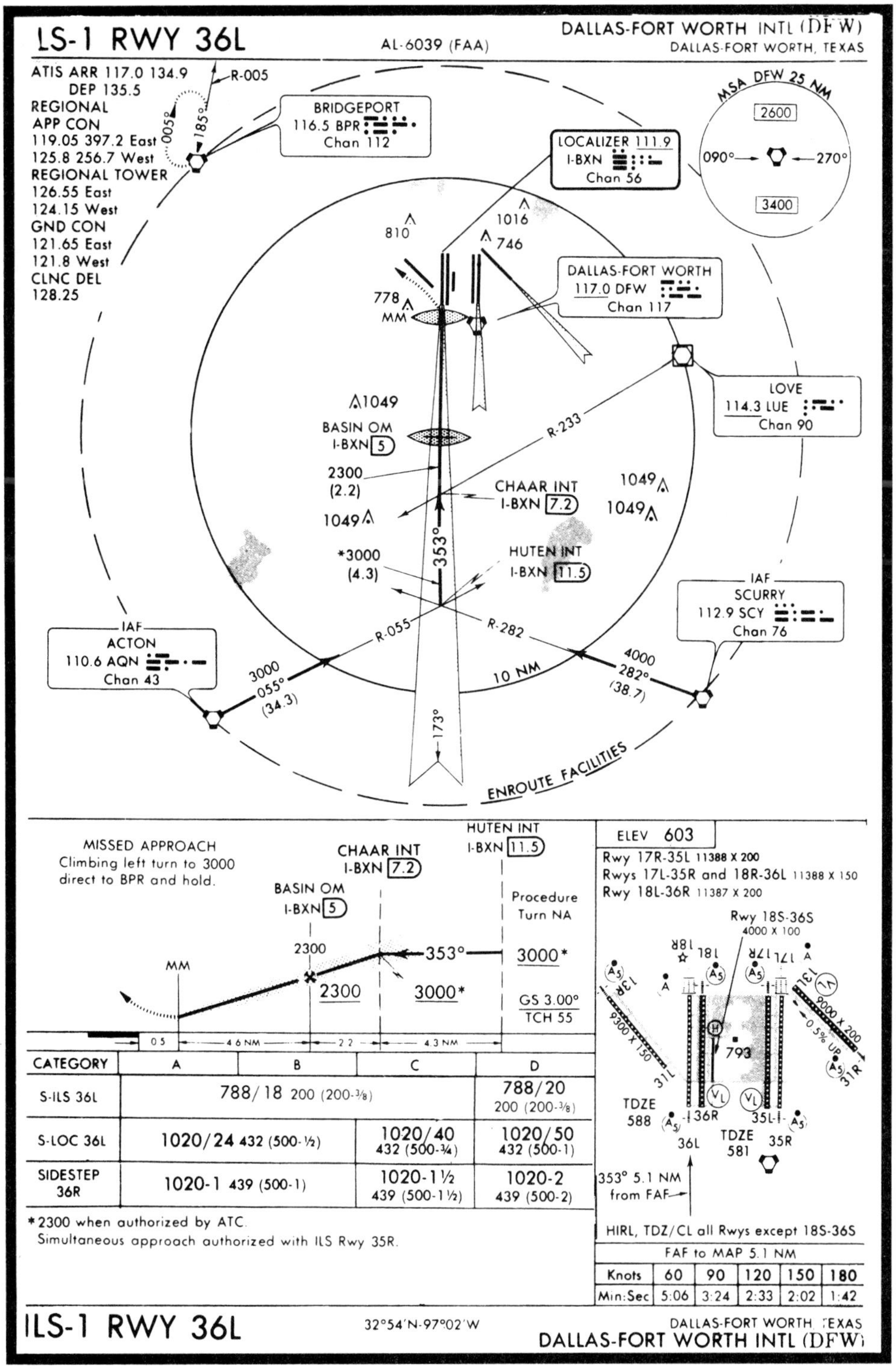

FIGURE 42A.—ILS RWY 36L.

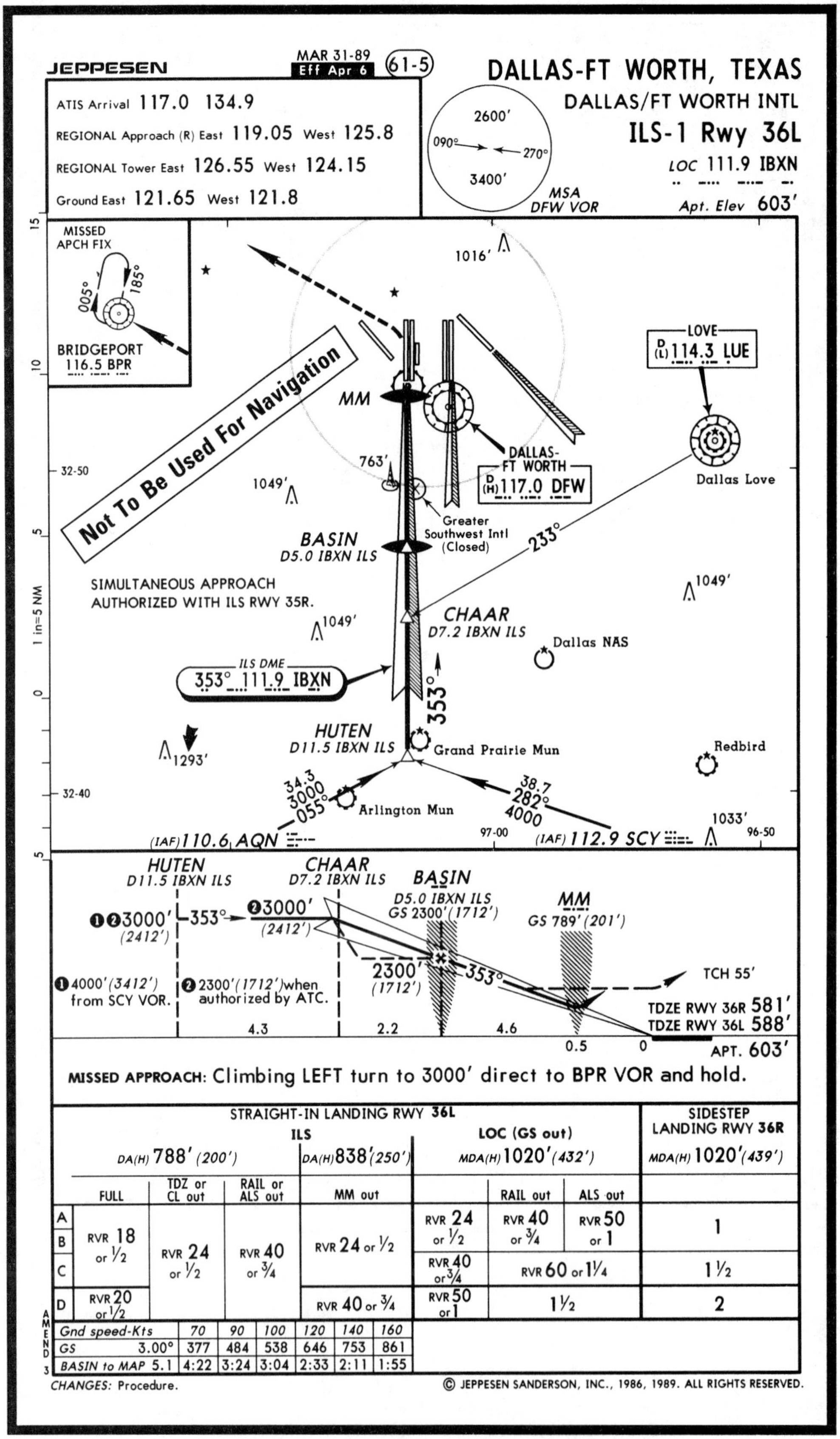

Appendix 3

FIGURE 42B. — ILS-1 RWY 36L (DFW).

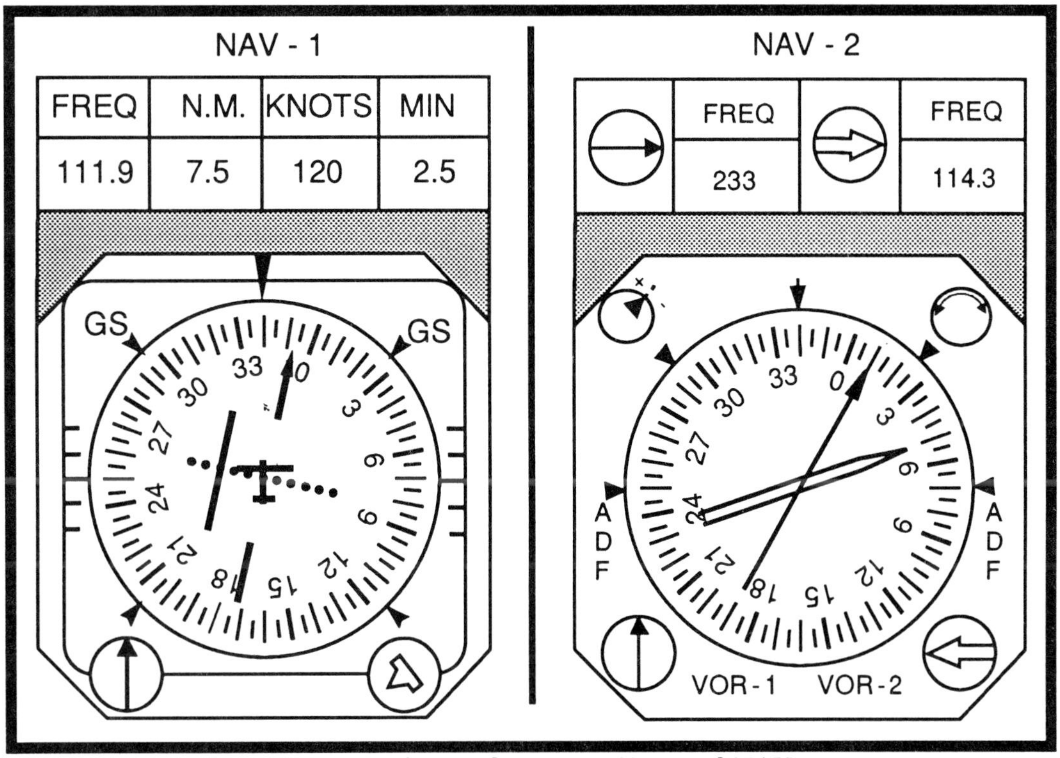

FIGURE 43.—CDI and RMI – NAV 1 and NAV 2.

Appendix 3

```
                                                               Form Approved: OMB No. 2120-0034
 U.S. DEPARTMENT OF TRANSPORTATION  (FAA USE ONLY)   ☐ PILOT BRIEFING   ☐ VNR   TIME STARTED   SPECIALIST
 FEDERAL AVIATION ADMINISTRATION                                                               INITIALS
      FLIGHT PLAN                                    ☐ STOPOVER
```

1. TYPE	2. AIRCRAFT IDENTIFICATION	3. AIRCRAFT TYPE/ SPECIAL EQUIPMENT	4. TRUE AIRSPEED	5. DEPARTURE POINT	6. DEPARTURE TIME		7. CRUISING ALTITUDE
☐ VFR					PROPOSED (Z)	ACTUAL (Z)	
X IFR	N3678A	PA31/	180 KTS	YKM			12000
☐ DVFR							

8. ROUTE OF FLIGHT

GROMO 2, HITCH, V468 BTG, DIRECT

9. DESTINATION (Name of airport and city)	10. EST. TIME ENROUTE		11. REMARKS
PORTLAND INTL. AIRPORT PDX	HOURS	MINUTES	INSTRUMENT TRAINING FLIGHT

12. FUEL ON BOARD		13. ALTERNATE AIRPORT(S)	14. PILOT'S NAME, ADDRESS & TELEPHONE NUMBER & AIRCRAFT HOME BASE	15. NUMBER ABOARD
HOURS	MINUTES			
			17. DESTINATION CONTACT/TELEPHONE (OPTIONAL)	2
		N/A		

16. COLOR OF AIRCRAFT	CIVIL AIRCRAFT PILOTS. FAR Part 91 requires you file an IFR flight plan to operate under instrument flight rules in controlled airspace. Failure to file could result in a civil penalty not to exceed $1,000 for each violation (Section 901 of the Federal Aviation Act of 1958, as amended). Filing of a VFR flight plan is recommended as a good operating practice. See also Part 99 for requirements concerning DVFR flight plans.
GOLD/WHITE	

FAA Form 7233-1 (8-82)   CLOSE VFR FLIGHT PLAN WITH _____ FSS ON ARRIVAL

AIRCRAFT INFORMATION

MAKE Piper   MODEL PA-31

N 3678A   Vso 77

AIRCRAFT EQUIPMENT/STATUS**

**NOTE: X= OPERATIVE   INOP= INOPERATIVE   N/A= NOT APPLICABLE
TRANSPONDER: X (MODE C) X ILS: (LOCALIZER) X (GLIDE SLOPE) X
VOR NO. 1 X (NO. 2) X ADF: X RNAV: X
VERTICAL PATH COMPUTER: N/A DME: X
MARKER BEACON: X (AUDIO) INOP (VISUAL) X

FIGURE 44.—Flight Plan and Aircraft Information.

Appendix 3

FLIGHT LOG

YAKIMA AIR TERMINAL TO PORTLAND, INTL.

CHECK POINTS		ROUTE	COURSE	WIND	SPEED-KTS		DIST	TIME		FUEL	
FROM	TO	ALTITUDE		TEMP	TAS	GS	NM	LEG	TOT	LEG	TOT
YKM	HITCH	GROMO 2 CLIMB	206°					:10.			
	VOR C.O.P.	V468 12,000	206°		180						
	BTG	V468 12,000	234°								
	PDX	DIRECT	160°								
APPROACH & LANDING	PDX AIRPORT							:13.			

OTHER DATA:
NOTE: MAG. VAR. 20° E.

FLIGHT SUMMARY

TIME	FUEL (LB)	
		EN ROUTE
		RESERVE
		MISSED APPR.
		TOTAL

FIGURE 45.—Flight Planning Log.

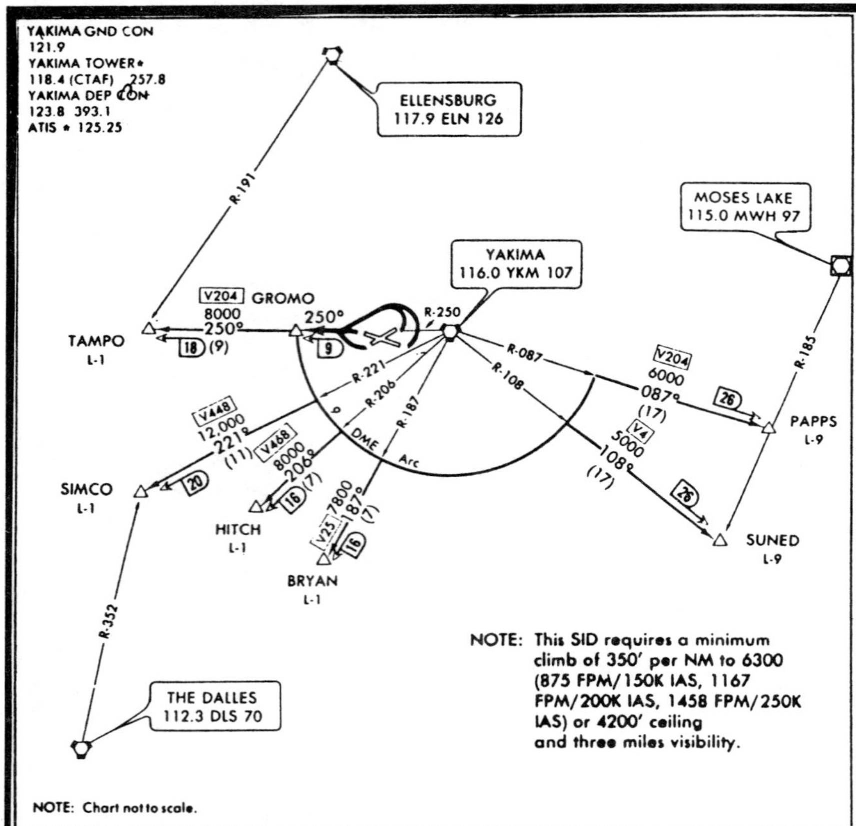

▽ DEPARTURE ROUTE DESCRIPTION

TAKE-OFF RUNWAY 22: Turn right thence . . . .
TAKE-OFF RUNWAY 4, 9: Turn left thence . . . .
TAKE-OFF RUNWAY 27: Climb runway heading thence . . . .
. . . .intercept and proceed via YKM R-250 to the GROMO DME FIX (YKM R-250/9), thence via (assigned transition).
TAMPO TRANSITION (GROMO2.TAMPO): From GROMO DME Fix via V204 to TAMPO INT.
NOTE: Climb in holding pattern east of TAMPO INT, right turns, 250° inbound to 8000′ before proceeding on course.

(Continued on next page)

ELEV 1095

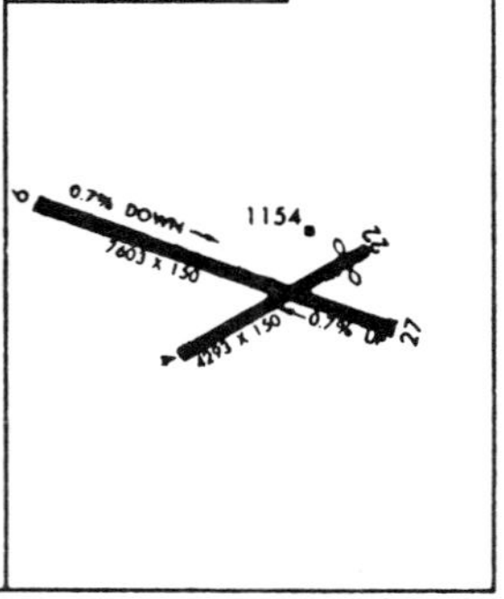

GROMO TWO DEPARTURE (PILOT NAV)
(GROMO2.GROMO)
YAKIMA, WASHINGTON
YAKIMA AIR TERMINAL

(GROMO2.GROMO)
GROMO TWO DEPARTURE (PILOT NAV)
YAKIMA AIR TERMINAL
YAKIMA, WASHINGTON

DEPARTURE ROUTE DESCRIPTION
(Continued)

SIMCO TRANSITION (GROMO2.SIMCO): From over GROMO DME Fix via 9 DME Arc and V448 to SIMCO INT. NOTE: Climb in holding pattern NE of SIMCO INT, right turns, 221° inbound to 12000 feet before proceeding on course.
HITCH TRANSITION (GROMO2.HITCH): From over GROMO DME Fix via 9 DME Arc and V468 to HITCH DME Fix. NOTE: Climb in holding pattern NE of HITCH DME Fix, right turns, 206° inbound to 8000 feet before proceeding on course.
BRYAN TRANSITION (GROMO2.BRYAN): From over GROMO DME Fix via 9 DME Arc and V25 to BRYAN DME Fix.
SUNED TRANSITION (GROMO2.SUNED): From over GROMO DME Fix via 9 DME Arc and V4 to SUNED INT.
PAPPS TRANSITION (GROMO2.PAPPS): From over GROMO DME Fix via 9 DME Arc and V204 to PAPPS INT.

GROMO TWO DEPARTURE (PILOT NAV)
(GROMO2.GROMO)
YAKIMA, WASHINGTON
YAKIMA AIR TERMINAL

§ **YAKIMA AIR TERMINAL** (YKM) 3 S GMT−8(−7DT) 46°34′06″N 120°32′33″W **SEATTLE**
1095 B S4 **FUEL** 80, 100, 100LL, JET A OX 1, 3 CFR Index A **H-1A, L-1C, 9A**
RWY 09-27: H7603X150 (ASPH-PFC) S-95, D-110, DT-175 HIRL .6% up NW **IAP**
RWY 09: VASI(V4L)—GA 3.0° TCH 50′. Antenna. **RWY 27:** MALSR. Trees.
RWY 04-22: H4293X150 (ASPH) S-70, D-80, DT-120 MIRL
RWY 04: Trees. **RWY 22:** VASI(V2L)—GA 3.03° TCH 61′. Thld dsplcd 469′. Tree.
AIRPORT REMARKS: Attended continuously. CLOSED 0600-1400Z‡ to Part 121 non-scheduled operations and Part 121 scheduled charters operations without prior approval, call (509) 575-6150/6014. Bird hazard. ACTIVATE MALSR Rwy 27—118.4.
COMMUNICATIONS: CTAF 118.4 **ATIS** 125.25 (1400-0600Z‡) **UNICOM** 122.95
SEATTLE FSS (SEA) LC 965-1840 NOTAM FILE YKM
RCO 122.5 122.1R 116.0T (SEATTLE FSS)
APP/DEP CON 123.8 (1400-0600Z‡) **SEATTLE CENTER APP/DEP CON** 132.6 (0600-1400Z‡)
TOWER 118.4 (1400-0600Z‡) **GND CON** 121.9
VFR ADVSY SVC 123.8
RADIO AIDS TO NAVIGATION:
(H) **VORTAC** 116.0 YKM Chan 107 46°34′14″N 120°26′36″W 244° 3.6 NM to fld. 980/21E
DME portion unusable:

350°-065° beyond 20 NM below 9000′	025°-065° beyond 15 NM below 8000′
115°-135° beyond 25 NM below 7000′	135°-150° beyond 30 NM below 7500′
195°-230° beyond 22 NM below 8000′	300°-325° beyond 29 NM below 9000′
325°-335° beyond 20 NM below 9000′	335°-350° beyond 25 NM below 10,000′

VOR portion unusable:

350°-080° beyond 25 NM below 9000′	025°-035° beyond 5 NM below 10,000′
080°-105° beyond 35 NM below 6000′	105°-107° beyond 25 NM below 6000′
109°-135° beyond 25 NM below 6000′	135°-180° beyond 30 NM below 7500′
195°-225° beyond 30 NM below 8500′	305°-335° beyond 30 NM below 9000′

DONNY NDB (LOM) 371 YK 46°31′33″N 120°22′16″W 269° 7 NM to fld
ILS 110.1 I-YKM Rwy 27 LOM DONNY NDB. ILS unmonitored when tower closed. Localizer unusable inside threshold.

FIGURE 46.—GROMO Two Departure and Excerpt from Airport/Facility Directory.

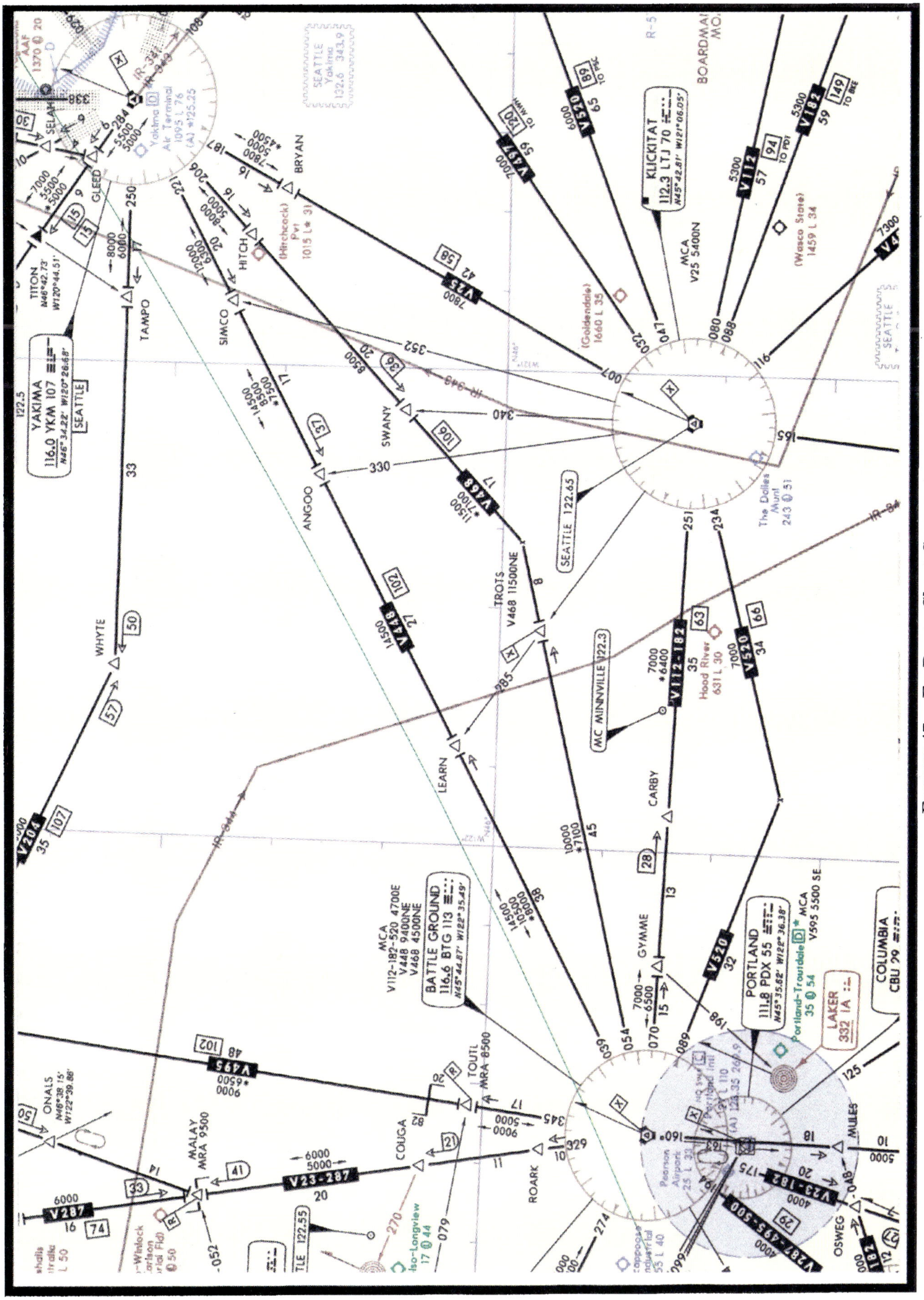

Appendix 3

FIGURE 47.—En Route Chart Segment.

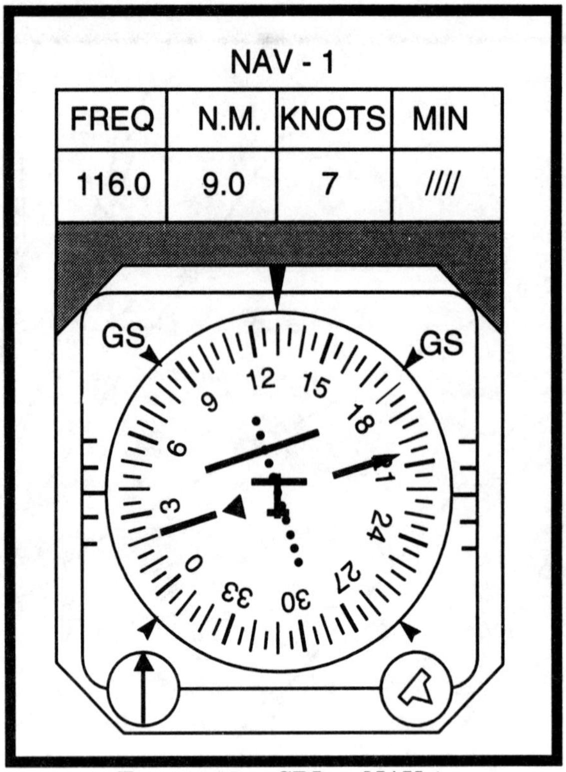

Appendix 3

FIGURE 48.—CDI — NAV 1.

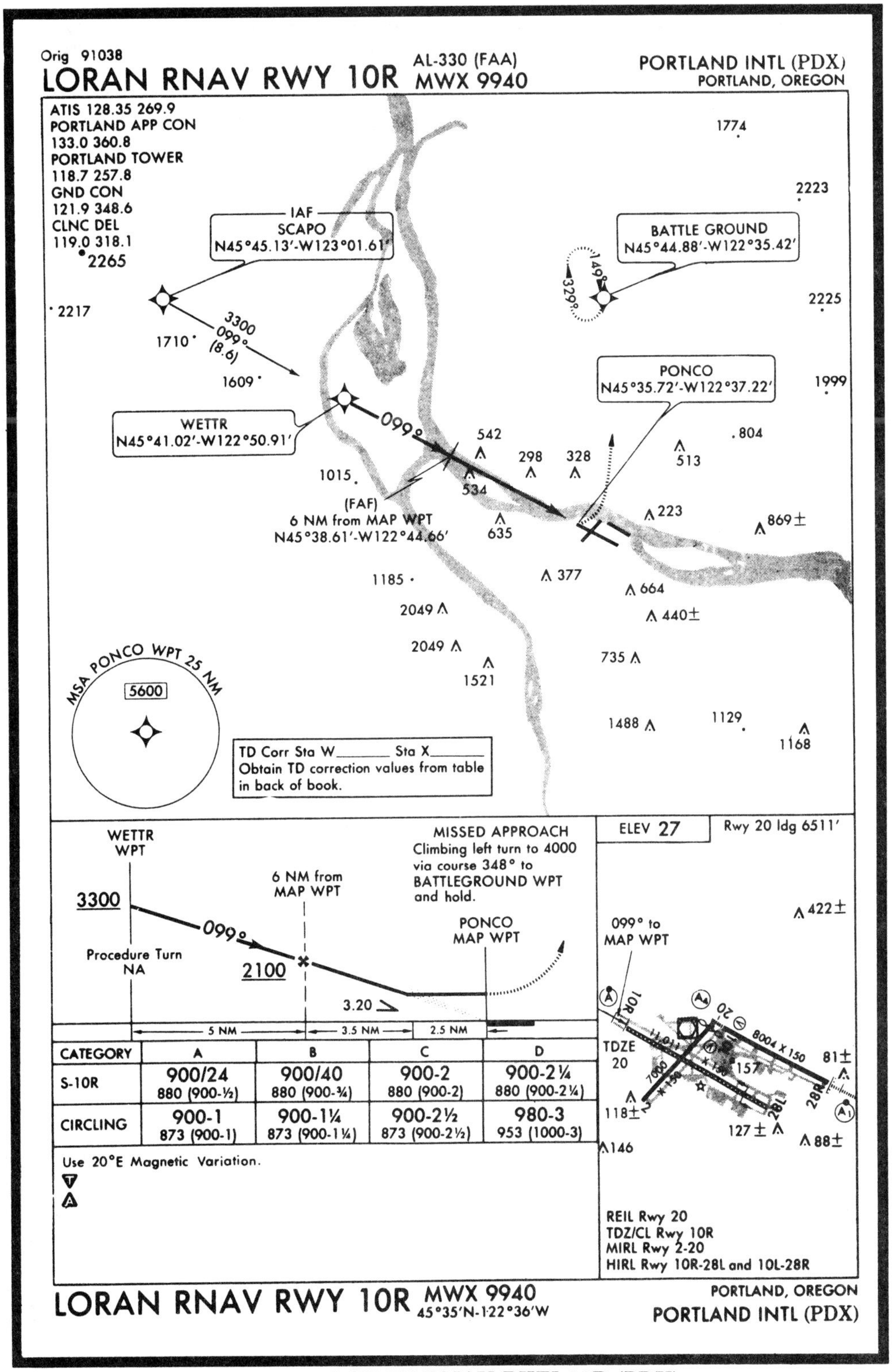

FIGURE 49.—LORAN RNAV RWY 10R (PDX).

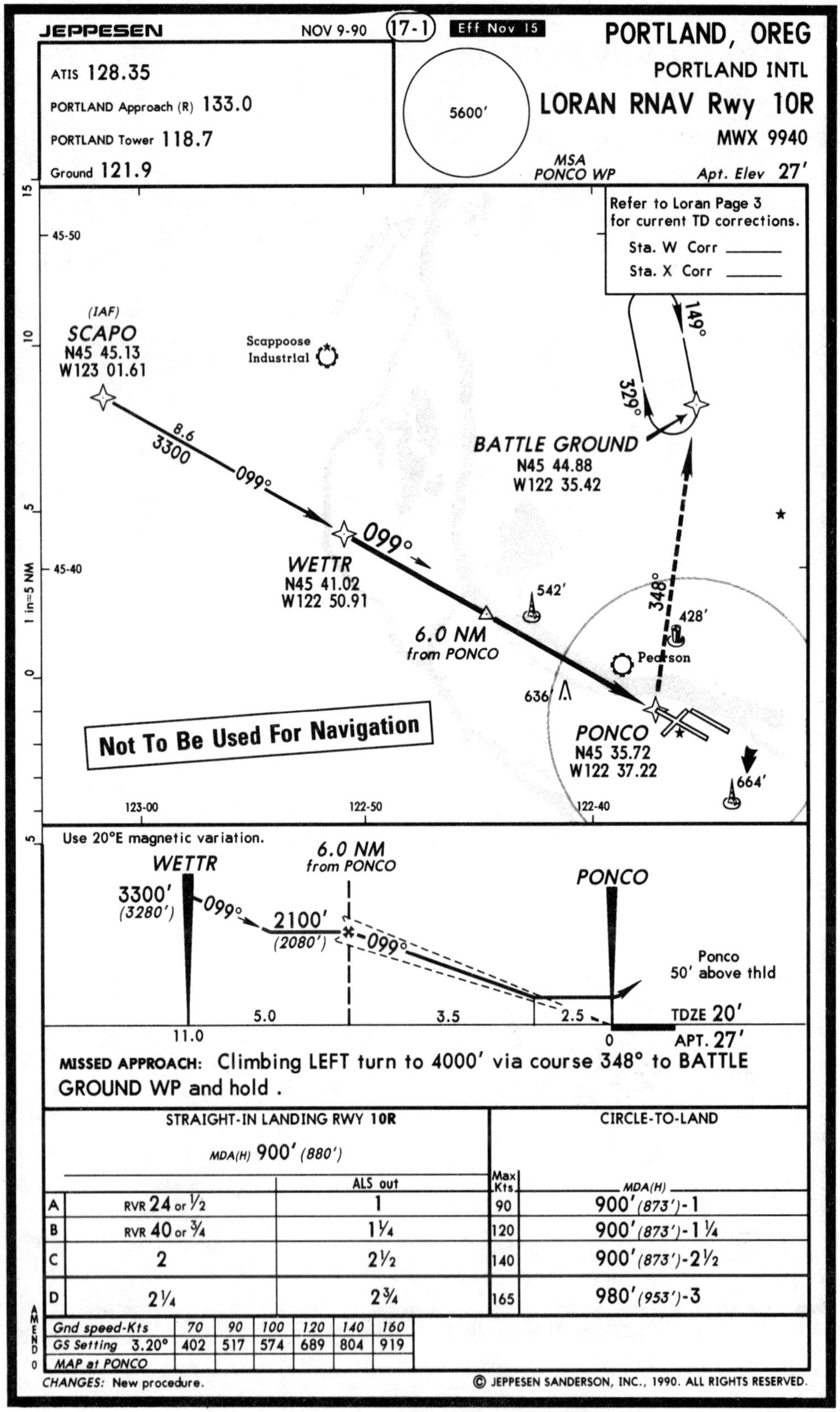

Appendix 3

FIGURE 49A.—LORAN RNAV RWY 10R.

Appendix 3

U.S. DEPARTMENT OF TRANSPORTATION FEDERAL AVIATION ADMINISTRATION **FLIGHT PLAN**	(FAA USE ONLY)	☐ PILOT BRIEFING ☐ STOPOVER	☐ VNR	TIME STARTED	SPECIALIST INITIALS

1. TYPE	2. AIRCRAFT IDENTIFICATION	3. AIRCRAFT TYPE/ SPECIAL EQUIPMENT	4. TRUE AIRSPEED	5. DEPARTURE POINT	6. DEPARTURE TIME	7. CRUISING ALTITUDE
☐ VFR X IFR ☐ DVFR	N2468	A36/	158 KTS	SBA	PROPOSED (Z) / ACTUAL (Z)	8000

8. ROUTE OF FLIGHT
HABUTI GVO, V27 MQO, V113 PRB

9. DESTINATION (Name of airport and city)	10. EST. TIME ENROUTE HOURS / MINUTES	11. REMARKS
PASO ROBLES MUNI PRB		IFR TRAINING FLIGHT

12. FUEL ON BOARD HOURS / MINUTES	13. ALTERNATE AIRPORT(S)	14. PILOT'S NAME, ADDRESS & TELEPHONE NUMBER & AIRCRAFT HOME BASE	15. NUMBER ABOARD
		17. DESTINATION CONTACT/TELEPHONE (OPTIONAL) N/A	2

16. COLOR OF AIRCRAFT	CIVIL AIRCRAFT PILOTS. FAR Part 91 requires you file an IFR flight plan to operate under instrument flight rules in controlled airspace. Failure to file could result in a civil penalty not to exceed $1,000 for each violation (Section 901 of the Federal Aviation Act of 1958, as amended). Filing of a VFR flight plan is recommended as a good operating practice. See also Part 99 for requirements concerning DVFR flight plans.
GOLD/WHITE	

FAA Form 7233-1 (8-82)   CLOSE VFR FLIGHT PLAN WITH _____ FSS ON ARRIVAL

AIRCRAFT INFORMATION

MAKE Beechcraft   MODEL A-36

N 2468   Vso 52

AIRCRAFT EQUIPMENT/STATUS**

**NOTE: X= OPERATIVE   INOP= INOPERATIVE   N/A= NOT APPLICABLE
TRANSPONDER: X (MODE C) X ILS: (LOCALIZER) X (GLIDE SLOPE) X
VOR NO. 1 X (NO. 2) X ADF: X RNAV: X
VERTICAL PATH COMPUTER: N/A DME: X
MARKER BEACON: X (AUDIO) X (VISUAL) INOP

FIGURE 50.—Flight Plan and Aircraft Information.

Appendix 3

FLIGHT LOG
SANTA BARBARA MUNI TO PASO ROBLES MUNI

| CHECK POINTS || ROUTE | COURSE | WIND | SPEED-KTS || DIST | TIME || FUEL ||
FROM	TO	ALTITUDE		TEMP	TAS	GS	NM	LEG	TOT	LEG	TOT
SBA	HABUT	HABUT 1 CLIMB	253°					:08:00			
	GVO	163°R 8000	343°		158						
	MQO	V27 8000	306°								
	PRB	V113	358°								
APPROACH & LANDING		DESCENT						:10:00			
	PRB AIRPORT										

OTHER DATA:
 NOTE: MAG. VAR. 16° E.

FLIGHT SUMMARY

TIME	FUEL (LB)	
		EN ROUTE
		RESERVE
		MISSED APPR.
		TOTAL

FIGURE 51.—Flight Planning Log.

HABUT ONE DEPARTURE (HABUT1.GVO)

SANTA BARBARA MUNI
SANTA BARBARA, CALIFORNIA

SANTA BARBARA GND CON
121.7
SANTA BARBARA TOWER *
119.7 242.4
SANTA BARBARA DEP CON
120.55 321.4
ATIS * 125.1

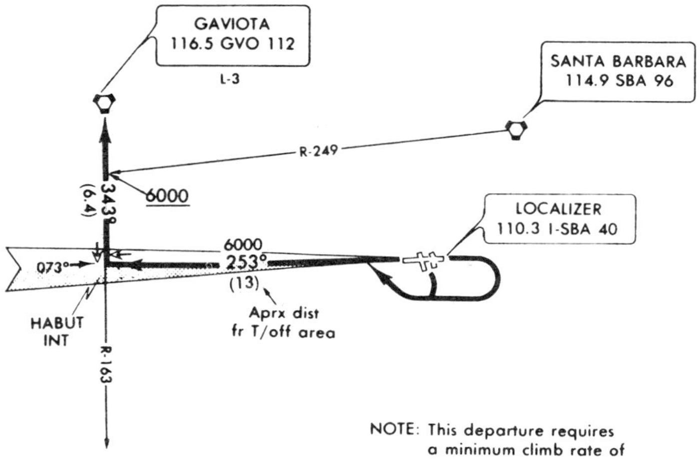

NOTE: This departure requires a minimum climb rate of 385′ per NM to 6000

NOTE: IFR departure Rwys 33L/R not authorized.

NOTE: Chart not to scale

DEPARTURE ROUTE DESCRIPTION

TAKE-OFF RUNWAY 7: Maintain runway heading to at least 650′, then turn right, thence intercept and climb westbound via I-SBA localizer west course to HABUT INT, thence via GVO R-163 to GVO VORTAC. Cross SBA R-249 at or above 6000′.

TAKE-OFF RUNWAY 15: Maintain runway heading to at least 310′, then turn right, thence intercept and climb westbound via I-SBA localizer west course to HABUT INT, thence via GVO R-163 to GVO VORTAC. Cross SBA R-249 at or above 6000′.

(Continued on next page)

ELEV 10

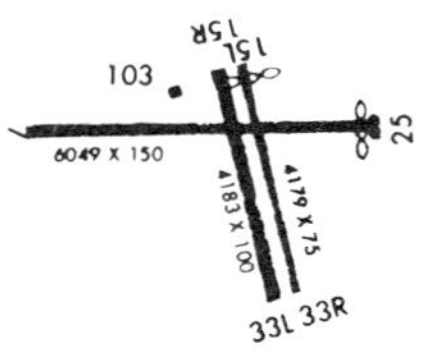

HABUT ONE DEPARTURE (HABUT1.GVO)

SANTA BARBARA, CALIFORNIA
SANTA BARBARA MUNI

HABUT ONE DEPARTURE (HABUT1.GVO)

SANTA BARBARA MUNI
SANTA BARBARA, CALIFORNIA

DEPARTURE ROUTE DESCRIPTION
(Continued)

TAKE-OFF RUNWAY 25: Climb westbound via I-SBA localizer west course to HABUT INT, thence via GVO R-163 to GVO VORTAC. Cross SBA R-249 at or above 6000′.

HABUT ONE DEPARTURE (HABUT1.GVO)

SANTA BARBARA, CALIFORNIA
SANTA BARBARA MUNI

§ **SANTA BARBARA MUNI** (SBA) 7 W GMT–8(–7DT) 34°25′34″N 119°50′22″W **LOS ANGELES H-2F, L-3B IAP**
10 B S4 **FUEL** 80, 100, 100LL, JET A OX 1, 2, 3, 4 TPA—See Remarks
CFR Index C
RWY 07-25: H6049X150 (ASPH-GRVD) S-110, D-160, DT-245 HIRL
RWY 07: MALSR. Tree. Rgt tfc. **RWY 25:** VASI(V4L)—GA 3.0°TCH 46′. Thld dsplcd 324′. Road.
RWY 15R-33L: H4183X100 (ASPH) S-48, D-63, DT-100 MIRL
RWY 15R: REIL. Pole. **RWY 33L:** Road. Rgt tfc.
RWY 15L-33R: H4179X75 (ASPH) S-35, D-41, DT-63
RWY 15L: Thld dsplcd 225′. Tree. **RWY 33R:** Pole. Rgt tfc.
AIRPORT REMARKS: Attended 1330-0600Z‡. Fee after hours. Numerous flocks of birds on and in vicinity of arpt. TPA—1000(990) small acft, 1500(1490) large acft. Pure jet touch/go or low approaches prohibited.
COMMUNICATIONS: CTAF 119.7 **ATIS** 125.1 (1430-0600Z‡) **UNICOM** 122.95
SANTA BARBARA FSS (SBA) on arpt 123.65, 122.3, 122.2, 122.1R, 116.5T LD (805) 967-2305, DL. NOTAM FILE SBA.
Ⓡ **APP CON** 125.4 (1430-0600Z‡) Ⓡ **DEP CON** 120.55 (1430-0600Z‡)
Ⓡ **LOS ANGELES CENTER APP/DEP CON** 128.05 (0600-1430Z‡)
TOWER 119.7 (1430-0600Z‡) **GND CON** 121.7
VFR ADVSY SVC ctc TOWER
RADIO AIDS TO NAVIGATION: NOTAM FILE SBA. VHF/DF ctc SANTA BARBARA FSS
(H) ABVORTAC 114.9 ■ SBA Chan 96 34°30′34″N 119°46′12″W 198° 5.6 NM to fld. 3620/16E.
GAVIOTA (L) VORTAC 116.5 GVO Chan 112 34°31′53″N 120°05′24″W 099° 14.0 NM to fld. 2620/16E
ILS/DME 110.3 I-SBA Chan 40 Rwy 07

CALIFORNIA

VOR RECEIVER CHECK POINTS

Facility Name (Arpt Name)	Freq/Ident	Type Check Pt. Gnd. AB/ALT	Azimuth from Fac. Mag	Dist. from Fac. N.M.	Check Point Description
Sacramento (Sacramento Executive)	115.2/SAC	A/1000	015		Over apch end rwy 02.
Salinas (Salinas Muni)	117.3/SNS	G	247		0.4 NM on Compass rose.
Santa Ana (John Wayne Airport/Orange County)	109.4/SNA	G	186		On runup pad rwy 01R.
Santa Barbara	114.9/SBA	A/2000	277	11	Over Lake Cachuma Dam spillway.
Santa Barbara (Santa Barbara Muni)	114.9/SBA	G	200	5.9	On runup area end rwy 15

FIGURE 52.—HABUT One Departure and Excerpt from Airport/Facility Directory.

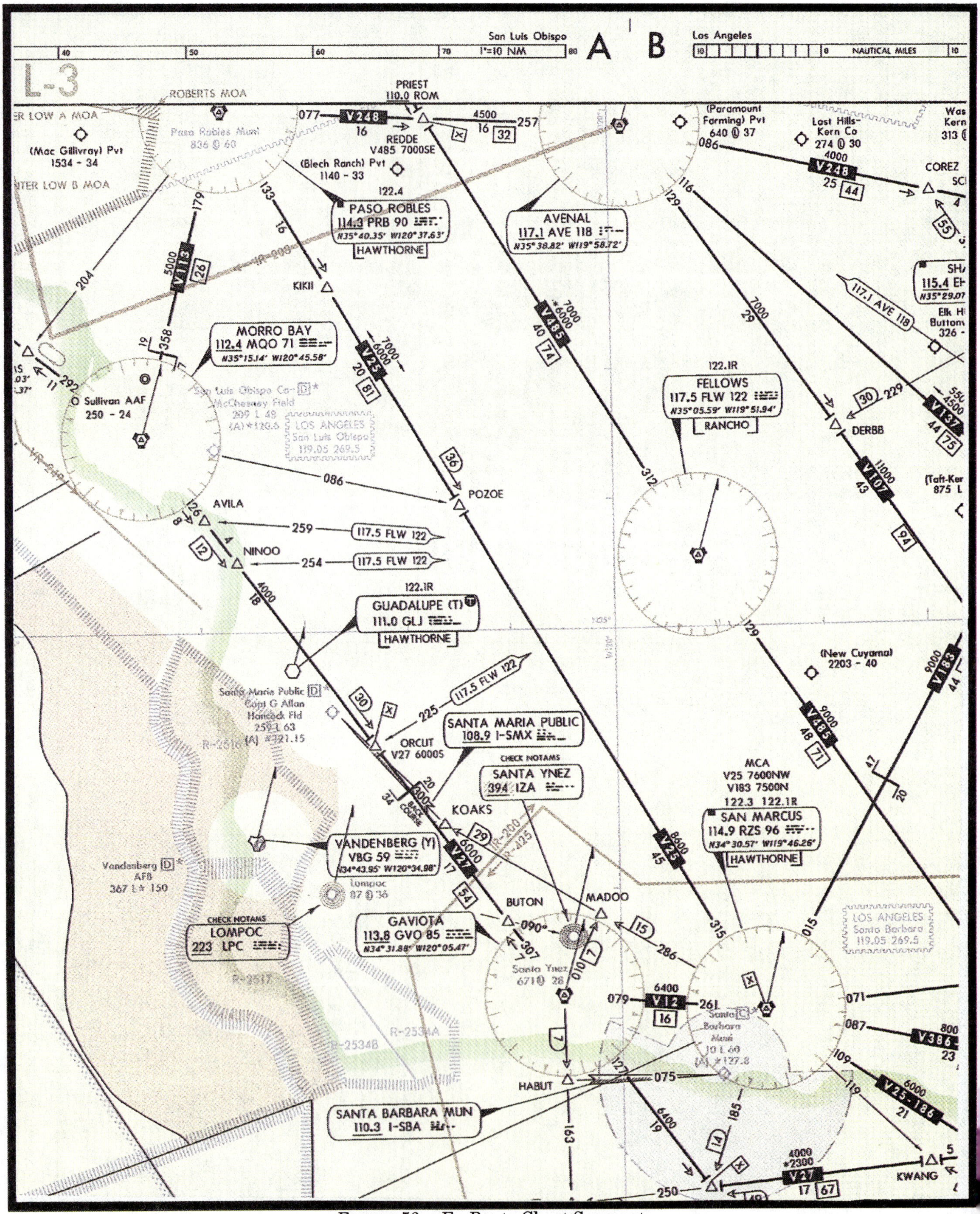

Appendix 3

FIGURE 53.—En Route Chart Segment.

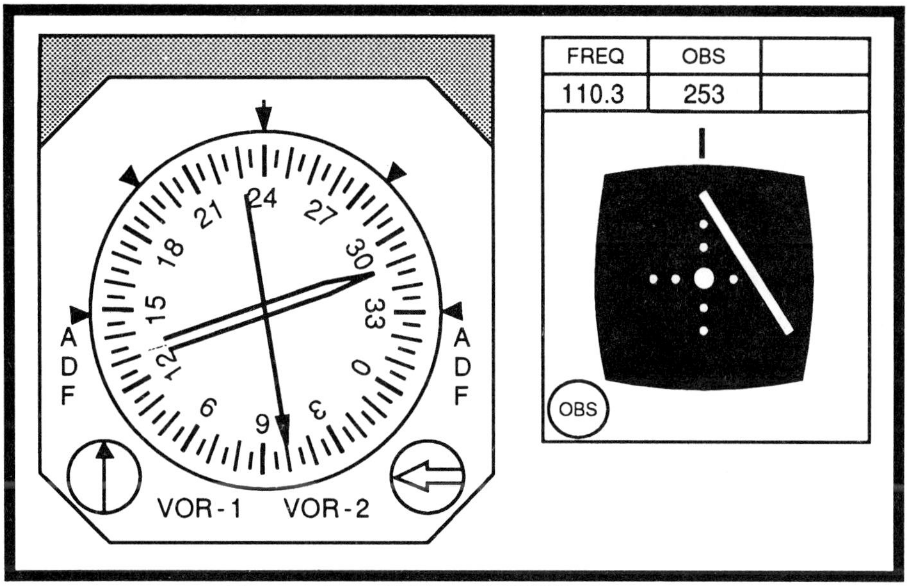

Appendix 3

FIGURE 54.—RMI and CDI Indicators.

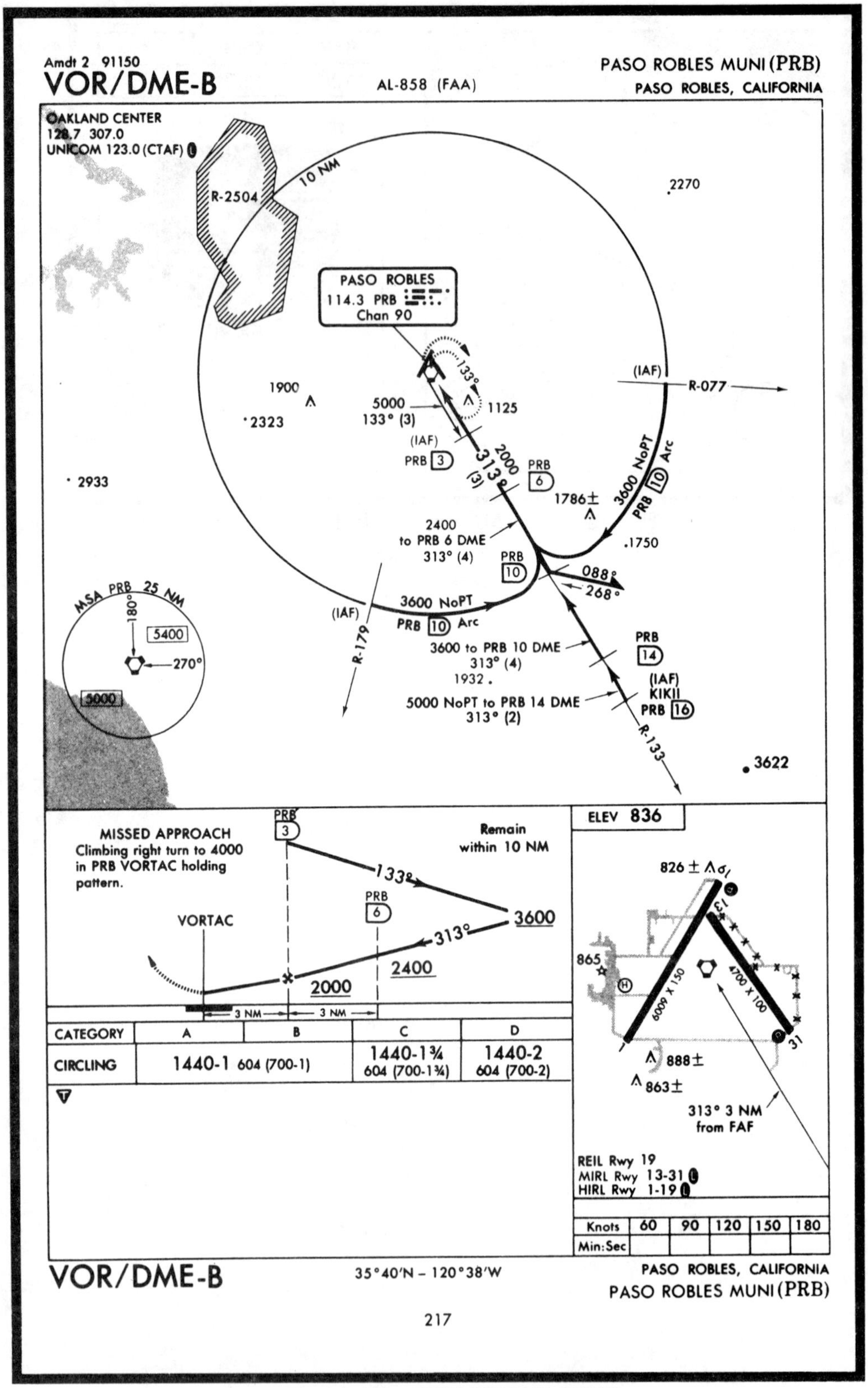

Appendix 3

FIGURE 55.—VOR/DME-B (PRB).

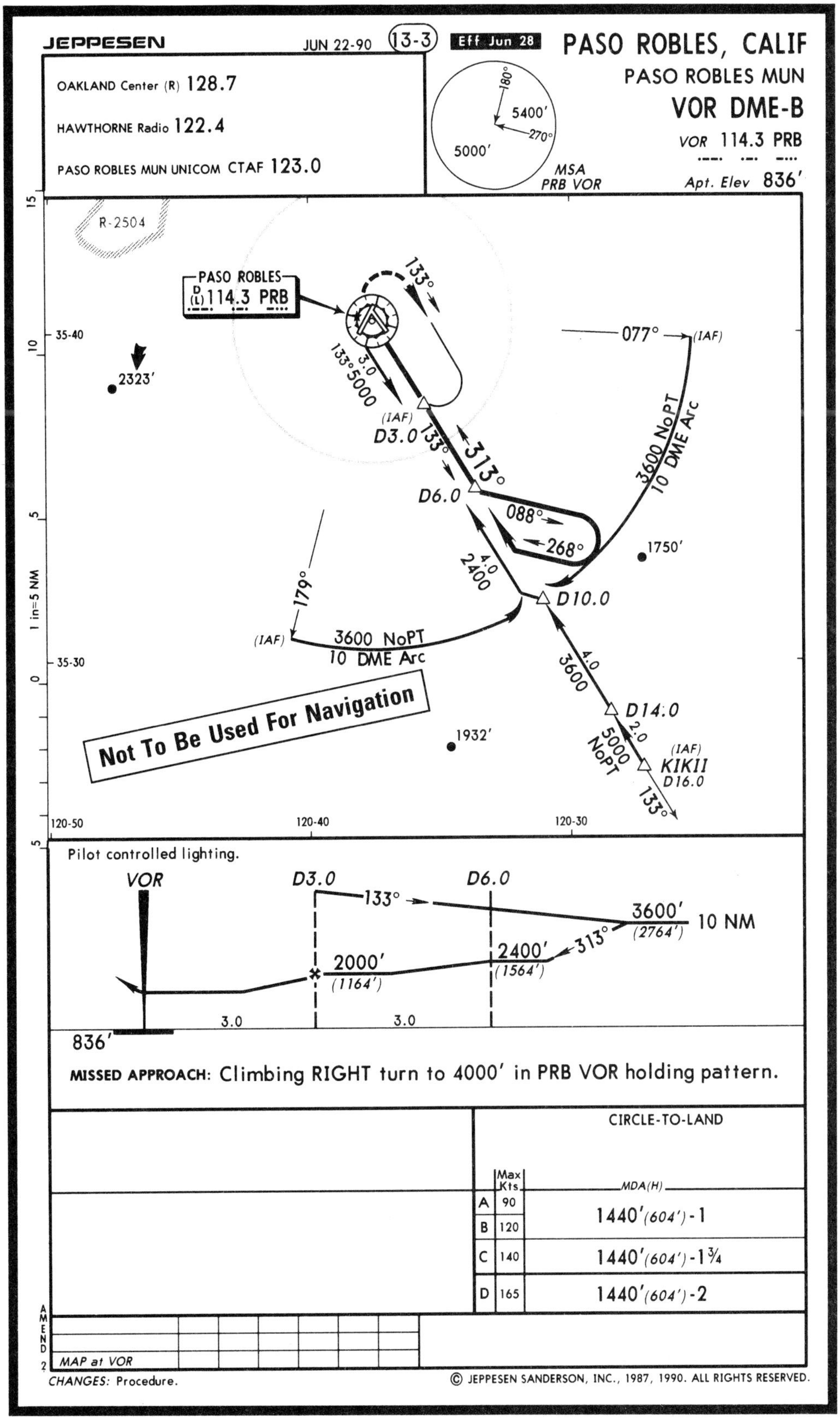

FIGURE 55A.—VOR/DME-B (PRB).

Appendix 3

U.S. DEPARTMENT OF TRANSPORTATION FEDERAL AVIATION ADMINISTRATION **FLIGHT PLAN**	(FAA USE ONLY)	☐ PILOT BRIEFING ☐ STOPOVER	☐ VNR	TIME STARTED	SPECIALIST INITIALS

Form Approved: OMB No. 2120-0034

| 1. TYPE
☐ VFR
X IFR
☐ DVFR | 2. AIRCRAFT IDENTIFICATION
N12193 | 3. AIRCRAFT TYPE/ SPECIAL EQUIPMENT
BH 206/ | 4. TRUE AIRSPEED
110 KTS | 5. DEPARTURE POINT
EASTERWOOD FIELD | 6. DEPARTURE TIME
PROPOSED (Z) | ACTUAL (Z) | 7. CRUISING ALTITUDE
7000 |

8. ROUTE OF FLIGHT
DIRECT CLL, V15 TNV, V571 IAH, DIRECT

9. DESTINATION (Name of airport and city)
WILLIAM P HOBBY AIRPORT
HOUSTON, TX

10. EST. TIME ENROUTE HOURS MINUTES

11. REMARKS

12. FUEL ON BOARD HOURS MINUTES

13. ALTERNATE AIRPORT(S) N/A

14. PILOT'S NAME, ADDRESS & TELEPHONE NUMBER & AIRCRAFT HOME BASE

17. DESTINATION CONTACT/TELEPHONE (OPTIONAL)

15. NUMBER ABOARD 2

16. COLOR OF AIRCRAFT
TAN/GOLD/WHITE

CIVIL AIRCRAFT PILOTS. FAR Part 91 requires you file an IFR flight plan to operate under instrument flight rules in controlled airspace. Failure to file could result in a civil penalty not to exceed $1,000 for each violation (Section 901 of the Federal Aviation Act of 1958, as amended). Filing of a VFR flight plan is recommended as a good operating practice. See also Part 99 for requirements concerning DVFR flight plans.

FAA Form 7233-1 (8-82)   CLOSE VFR FLIGHT PLAN WITH _____ FSS ON ARRIVAL

AIRCRAFT INFORMATION

MAKE Bell   MODEL 206L

N 12193   Vso N/A

AIRCRAFT EQUIPMENT/STATUS**

**NOTE: X= OPERATIVE   INOP= INOPERATIVE   N/A= NOT APPLICABLE
TRANSPONDER: X (MODE C) X ILS: (LOCALIZER) X (GLIDE SLOPE) X
VOR NO. 1 X (NO. 2) X ADF: X RNAV: X
VERTICAL PATH COMPUTER: N/A DME: X
MARKER BEACON: X (AUDIO) X (VISUAL) X

FIGURE 56.—IFR Flight Plan and Aircraft Information.

Appendix 3

FLIGHT LOG

EASTERWOOD FIELD TO WILLIAM P HOBBY AIRPORT

CHECK POINTS		ROUTE	COURSE	WIND	SPEED-KTS		DIST	TIME		FUEL	
FROM	TO	ALTITUDE		TEMP	TAS	GS	NM	LEG	TOT	LEG	TOT
EASTERWOOD	CLL	DIRECT CLIMB	DIRECT					:05:			
	TNV	V15 7000	127°		110		27				
	IAH	V571 7000	110°				42				
	HUB	DIRECT 7000	161°				18				
APPROACH & LANDING								:15:			
	HOBBY AIRPORT										

OTHER DATA:
NOTE: MAG. VAR. 6° E.

FLIGHT SUMMARY

TIME	FUEL (LB)	
		EN ROUTE
		RESERVE
		MISSED APPR.
		TOTAL

FIGURE 57.—Flight Planning Log.

Appendix 3

140   TEXAS

COLLEGE STATION
EASTERWOOD FLD (CLL) 3 SW UTC−6(−5DT) 30°35'18"N 96°21'49"W   HOUSTON
320 B S4 FUEL 100LL, JET A OX 2 ARFF Index A   H-2K, 5B, L-17A
RWY 16-34: H7000X150 (ASPH–GRVD) S-70, D-90, DT-150 MIRL   IAP
  RWY 16: VASI(V4R)—GA 3.0°TCH 51'. Tree.   RWY 34: MALSR.
RWY 10-28: H5160X150 (CONC) S-27, D-50, DT-87 MIRL
  RWY 10: VASI(V4L)—GA 3.0°TCH 50'. Tree.   RWY 28: REIL VASI(V4L)—GA 3.0° TCH 54'. Tree.
RWY 04-22: H5149X150 (CONC) S-27, D-50, DT-87
  RWY 04: Tree.   RWY 22: Tree.
AIRPORT REMARKS: Attended 1200-0500Z‡. CAUTION: deer on rwys. CAUTION: Rwy 10-28 taxiway B and taxiway E
  have uneven surfaces. Birds on and in vicinity of arpt. MIRL Rwy 10-28 preset medium ints when twr clsd, to
  increase ints and ACTIVATE MIRL Rwy 16-34 and MALSR Rwy 34—CTAF. CLOSED to unscheduled air carrier
  ops with more than 30 passenger seats except 24 hours PPR call, arpt manager 409-845-4811. Rwy 04-22
  day VFR ops only. Itinerant acft park North of twr, overnight parking fee. Ldg fee scheduled FAR 135 and all FAR
  121 ops. For fuel after hours PPR call 409-845-4811/823 -0690 or ctc Texas A and M University police
  409-845-2345; late ngt fee. Rwy 16-34 grvd except south 200'. Rwy 04-22 deteriorating and vegetation
  growing through cracks. NOTE: See SPECIAL NOTICE—Simultaneous Operations on Intersecting Runways.
COMMUNICATIONS: CTAF 118.5 ATIS 126.85 (1200-0400Z‡) UNICOM 122.95
  MONTGOMERY COUNTY FSS (CXO) TF 1-800-WX-BRIEF. NOTAM FILE CLL.
  COLLEGE STATION RCO 122.65 122.2 (MONTGOMERY COUNTY FSS).
®HOUSTON CENTER APP/DEP CON: 120.4
  TOWER: 118.5 (1200-0400Z‡) (VFR only)   GND CON: 121.7
RADIO AIDS TO NAVIGATION: NOTAM FILE CLL. VHF/DF ctc FSS
  COLLEGE STATION (L) VORTACW 113.3   CLL   Chan 80   30°36'17"N 96°25'13"W   100° 3.1 NM to fld.
    370/08E. HIWAS.
  ROWDY NDB (LOM) 260   CL   30°29'36"N 96°20'16"W   341° 5.9 NM to fld.
  ILS 111.7 I-CLL Rwy 34 LOM ROWDY NDB. ILS unmonitored when twr closed.

COLLEGE STATION   30°36'17"N 96°25'13"W   NOTAM FILE CLL.   HOUSTON
  (L) VORTACW 113.3   CLL   Chan 80   100° 3.1 NM to Easterwood Fld. 370/08E. HIWAS.   H-2K, 5B, L-17A
  RCO 122.65 122.2 (MONTGOMERY COUNTY FSS)

VOR RECEIVER CHECK   259

TEXAS

VOR RECEIVER CHECK POINTS

Facility Name (Arpt Name)	Freq/Ident	Type Check Pt. Gnd. AB/ALT	Azimuth from Fac. Mag	Dist. from Fac. N.M.	Check Point Description
Abilene (Abilene Regional)	113.7/ABI	A/2800	047	10.1	Over silos in center of Ft Phantom Lake.
Alice (Alice International)	114.5/ALI	G	270	0.5	On twy N of hangar.
Amarillo (Amarillo Internationl)	117.2/AMA	G	210	4.5	On east runup pad Rwy 22.
Austin (Robert Mueller Muni)	114.6/AUS	G	118	0.6	On runup area on twy to Rwy 31L.
Beaumont (Jefferson County)	114.5/BPT	G	310	1.0	On runup area for Rwy 12.
Big Spring (Big Spring McMahon-Wrinkle)	114.3/BGS	A/3500	107	10.5	Over red and white water tank.
Borger (Hutchinson Co)	108.6/BGD	G	175	6.7	On intersecting twy in front of terminal.
Brownsville (Brownsville/South Padre Island Intl)	116.3/BRO	G	248	3.2	On NE corner of parking ramp.
Brownwood (Brownwood Muni)	108.6/BWD	A/2600	169	6.2	Over rotating bcn.
Childress (Childress Muni)	117.6/CDS	G	353	3.7	At intersection of edge of ramp at center twy.
College Station (Easterwood Field)	113.3/CLL	G	097	3.2	On W edge of parking ramp.
Corpus Christi (Corpus Christi Intl)	115.5/CRP	A/1100	187	7.5	Over grain elevator.
Corpus Christi (San Patricio County)	115.5/CRP	A/1000	318	9.5	Over rotating beacon on arpt.
Daisetta (Liberty Muni)	116.9/DAS	A/1200	195	7.5	Over hangar S of arpt.
Dalhart (Dalhart Muni)	112.0/DHT	G	170	3.9	On SE corner of main ramp.
Eagle Lake (Eagle Lake)	116.4/ELA	A/1200	180	4.5	Over water tank 0. NM SW

FIGURE 58.—Excerpts from Airport/Facility Directory.

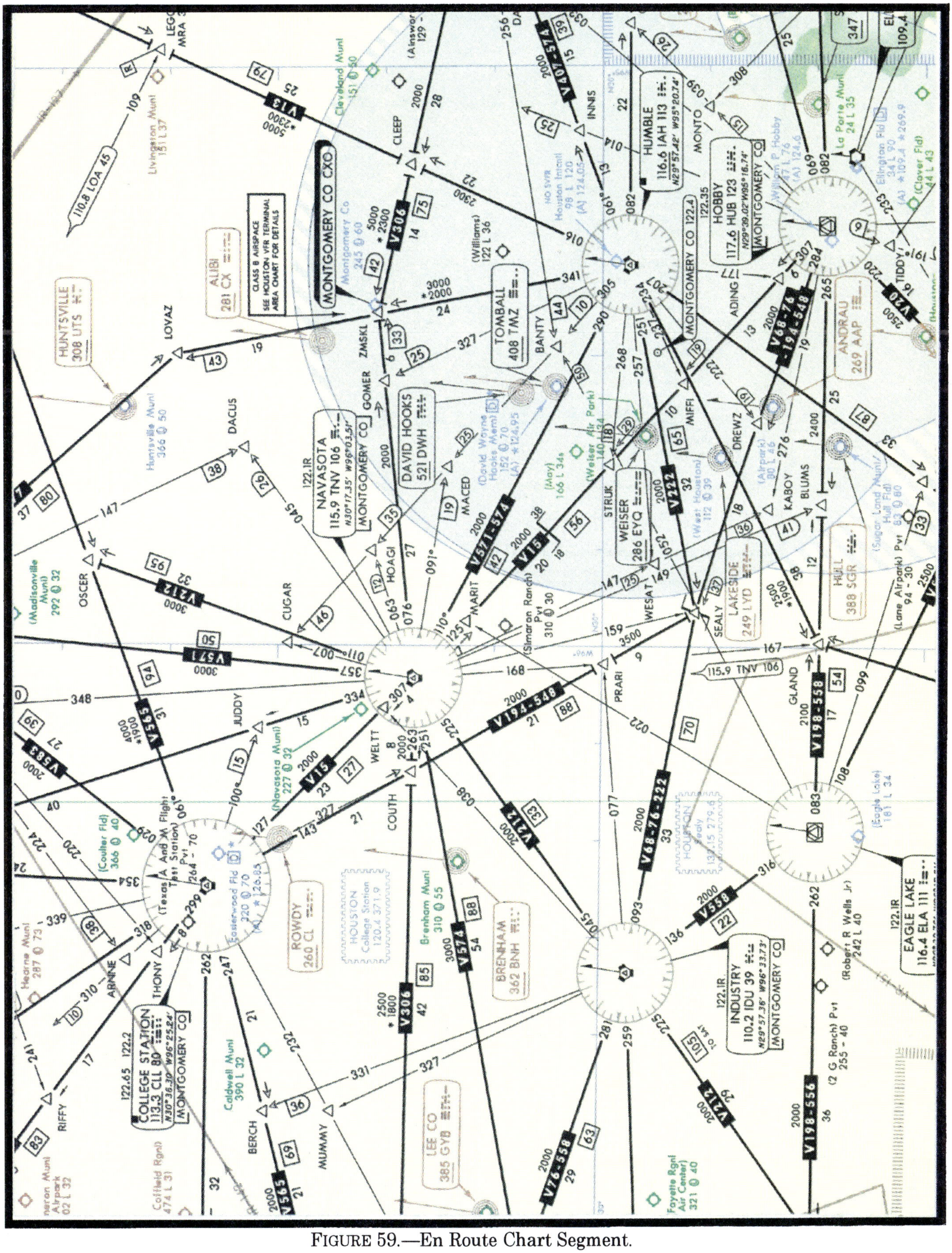

FIGURE 59.—En Route Chart Segment.

Appendix 3

```
'172                          TEXAS
 ─────────────────────────────────────────────────────────
    WILLIAM P. HOBBY    (HOU)  8 SE  UTC−6(−5DT)   29°38'43"N 95°16'43"W              HOUSTON
    47   B   S4   FUEL 100, JET A   OX 1, 2, 3, 4   LRA   ARFF Index C                H−5B, L−17B
      RWY 04−22: H7602X150 (CONC-GRVD)   S−75, D−200, DT−400   HIRL   CL              IAP
        RWY 04: MALSR. TDZ.         RWY 22: MALS. VASI(V4L)—GA 3.0° TCH 52'. Pole.
      RWY 12R−30L: H7601X150 (ASPH-GRVD)   S−75, D−195, DT−220   HIRL   CL
        RWY 12R: MALSR. VASI(V4R)—GA 3.0°TCH 49'. Thld dsplcd 1032'. Pole.
        RWY 30L: REIL. Thld dsplcd 200'. Road.
      RWY 17−35: H6000X150 (CONC-ASPH-GRVD)   S−75, D−121, DT−195   MIRL
        RWY 17: VASI(V4L)—GA 3.0°TCH 38'. Antenna.     RWY 35: VASI(V4R)—GA 3.0°TCH 41'. Building.
      RWY 12L−30R: H5149X100 (CONC-GRVD)   S−30, D−45, DT−80   MIRL
        RWY 12L: VASI(V4L)—GA 3.0°TCH 52'.    RWY 30R: Antenna.
      AIRPORT REMARKS: Attended continuously. Arpt CLOSED to acft with wing span over 117' except 24 hours PPR, call
        arpt manager 713−643−4597. CAUTION: numerous birds on and in vicinity of arpt. CAUTION to larger acft: W
        ramp twy centerline to parked acft on W side only 68'. W ramp twy centerline to edge of adjacent svc vehicle road
        on W side only 48'. PPR to taxi to main terminal bldg, call 713−643−4597. Flight Notification Service (ADCUS)
        available. NOTE: See SPECIAL NOTICE—Simultaneous Operations on Intersecting Runways.
      WEATHER DATA SOURCES: LLWAS.
      COMMUNICATIONS: ATIS 124.6   UNICOM 122.95
        MONTGOMERY COUNTY FSS (CXO) TF 1−800−WX−BRIEF. NOTAM FILE HOU.
        HOBBY RCO 122.35 (MONTGOMERY COUNTY FSS)
      ®HOUSTON APP CON 120.8 (South) 124.35 (West) 120.05(North and East)
        HOBBY TOWER 118.7   HOUSTON GND CON 121.9   CLNC DEL 125.45   PRE-TAXI CLNC 125.45
      ®HOUSTON DEP CON 120.8 (South) 123.8 (West) 119.7 (North and East)
        ARSA ctc APP CON
      RADIO AIDS TO NAVIGATION: NOTAM FILE HOU.
        HOBBY (H) VORW/DME 117.6   HUB   Chan 123   29°39'00"N 95°16'44"W   at fld. 50/06E.
        TUTTE NDB (LOM) 395   HU   29°35'20"N 95°20'25"W   038°  4.7 NM to fld.
        ILS/DME 111.3 I-PRQ Chan 50 Rwy 12R.
        ILS/DME 109.9 I-HUB Chan 36 Rwy 04 LOM TUTTE NDB. BC unusable beyond 25° SE of centerline.
        ILS/DME 111.3 I-UPU Chan 50 Rwy 30L.
```

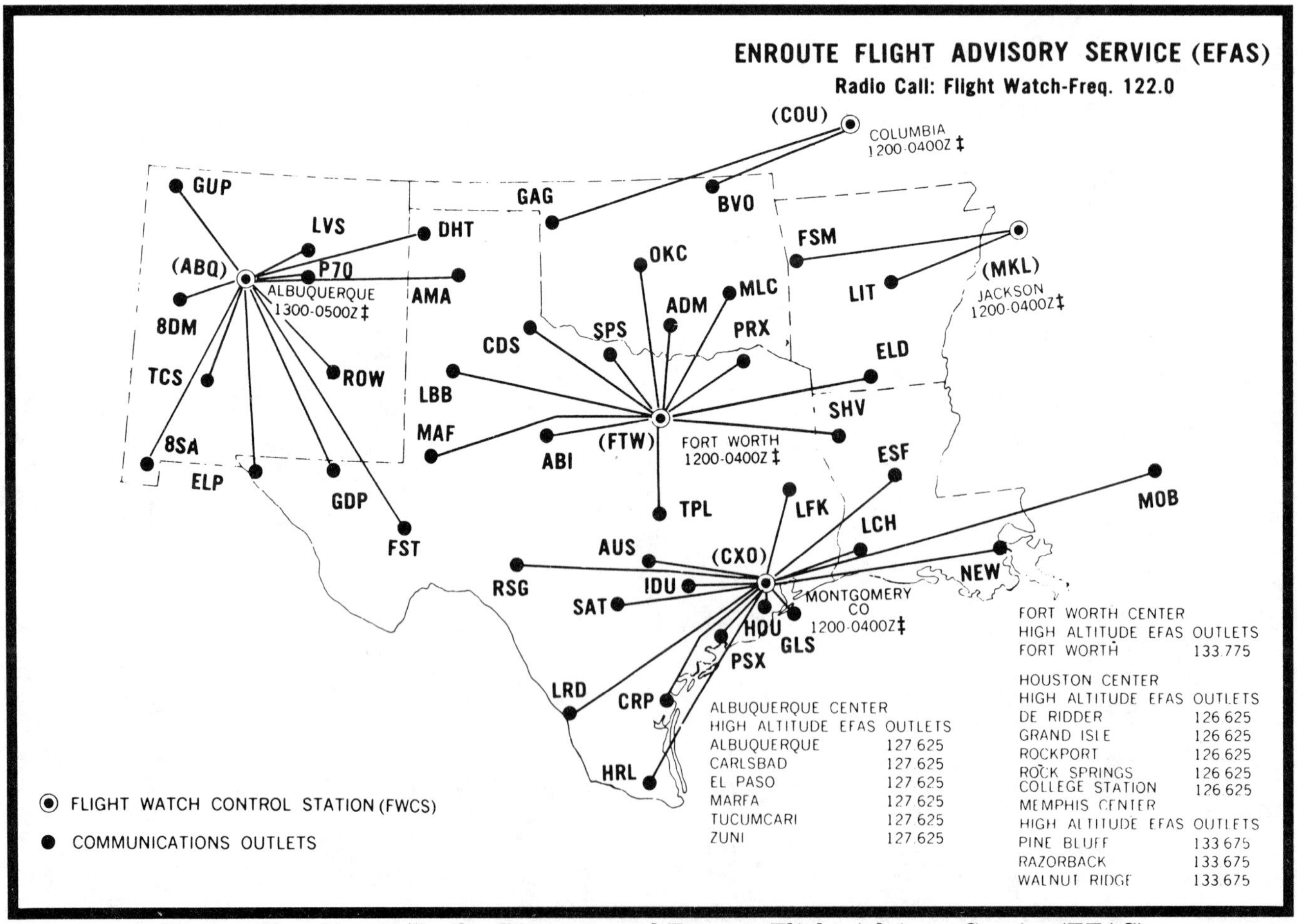

FIGURE 60.—Airport/Facilty Directory and Enroute Flight Advisory Service (EFAS).

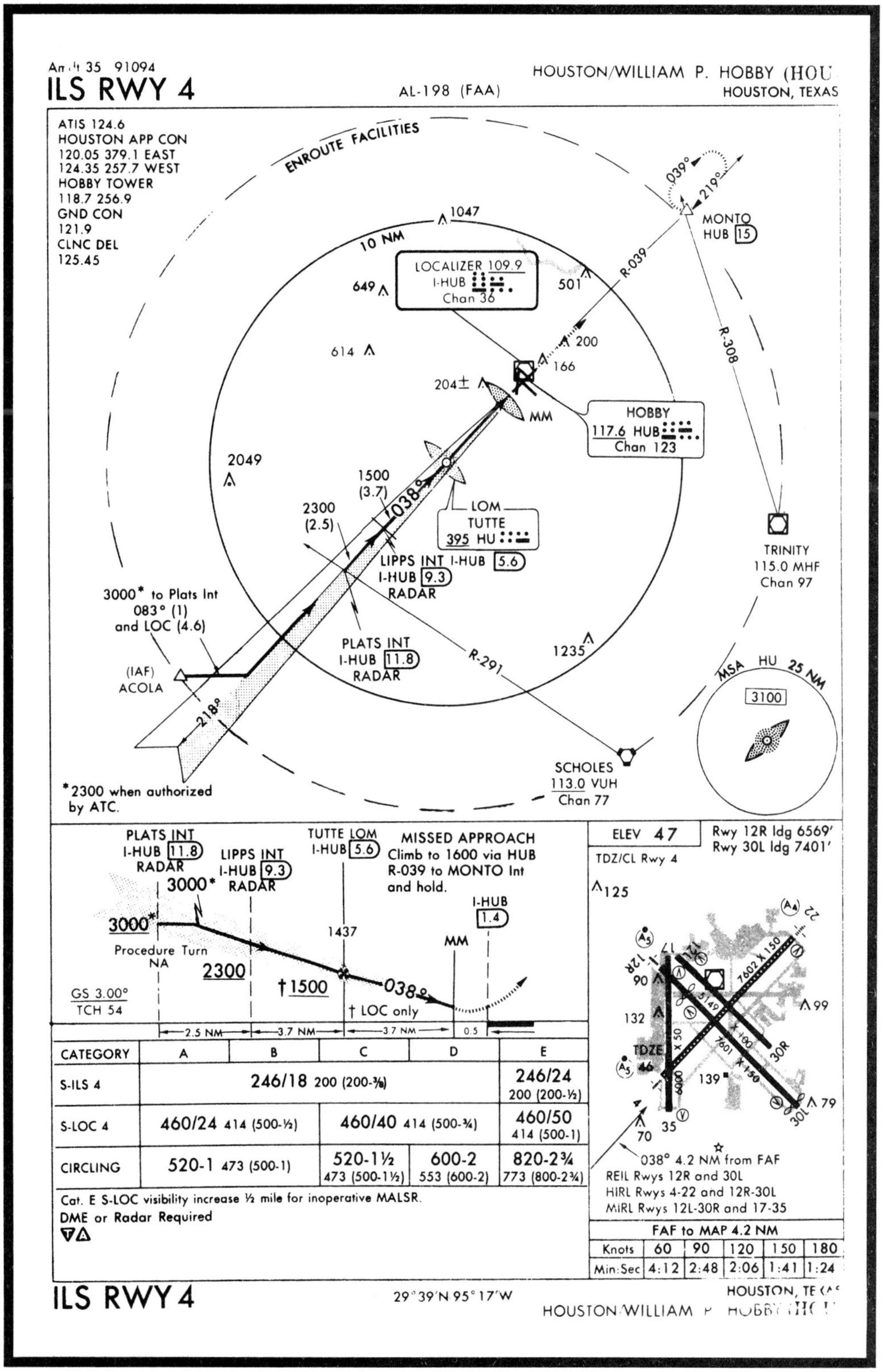

FIGURE 60A.—ILS RWY 4 (HOU).

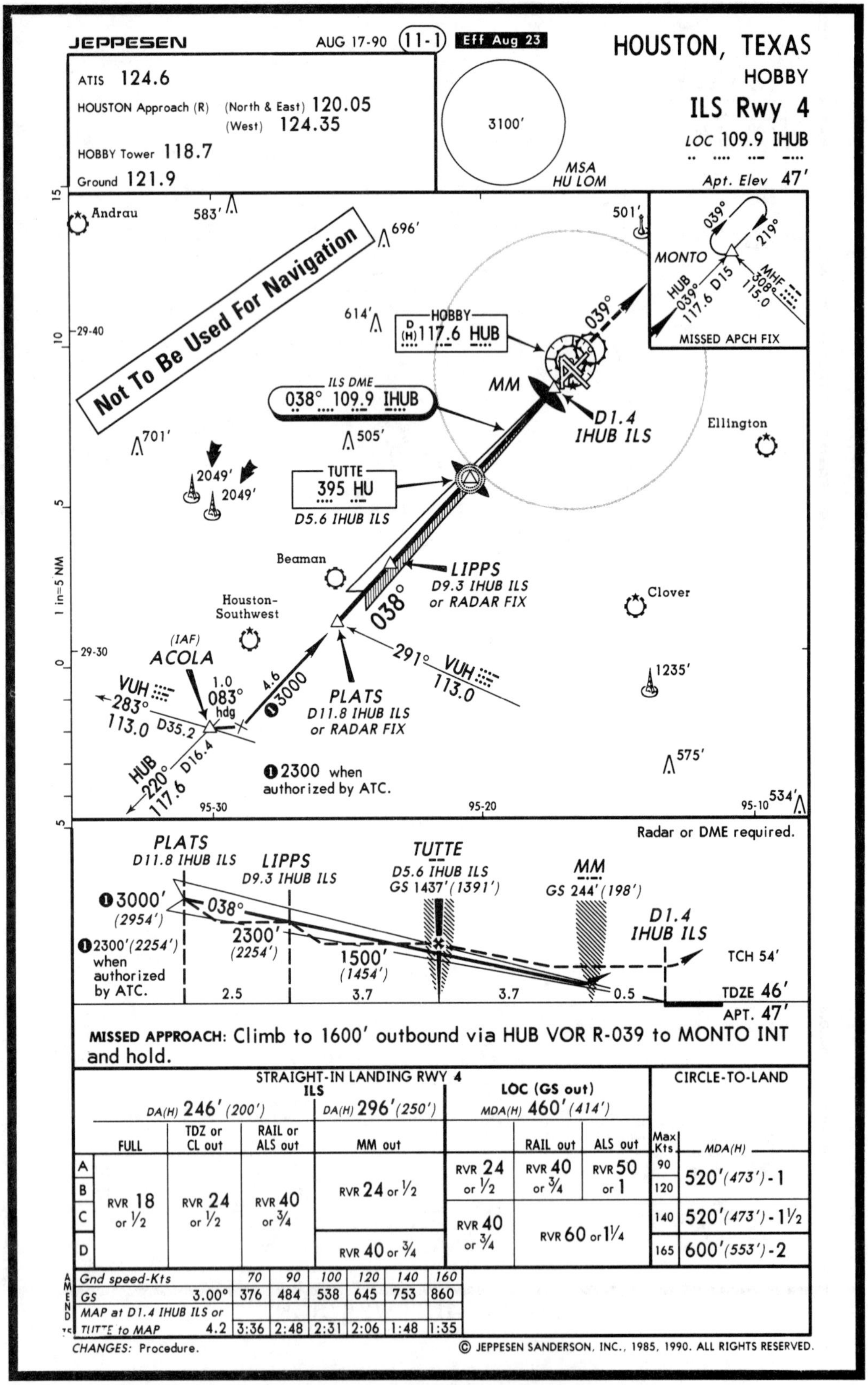

Appendix 3

FIGURE 60B.— ILS RWY 4 (HOU).

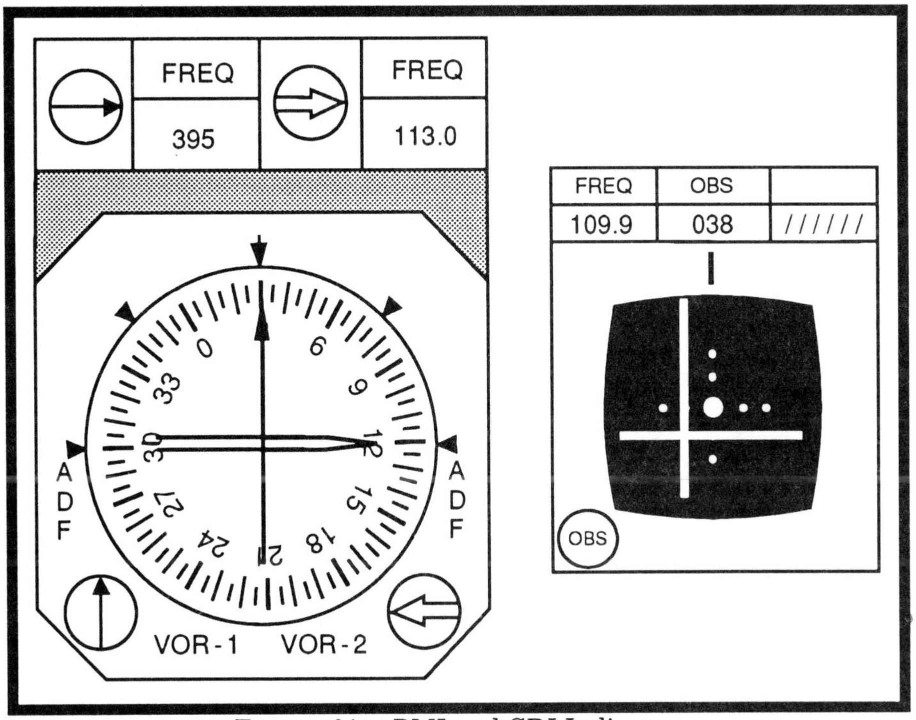

Appendix 3

FIGURE 61.—RMI and CDI Indicators.

Appendix 3

U.S. DEPARTMENT OF TRANSPORTATION FEDERAL AVIATION ADMINISTRATION **FLIGHT PLAN**	(FAA USE ONLY)	☐ PILOT BRIEFING ☐ STOPOVER	☐ VNR	TIME STARTED	SPECIALIST INITIALS

Form Approved: OMB No. 2120-0034

1. TYPE	2. AIRCRAFT IDENTIFICATION	3. AIRCRAFT TYPE/ SPECIAL EQUIPMENT	4. TRUE AIRSPEED	5. DEPARTURE POINT	6. DEPARTURE TIME		7. CRUISING ALTITUDE
					PROPOSED (Z)	ACTUAL (Z)	
VFR X IFR DVFR	N321JL	HU369/	105 KTS	LFT			5000

8. ROUTE OF FLIGHT: DIRECT LFT, V552 TBD

9. DESTINATION (Name of airport and city)	10. EST. TIME ENROUTE		11. REMARKS
HOUMA TERREBONNE LA (HUM)	HOURS	MINUTES	

12. FUEL ON BOARD		13. ALTERNATE AIRPORT(S)	14. PILOT'S NAME, ADDRESS & TELEPHONE NUMBER & AIRCRAFT HOME BASE	15. NUMBER ABOARD
HOURS	MINUTES			
		N/A	17. DESTINATION CONTACT/TELEPHONE (OPTIONAL)	2

16. COLOR OF AIRCRAFT	CIVIL AIRCRAFT PILOTS. FAR Part 91 requires you file an IFR flight plan to operate under instrument flight rules in controlled airspace. Failure to file could result in a civil penalty not to exceed $1,000 for each violation (Section 901 of the Federal Aviation Act of 1958, as amended). Filing of a VFR flight plan is recommended as a good operating practice. See also Part 99 for requirements concerning DVFR flight plans.
ORANGE/BLACK/WHITE	

FAA Form 7233-1 (8-82)   CLOSE VFR FLIGHT PLAN WITH _____ FSS ON ARRIVAL

AIRCRAFT INFORMATION

MAKE Hughes   MODEL 369

N 321JL   Vso N/A

AIRCRAFT EQUIPMENT/STATUS**

**NOTE: X= OPERATIVE   INOP= INOPERATIVE   N/A= NOT APPLICABLE
TRANSPONDER: X (MODE C) X ILS: (LOCALIZER) X (GLIDE SLOPE) X
VOR NO. 1 X (NO. 2) X ADF: X RNAV: X
VERTICAL PATH COMPUTER: N/A DME: X
MARKER BEACON: X (AUDIO) X (VISUAL) X

FIGURE 62.—Flight Plan and Aircraft Information.

Appendix 3

FLIGHT LOG

LAFAYETTE REGIONAL TO HOUMA TERREBONNE (HUM)

CHECK POINTS		ROUTE	COURSE	WIND	SPEED-KTS		DIST	TIME		FUEL	
FROM	TO	ALTITUDE		TEMP	TAS	GS	NM	LEG	TOT	LEG	TOT
LFT AIRPORT	LFT VOR	DIRECT CLIMB						:05:0			
	HATCH	V552 5000	109°		105						
	GRICE	V552 5000	110°								
	TBD	V552 5000	110°								
APPROACH & LANDING		DESCENT	117°					:10:0			
	HUM AIRPORT										

OTHER DATA:
NOTE: MAG. VAR. 6° E.

FLIGHT SUMMARY

TIME	FUEL (LB)	
		EN ROUTE
		RESERVE
		MISSED APPR.
		TOTAL

FIGURE 63.—Flight Planning Log.

Appendix 3

LOUISIANA

VOR RECEIVER CHECK POINTS

Facility Name (Arpt Name)	Freq/Ident	Type Check Pt. Gnd. AB/ALT	Azimuth from Fac. Mag	Dist. from Fac. N.M.	Check Point Description
Baton Rouge (Baton Rouge Metro, Ryan)	116.5/BTR	A/1500	063	7.7	Over water tank W side of arpt.
Downtown	108.6/DTN	A/1500	290	10	Over white water tower.
Esler (Esler Regional)	108.8/ESF	G	151	3.5	On ramp in front of admin bldg.
Hammond (Hammond Muni)	109.6/HMU	G	342	.6	On twy W side app end Rwy 18.
Lafayette (Lafayette Regional)	110.8/LFT	A/1000	340	25	Over rotating beacon.
Lake Charles (Lake Charles Muni)	113.4/LCH	A/1000	253	6.2	Over rotg bcn on atct.
Monroe (Monroe Muni)	117.2/MLU	G	209	0.9	On ramp SE of atct.
Natchez (Concordia Parish)	110.0/HEZ	A/1000	247	10.5	Over hangar NW end of field.
New Orleans (Lakefront)	113.2/MSY	A/1000	081	7.7	Over lakefront atct.
Ruston	112.8/RSN	A/2000	343	14	Over hwy & RR crossing at Dubash.
Shreveport (Shreveport Downtown)	108.6/DTN	G	307	.5	On runup area N side of rwy 14.
Shreveport (Shreveport Regional)	117.4/SHV	A/1200	175	19.3	Over old terminal building.
Tibby (Thibodaux Muni)	112.0/TBD	A/1000	006	5.0	Over railroad bridge off apch end rwy 26.
	112.0/TBD	A/1000	117	10.0	Over intersection of rwys 17-35 and 12-30.

§ **LAFAYETTE REGIONAL** (LFT) 2 SE GMT−6(−5DT) 30°12'14"N 91°59'16"W   **HOUSTON**
42 B S4 **FUEL** 100LL, JET A OX 1   CFR Index B   H-4F, L-17C
 RWY 03-21: H7651X150 (ASPH-GRVD)   S-75, D-170, DT-290   HIRL   IAP
  RWY 03: REIL. VASI(V4L)—GA 3.0°TCH 35'. Tree.
  RWY 21: MALSR. VASI(V4L)—GA 3.0°TCH 44'. Tree.
 RWY 10-28: H5401X150 (ASPH)   S-85, D-110, DT-175   MIRL
  RWY 10: REIL (out of svc indefinitely). VASI(V4L)—GA 3.0° TCH 35.33'. Tree.
  RWY 28: REIL. VASI(V4L)—GA 3.0°TCH 55'. Thld dsplcd 202'. Tree.
 RWY 01-19: H5069X150 (ASPH)   S-25, D-45
  RWY 01: VASI(V4R)—GA 3.0°TCH 50'. Tree.
 AIRPORT REMARKS: Attended continuously. Rwy 01-19 closed to air carriers. ACTIVATE MALSR Rwy 21—118.5.
 COMMUNICATIONS: CTAF 118.5   **ATIS** 120.5 Opr 1200-0500Z‡   **UNICOM** 122.95
  LAFAYETTE FSS (LFT) on arpt. 122.35, 122.2, 122.1R, 110.8T LD 318-233-4952 NOTAM FILE LFT.
 ® **APP/DEP CON** 121.1 (011°-190°) 124.0 (191°-010°) (1200-0400Z‡)
  HOUSTON CENTER APP/DEP CON 133.65 (0400-1200Z‡)
  TOWER 118.5, 121.35 (Helicopter ops) (1200-0400Z‡)   **GND CON** 121.8   **CLNC DEL** 125.55
  STAGE III ctc APP CON within 25 NM below 7000'
 RADIO AIDS TO NAVIGATION: NOTAM FILE LFT. VHF/DF ctc LAFAYETTE FSS
  (L) VORTAC 110.8   LFT   Chan 45   30°08'45"N 91°59'00"W   344°3.0 NM to fld. 40/06E
  LAFFS NDB (LOM) 375   LF   30°17'21"N 91°54'29"W   215° 5.8 NM to fld
  LAKE MARTIN NDB (MHW) 362   LKM   30°11'33"N 91°52'58"W   270° 5.2 NM to fld
  ILS/DME 109.5 I-LFT Chan 32 Rwy 21 LOM LAFFS NDB. Unmonitored when twr clsd.
  ASR

FIGURE 64.—Excerpt from Airport/Facility Directory (LFT).

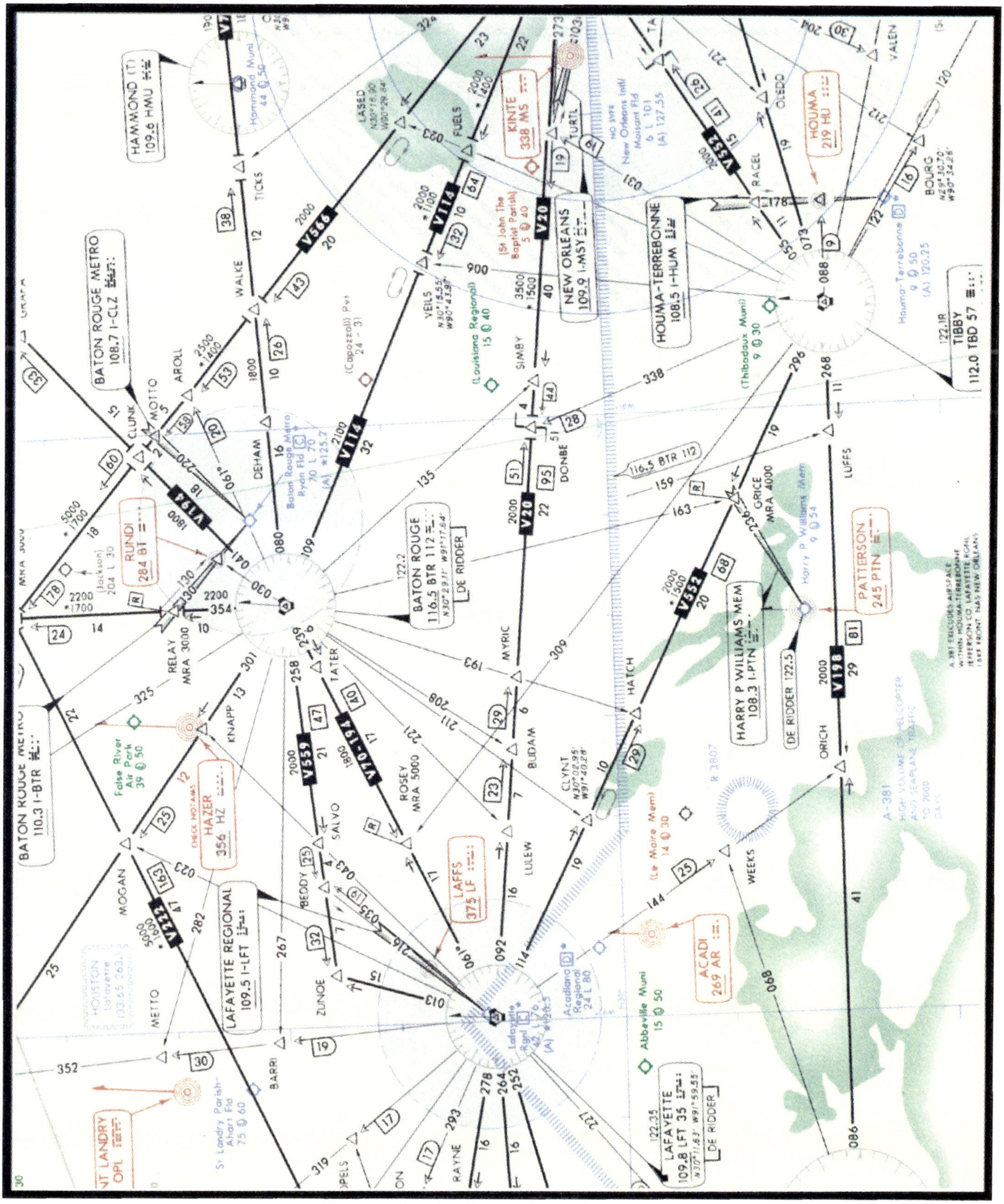

FIGURE 65.—En Route Chart Segment.

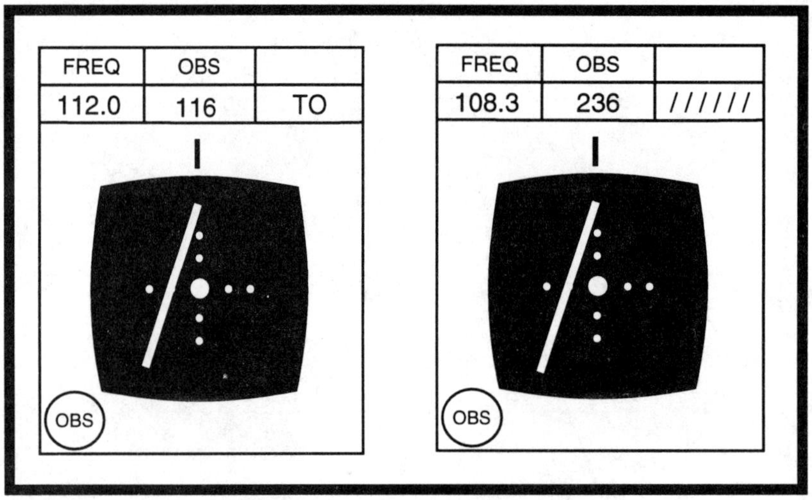

Appendix 3

FIGURE 66.—CDI and OBS Indicators.

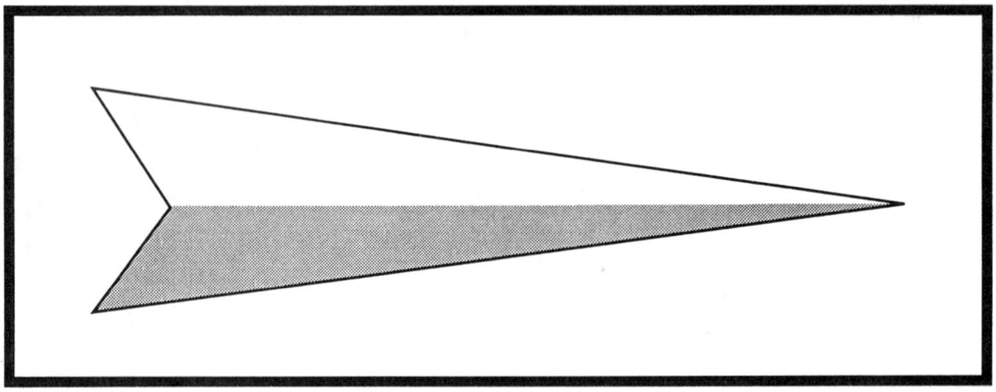

FIGURE 67.—Localizer Symbol.

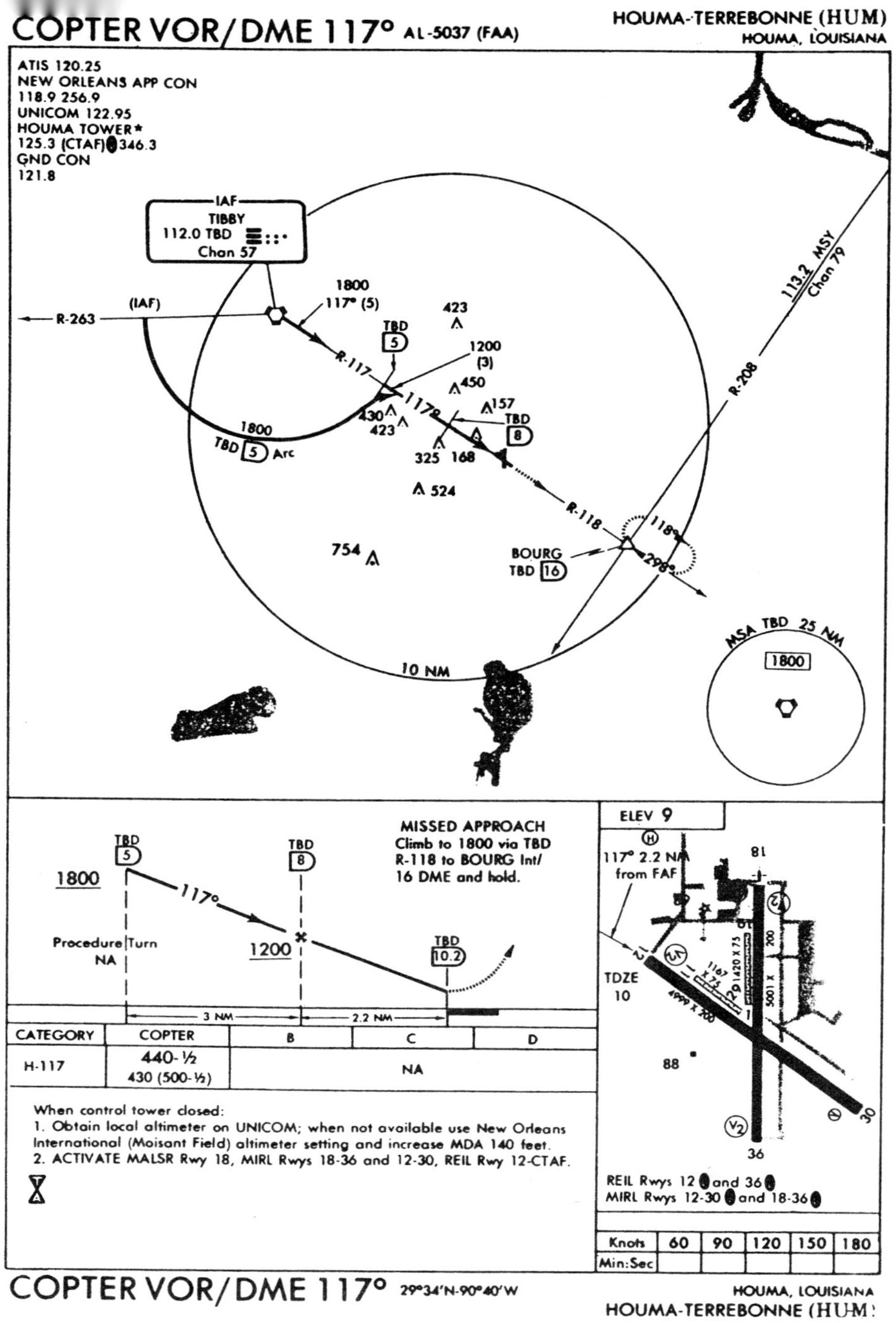

HOUMA-TERREBONNE (HUM) 3 SE UTC–6(–5DT) 29°34′04″N 90°39′38″W **NEW ORLEANS**
9 B S4 **FUEL** 100LL, JET A OX 1, 4 TPA—(See Remarks) **H-5C, L-17C**
RWY 18-36: H5001X200 (CONC) S-50, D-70, DT-137 MIRL **IAP**
RWY 18: MALSR. PVASI(PSIL)—GA 3.0°TCH 52′. Tree. **RWY 36:** REIL. PVASI(PSIL)—GA 3.0°TCH 39′. Tree.
RWY 12-30: H4999X200(CONC) S-50, D-70, DT-137 MIRL
RWY 12: REIL. PVASI(PSIL)—GA 3.0°TCH 42′. **RWY 30:** VASI(V2L)—GA 3.0°TCH 39′.
RWY 01-19: 1420X75 (TURF)
RWY 11-29: 1167X75 (TURF)
AIRPORT REMARKS: Attended dawn-dusk. Birds on and in vicinity of arpt. Extensive helicopter ops south thru west of arpt. Rwy 01–19 and Rwy 11–29 soft and unusable when wet. Rwy 01–19 marked with white tires. Rwy 11–29 marked with white tires. Rwys 12–30 and 18–36 Sfc skid resistance fair to poor when wet. Oxygen avbl by prior request 504-876-0584. TPA—1009′(1000′), turbine powered 1509′ (1500′). ACTIVATE MIRL Rwy 12–30 and Rwy 18–36 and MALSR Rwy 18 and REIL Rwy 12 and Rwy 36—CTAF. Control Zone effective 1200-0300Z‡.
WEATHER DATA SOURCES: LAWRS
COMMUNICATIONS: **CTAF** 125.3 **ATIS** 120.25 **UNICOM** 122.95
DE RIDDER FSS (DRI) TF 1–800–WX–BRIEF. NOTAM FILE HUM.
TIBBY RCO 122.1R 112.0T (DE RIDDER FSS)
Ⓡ **NEW ORLEANS APP/DEP CON** 118.9
TOWER 125.3 (1200-0300Z‡) **GND CON** 121.8 **CLNC DEL** 118.35
RADIO AIDS TO NAVIGATION: NOTAM FILE DRI.
TIBBY (L) VORTAC 112.0 TBD Chan 57 29°39′51″N 90°49′44″W 117° 10.5 NM to fld. 10/06E
NDB (LOM) 219 HU 29°39′47″N 90°39′34″W 177° 5.7 NM to fld. NOTAM FILE HUM.
ILS 108.5 I-HUM RWY 18 LOM HOUMA NDB.

FIGURE 68.—COPTER VOR DME-117 Degrees (HUM).

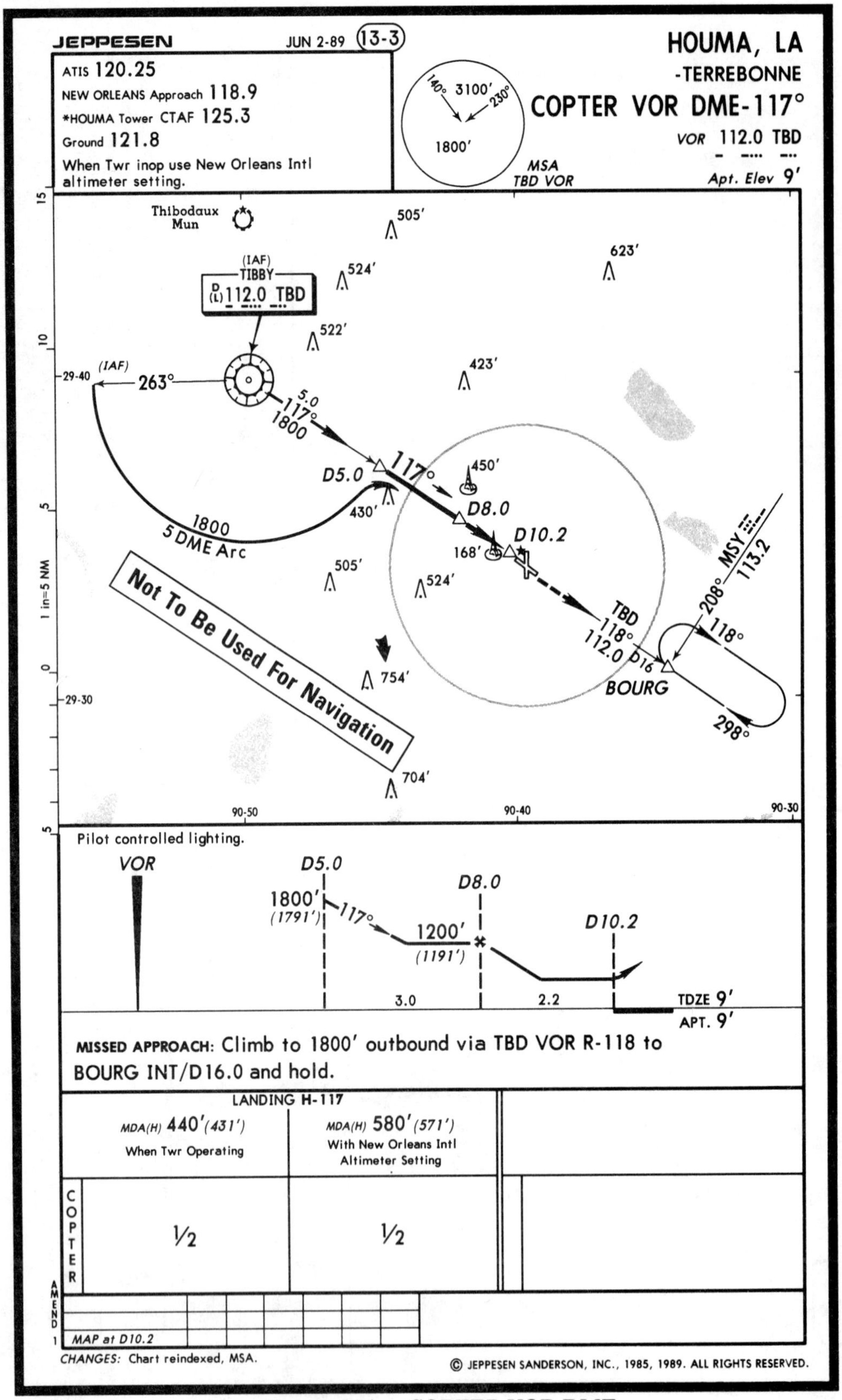

Appendix 3

FIGURE 68A.—COPTER VOR DME.

FLIGHT PLAN

U.S. DEPARTMENT OF TRANSPORTATION
FEDERAL AVIATION ADMINISTRATION

Form Approved: OMB No. 2120-0034

(FAA USE ONLY) □ PILOT BRIEFING □ VNR TIME STARTED SPECIALIST INITIALS
□ STOPOVER

1. TYPE	2. AIRCRAFT IDENTIFICATION	3. AIRCRAFT TYPE/ SPECIAL EQUIPMENT	4. TRUE AIRSPEED	5. DEPARTURE POINT	6. DEPARTURE TIME PROPOSED (Z) / ACTUAL (Z)	7. CRUISING ALTITUDE
□ VFR [X] IFR □ DVFR	N2142S	C172/	128 KTS	GREENWOOD LAKE 4N1		5000

8. ROUTE OF FLIGHT
DIRECT SHAFF INT., V213 HELON INT., V58 JUDDS INT., JUDDS2

9. DESTINATION (Name of airport and city)	10. EST. TIME ENROUTE HOURS / MINUTES	11. REMARKS
BRADLEY INTL. BDL		INSTRUMENT TRAINING FLIGHT

12. FUEL ON BOARD HOURS / MINUTES	13. ALTERNATE AIRPORT(S)	14. PILOT'S NAME, ADDRESS & TELEPHONE NUMBER & AIRCRAFT HOME BASE	15. NUMBER ABOARD
	N/A	17. DESTINATION CONTACT/TELEPHONE (OPTIONAL)	2

16. COLOR OF AIRCRAFT
BROWN/TAN/WHITE

CIVIL AIRCRAFT PILOTS. FAR Part 91 requires you file an IFR flight plan to operate under instrument flight rules in controlled airspace. Failure to file could result in a civil penalty not to exceed $1,000 for each violation (Section 901 of the Federal Aviation Act of 1958, as amended). Filing of a VFR flight plan is recommended as a good operating practice. See also Part 99 for requirements concerning DVFR flight plans.

FAA Form 7233-1 (8-82)   CLOSE VFR FLIGHT PLAN WITH _____ FSS ON ARRIVAL

AIRCRAFT INFORMATION

MAKE Cessna   MODEL 172

N 2142S   Vso 33

AIRCRAFT EQUIPMENT/STATUS**

**NOTE: X= OPERATIVE   INOP= INOPERATIVE   N/A= NOT APPLICABLE
TRANSPONDER: X (MODE C) X ILS: (LOCALIZER) X (GLIDE SLOPE) X
VOR NO. 1 X (NO. 2) X ADF: X RNAV: N/A
VERTICAL PATH COMPUTER: N/A DME: X
MARKER BEACON: X (AUDIO) INOP (VISUAL) X

FIGURE 69.—Flight Plan and Aircraft Information.

Appendix 3

FLIGHT LOG
GREENWOOD LAKE (4N1) TO BRADLEY INTL. (BDL)

| CHECK POINTS || ROUTE | COURSE | WIND || SPEED-KTS || DIST | TIME || FUEL ||
FROM	TO	ALTITUDE		TEMP	TAS	GS	NM	LEG	TOT	LEG	TOT
4N1	SHAFF	DIRECT CLIMB	350°					:08:0			
	HELON	V213 5000	029°		128						
	IGN	V58 5000	102°								
		JUDDS2	112°								
	JUDDS	JUDDS2	100°								
	BRISS	JUDDS2	057°								
APPROACH & LANDING	BDL INTL							:12:0			

OTHER DATA:
   NOTE: MAG. VAR. 14° W.

FLIGHT SUMMARY

TIME	FUEL (LB)	
		EN ROUTE
		RESERVE
		MISSED APPR.
		TOTAL

FIGURE 70.—Flight Planning Log.

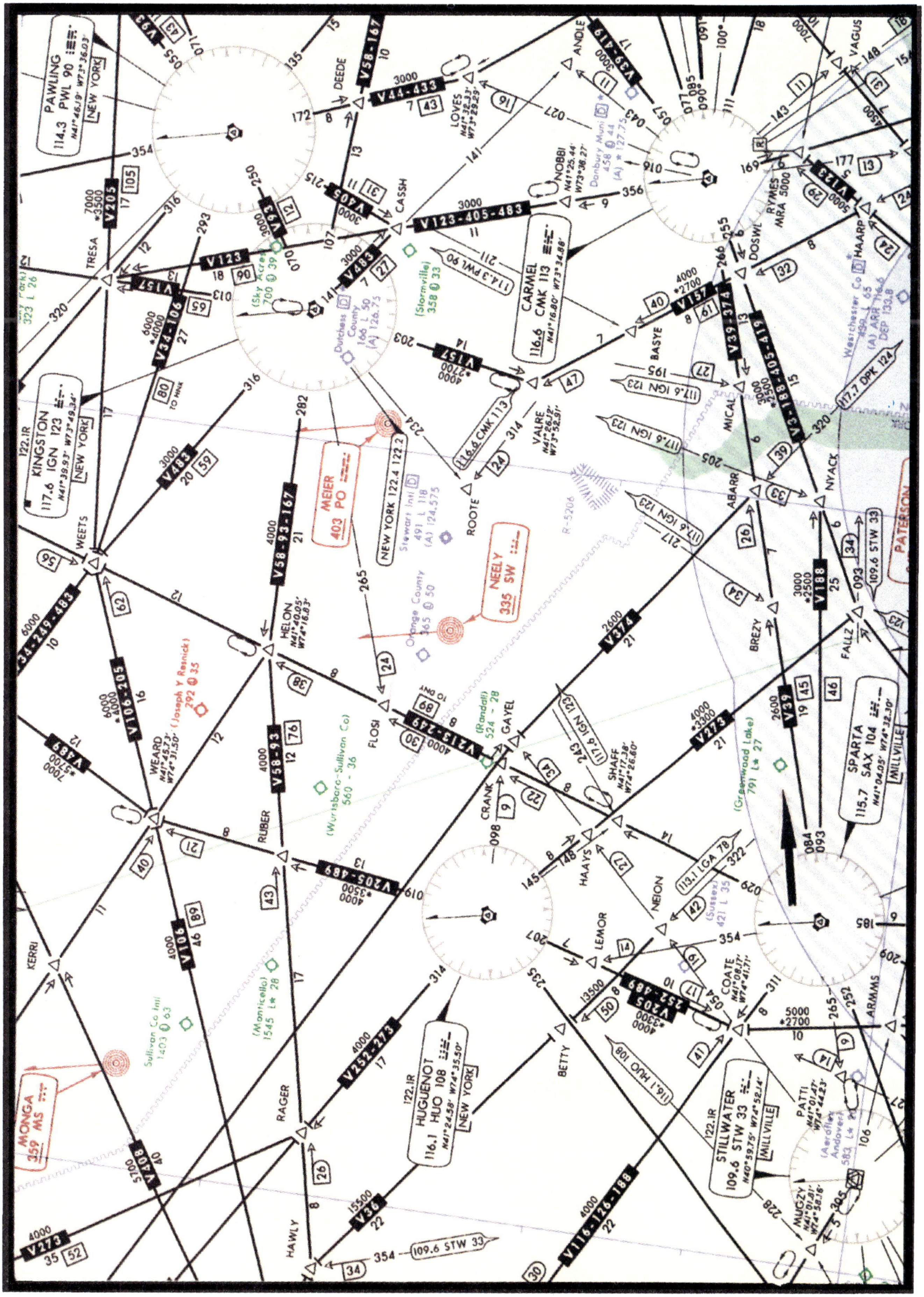

Appendix 3

FIGURE 71.—En Route Chart Segment.

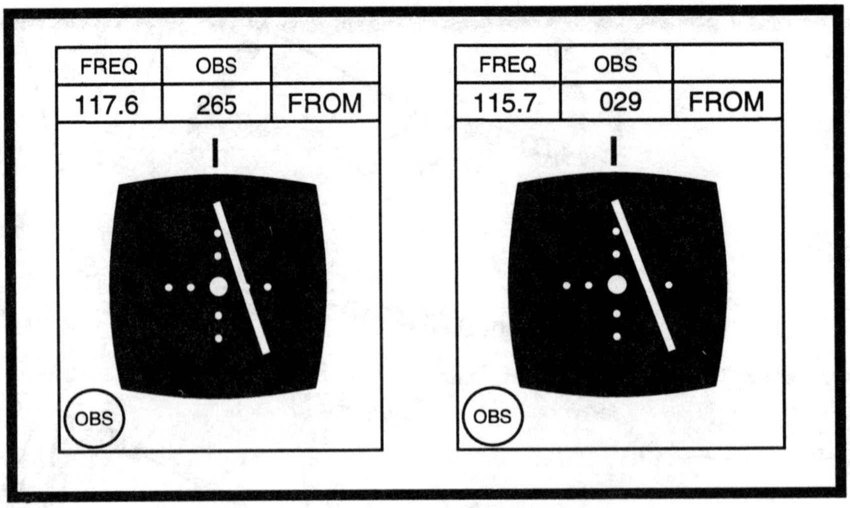

Appendix 3

FIGURE 71A.—CDI and OBS Indicators.

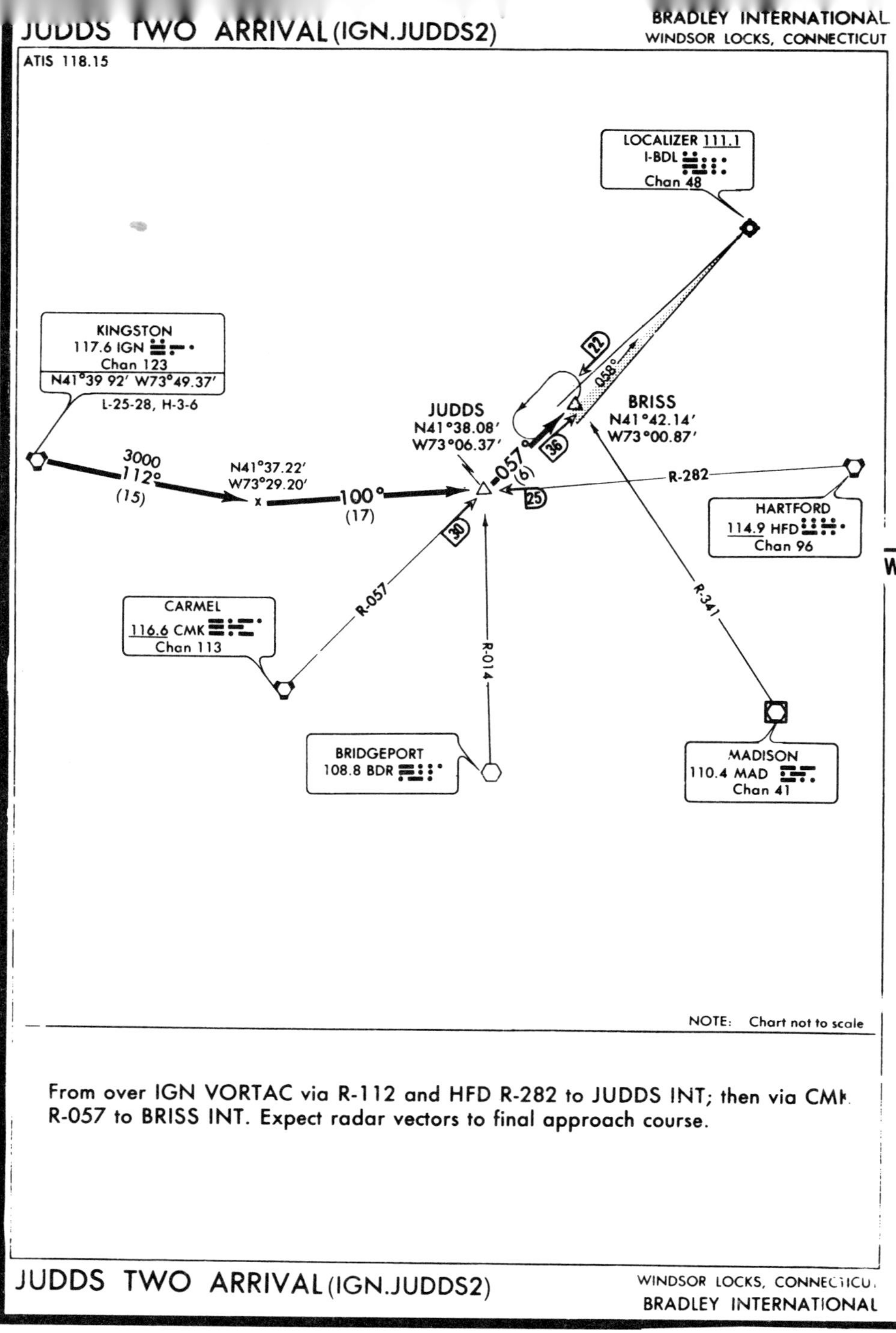

Appendix 3

WINDSOR LOCKS

CONNECTICUT

BRADLEY INTL (BDL) 3 W UTC−5(−4DT) 41°56'20"N 72°41'01"W NEW YORK
174 B S4 FUEL 100LL, JET A OX 1, 2, 3, 4 TPA—See Remarks H-3D, 6J, L-25C, 28I
LRA ARFF Index D IAP
RWY 06-24: H9502X200 (ASPH-GRVD) S-200, D-200, DT-350,DDT-710 HIRL CL
RWY 06: ALSF2 TDZ. Trees. RWY 24: MALSR. VASI(V4L)—GA 3.0°TCH 56'.
RWY 15-33: H6846X200 (ASPH) S-200, D-200, DT-350 HIRL
RWY 15: REIL. VASI(V4L)—GA 3.5°TCH 59'. Trees. RWY 33: MALSF. VASI(V4R)—GA 3.0°TCH 59'. Trees.
RWY 01-19: H5141X100 (ASPH) S-60, D-190, DT-328 MIRL
RWY 01: Building. RWY 19: Trees.
AIRPORT REMARKS: Attended continuously. Rwy 01–19 restricted to ldg and tkf with maximum tkf gross weight of 73,000 pounds. This restriction does not apply to acft emergency. Numerous birds frequently on or in vicinity or arpt. Portions of taxiway Alpha not visible from tower. TPA—1174(1000) light acft, 1874(1700) heavy acft. Landing fee for unscheduled air carrier ops with more than 30 passenger seats call arpt manager 203-627-3001/3008. This does not include delayed regularly schedule air carrier ops or diversions. Rwy 15 REIL out of svc indefinitely. Flight Notification Service (ADCUS) available. NOTE: See SPECIAL NOTICE— Simultaneous Operations on Intersecting Runways.
WEATHER DATA SOURCES: LLWAS.
COMMUNICATIONS: ATIS 118.15 UNICOM 122.95
BRIDGEPORT FSS (BDR) TF 1–800–WX–BRIEF. NOTAM FILE BDL.
WINDSOR LOCKS RCO 122.3 (BRIDGEPORT FSS)
ⓇBRADLEY APP CON 125.8 (within 20 miles)
ⓇBRADLEY DEP CON 121.05 (South) 125.35 (North and West) 123.95 (Northeast)
TOWER 120.3 GND CON 121.9 CLNC DEL 121.75
ARSA ctc APP CON
RADIO AIDS TO NAVIGATION: NOTAM FILE BDL.
(T) VORTACN 109.0 BDL Chan 27 41°56'27"N 72°41'21"W at fld. 165/14W.
  VOR portion unusable 090°–103° beyond 24 NM below 5000' 104°–170° beyond 10 NM below 6000'.
  260°–290° beyond 15 NM below 6000'.
  DME portion unusable:
    040°–085° beyond 13 NM below 2000'
    130°–150° beyond 10 NM below 3000'
    170°–195° beyond 14 NM below 3000'
    250°–290° beyond 18 NM below 6000'
CHUPP NDB (LOM) 388 BD 41°52'38"N 72°46'00"W 058° 5.2 NM to fld.
ILS/DME 111.1 I-BDL Chan 48 Rwy 06. LOM CHUPP NDB.
ILS/DME 108.55 I-IKX Chan 22Y Rwy 33.
ILS/DME 111.1 I-MYQ Chan 48 Rwy 24.

JUDDS TWO ARRIVAL (IGN.JUDDS2)
ATIS 118.15
BRADLEY INTERNATIONAL
WINDSOR LOCKS, CONNECTICUT

From over IGN VORTAC via R-112 and HFD R-282 to JUDDS INT; then via CMK R-057 to BRISS INT. Expect radar vectors to final approach course.

NOTE: Chart not to scale.

JUDDS TWO ARRIVAL (IGN.JUDDS2)
WINDSOR LOCKS, CONNECTICUT
BRADLEY INTERNATIONAL

FIGURE 72.— JUDDS TWO ARRIVAL.

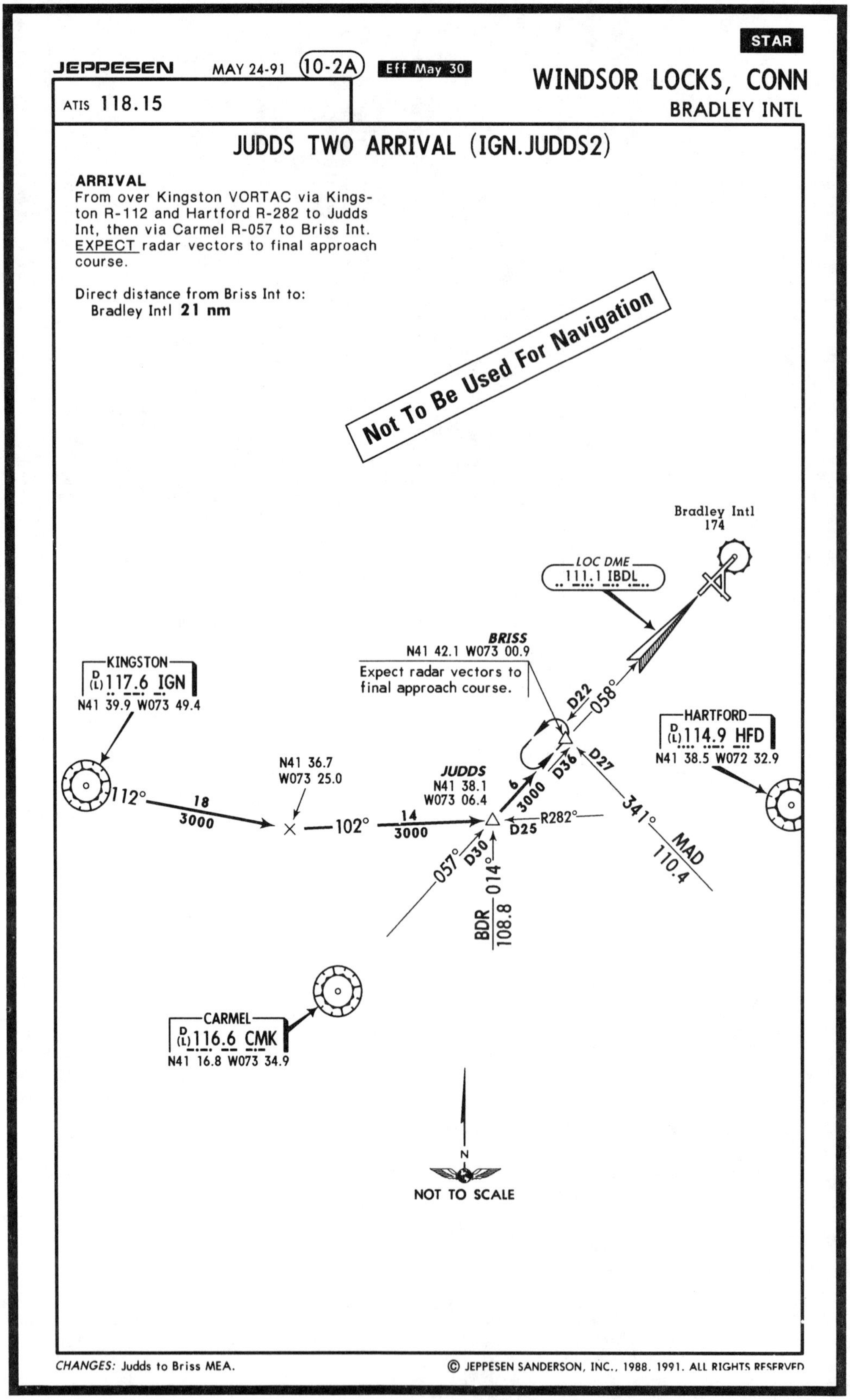

Appendix 3

FIGURE 72A.— JUDDS TWO ARRIVAL.

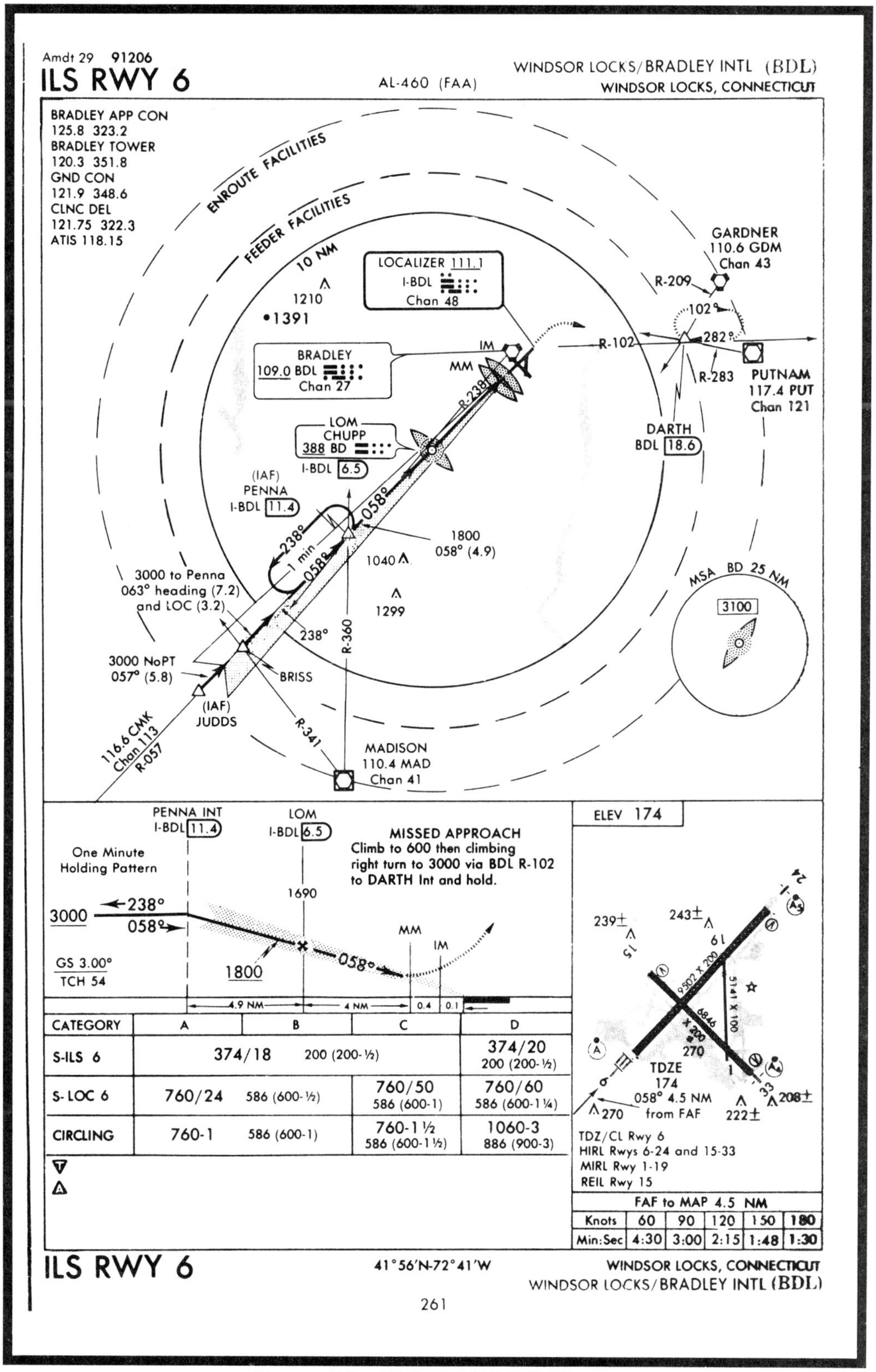

FIGURE 73.—ILS RWY 6 (BDL).

JEPPESEN AUG 17-90 (11-1) Eff Aug 23

WINDSOR LOCKS, CONN

BRADLEY INTL

ILS Rwy 6

LOC 111.1 IBDL

Apt. Elev 174'

ATIS 118.15
BRADLEY Approach (R) 125.8
BRADLEY Tower 120.3
Ground 121.9

MSA BD LOM 3100'

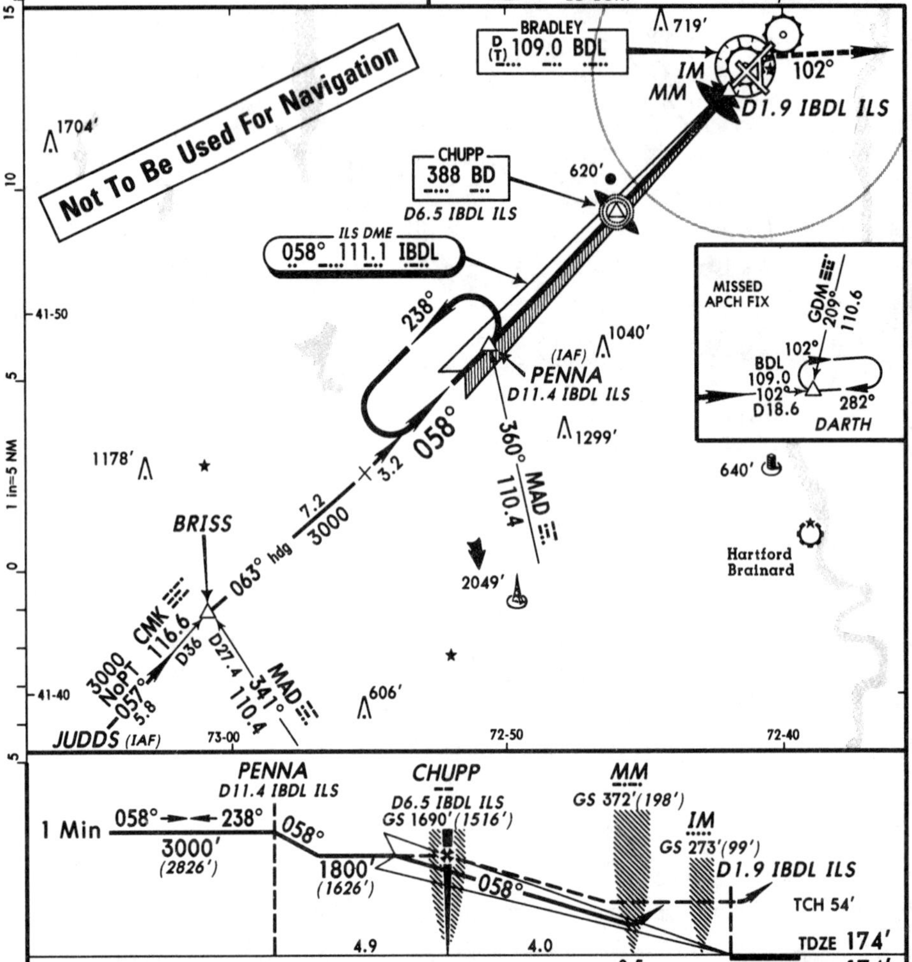

MISSED APPROACH: Climb to 600' then climbing RIGHT turn to 3000' outbound via BDL VOR R-102 to DARTH INT and hold.

	STRAIGHT-IN LANDING RWY 6 ILS DA(H) 374'(200') FULL	TDZ or CL out	ALS out	DA(H) 424'(250') MM out	LOC (GS out) MDA(H) 760'(586')	ALS out	CIRCLE-TO-LAND Max Kts	MDA(H)
A							90	
B	RVR 18 or 1/2	RVR 24 or 1/2	RVR 40 or 3/4	RVR 24 or 1/2	RVR 24 or 1/2	RVR 50 or 1	120	760'(586')-1
C					RVR 50 or 1	1 1/2	140	760'(586')-1 1/2
D	RVR 20 or 1/2			RVR 40 or 3/4	RVR 60 or 1 1/4	1 3/4	165	1060'(886')-3

Gnd speed-Kts		70	90	100	120	140	160
GS	3.00°	377	484	538	646	754	861
MAP at D1.9 IBDL ILS or CHUPP to MAP	4.5	3:51	3:00	2:42	2:15	1:56	1:41

AMEND 29

CHANGES: Printing sequence.

FIGURE 73A.—ILS RWY 6 (BDL).

Appendix 3

							Form Approved: OMB No. 2120-0034	

U.S. DEPARTMENT OF TRANSPORTATION FEDERAL AVIATION ADMINISTRATION **FLIGHT PLAN**	(FAA USE ONLY)	☐ PILOT BRIEFING ☐ STOPOVER	☐ VNR	TIME STARTED	SPECIALIST INITIALS

1. TYPE	2. AIRCRAFT IDENTIFICATION	3. AIRCRAFT TYPE/ SPECIAL EQUIPMENT	4. TRUE AIRSPEED	5. DEPARTURE POINT	6. DEPARTURE TIME		7. CRUISING ALTITUDE
☐ VFR ☒ IFR ☐ DVFR	N242T	C310/	160 KTS	HLN	PROPOSED (Z)	ACTUAL (Z)	11000

8. ROUTE OF FLIGHT
STAKK2, V365 BZN, V86

9. DESTINATION (Name of airport and city)	10. EST. TIME ENROUTE		11. REMARKS
LOGAN INTL. AIRPORT (BIL)	HOURS	MINUTES	

12. FUEL ON BOARD		13. ALTERNATE AIRPORT(S)	14. PILOT'S NAME, ADDRESS & TELEPHONE NUMBER & AIRCRAFT HOME BASE	15. NUMBER ABOARD
HOURS	MINUTES			
		N/A	17. DESTINATION CONTACT/TELEPHONE (OPTIONAL)	2

16. COLOR OF AIRCRAFT	CIVIL AIRCRAFT PILOTS. FAR Part 91 requires you file an IFR flight plan to operate under instrument flight rules in controlled airspace. Failure to file could result in a civil penalty not to exceed $1,000 for each violation (Section 901 of the Federal Aviation Act of 1958, as amended). Filing of a VFR flight plan is recommended as a good operating practice. See also Part 99 for requirements concerning DVFR flight plans.
RED/BLACK/WHITE	

FAA Form 7233-1 (8-82)   CLOSE VFR FLIGHT PLAN WITH _____ FSS ON ARRIVAL

AIRCRAFT INFORMATION

MAKE   Cessna   MODEL   310R

N 242T   Vso 72

AIRCRAFT EQUIPMENT/STATUS**

**NOTE: X= OPERATIVE   INOP= INOPERATIVE   N/A= NOT APPLICABLE
TRANSPONDER: X (MODE C) X ILS: (LOCALIZER) X (GLIDE SLOPE) INOP
VOR NO. 1 X (NO. 2) X ADF: X RNAV: N/A
VERTICAL PATH COMPUTER: N/A DME: X
MARKER BEACON: X (AUDIO) X (VISUAL) X

FIGURE 74.—Flight Plan and Aircraft Information.

Appendix 3

FLIGHT LOG
HELENA REGIONAL AIRPORT TO BILLINGS LOGAN INTL.

CHECK POINTS		ROUTE	COURSE	WIND	SPEED-KTS		DIST	TIME		FUEL	
FROM	TO	ALTITUDE		TEMP	TAS	GS	NM	LEG	TOT	LEG	TOT
HLN	VESTS	STAKK2 CLIMB	103°					:15:0			
	BZN	V365 11000	140°		160						
	LVM	V86 11000	110° / 063°								
	REEPO	V86 11000	067°								
	BIL	V86	069°								
APPROACH & LANDING								:15:0			
	LOGAN INTL										

OTHER DATA:
   NOTE: MAG. VAR. 18° E.

FLIGHT SUMMARY

TIME	FUEL (LB)	
		EN ROUTE
		RESERVE
		MISSED APPR.
		TOTAL

FIGURE 75.—Flight Planning Log.

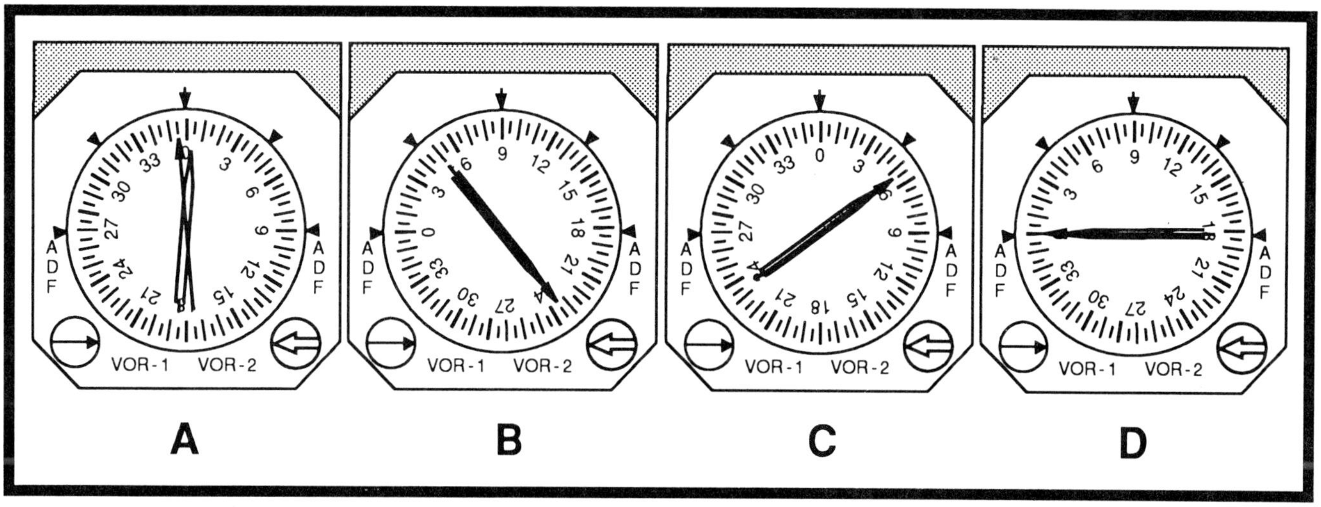

Appendix 3

HELENA REGIONAL (HLN) 2 NE UTC−7(−6DT) 46°36'25"N 111°58'55"W GREAT FALLS
3,873 B S4 FUEL 100LL, JET A OX 1,3 AOE ARFF Index B H-1C, L-9B
RWY 09-27: H9000X150 (ASPH-PFC) S-100, D-160, DT-250 HIRL IAP
  RWY 09: VASI(V4L)—GA 3.0°TCH 45'. Ground. RWY 27: MALSR. VASI(V4L)—GA 3.0°TCH 55'. Rgt tfc.
RWY 05-23: H4599X75 (ASPH-PFC) S-21, D-30
  RWY 05: Road. RWY 23: Fence. Rgt tfc.
RWY 16-34: H2979X75 (ASPH) S-21, D-30 MIRL
  RWY 34: Ground. Rgt tfc.
AIRPORT REMARKS: Attended 1200-0800Z‡. East 2400' Taxiway C and first 900' Rwy 27 not visible from tower.
  Prior permission for unscheduled FAR 121 operations, Call 406-442-2821. AOE, 1 hour prior notice required,
  phone 449-1569 1500-0000Z‡, 0000-1500Z‡ 449-1024. Twys A;B; high speed and C (between A and D)
  not available for air carrier use by acft with greater than 30 passenger seats. Rwy 16-34 and Rwy 05-23 (except
  between Rwy 09-27 and Twy D) not available for air carrier use by acft with greater than 30 passenger seats.
  When tower closed, ACTIVATE HIRL Rwy 09-27 and MALSR Rwy 27—CTAF, when twr closed MIRL Rwy 16-34
  are off. Ldg fee for all acft over 12,500 lbs. NOTE: See SPECIAL NOTICE—Simultaneous Operations on
  Intersecting Runways.
COMMUNICATIONS: CTAF 118.3   ATIS 120.4 (Mon-Fri 1300-0700Z‡, Sat-Sun 1300-0500Z‡)
  UNICOM 122.95
  GREAT FALLS FSS (GTF) TF 1-800-WX-BRIEF. NOTAM FILE HLN.
  RCO 122.2 122.1R 117.7T (GREAT FALLS FSS)
  APP/DEP CON 119.5 (Mon-Fri 1300-0700Z‡, Sat-Sun 1300-0500Z‡)
  SALT LAKE CENTER APP/DEP CON 133.4 (Mon-Fri 0700-1300Z‡, Sat-Sun 0500-1300Z‡)
  TOWER 118.3 (Mon-Fri 1300-0700Z‡, Sat-Sun 1300-0500Z‡) GND CON 121.9
RADIO AIDS TO NAVIGATION: NOTAM FILE HLN.
  (H) VORTAC 117.7   HLN   Chan 124   46°36'25"N 111°57'10"W   254° 1.2 NM to fld. 3810/16E.
    VORTAC unusable:
      006°-090° beyond 25 NM below 11,000'   091°-120° beyond 20 NM below 16,000'
      121°-240° beyond 25 NM below 10,000'   355°-006° beyond 15 NM below 17,500'
      241°-320° beyond 25 NM below 10,000'
  CAPITOL NDB (HW) 317   CVP   46°36'24"N 111°56'11"W   254° 1.9 NM to fld.
    NDB unmonitored when tower closed.
  HAUSER NDB (MHW) 386   HAU   46°34'08"N 111°45'26"W   268° 9.6 NM to fld.
  ILS 110.1 I-HLN Rwy 27 ILS unmonitored when tower closed.

VOR RECEIVER CHECK

Facility Name (Arpt Name)	Freq/Ident	Type Check Pt. Gnd. AB/ALT	Azimuth from Fac. Mag	Dist. from Fac. N.M.	Check Point Description
Helena (Helena Regional)	117.7/HLN	G	237	0.7	On Twy E midway between Twy C and Rwy 27.
Kalispell (Glacier Park Intl)	108.4/FCA	A/4000	316	6.4	Over apch end Rwy 29.
Lewistown (Lewistown Muni)	112.0/LWT	A/5200	072	5.4	Over apch end Rwy 07.
Livingston	116.1/LVM	A/6500	234	5.5	Over northern most radio twr NE of city.
Miles City (Frank Wiley Field)	112.1/MLS	G	036	4.2	On twy leading to Rwy 30.
Missoula (Missoula Intl)	112.8/MSO	G	340	0.6	On edge of ramp in front of Admin Building.

FIGURE 76.— VOR Indications and Excerpts from Airport/Facility Directory (HLN).

122

(PILOT NAV) (STAKK2.STAKK) 91038
STAKK TWO DEPARTURE SL-192 (FAA)

HELENA REGIONAL
HELENA, MONTANA

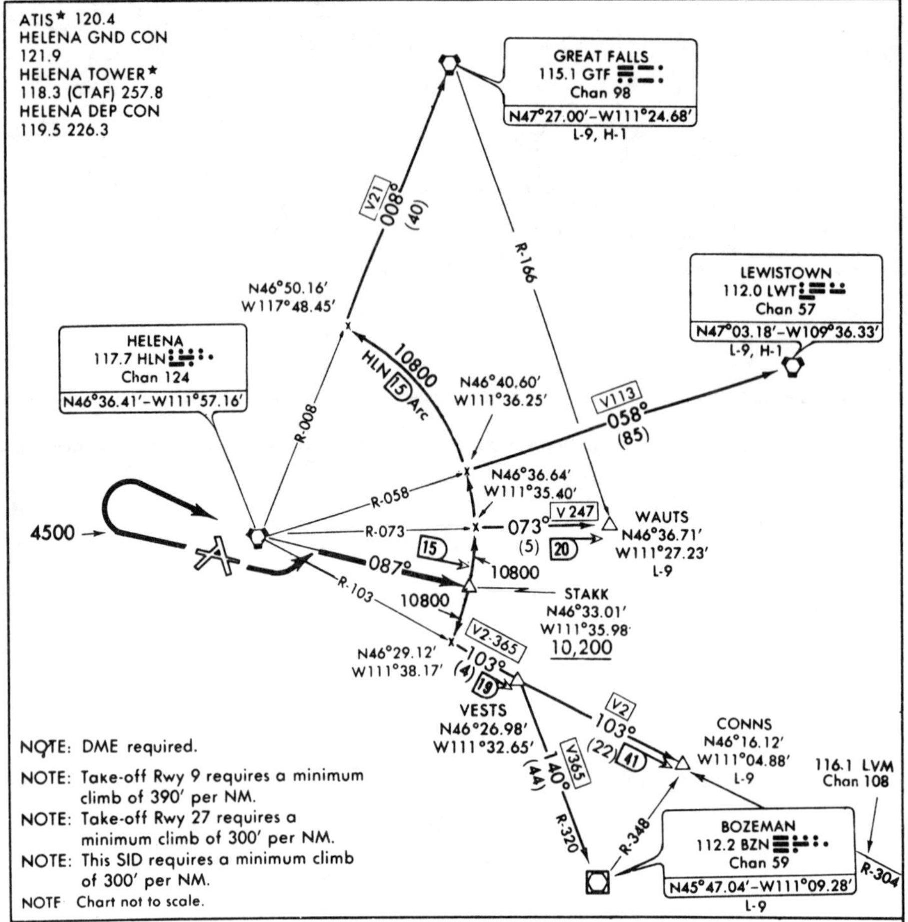

DEPARTURE ROUTE DESCRIPTION

TAKE-OFF RUNWAY 9: Climbing left turn to intercept HLN R-087 to cross STAKK INT at or above 10,200'. Thence via transition.

TAKE-OFF RUNWAY 27: Climb on runway heading to 4500' then climbing right turn direct HLN VORTAC. Continue climb on HLN R-087 to cross STAKK INT at or above 10,200'. Thence via transition.

BOZEMAN TRANSITION (STAKK2.BZN): From over STAKK INT via 15 DME Arc and V365 to BZN VOR/DME.

CONNS TRANSITION (STAKK2.CONNS): From over STAKK INT via 15 DME Arc and V2 to CONNS INT.

GREAT FALLS TRANSITION (STAKK2.GTF): From over STAKK INT via 15 DME Arc and V21 to GTF VORTAC.

LEWISTOWN TRANSITION (STAKK2.LWT): From over STAKK INT via 15 DME Arc and V113 to LWT VORTAC.

WAUTS TRANSITION (STAKK2.WAUTS): From over STAKK INT via 15 DME Arc and V247 to WAUTS INT.

STAKK TWO DEPARTURE
(PILOT NAV) (STAKK2.STAKK)

HELENA, MONTANA
HELENA REGIONAL

FIGURE 77.— STAKK TWO DEPARTURE.

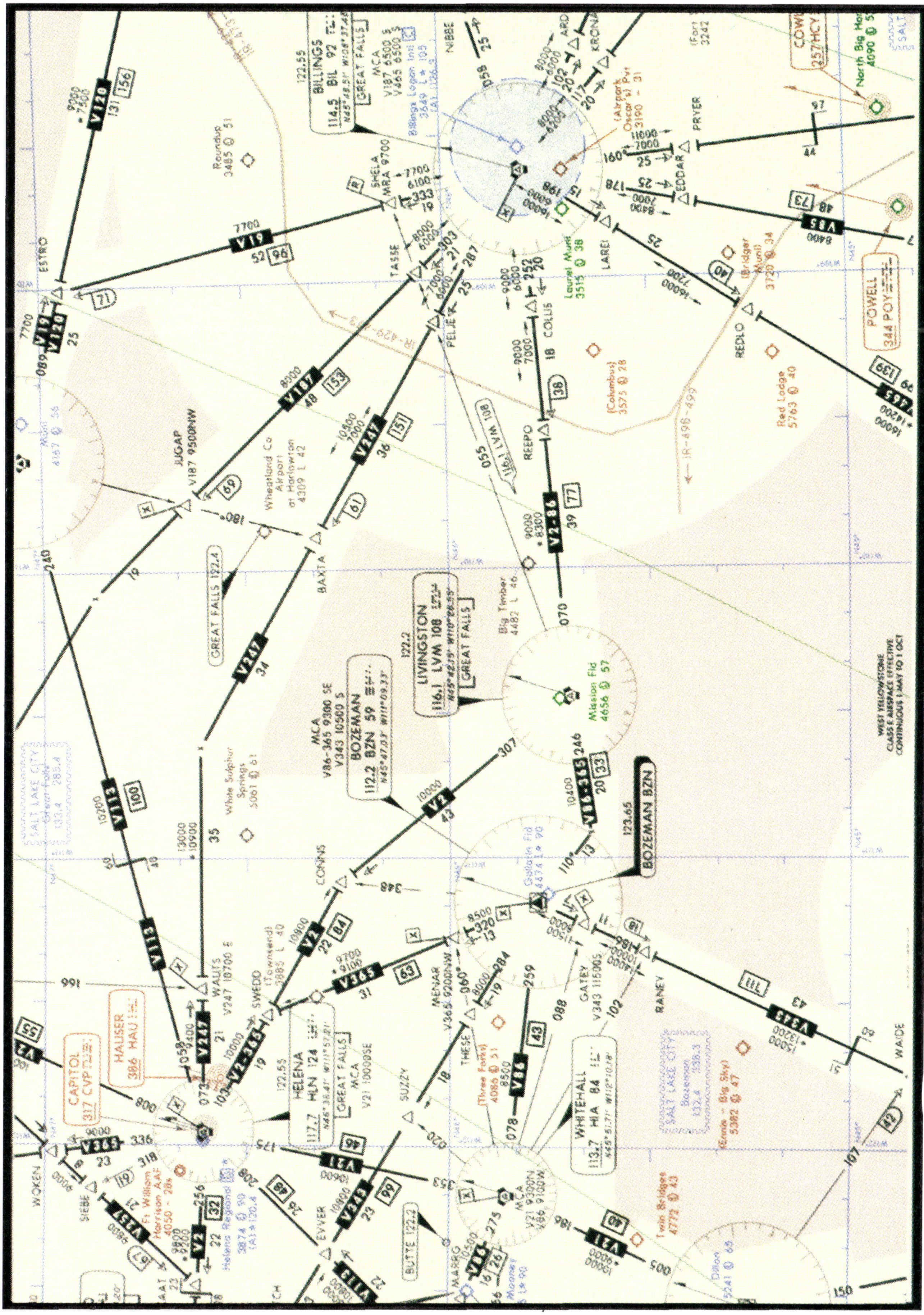

Appendix 3

FIGURE 78.—En Route Chart Segment.

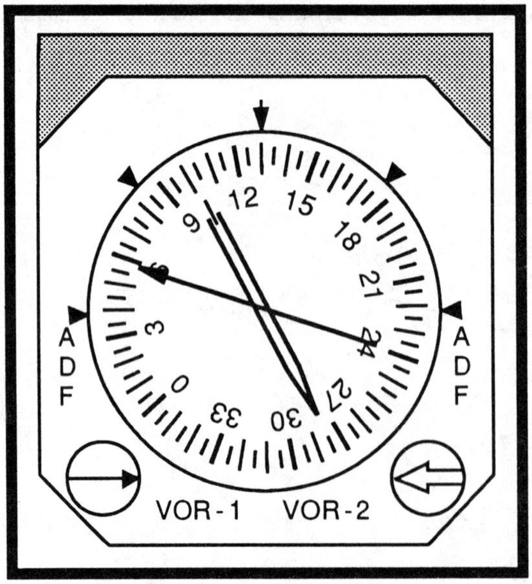

Appendix 3

FIGURE 79.—RMI Indicator.

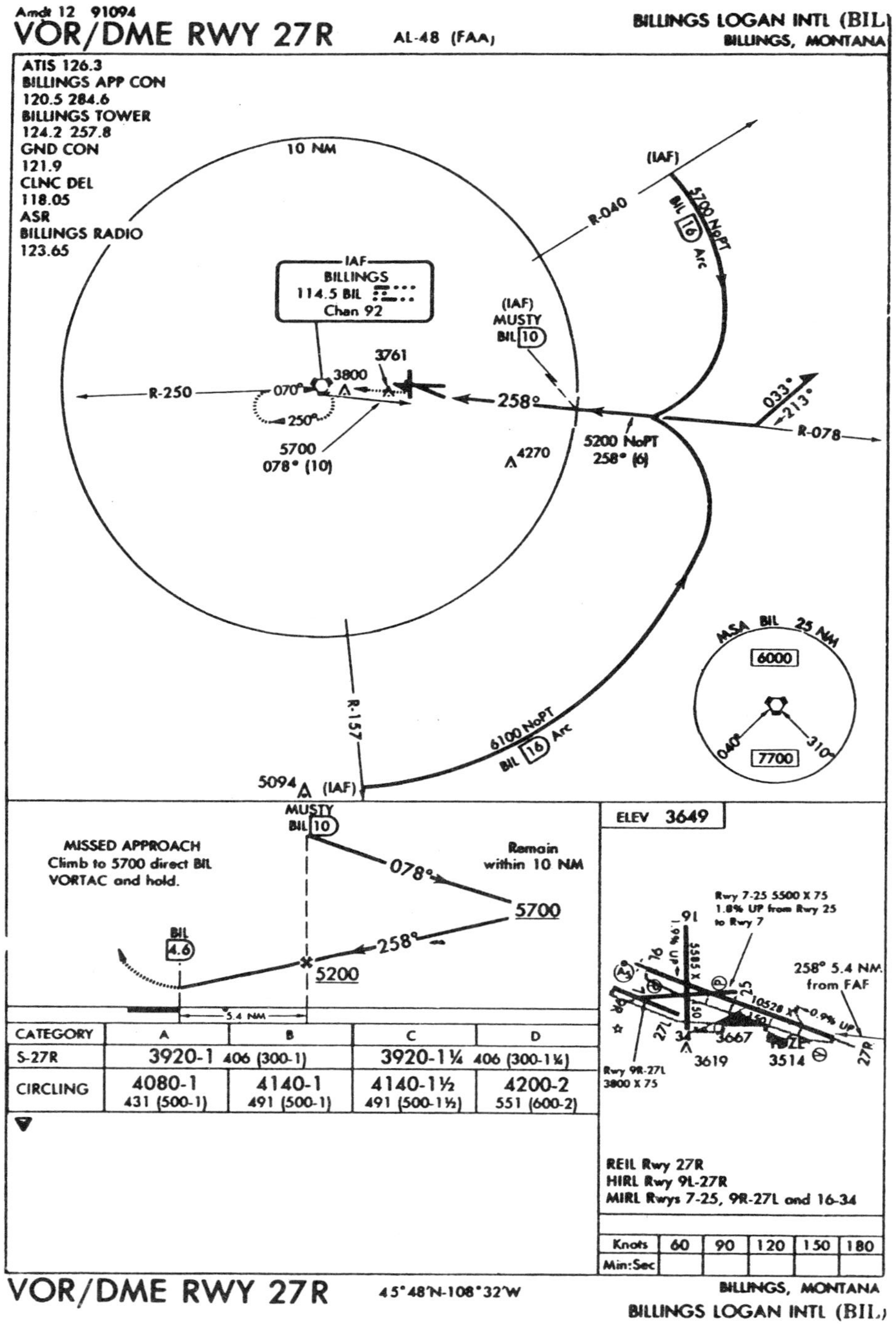

FIGURE 80.—VOR/DME RWY 27R and Airport/Facility Directory (BIL).

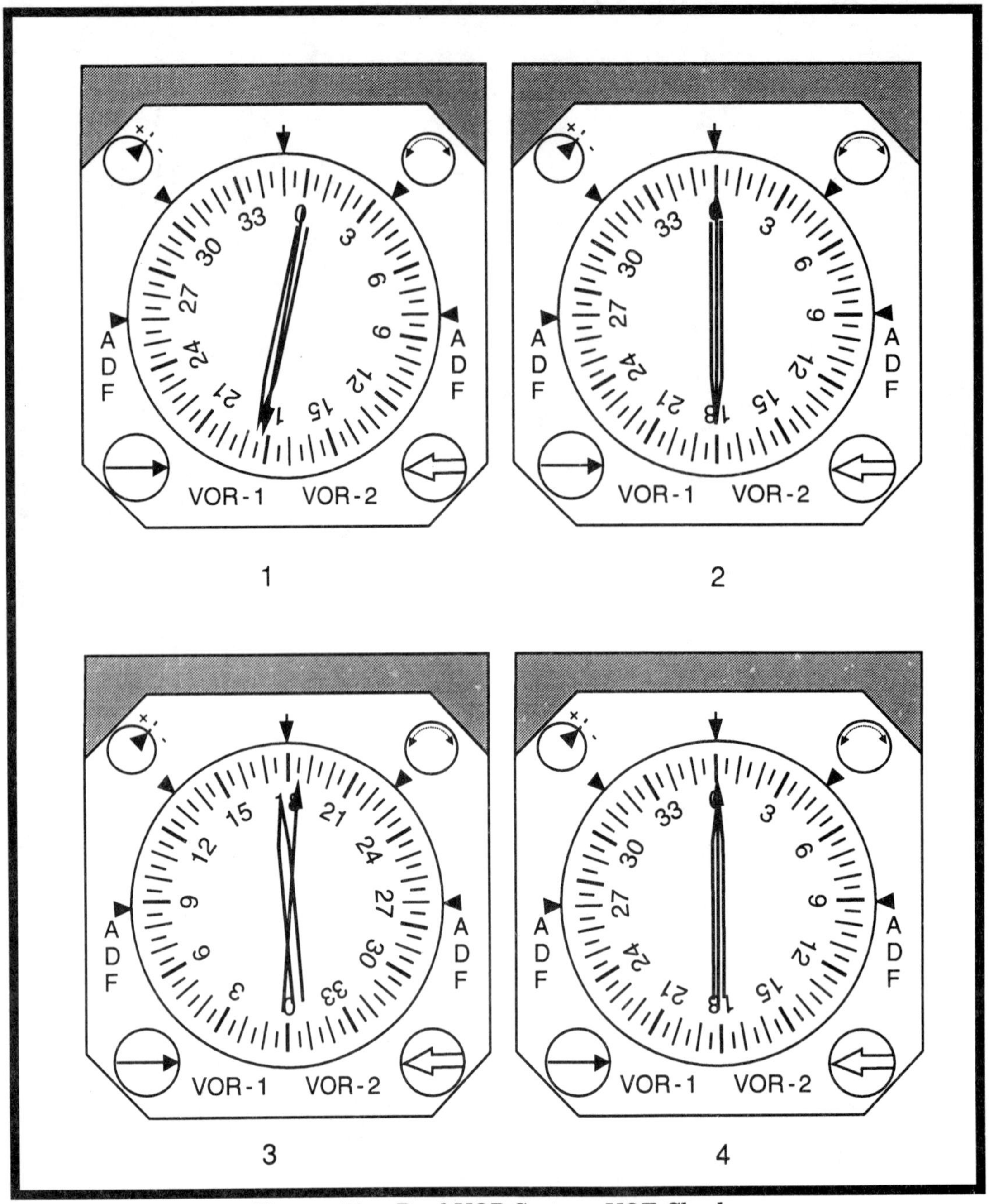

Appendix 3

FIGURE 81.—Dual VOR System, VOT Check.

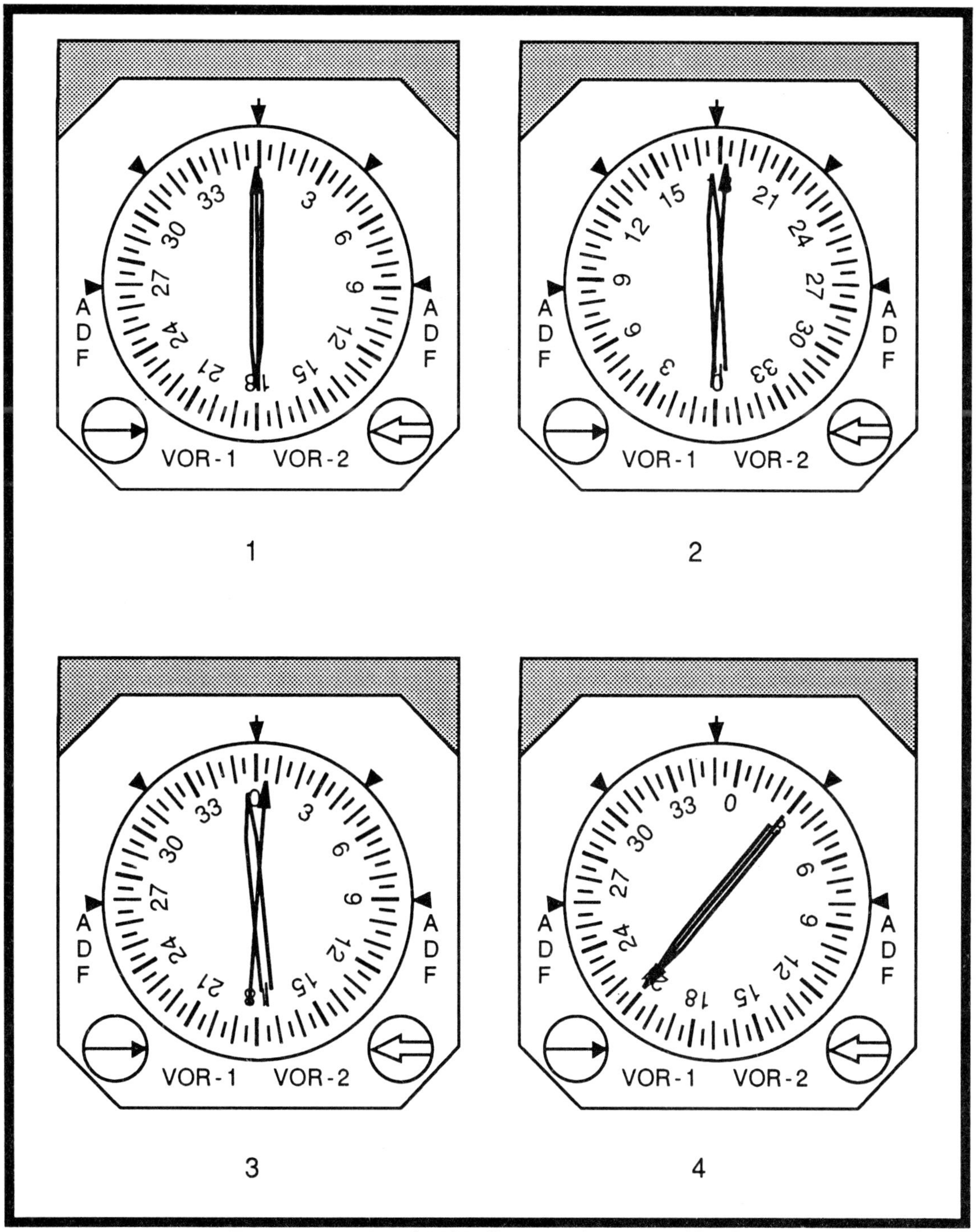

Appendix 3

FIGURE 82.—Dual VOR System, Accuracy Check.

Appendix 3

FIGURE 83.—Altimeter/12,000 Feet.

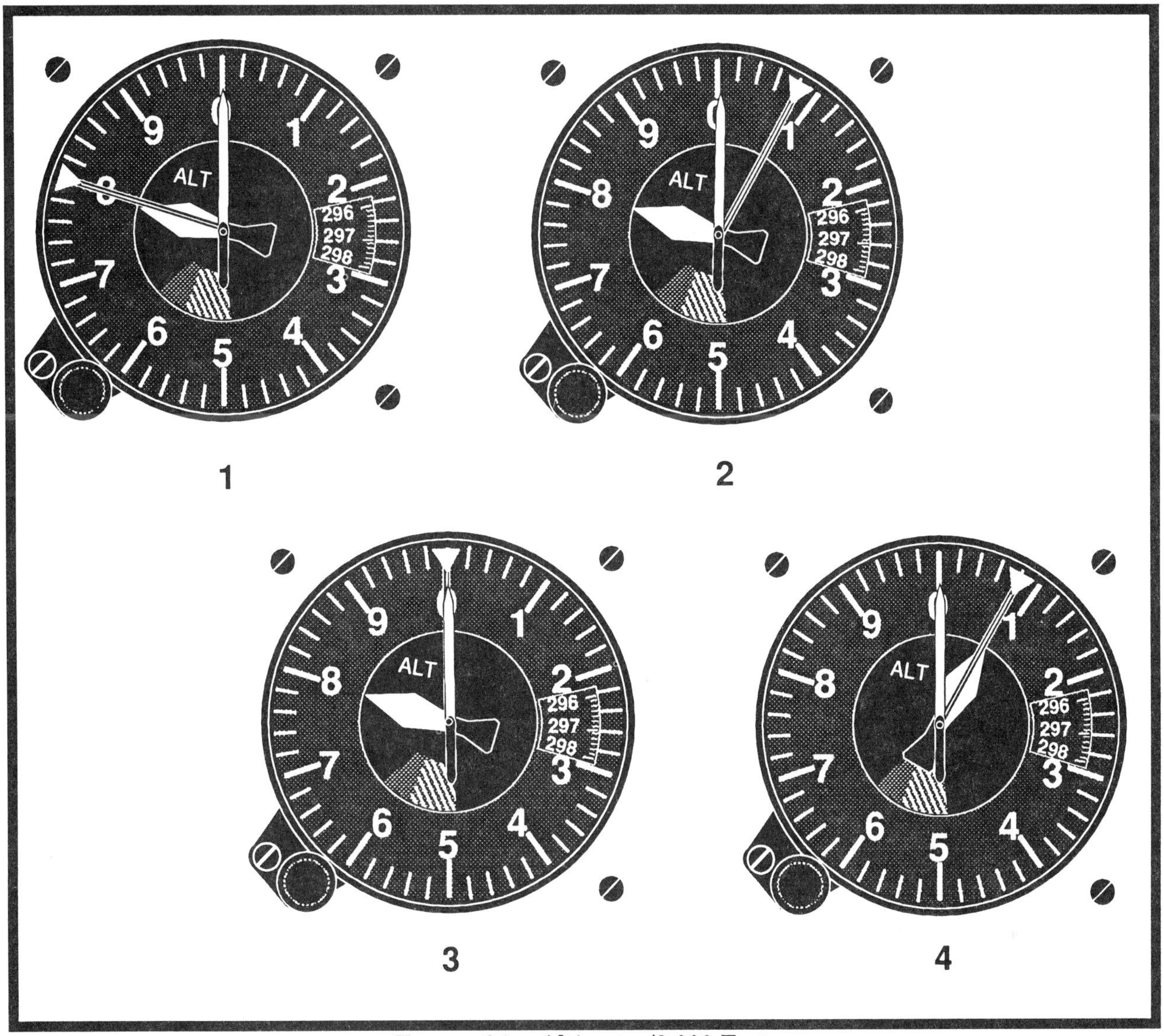

Appendix 3

FIGURE 84.—Altimeter/8,000 Feet.

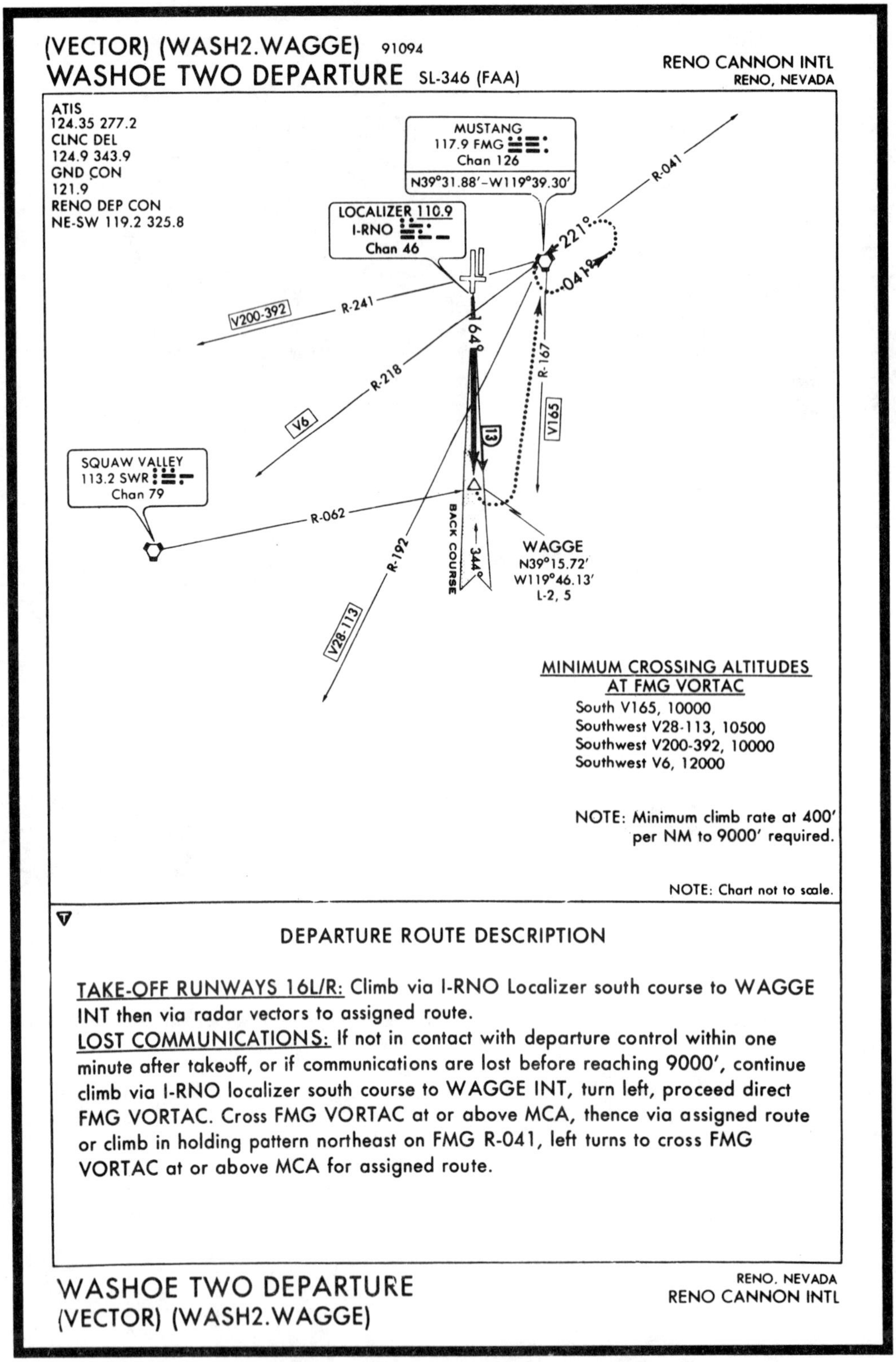

(VECTOR) (WASH2.WAGGE) 91094
WASHOE TWO DEPARTURE SL-346 (FAA)
RENO CANNON INTL
RENO, NEVADA
ATIS 124.35 277.2
CLNC DEL 124.9 343.9
GND CON 121.9
RENO DEP CON NE-SW 119.2 325.8
MUSTANG 117.9 FMG Chan 126
N39°31.88'-W119°39.30'
LOCALIZER 110.9 I-RNO Chan 46
221°
041°
R-041
R-241
V200-392
164°
R-218
V6
R-167
V165
13
SQUAW VALLEY 113.2 SWR Chan 79
R-062
BACK COURSE
344°
WAGGE
N39°15.72'
W119°46.13'
L-2, 5
R-192
V28-113
MINIMUM CROSSING ALTITUDES
AT FMG VORTAC
South V165, 10000
Southwest V28-113, 10500
Southwest V200-392, 10000
Southwest V6, 12000
NOTE: Minimum climb rate at 400' per NM to 9000' required.
NOTE: Chart not to scale.
DEPARTURE ROUTE DESCRIPTION
TAKE-OFF RUNWAYS 16L/R: Climb via I-RNO Localizer south course to WAGGE INT then via radar vectors to assigned route.
LOST COMMUNICATIONS: If not in contact with departure control within one minute after takeoff, or if communications are lost before reaching 9000', continue climb via I-RNO localizer south course to WAGGE INT, turn left, proceed direct FMG VORTAC. Cross FMG VORTAC at or above MCA, thence via assigned route or climb in holding pattern northeast on FMG R-041, left turns to cross FMG VORTAC at or above MCA for assigned route.
WASHOE TWO DEPARTURE
(VECTOR) (WASH2.WAGGE)
RENO, NEVADA
RENO CANNON INTL

FIGURE 85.—WASHOE TWO DEPARTURE.

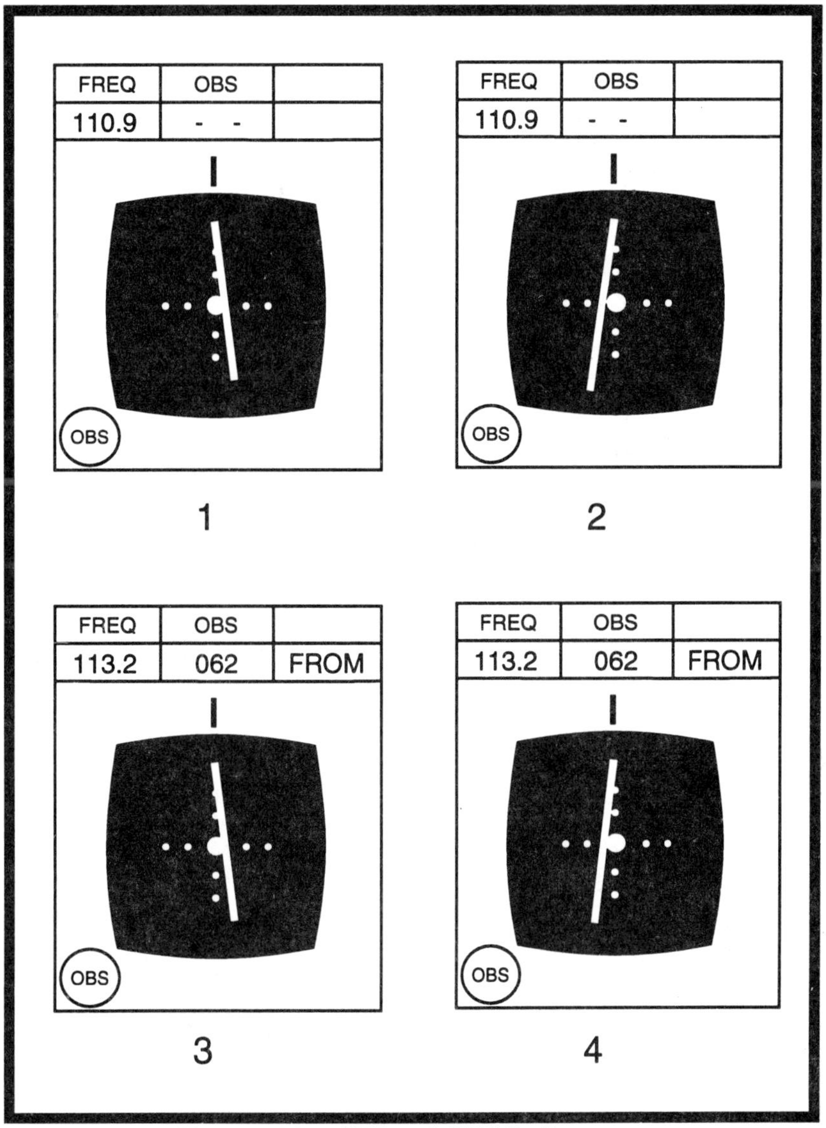

Appendix 3

FIGURE 86.—CDI and OBS Indicators.

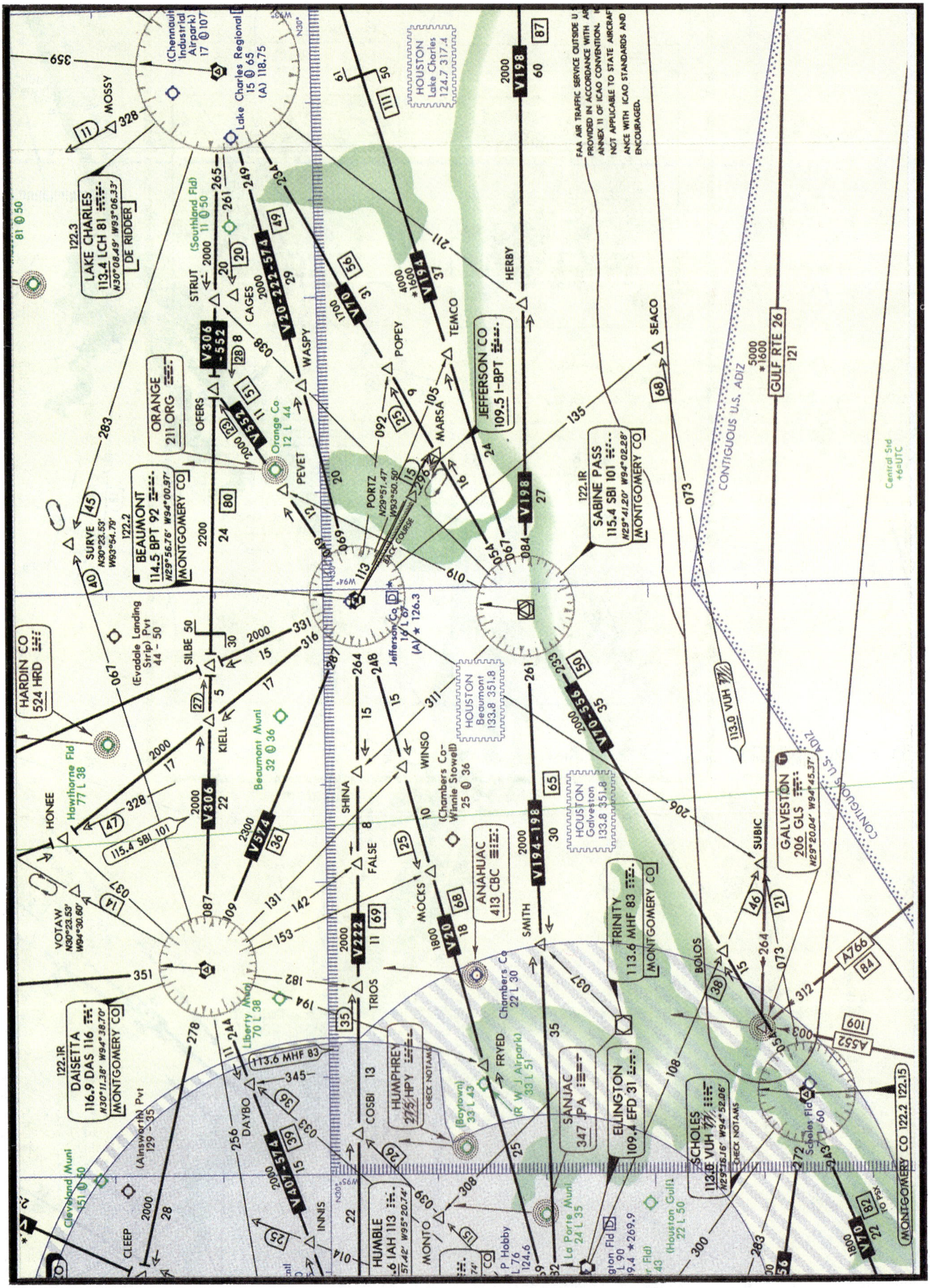

Appendix 3

FIGURE 87.—En Route Chart Segment.

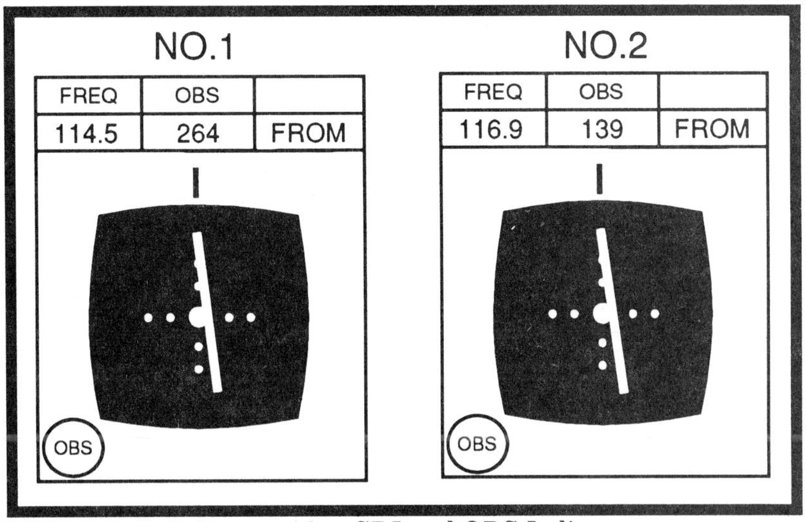

Appendix 3

FIGURE 88.—CDI and OBS Indicators.

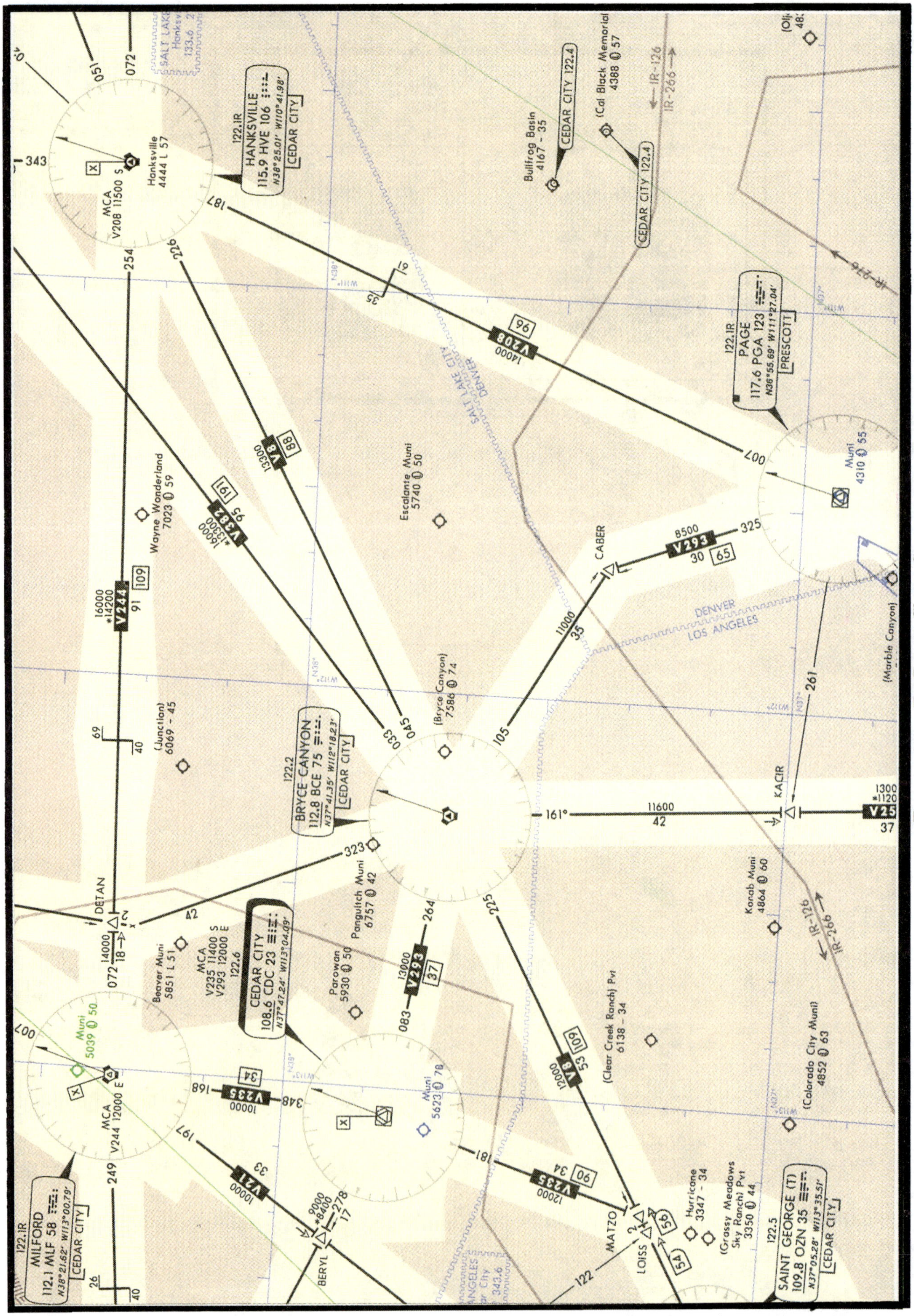

Appendix 3

FIGURE 89.—En Route Chart Segment.

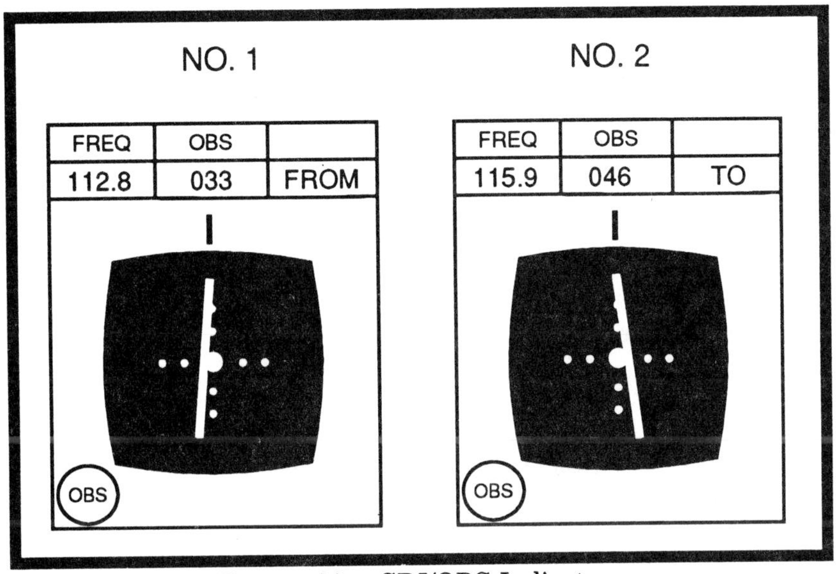

Appendix 3

FIGURE 90.—CDI/OBS Indicators.

111

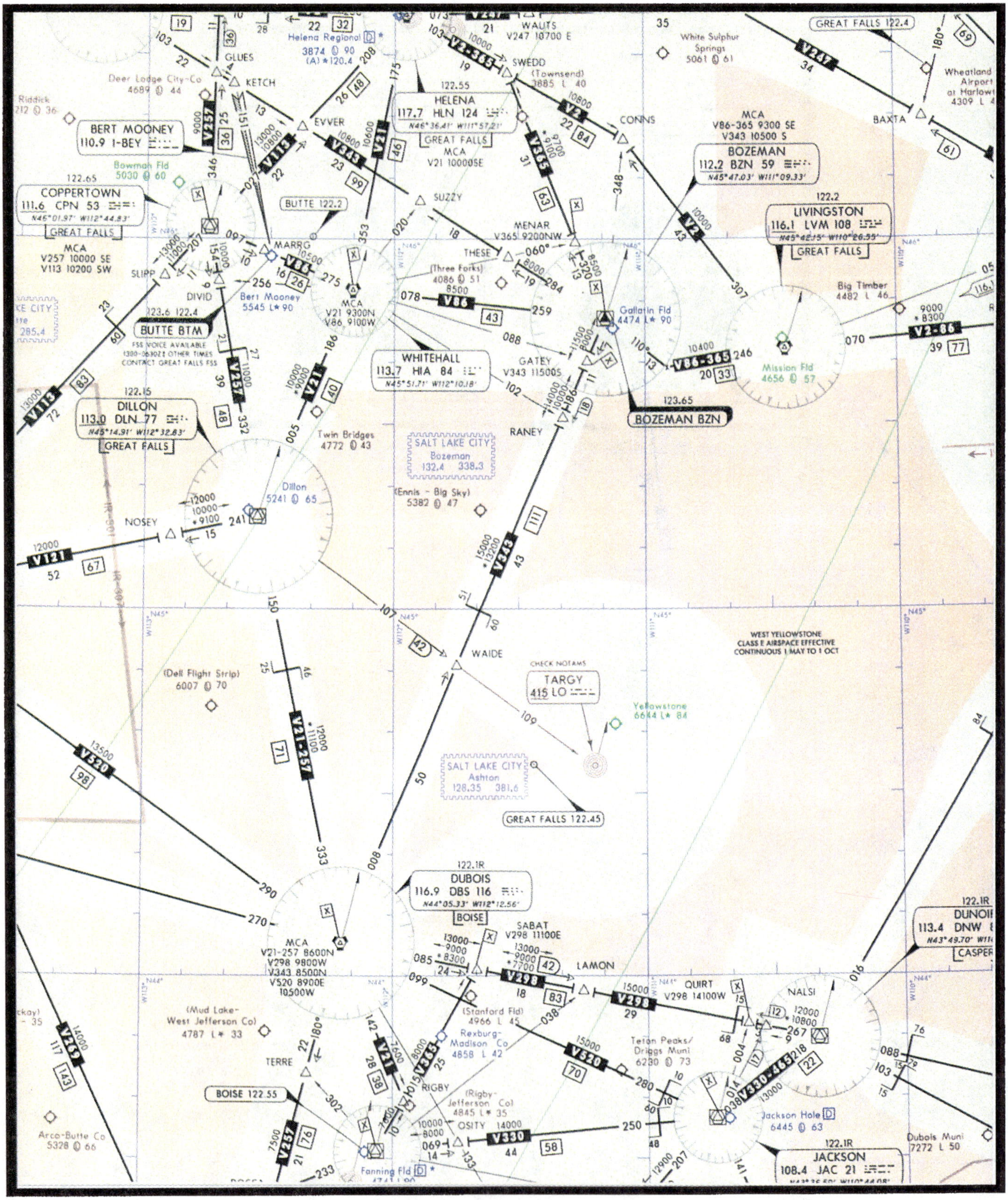

Appendix 3

FIGURE 91.—En Route Chart Segment.

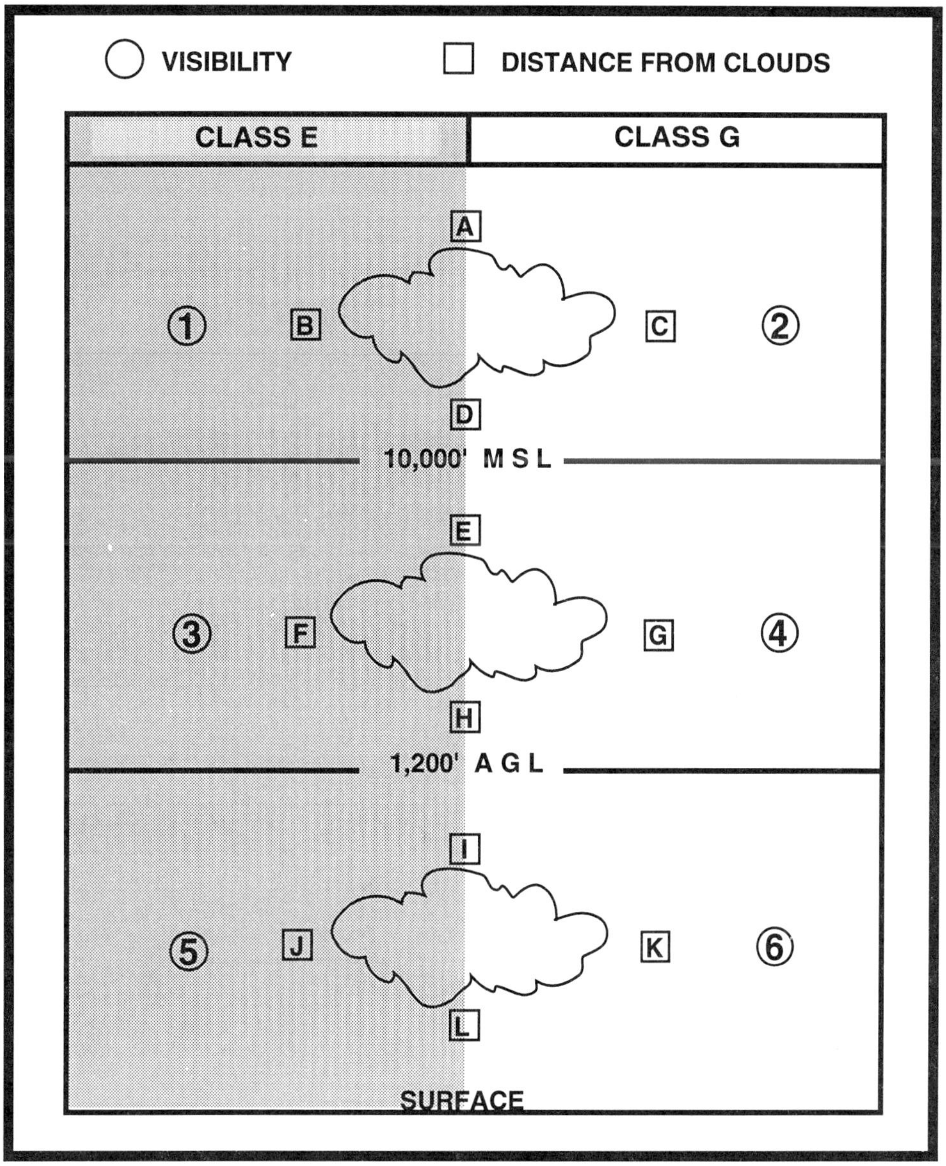

Appendix 3
Change 1

FIGURE 92.—Minimum In-Flight Visibility and Distance from Clouds.

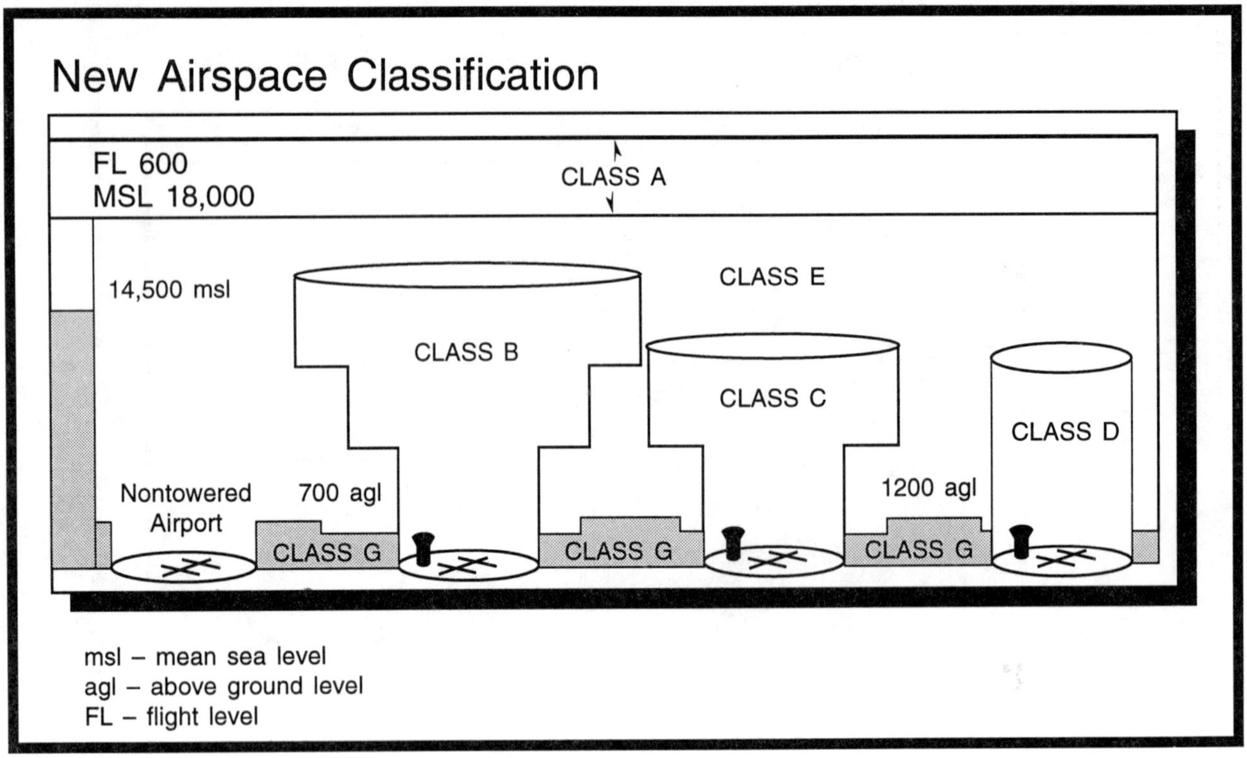

Appendix 3

FIGURE 93.—New Airspace Classification.

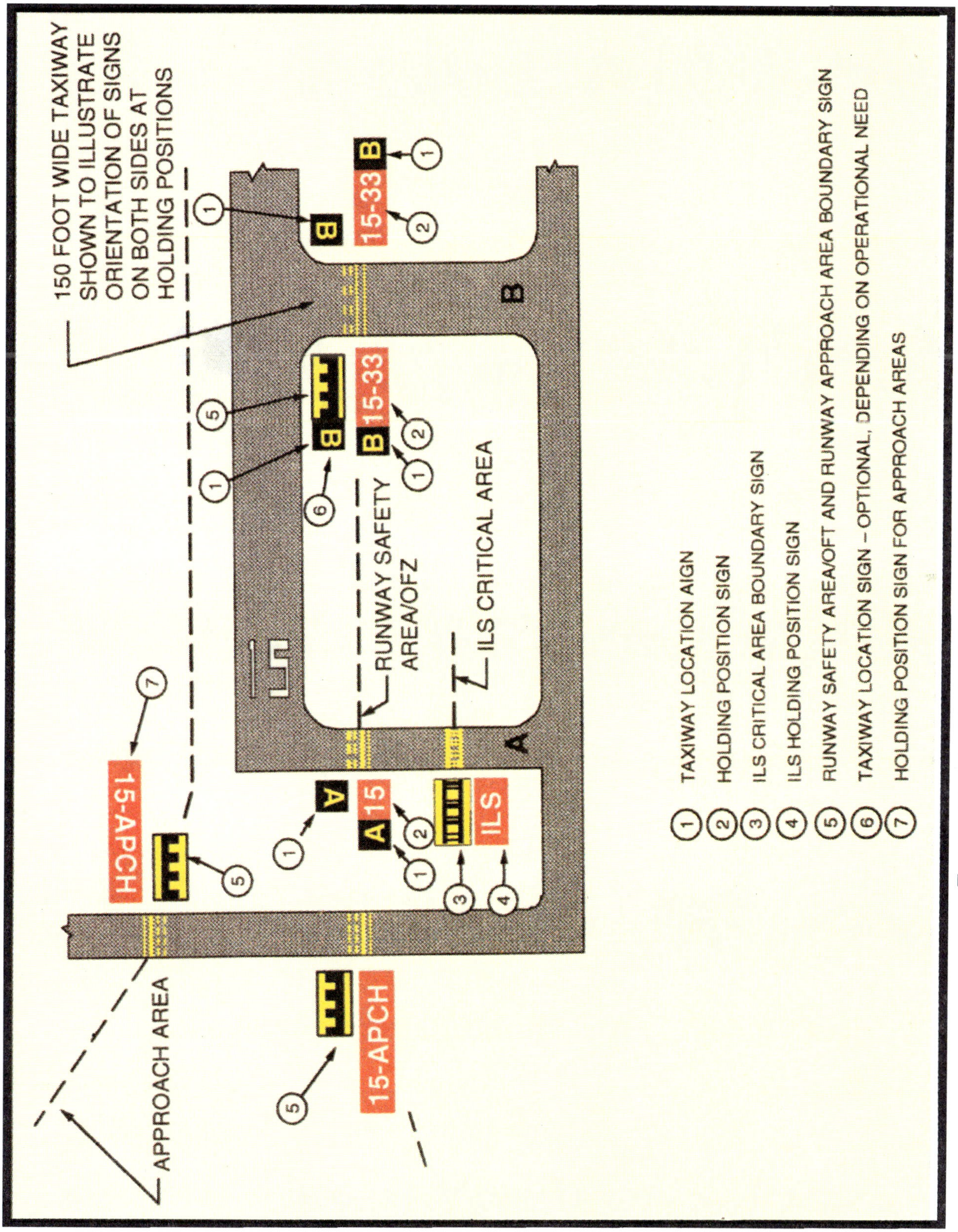

Appendix 3

FIGURE 94.—Application Examples for Holding Positions.

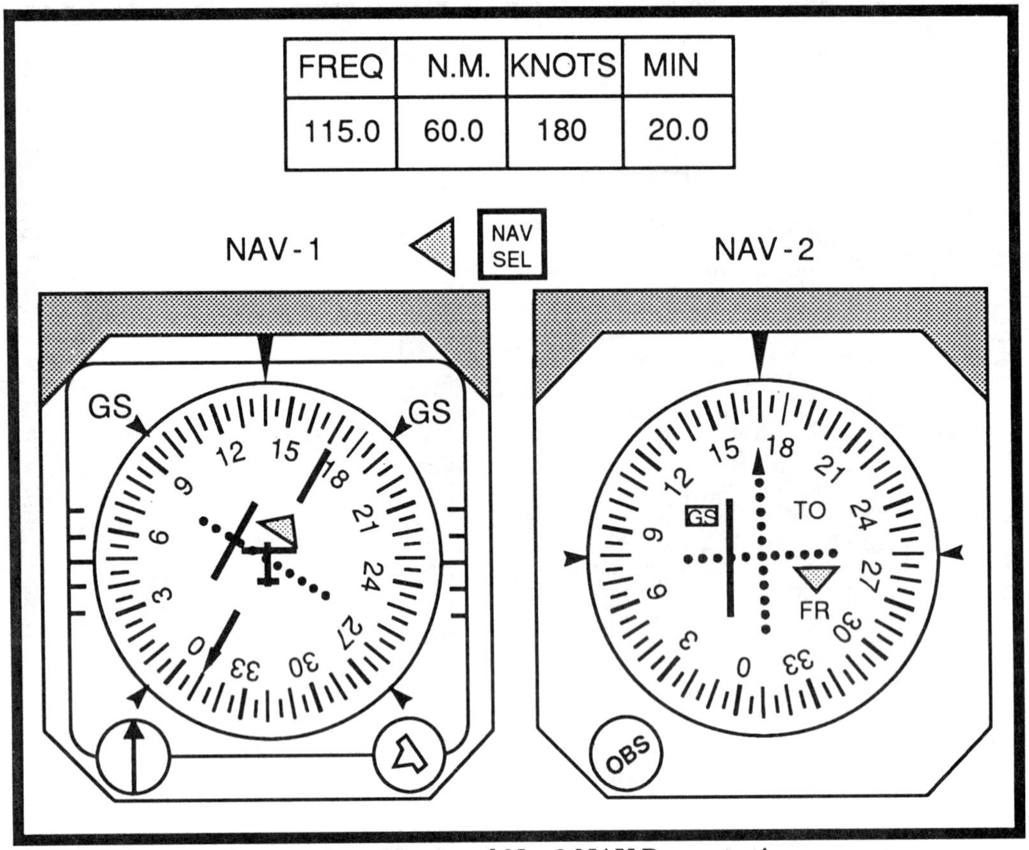

Appendix 3

FREQ	N.M.	KNOTS	MIN
115.0	60.0	180	20.0

NAV-1   NAV-2

FIGURE 95.—No. 1 and No. 2 NAV Presentation.

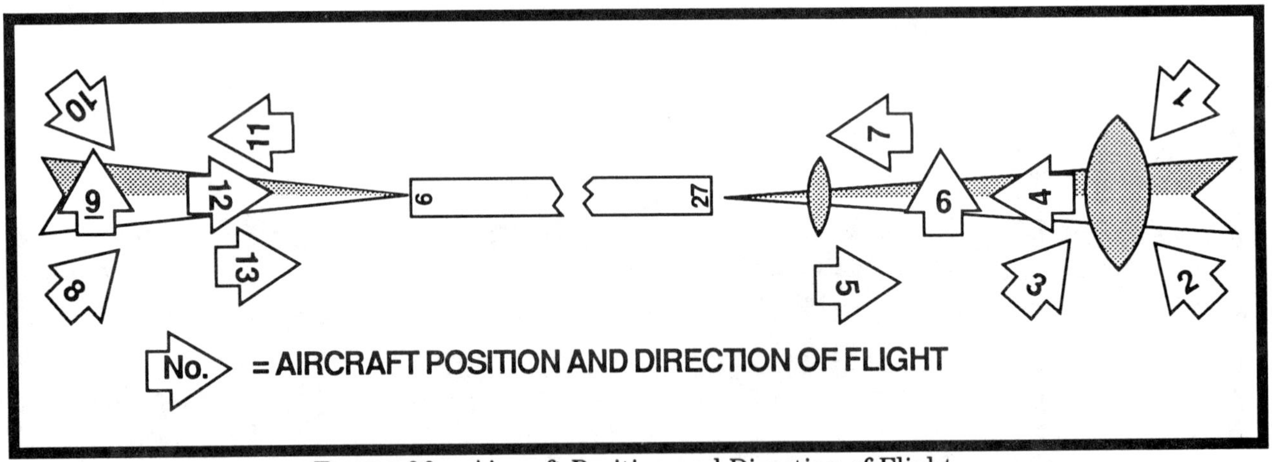

No.▷ = AIRCRAFT POSITION AND DIRECTION OF FLIGHT

FIGURE 96.—Aircraft Position and Direction of Flight.

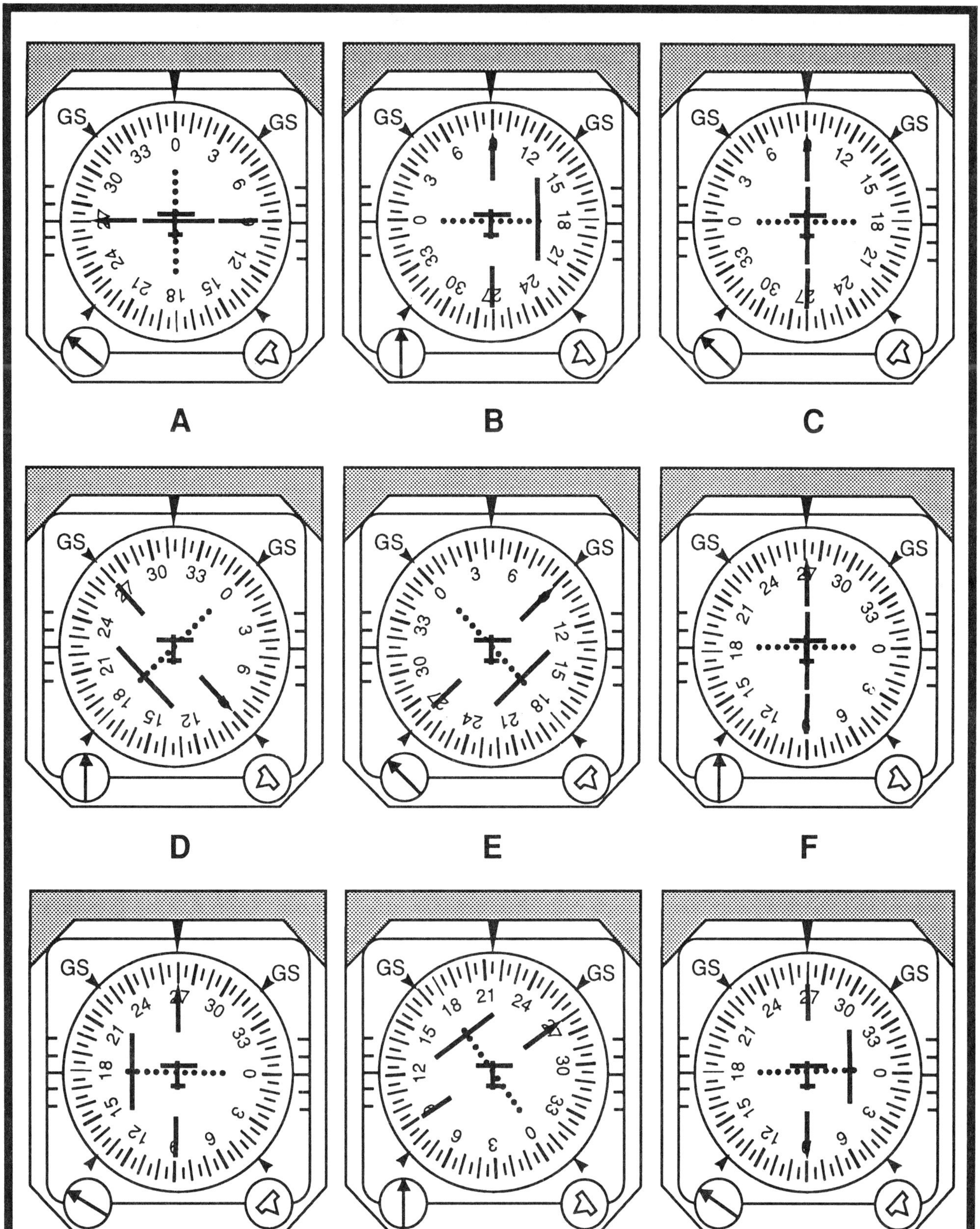

Appendix 3

FIGURE 97.—HSI Presentation.

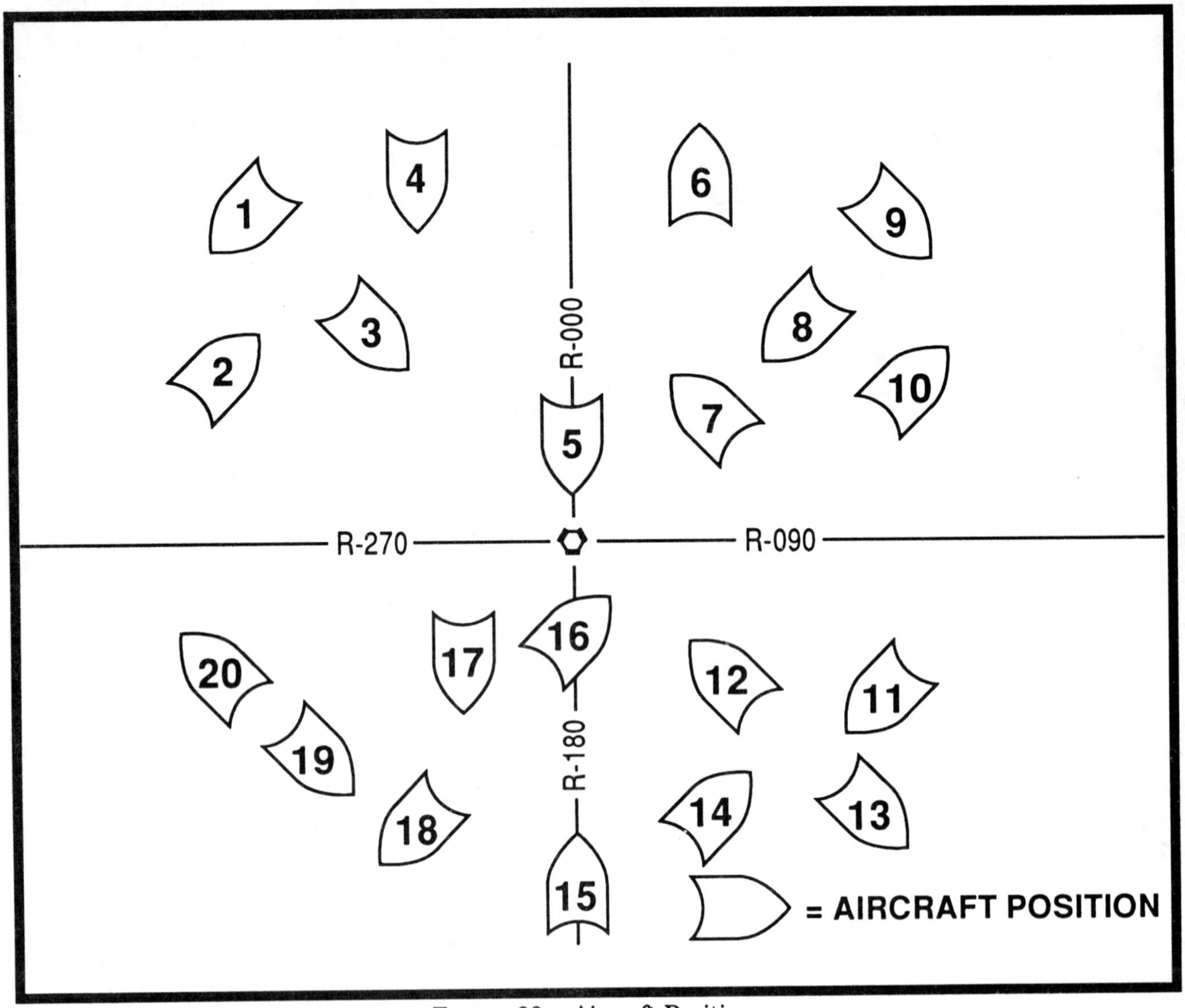

Appendix 3

FIGURE 98.—Aircraft Position.

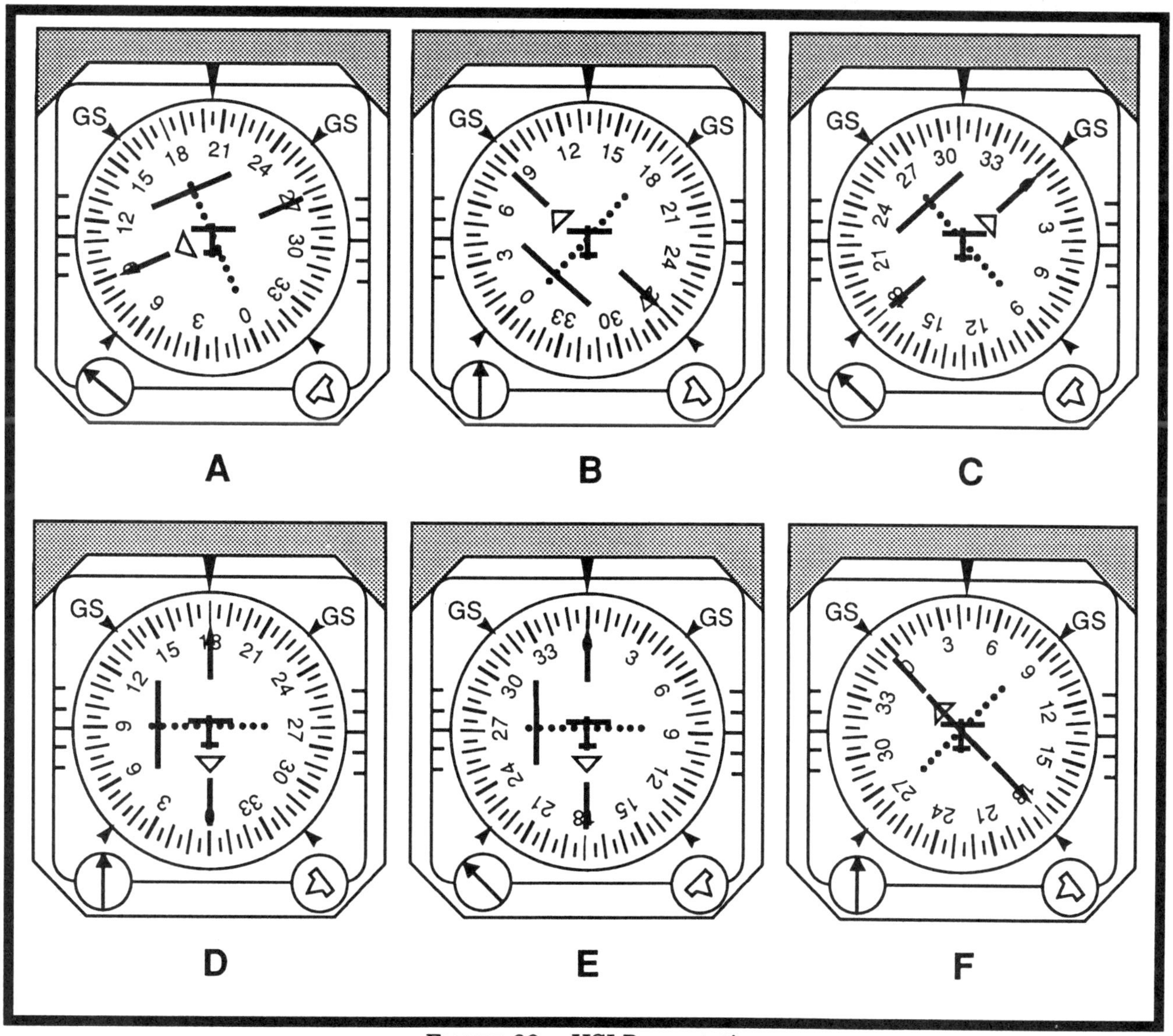

Appendix 3

FIGURE 99.—HSI Presentation.

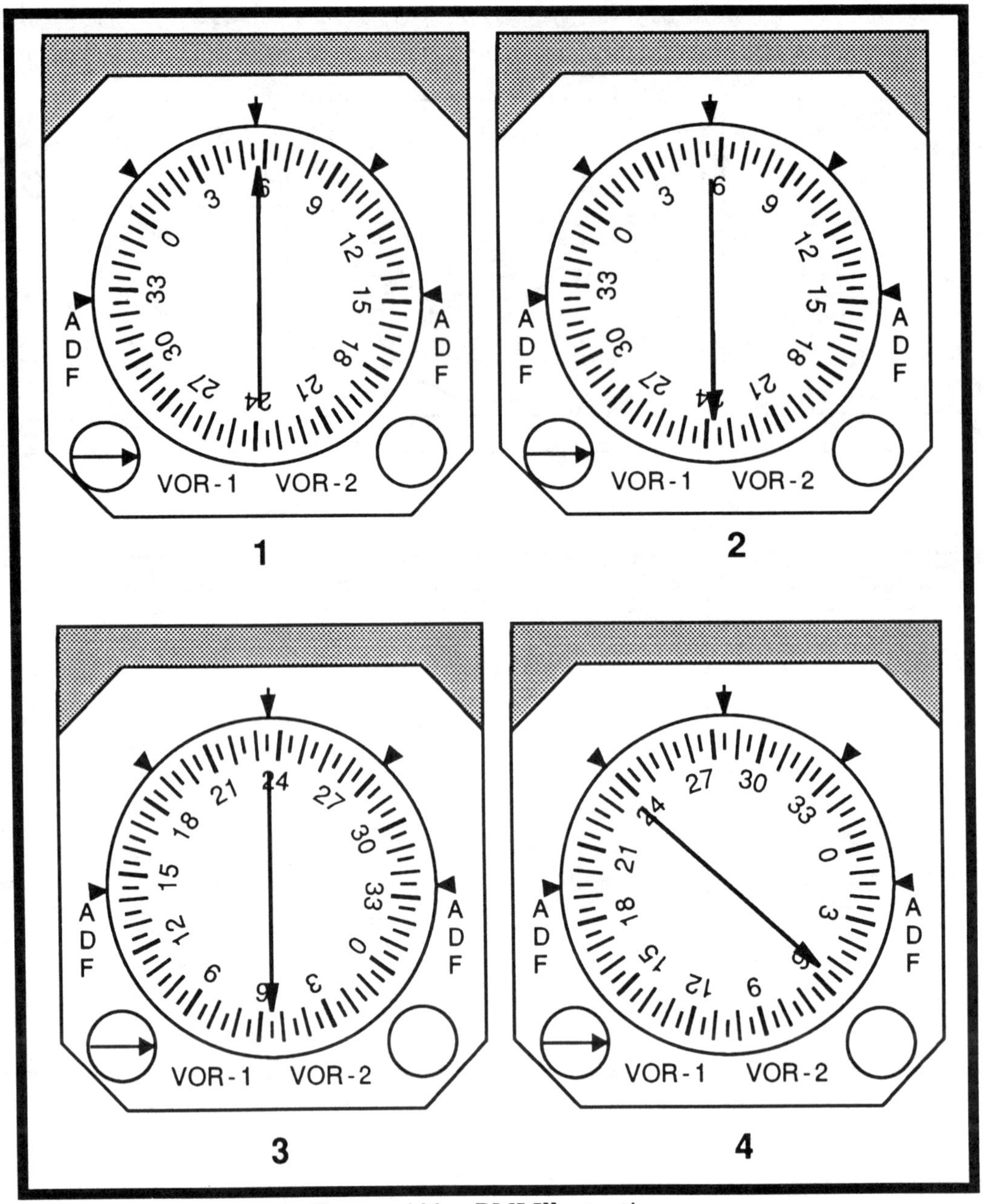

Appendix 3

FIGURE 100.—RMI Illustrations.

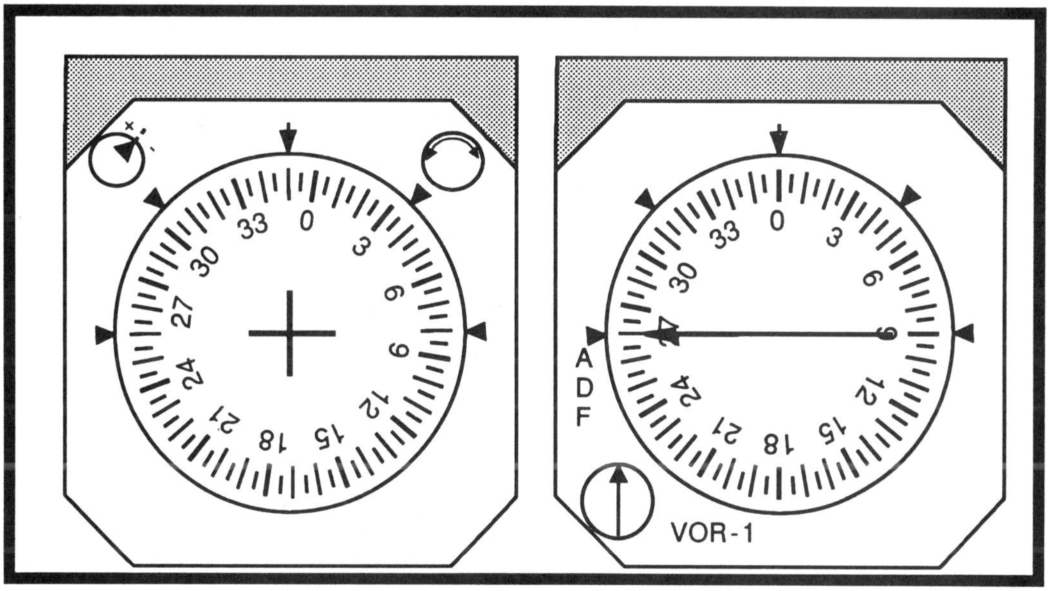

Appendix 3

FIGURE 101.—Directional Gyro and ADF Indicator.

FIGURE 102.—Directional Gyro and ADF Indicator.

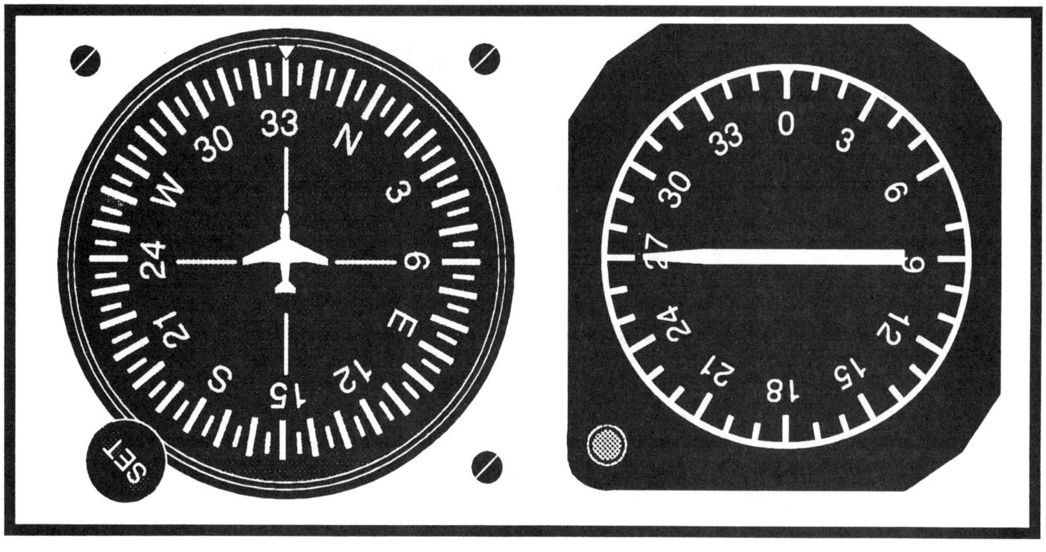

FIGURE 103.—Directional Gyro and ADF Indicator.

121

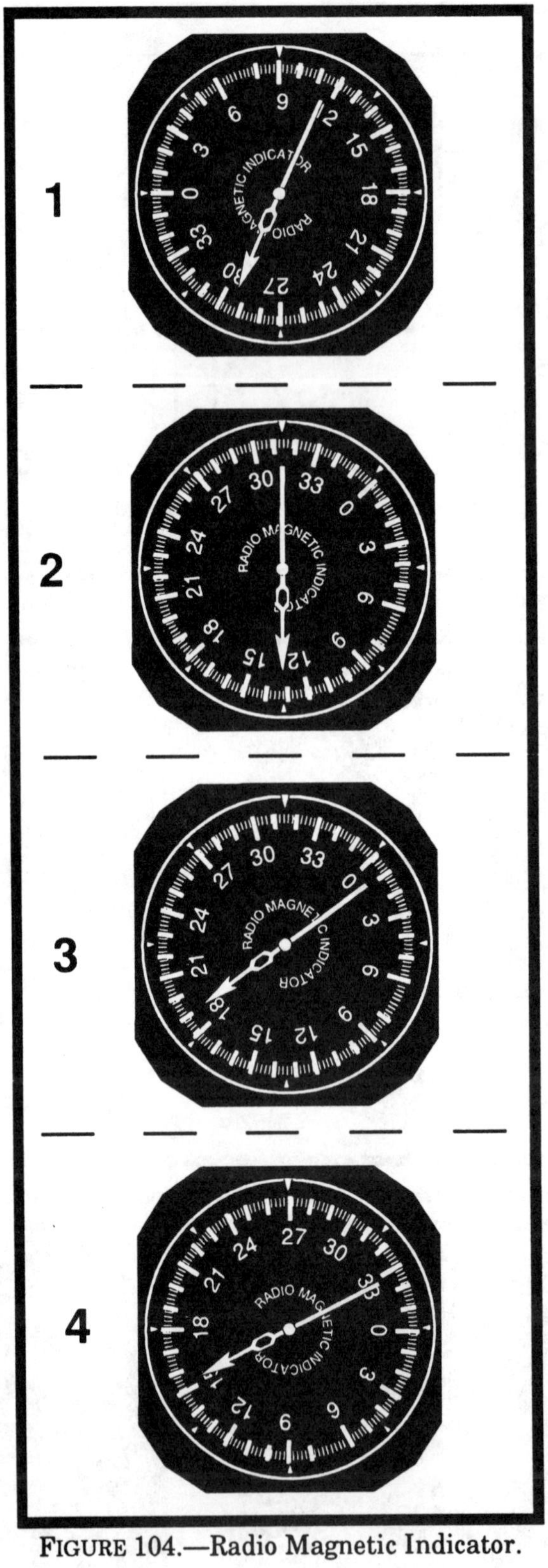

Appendix 3

FIGURE 104.—Radio Magnetic Indicator.

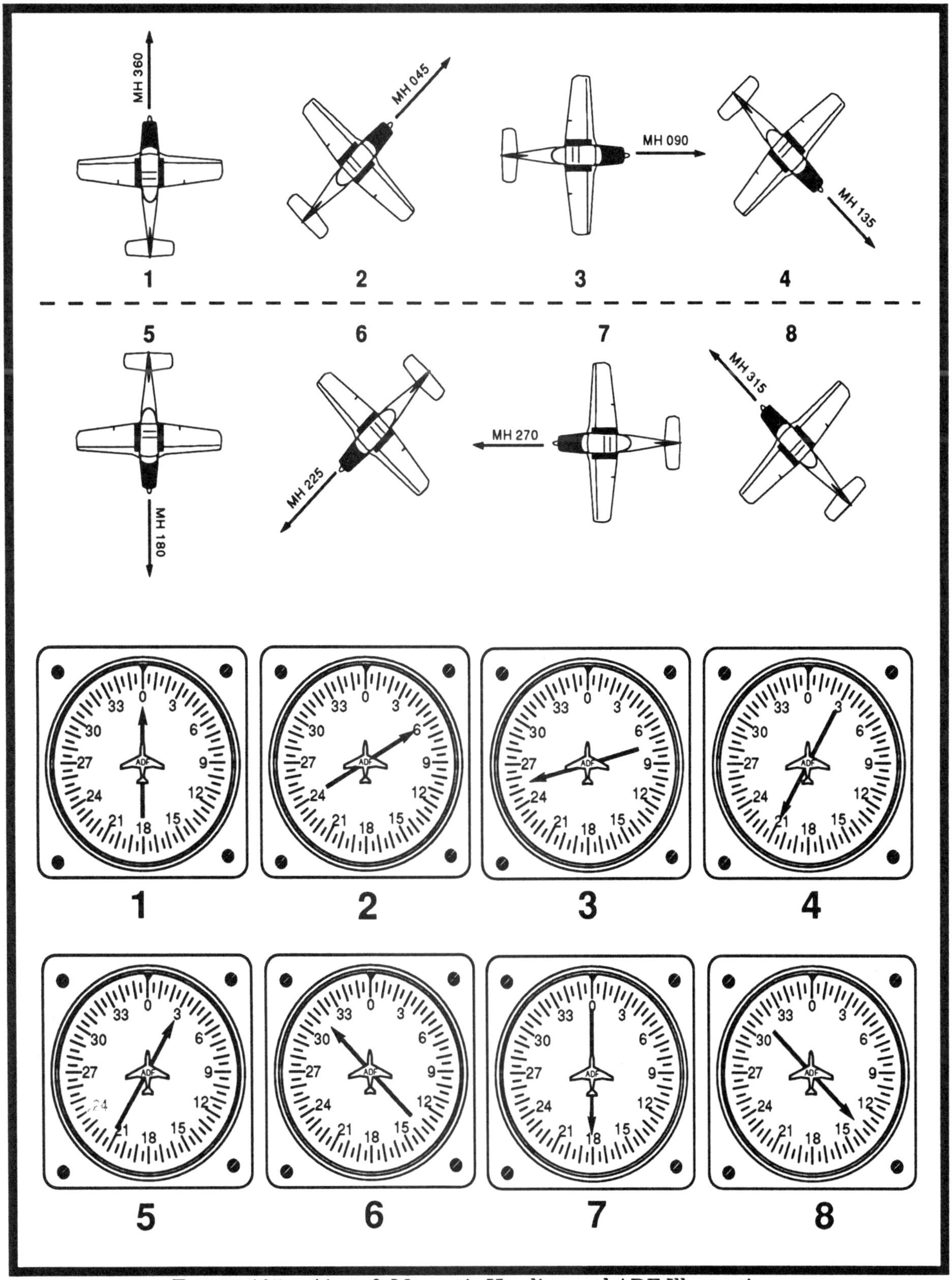

Appendix 3

FIGURE 105.—Aircraft Magnetic Heading and ADF Illustration.

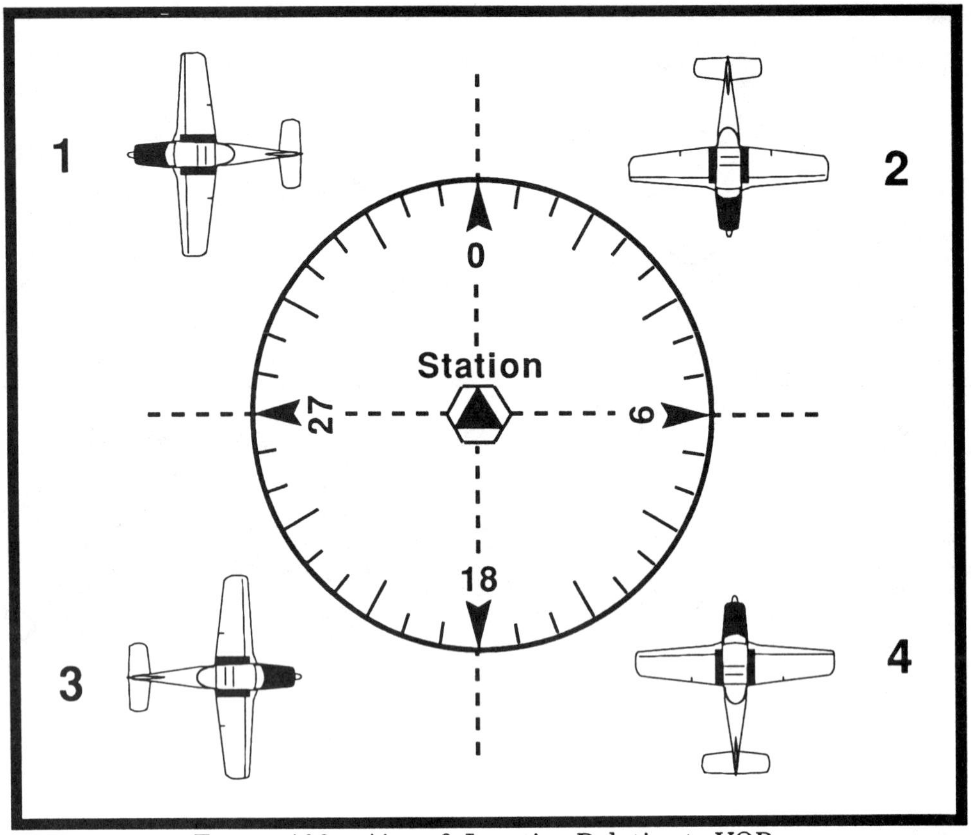

Appendix 3

FIGURE 106.—Aircraft Location Relative to VOR.

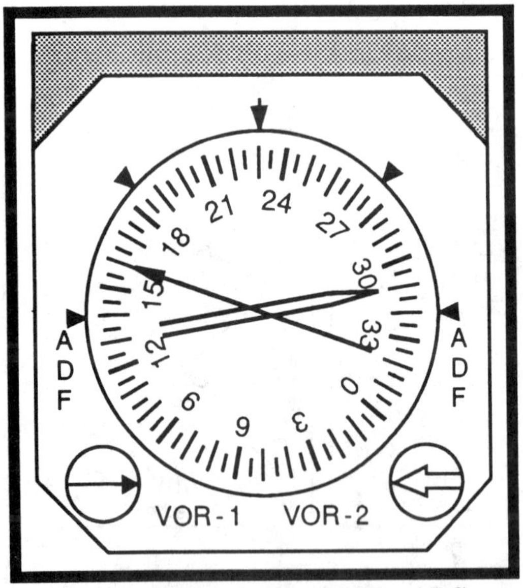

FIGURE 107.—RMI—DME—ARC Illustration Wind Component.

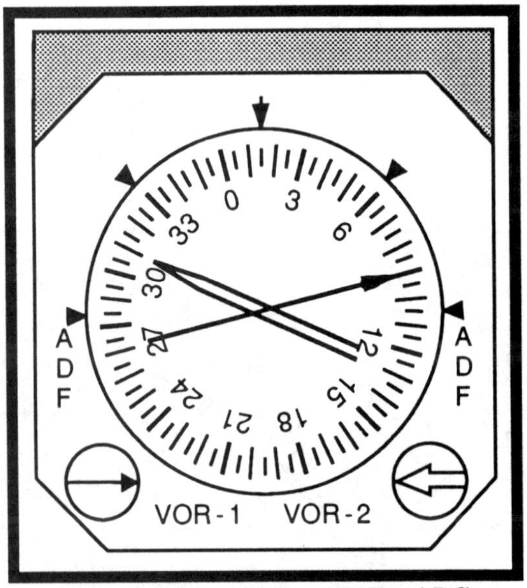

FIGURE 108.—RMI—DME—ARC Illustration Wind Component.

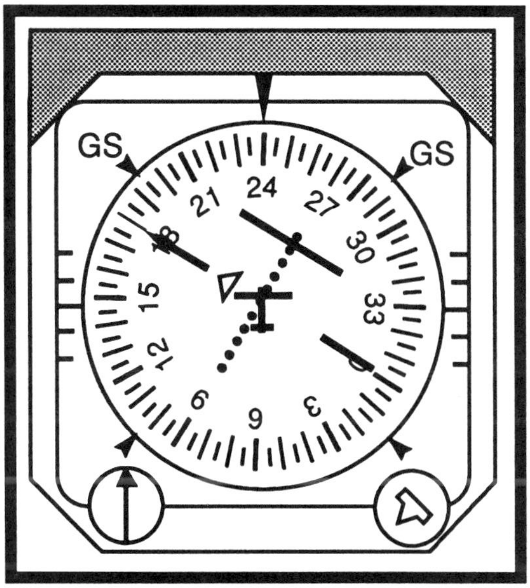

Appendix 3

FIGURE 109.—CDI Direction from VORTAC.

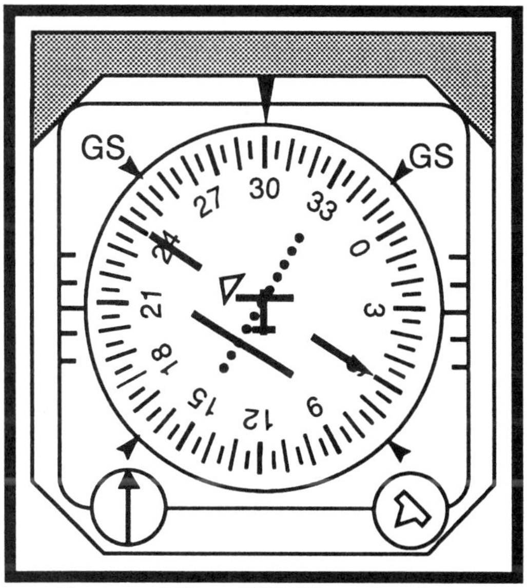

FIGURE 110.—CDI Direction from VORTAC.

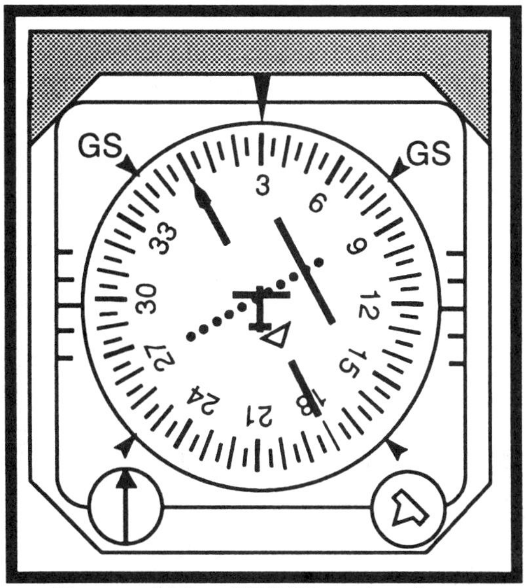

FIGURE 111.—CDI Direction from VORTAC.

125

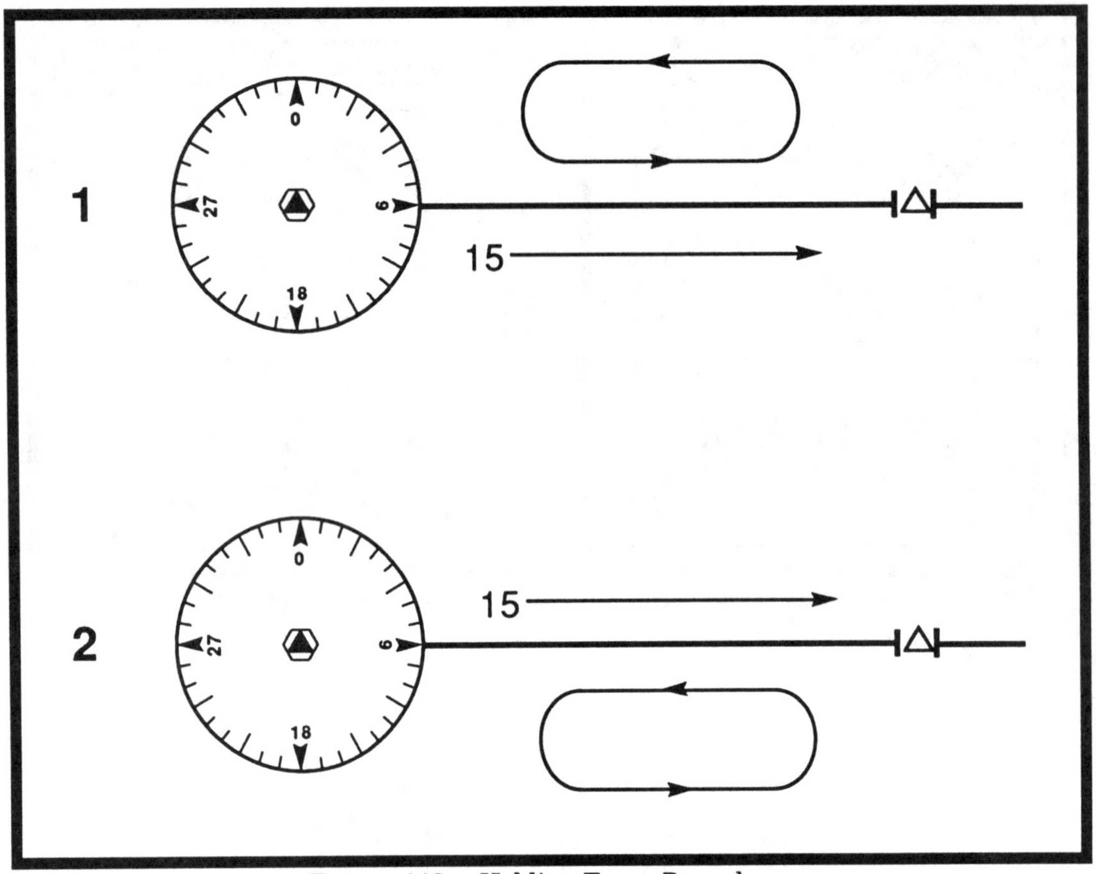

Appendix 3

FIGURE 112.—Holding Entry Procedure.

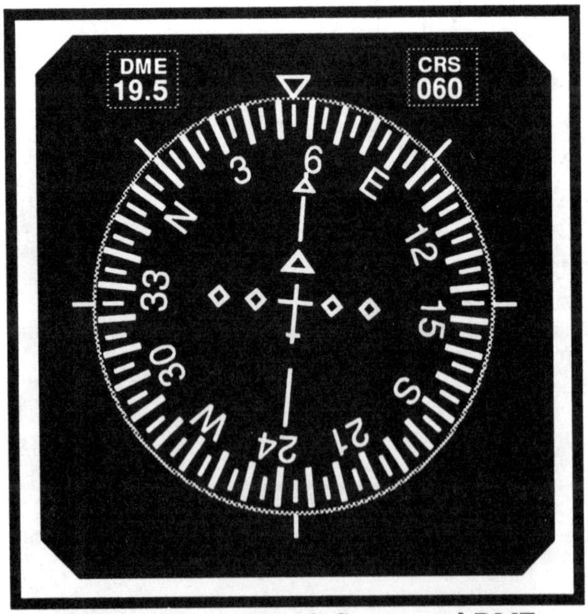

FIGURE 113.—Aircraft Course and DME Indicator.

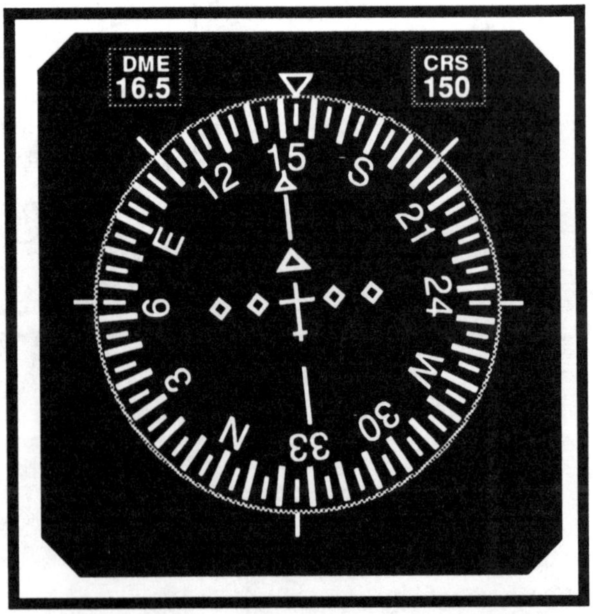

FIGURE 114.—Aircraft Course and DME Indicator.

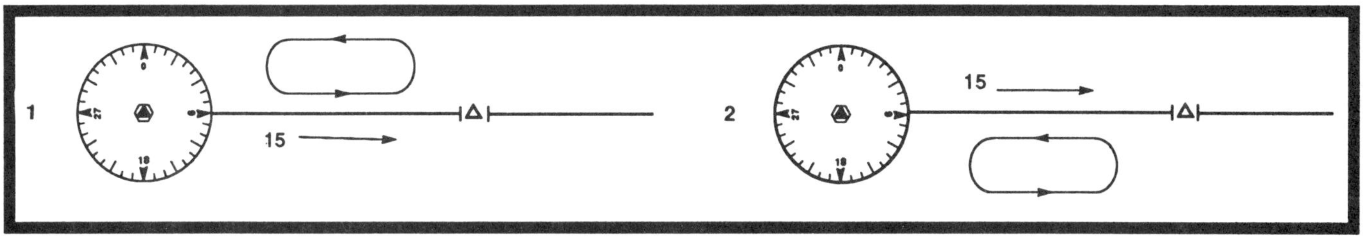

Appendix 3

FIGURE 115.—DME Fix with Holding Pattern.

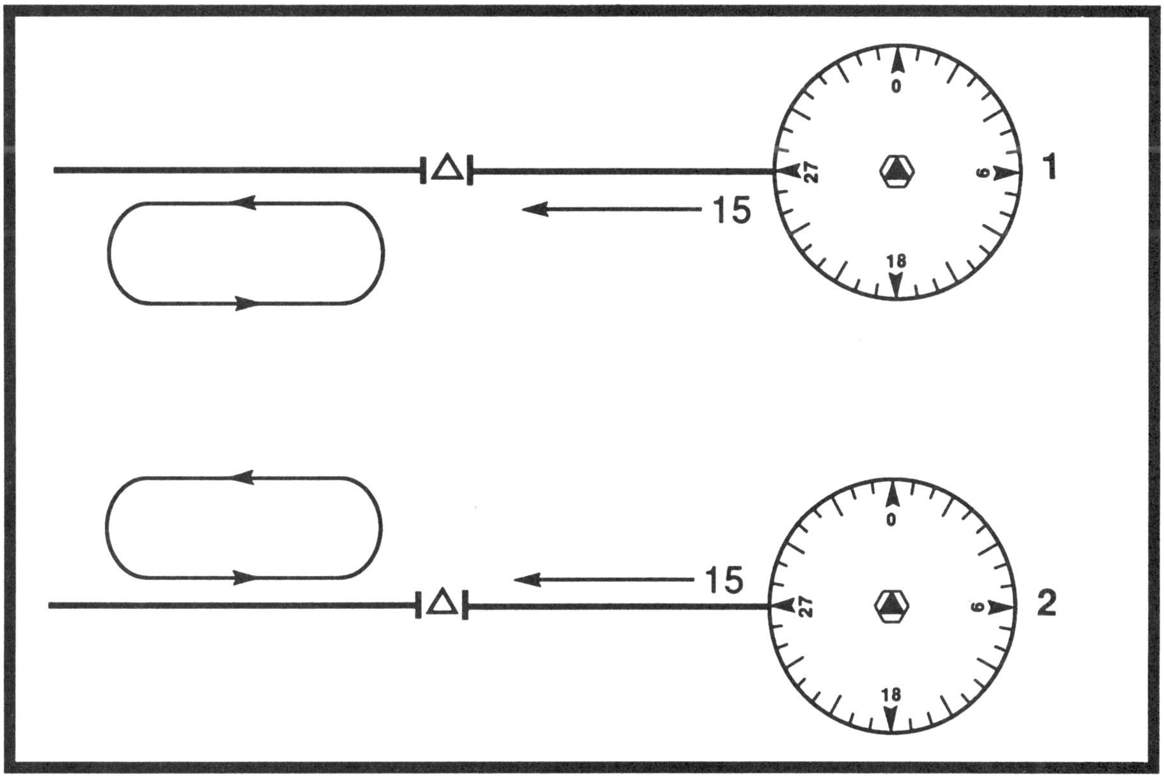

FIGURE 116.—Holding Entry Procedure.

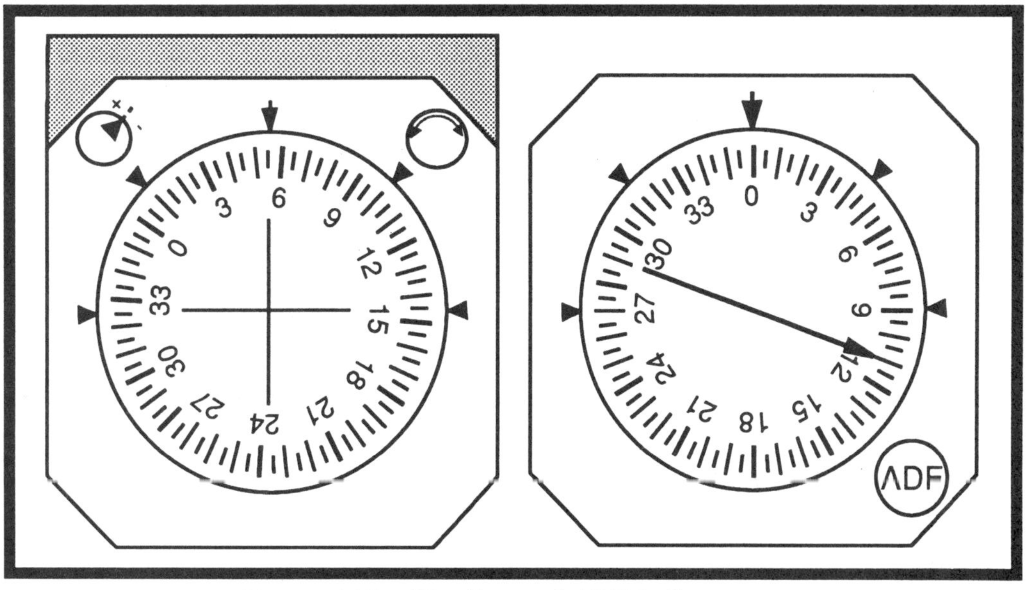

FIGURE 117.—Heading and ADF Indicators.

127

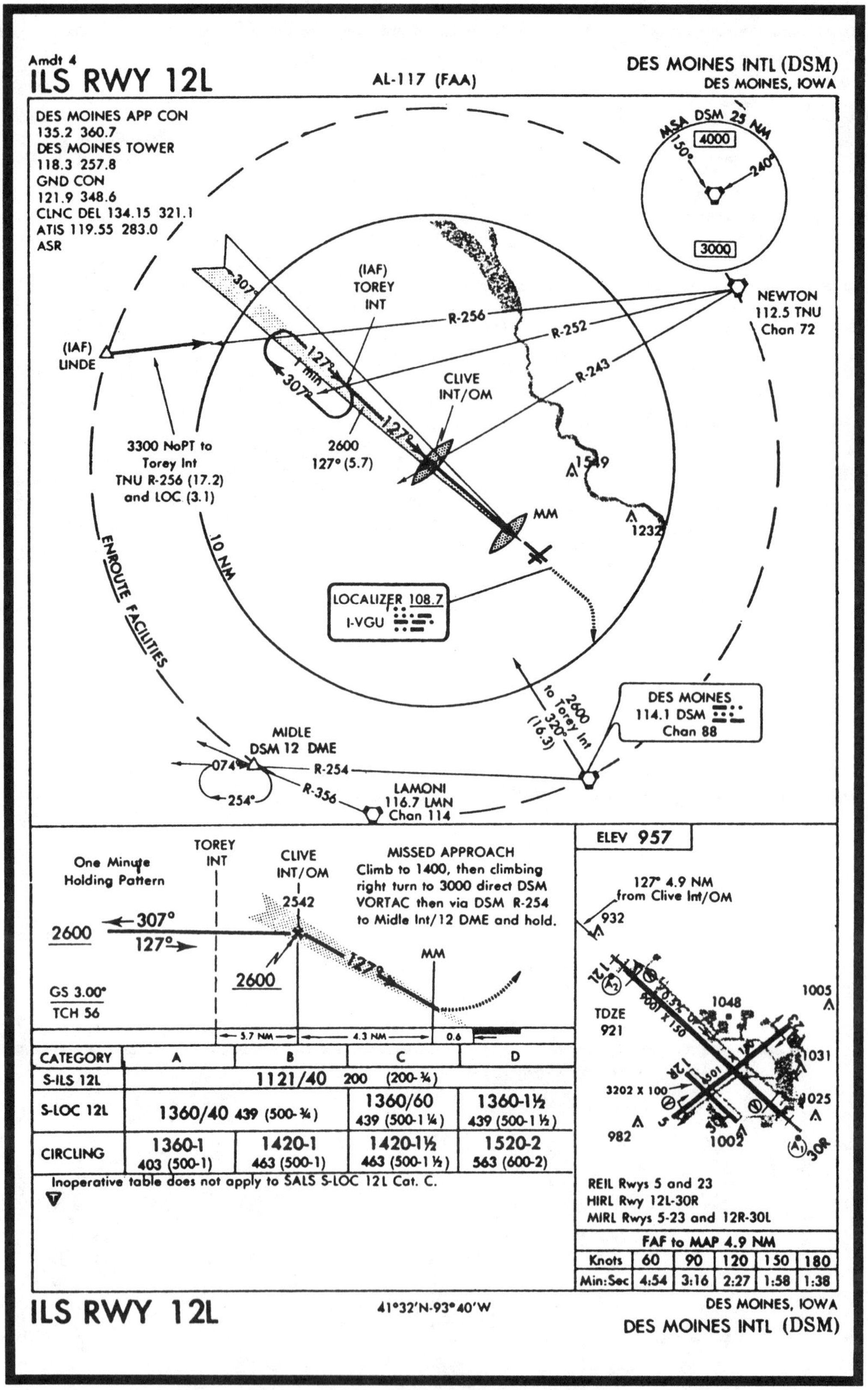

Appendix 3

FIGURE 118.—ILS RWY 12L (DSM).

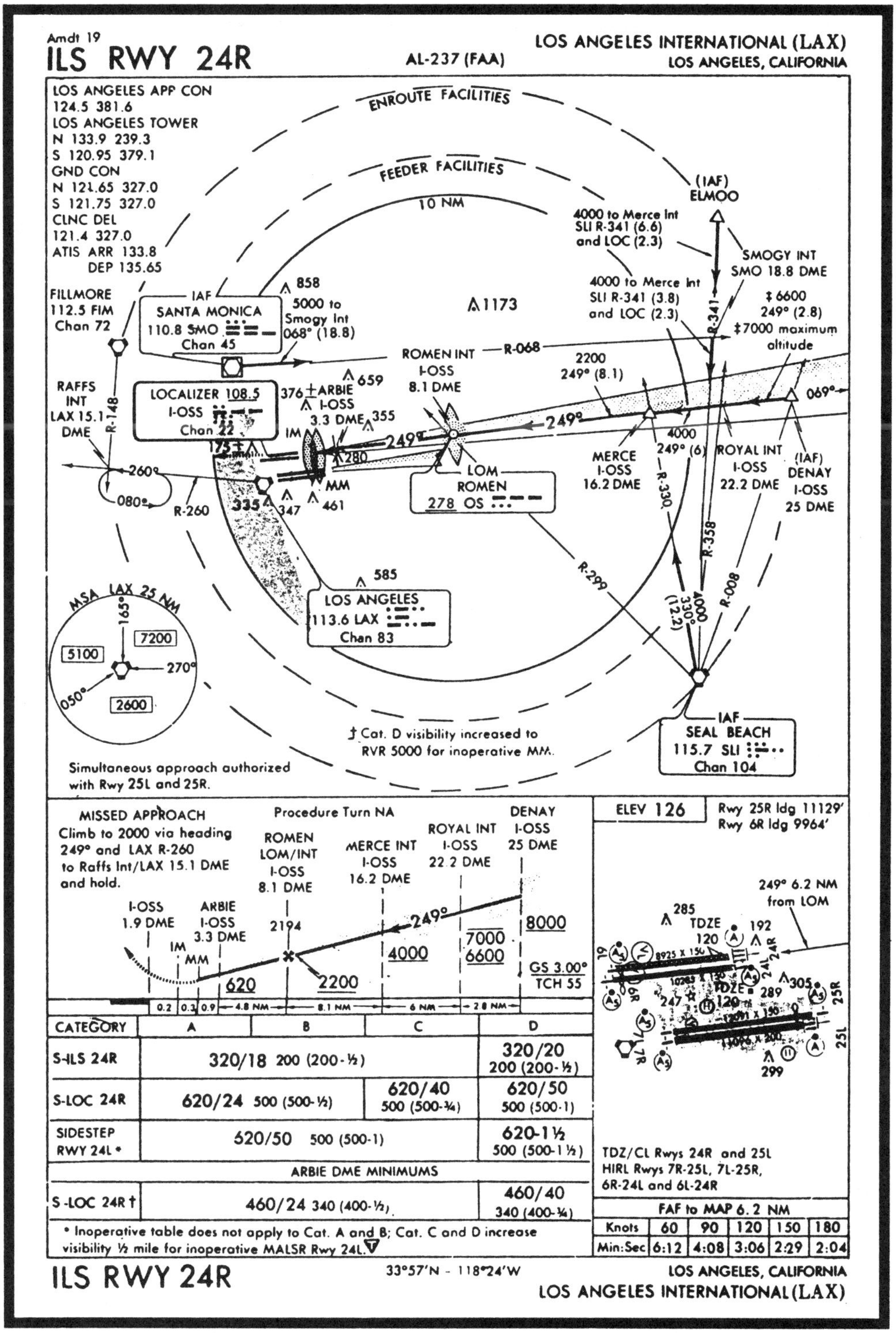

FIGURE 119.—ILS RWY 24R (LAX).

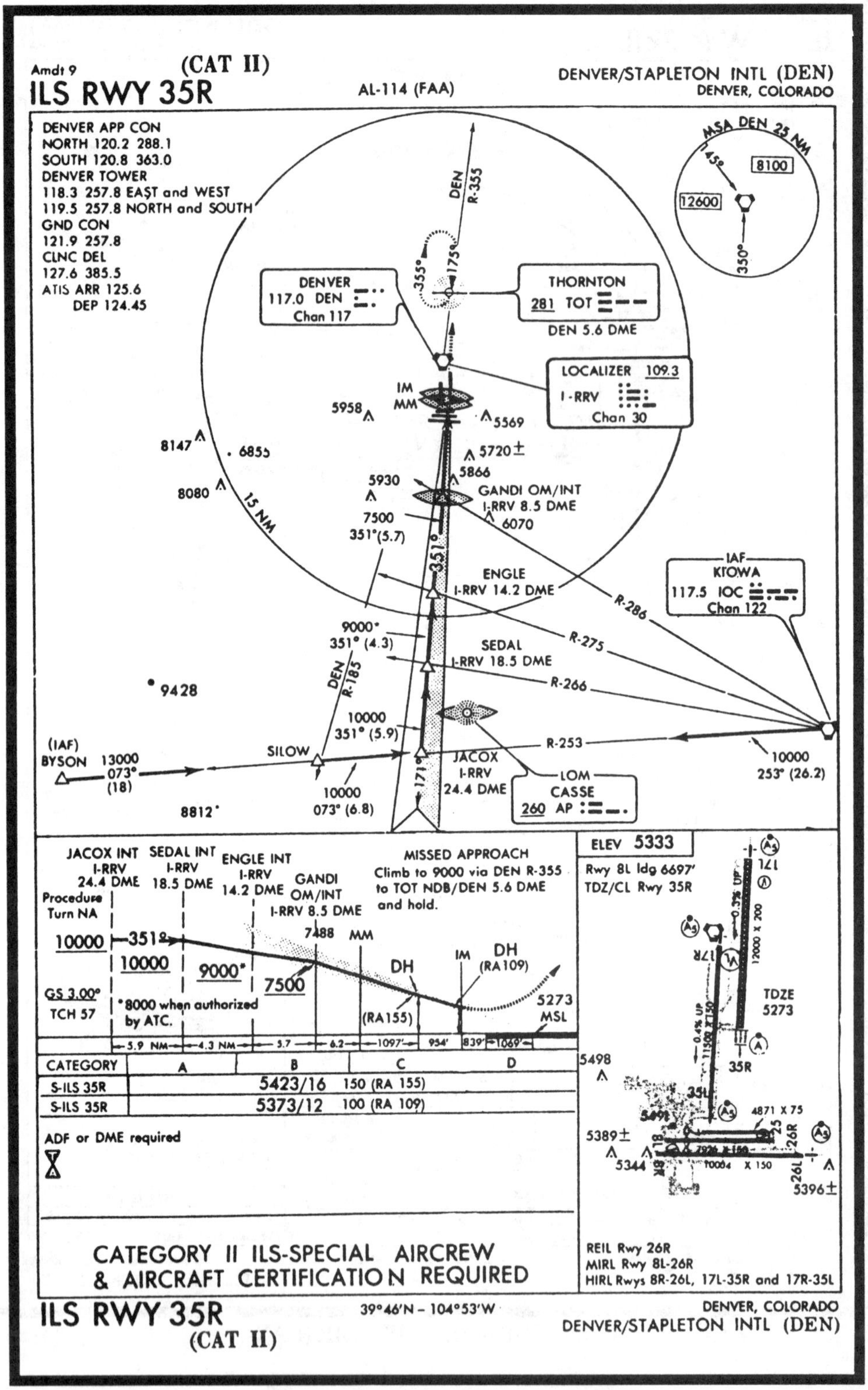

Appendix 3

FIGURE 120.—ILS RWY 35R (DEN).

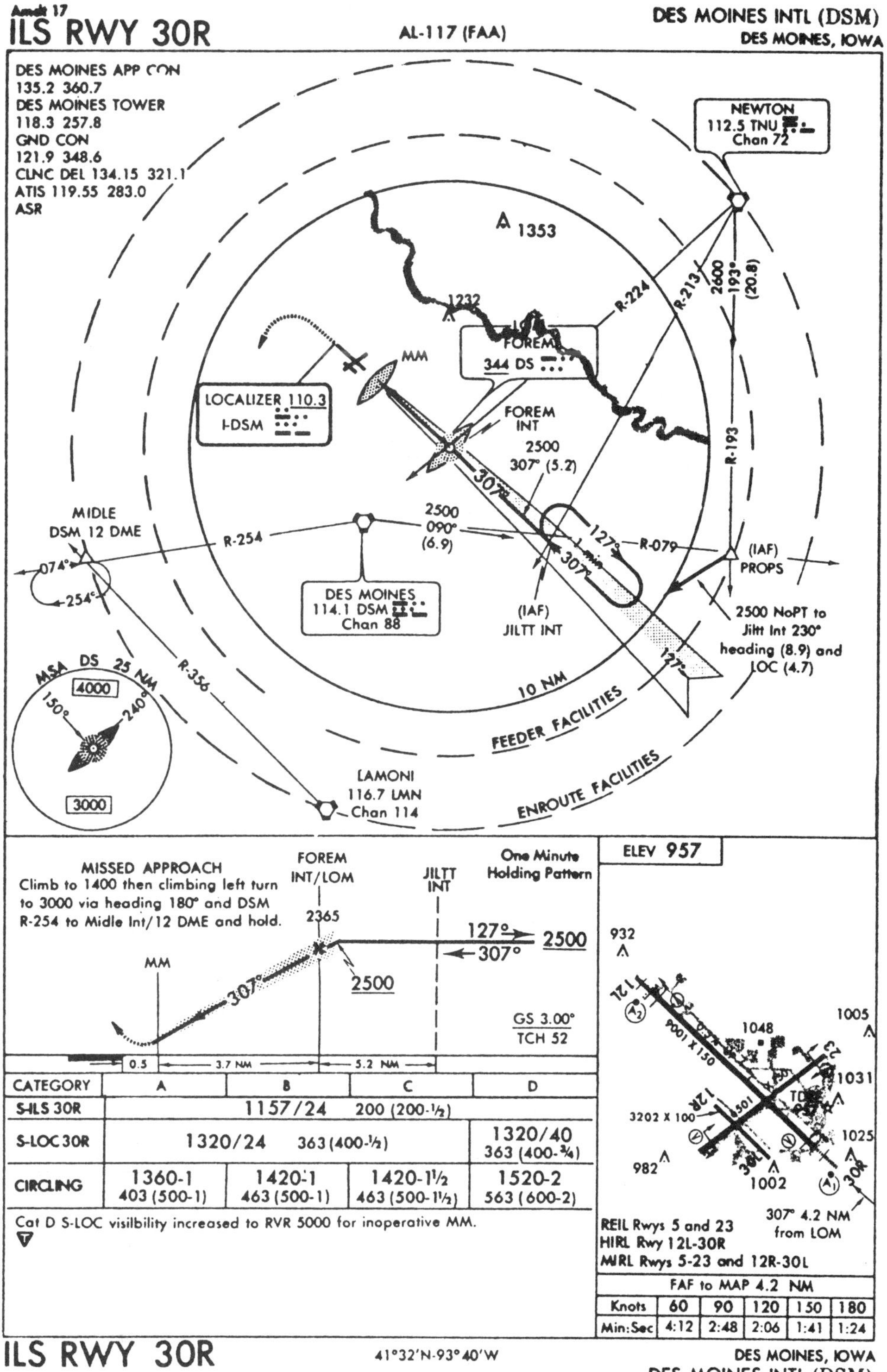

CATEGORY	A	B	C	D
S-ILS 30R	1157/24		200 (200-½)	
S-LOC 30R	1320/24	363 (400-½)		1320/40 363 (400-¾)
CIRCLING	1360-1 403 (500-1)	1420-1 463 (500-1)	1420-1½ 463 (500-1½)	1520-2 563 (600-2)

Cat D S-LOC visibility increased to RVR 5000 for inoperative MM.

FAF to MAP 4.2 NM					
Knots	60	90	120	150	180
Min:Sec	4:12	2:48	2:06	1:41	1:24

ILS RWY 30R

DES MOINES, IOWA
DES MOINES INTL (DSM)

FIGURE 121.—ILS RWY 30R (DSM).

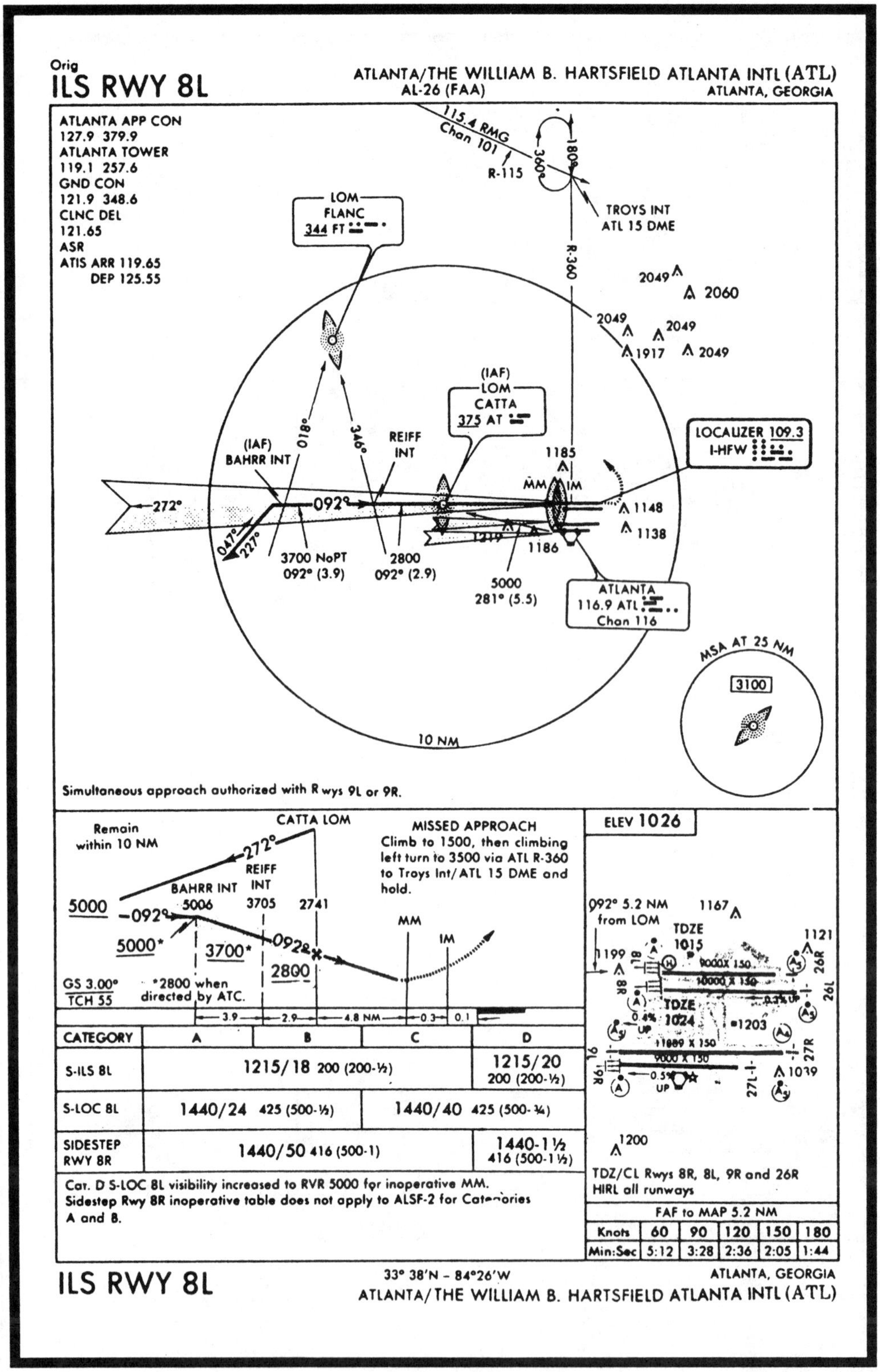

CATEGORY	A	B	C	D
S-ILS 8L	1215/18 200 (200-½)			1215/20 200 (200-½)
S-LOC 8L	1440/24 425 (500-½)		1440/40 425 (500-¾)	
SIDESTEP RWY 8R	1440/50 416 (500-1)			1440-1½ 416 (500-1½)

Cat. D S-LOC 8L visibility increased to RVR 5000 for inoperative MM.
Sidestep Rwy 8R inoperative table does not apply to ALSF-2 for Categories A and B.

FAF to MAP 5.2 NM

Knots	60	90	120	150	180
Min:Sec	5:12	3:28	2:36	2:05	1:44

FIGURE 122.—ILS RWY 8L (ATL).

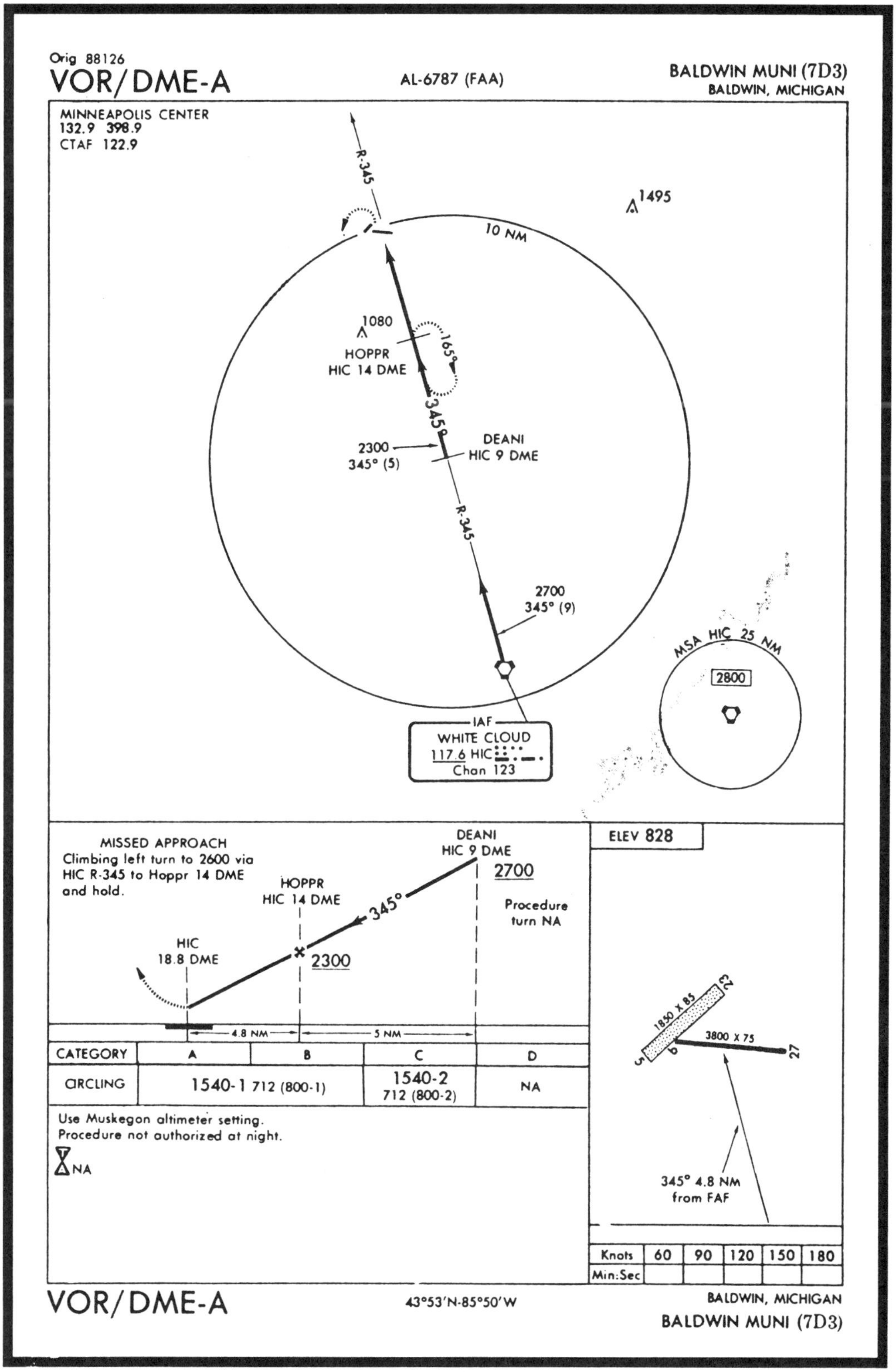

FIGURE 123.—VOR/DME-A (7D3).

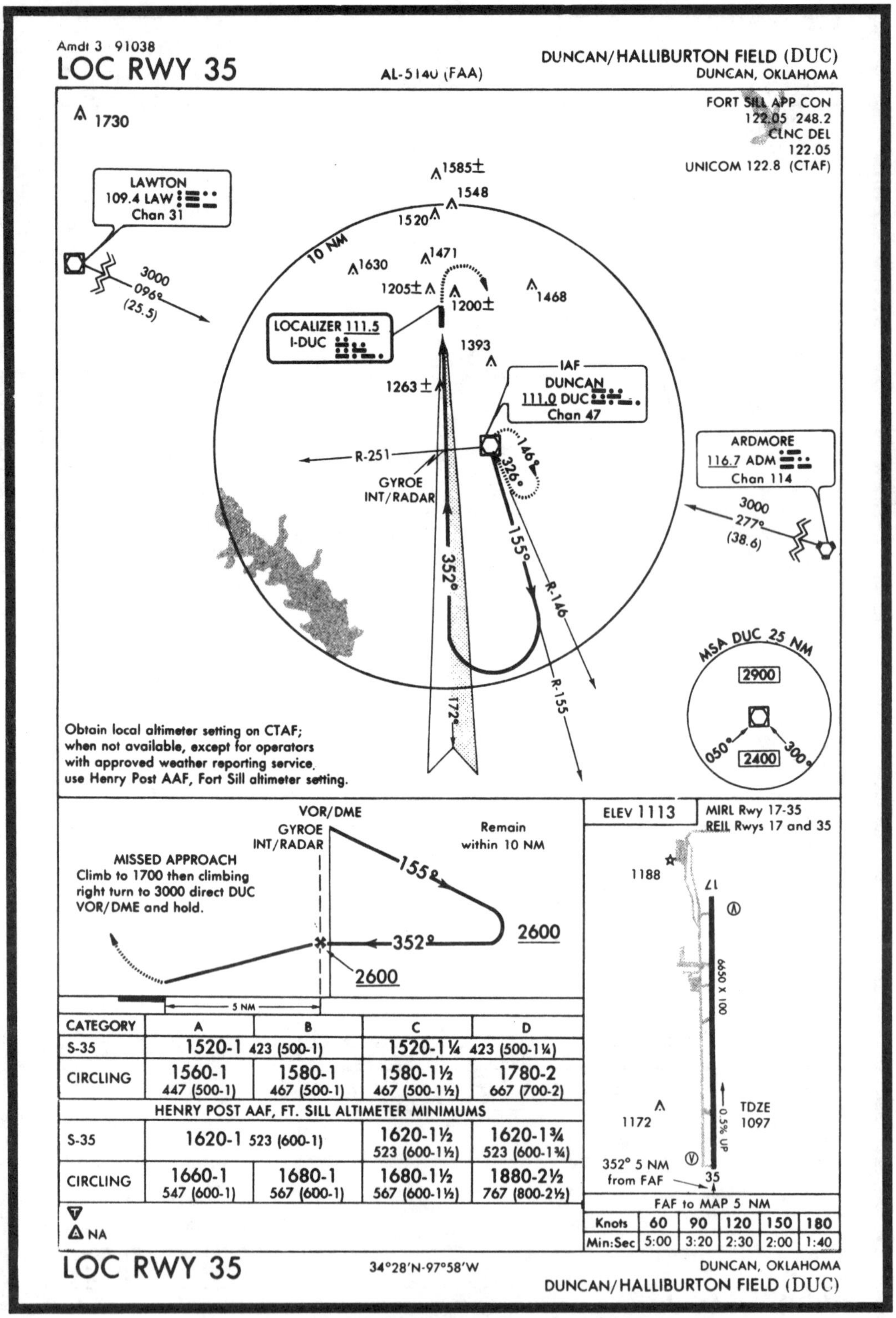

FIGURE 124.—LOC RWY 35, Duncan, Oklahoma.

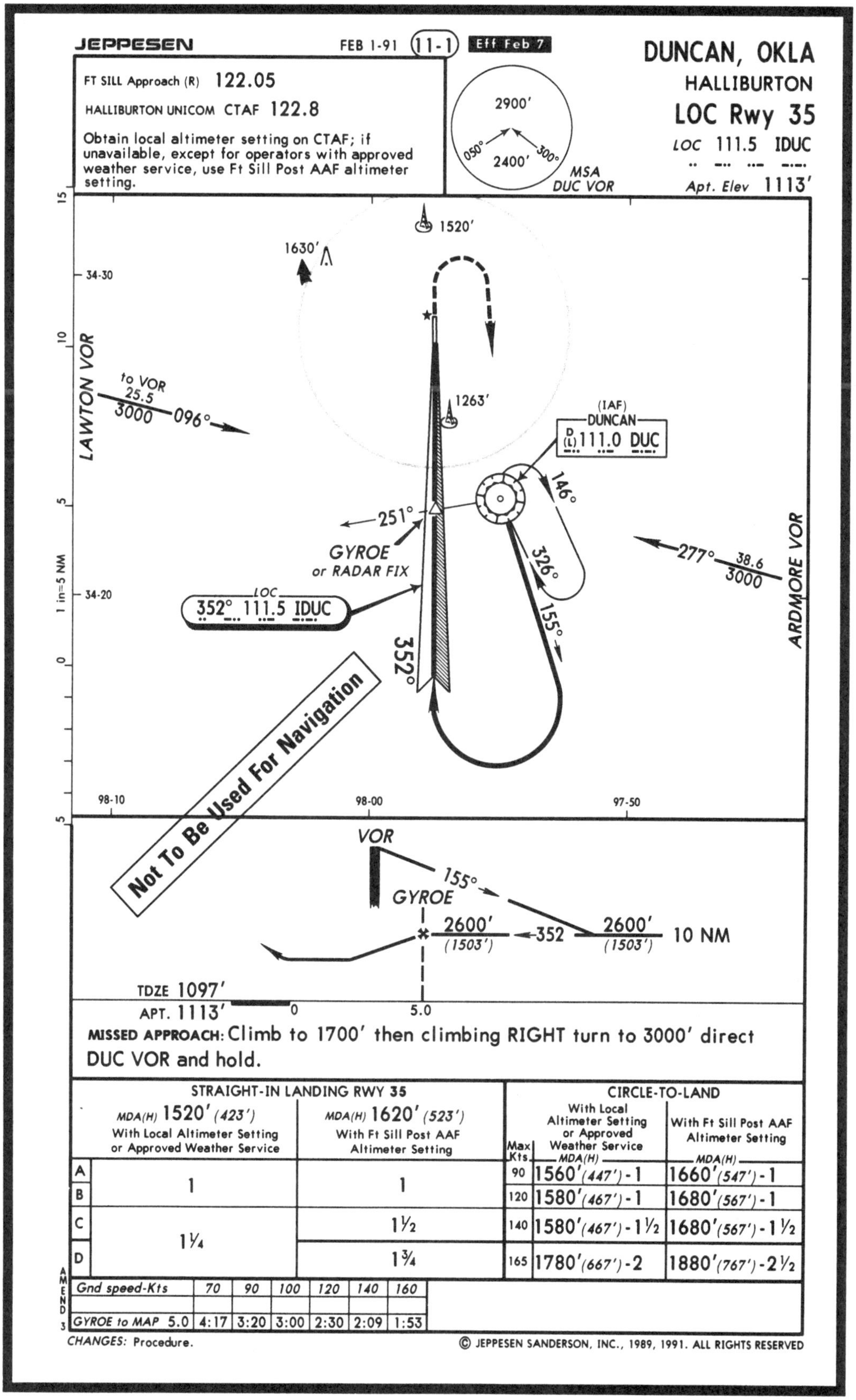

FIGURE 124A.—LOC RWY 35, Duncan, Oklahoma.

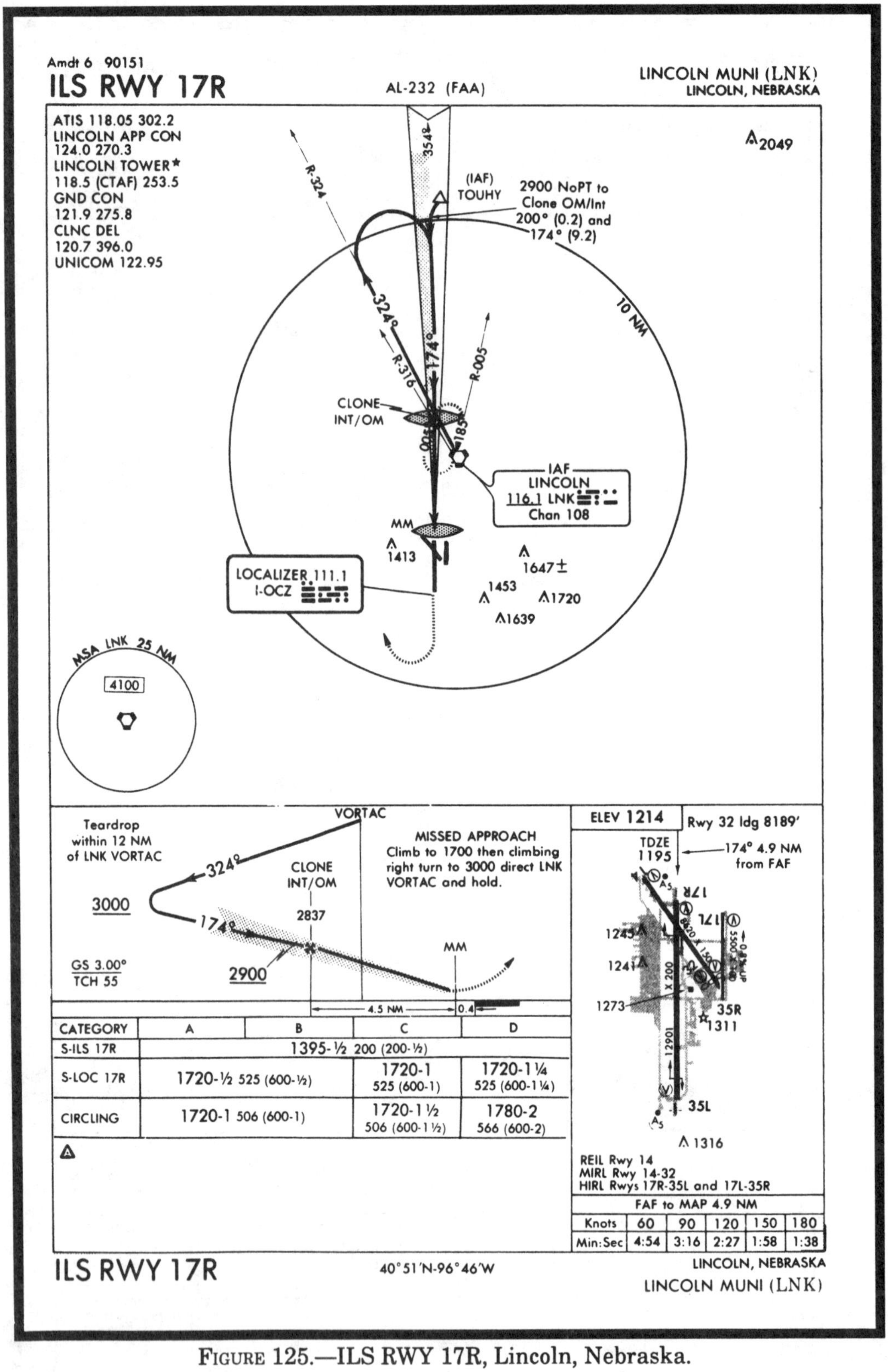

Appendix 3

FIGURE 125.—ILS RWY 17R, Lincoln, Nebraska.

JEPPESEN NOV 17-89 (11-2)

LINCOLN, NEBR
LINCOLN MUN
ILS Rwy 17R

LOC 111.1 IOCZ

Apt. Elev 1214'

*ATIS 118.05
*LINCOLN Approach (R) 124.0
MINNEAPOLIS Center (R) 128.75 when App inop.
*LINCOLN Tower CTAF 118.5
Ground 121.9

4100' MSA LNK VOR

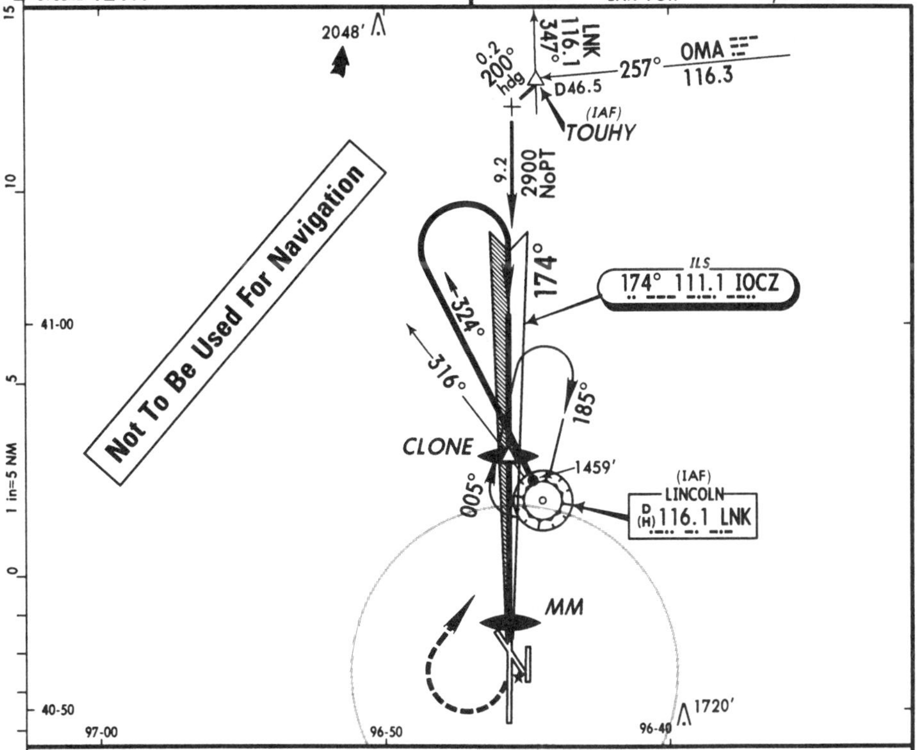

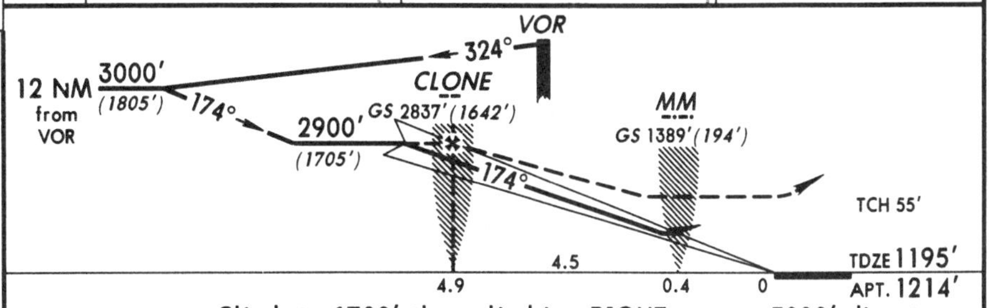

MISSED APPROACH: Climb to 1700' then climbing RIGHT turn to 3000' direct LNK VOR and hold.

<table>
<tr><th></th><th colspan="6">STRAIGHT-IN LANDING RWY 17R</th><th colspan="2">CIRCLE-TO-LAND</th></tr>
<tr><th></th><th colspan="3">ILS</th><th colspan="3">LOC (GS out)</th><th colspan="2"></th></tr>
<tr><th></th><th colspan="2">DA(H) 1395' (200')</th><th>DA(H) 1445' (250')</th><th colspan="3">MDA(H) 1720' (525')</th><th colspan="2"></th></tr>
<tr><th></th><th>FULL</th><th>RAIL or ALS out</th><th>MM out</th><th></th><th>RAIL out</th><th>ALS out</th><th>Max Kts</th><th>MDA(H)</th></tr>
<tr><td>A</td><td rowspan="4">1/2</td><td rowspan="4">3/4</td><td rowspan="3">1/2</td><td rowspan="2">1/2</td><td rowspan="2">3/4</td><td rowspan="2">1</td><td>90</td><td rowspan="2">1720'(506')-1</td></tr>
<tr><td>B</td><td>120</td></tr>
<tr><td>C</td><td>1</td><td colspan="2">1 1/2</td><td>140</td><td>1720'(506')-1 1/2</td></tr>
<tr><td>D</td><td>3/4</td><td>1 1/4</td><td colspan="2">1 3/4</td><td>165</td><td>1780'(566')-2</td></tr>
</table>

AMEND 6

Gnd speed-Kts	70	90	100	120	140	160
GS 3.00°	377	484	538	646	753	861
CLONE to MAP 4.9	4:12	3:16	2:56	2:27	2:06	1:50

CHANGES: Clone OM/Int formation.

FIGURE 125A.—ILS RWY 17R, Lincoln, Nebraska.

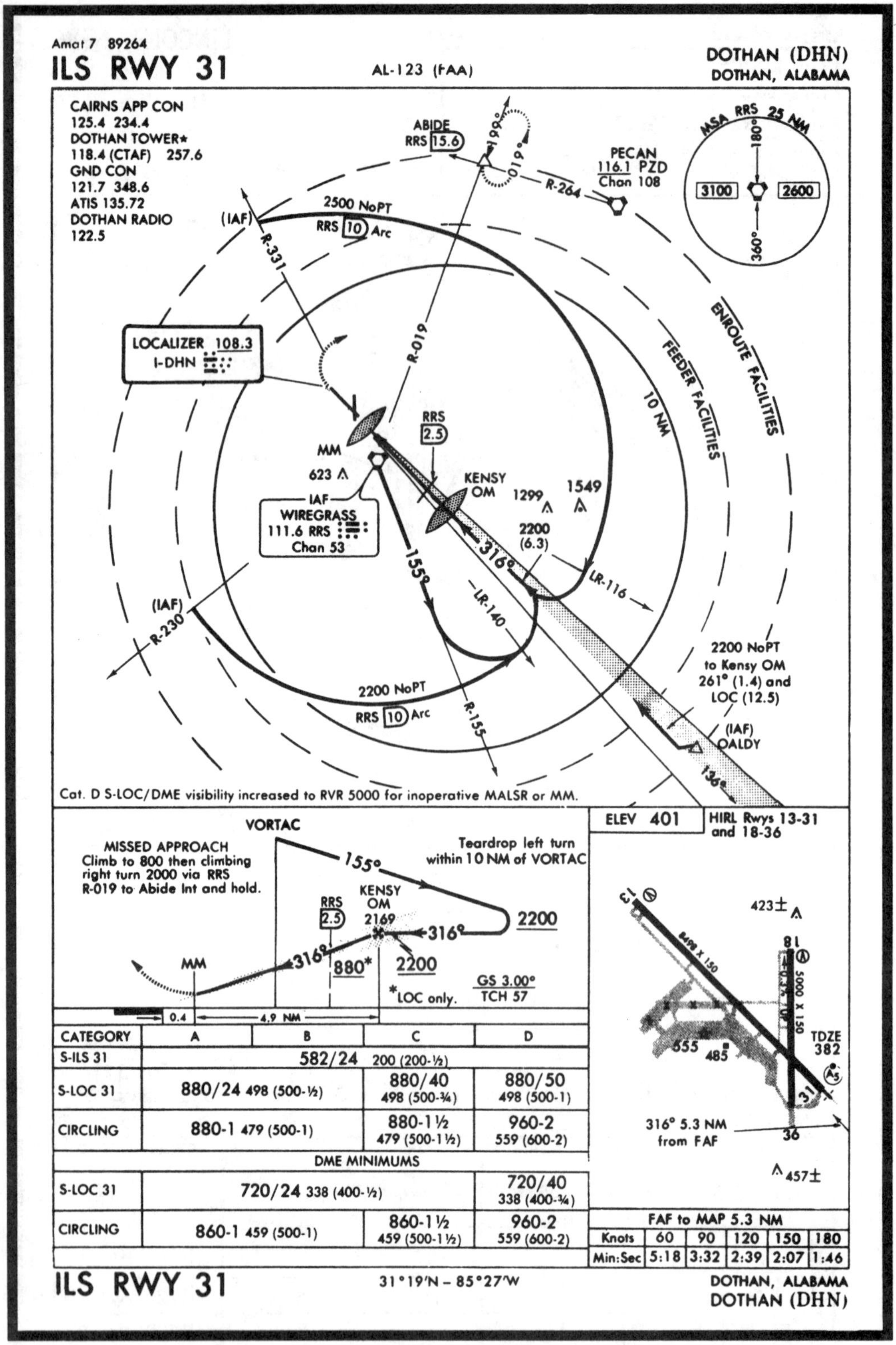

Appendix 3

FIGURE 126.—ILS RWY 31, Dothan, Alabama.

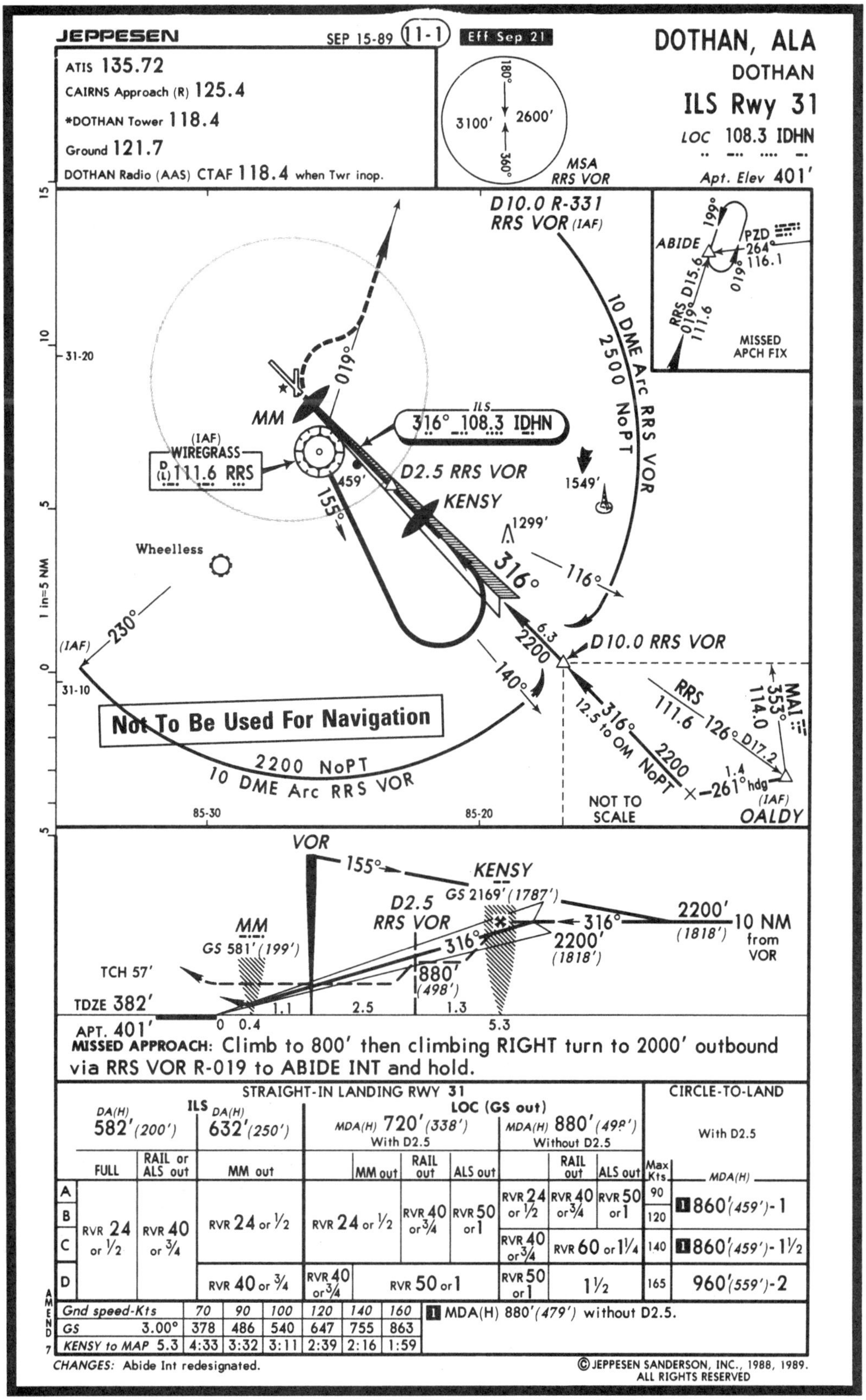

Appendix 3

FIGURE 126A.—ILS RWY 31, Dothan, Alabama.

NDB RWY 28

AL-6212 (FAA)

LANCASTER/FAIRFIELD COUNTY (I15)
LANCASTER, OHIO

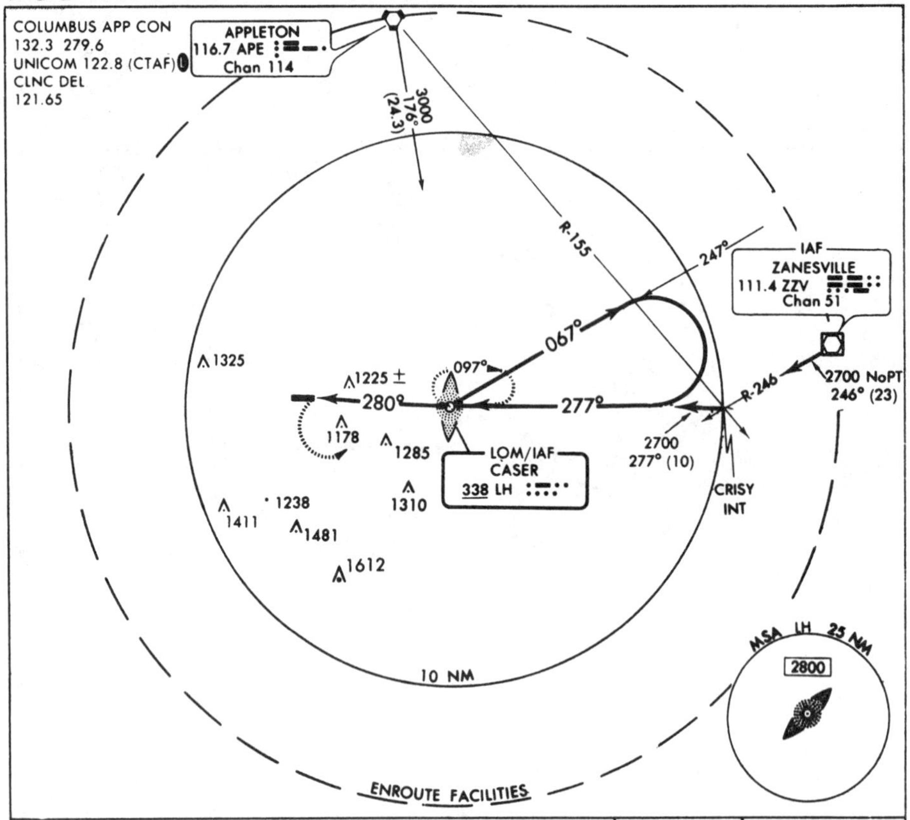

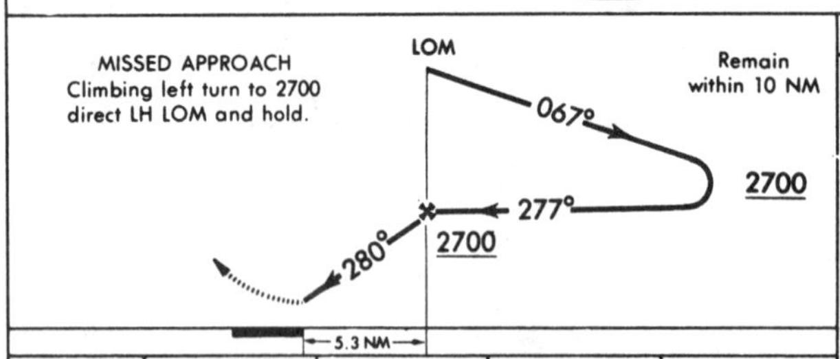

CATEGORY	A	B	C	D
S-28	1620-1 754 (800-1)	1620-1¼ 754 (800-1¼)	1620-2¼ 754 (800-2¼)	1620-2½ 754 (800-2½)
CIRCLING	1620-1 754 (800-1)	1620-1¼ 754 (800-1¼)	1620-2¼ 754 (800-2¼)	1620-2½ 754 (800-2½)

Use Columbus/Rickenbacker altimeter setting.

▽T

△A NA

ELEV 869

Rwy 28 ldg 4724'
Rwy 10 ldg 4874'

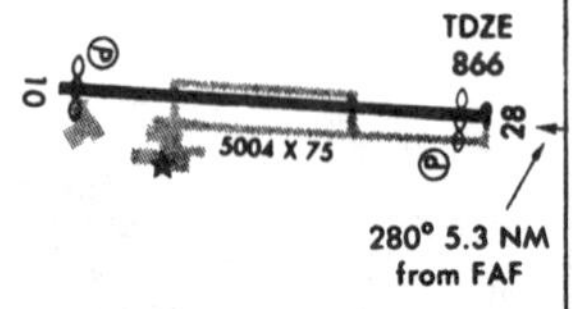

REIL Rwys 10 and 28
MIRL Rwy 10-28

FAF to MAP 5.3 NM					
Knots	60	90	120	150	180
Min:Sec	5:18	3:32	2:39	2:07	1:46

NDB RWY 28

39°45'N-82°39'W

LANCASTER, OHIO
LANCASTER/FAIRFIELD COUNTY (I15)

FIGURE 127.—NDB RWY 28, Lancaster/Fairfield County.

FIGURE 127A.—NDB RWY 28, Lancaster, Ohio.

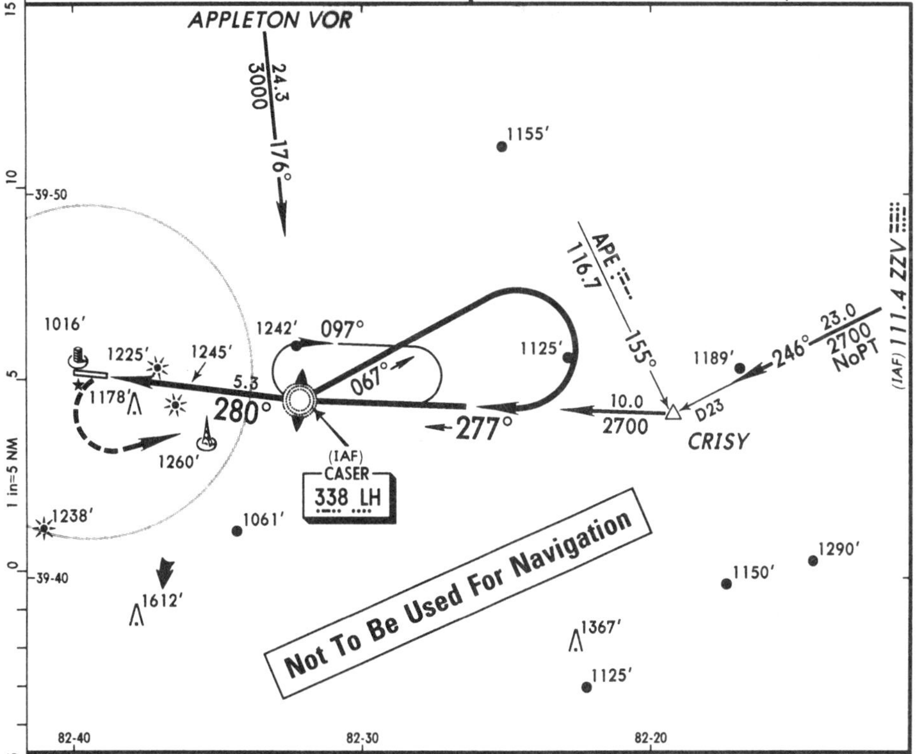

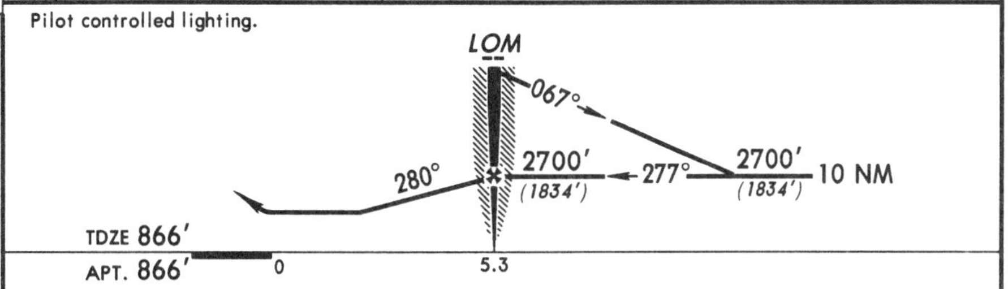

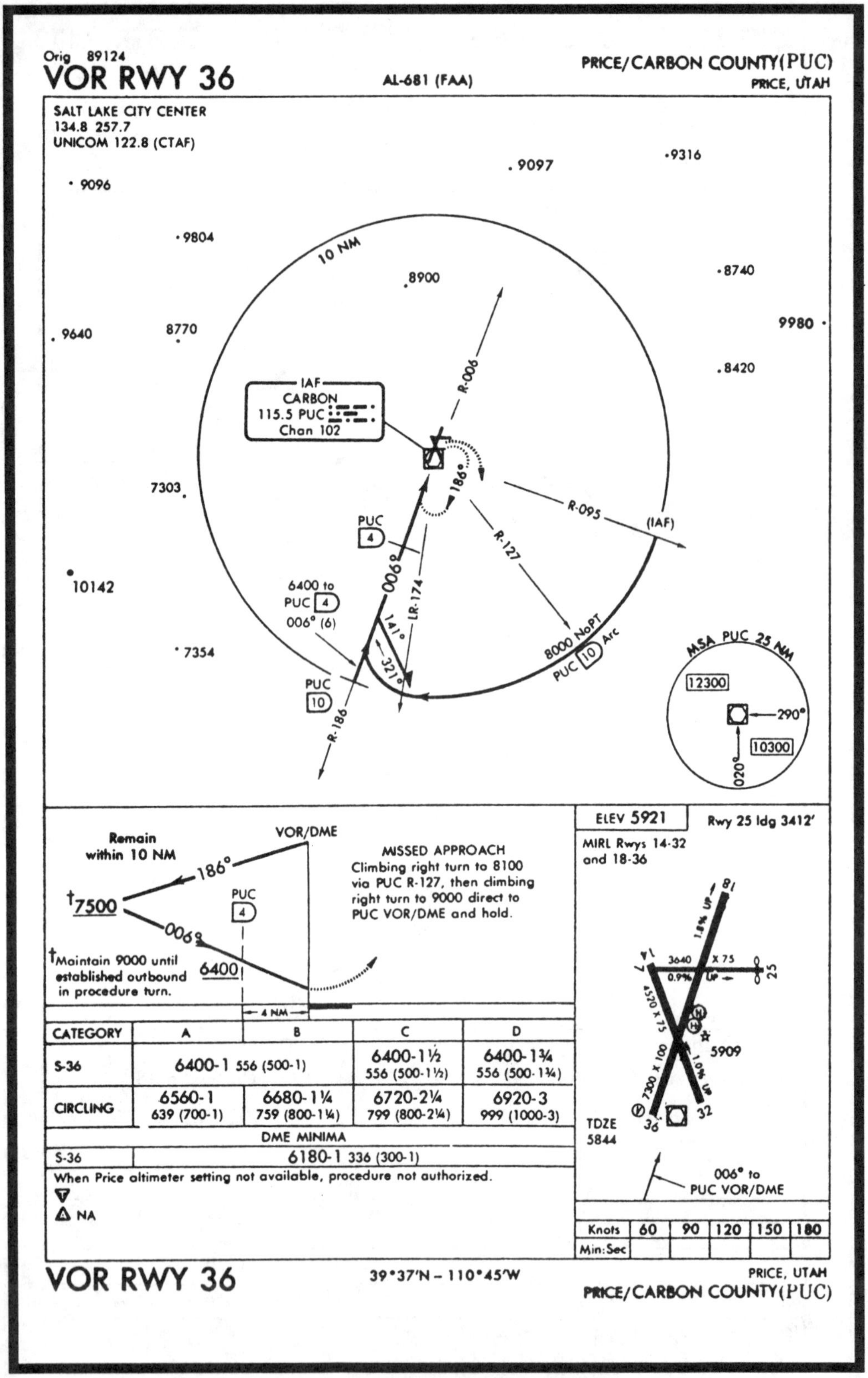

Appendix 3

FIGURE 128.—VOR RWY 36 (PUC).

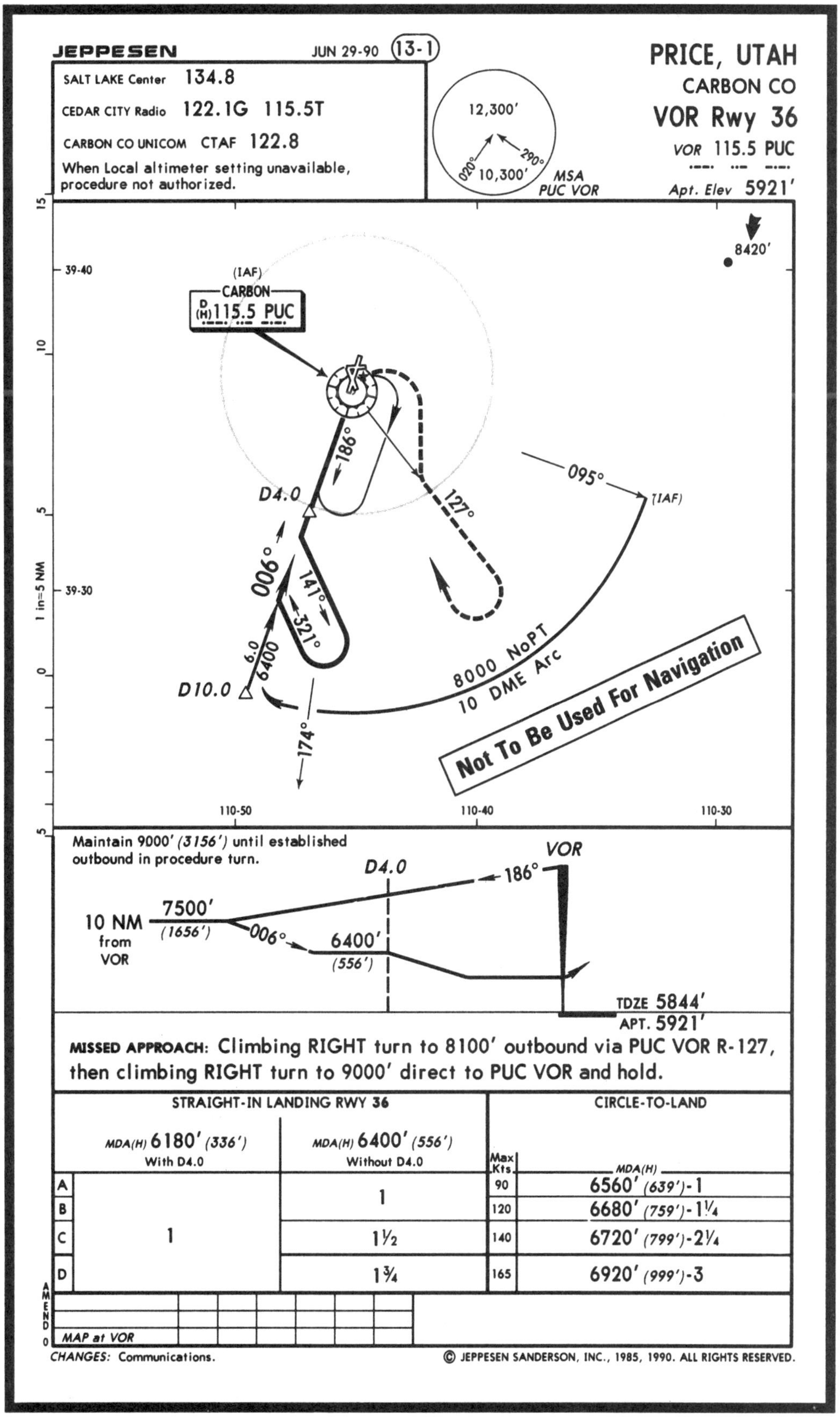

FIGURE 128A.—VOR RWY 36 (PUC).

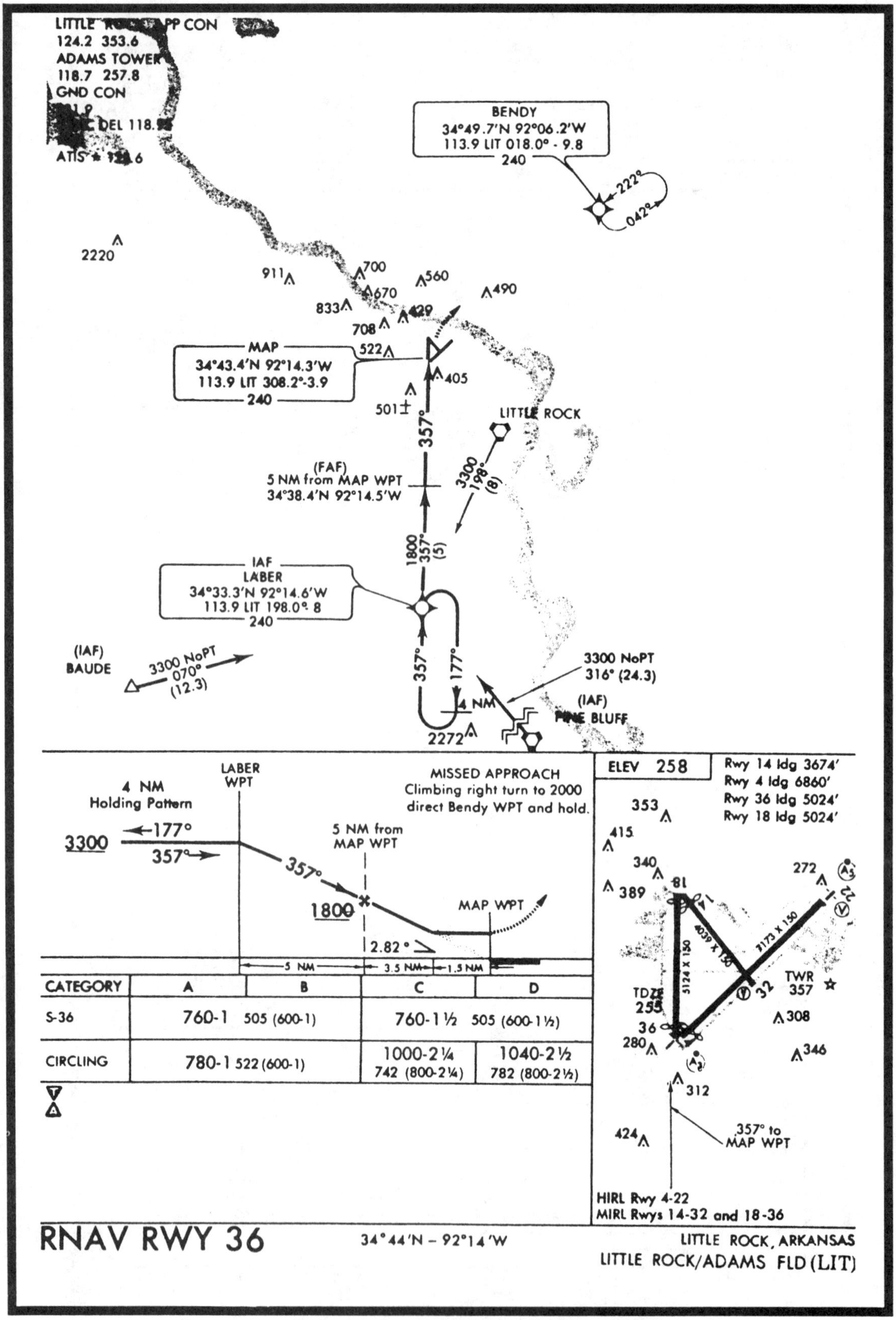

CATEGORY	A	B	C	D
S-36	760-1 505 (600-1)		760-1½ 505 (600-1½)	
CIRCLING	780-1 522 (600-1)		1000-2¼ 742 (800-2¼)	1040-2½ 782 (800-2½)

FIGURE 129.—RNAV RWY 36 (LIT).

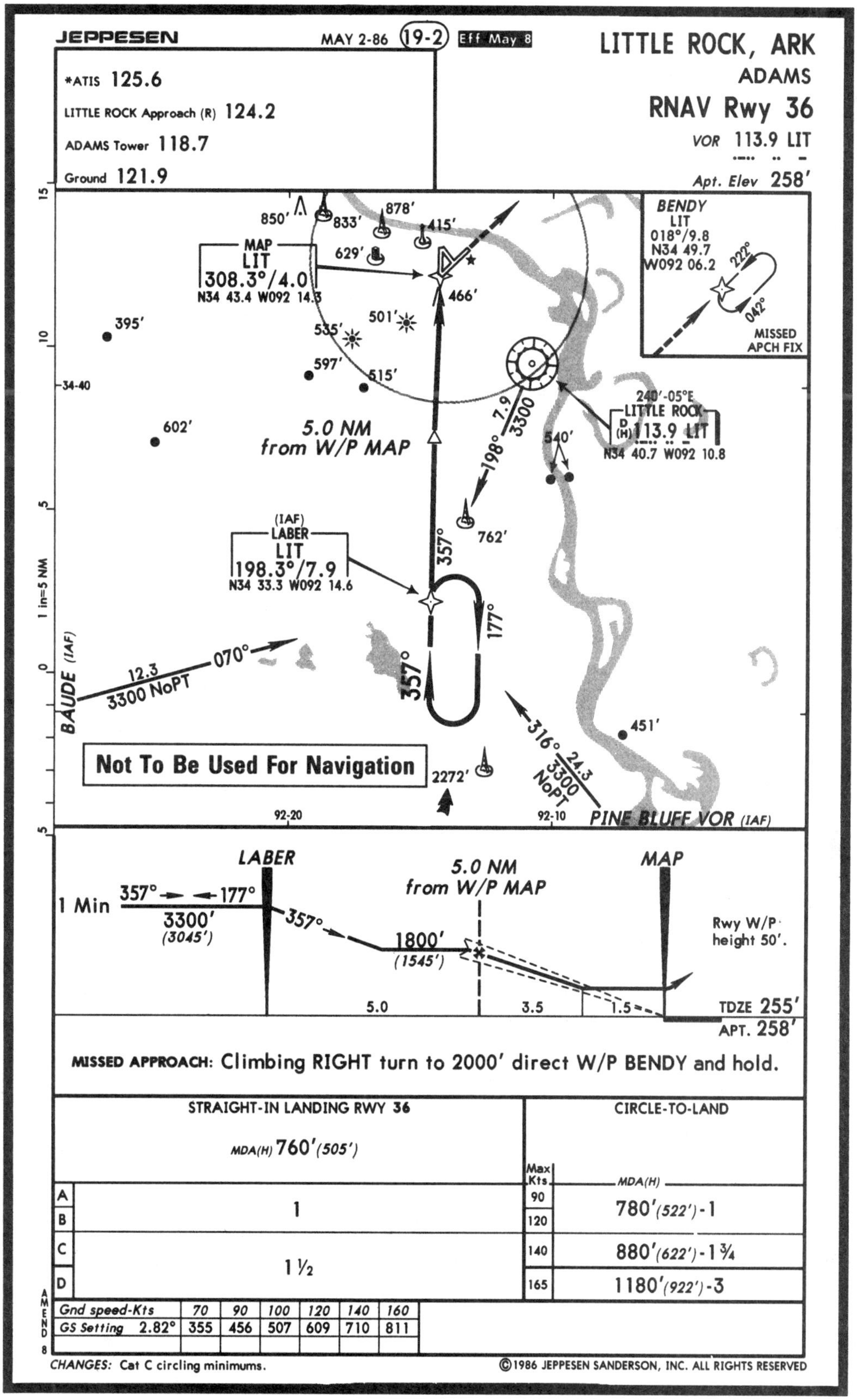

FIGURE 129A.—RNAV RWY 36 (LIT).

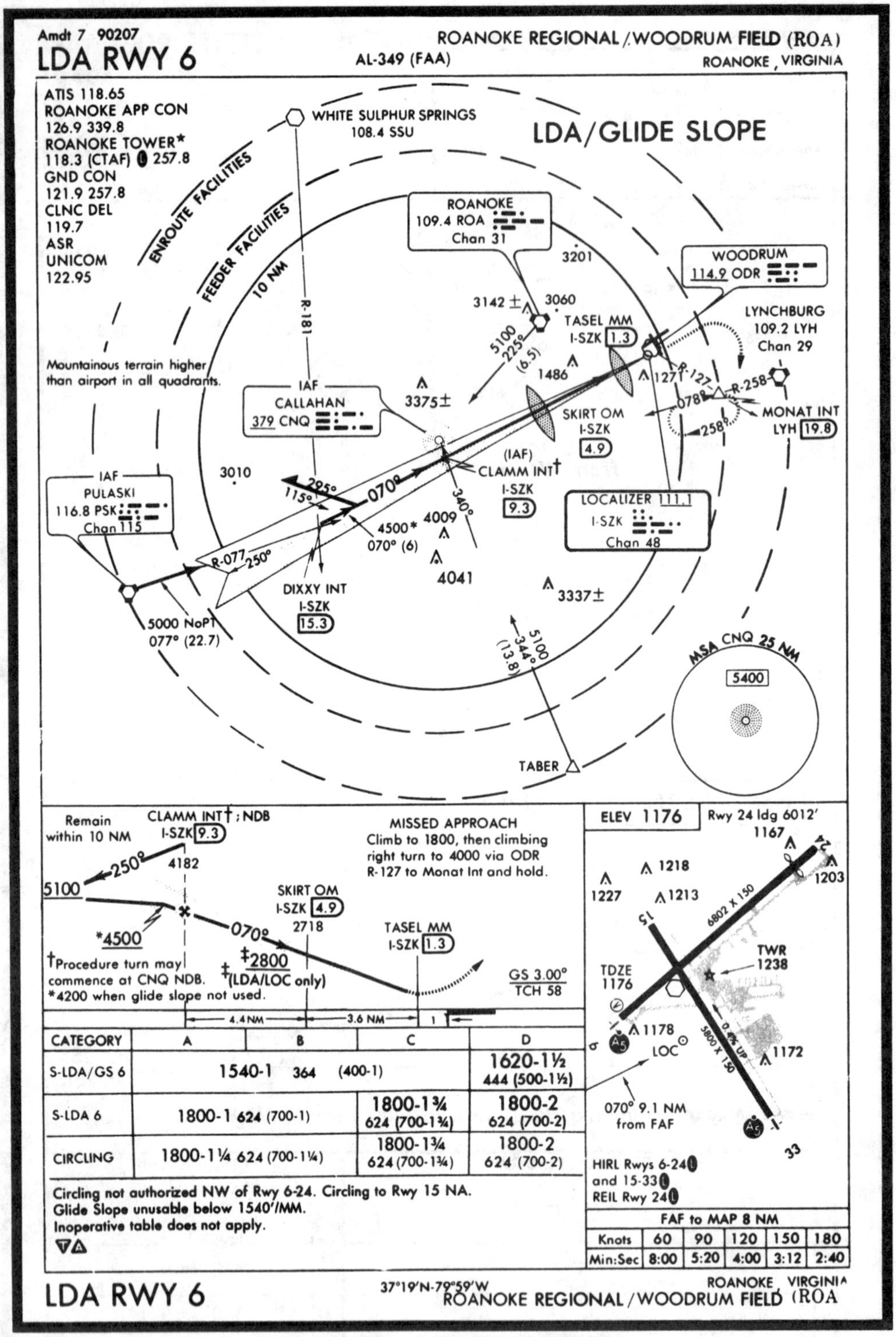

FIGURE 130.—LDA RWY 6 (ROA).

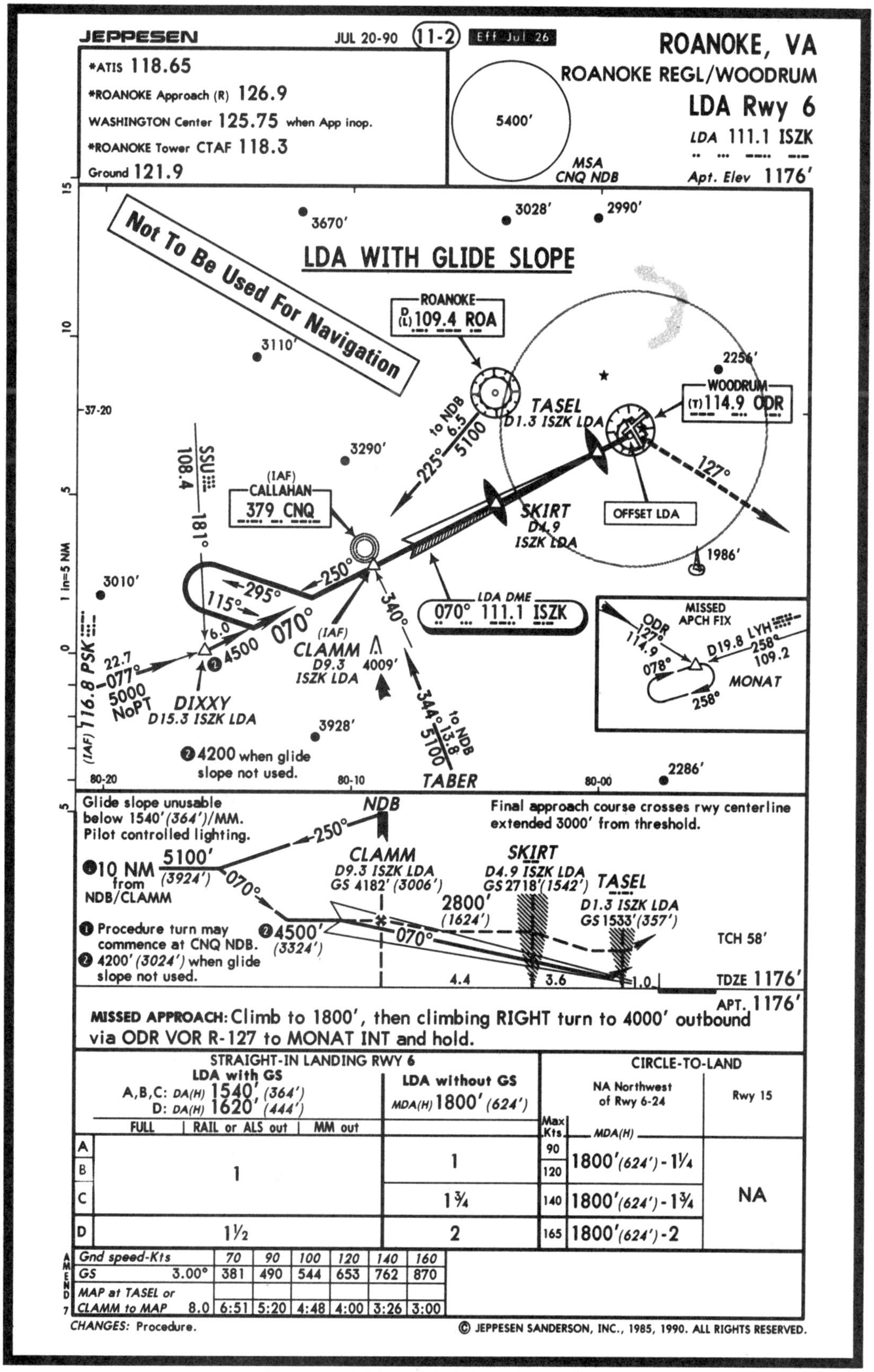

FIGURE 130A.—LDA RWY 6 (ROA).

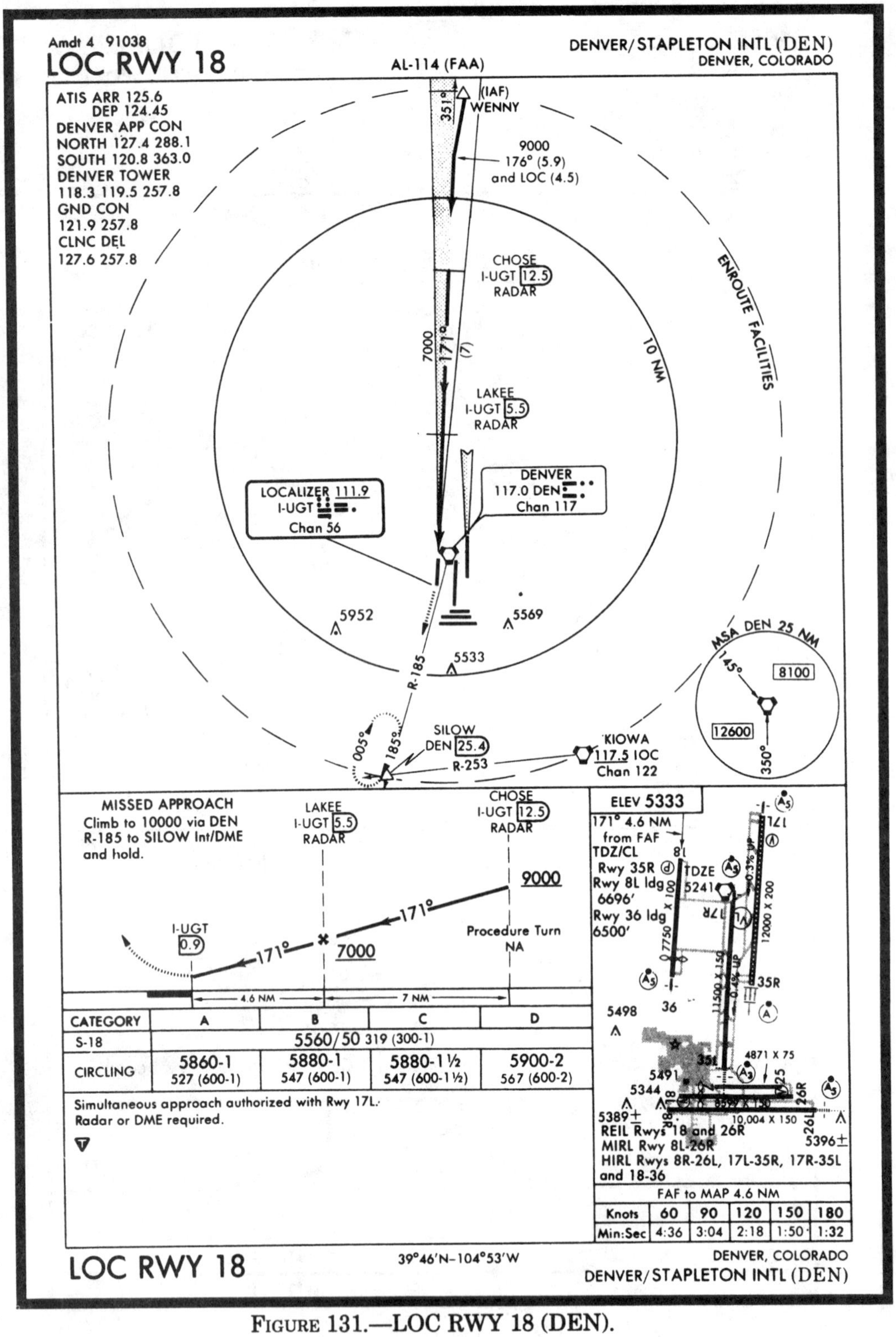

CATEGORY	A	B	C	D
S-18	5560/50 319 (300-1)			
CIRCLING	5860-1 527 (600-1)	5880-1 547 (600-1)	5880-1½ 547 (600-1½)	5900-2 567 (600-2)

FAF to MAP 4.6 NM					
Knots	60	90	120	150	180
Min:Sec	4:36	3:04	2:18	1:50	1:32

FIGURE 131.—LOC RWY 18 (DEN).

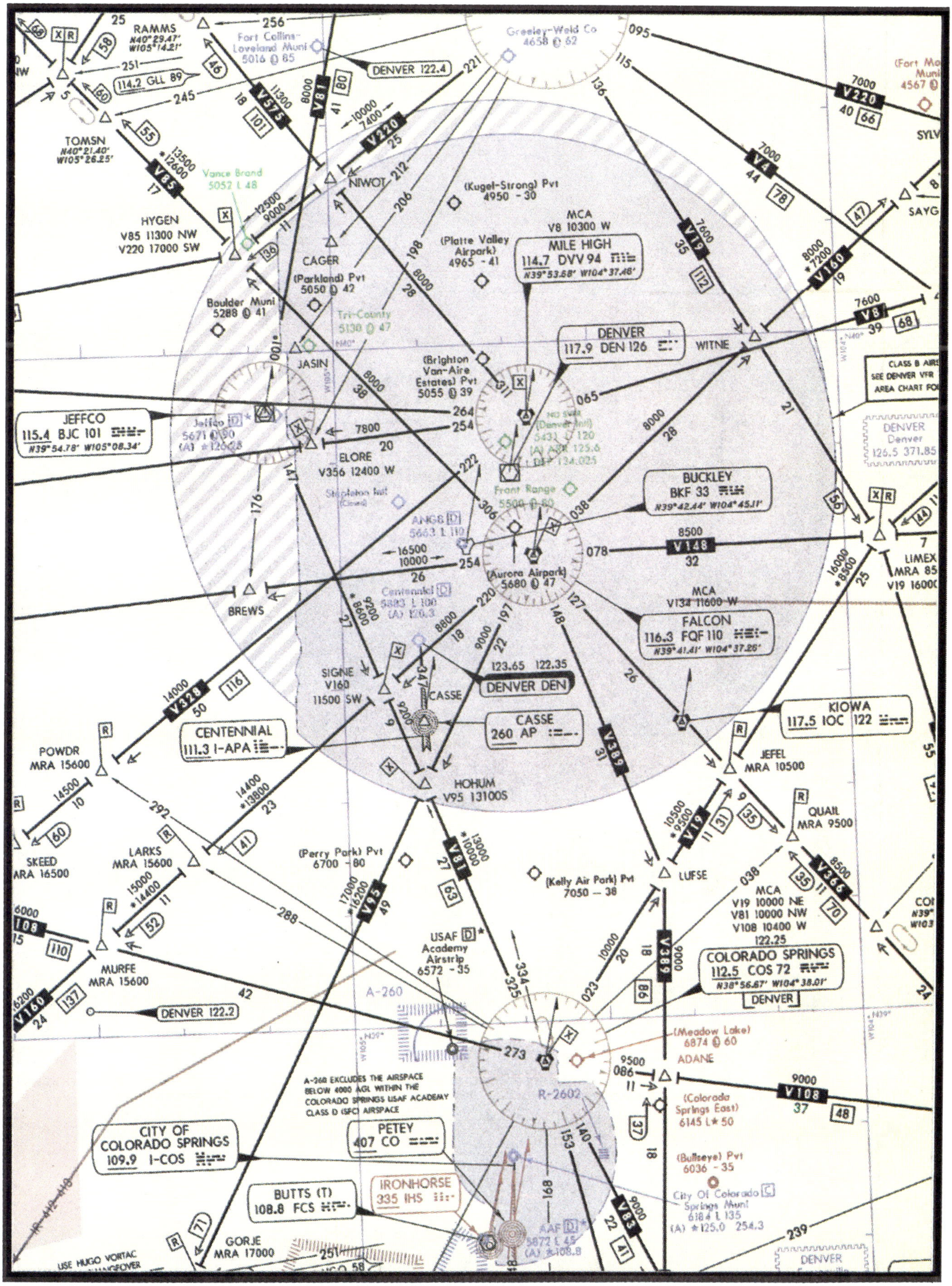

Appendix 3

FIGURE 132.—Terminal Area Chart.

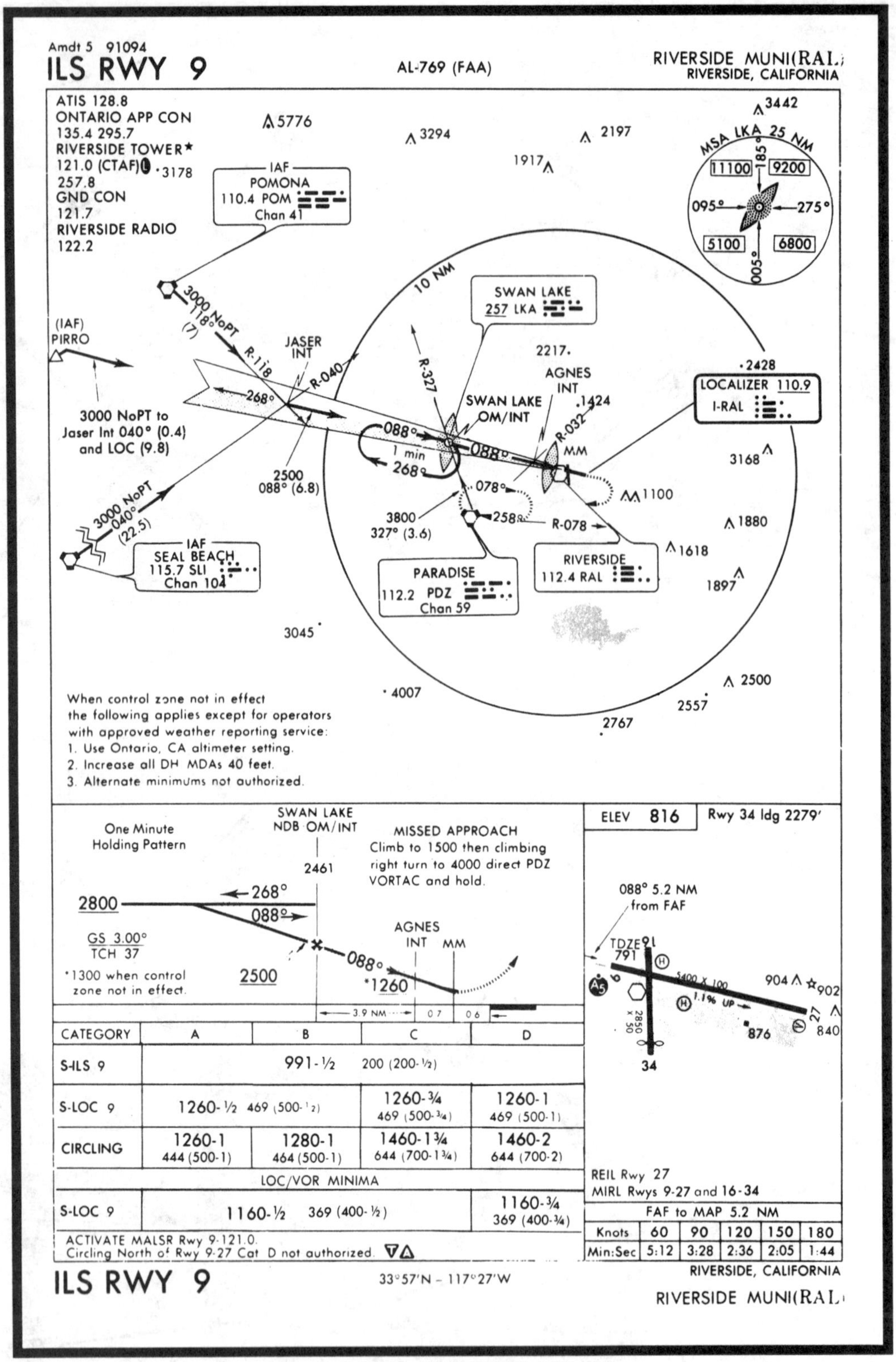

FIGURE 133.—ILS RWY 9 (RAL).

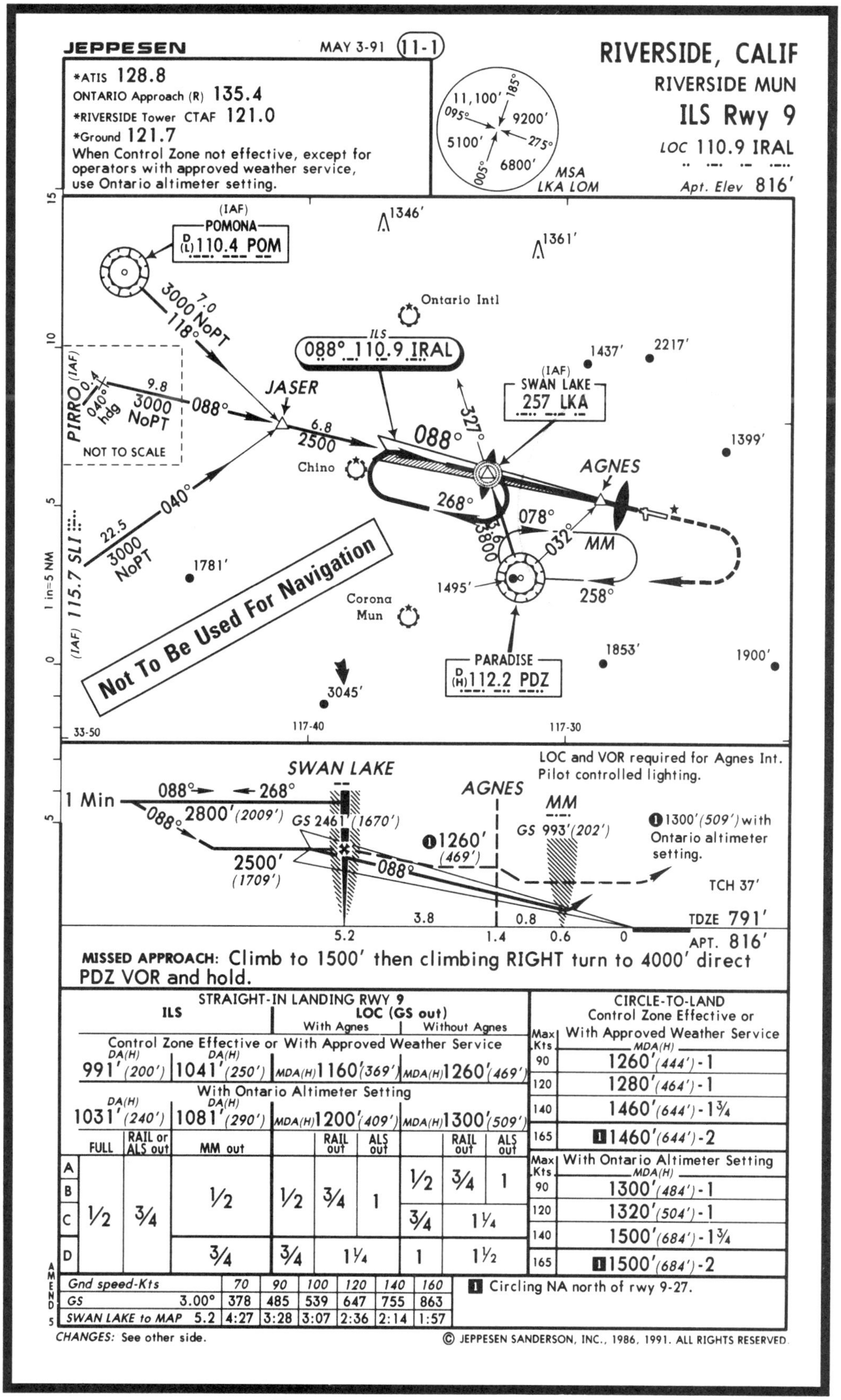

FIGURE 133A.—ILS RWY 9.

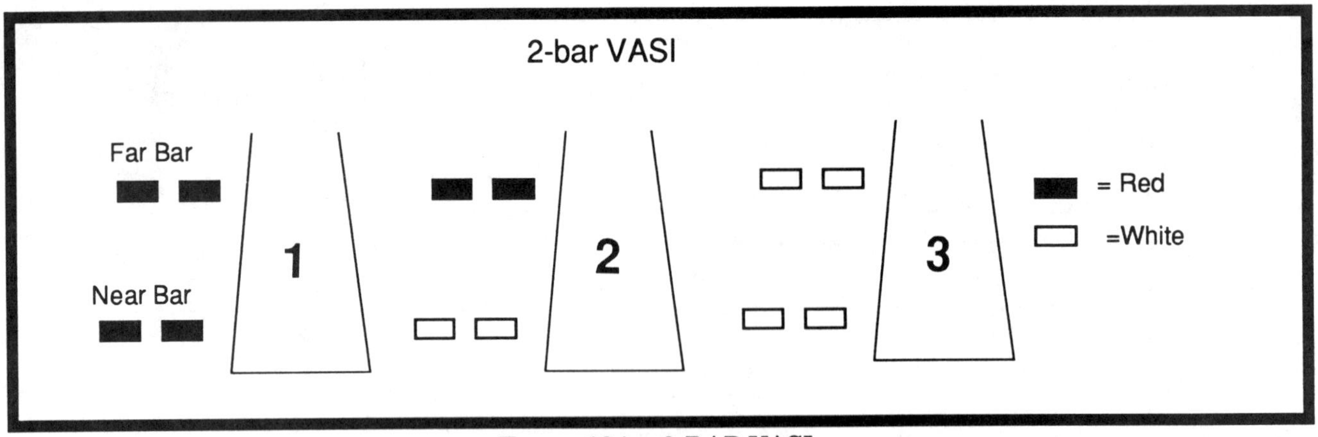

Appendix 3

FIGURE 134.—2-BAR VASI.

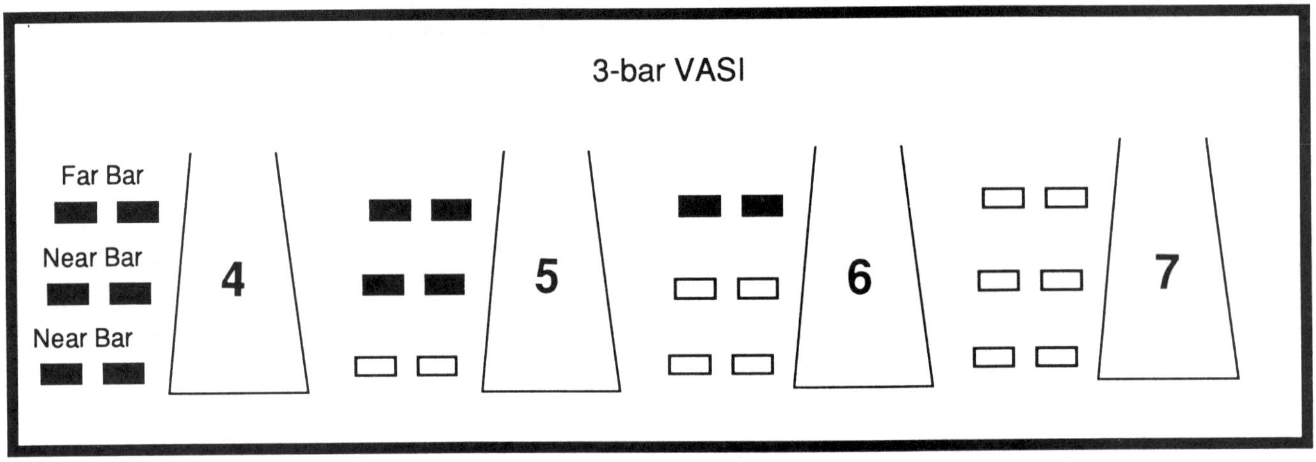

FIGURE 135.—3-BAR VASI.

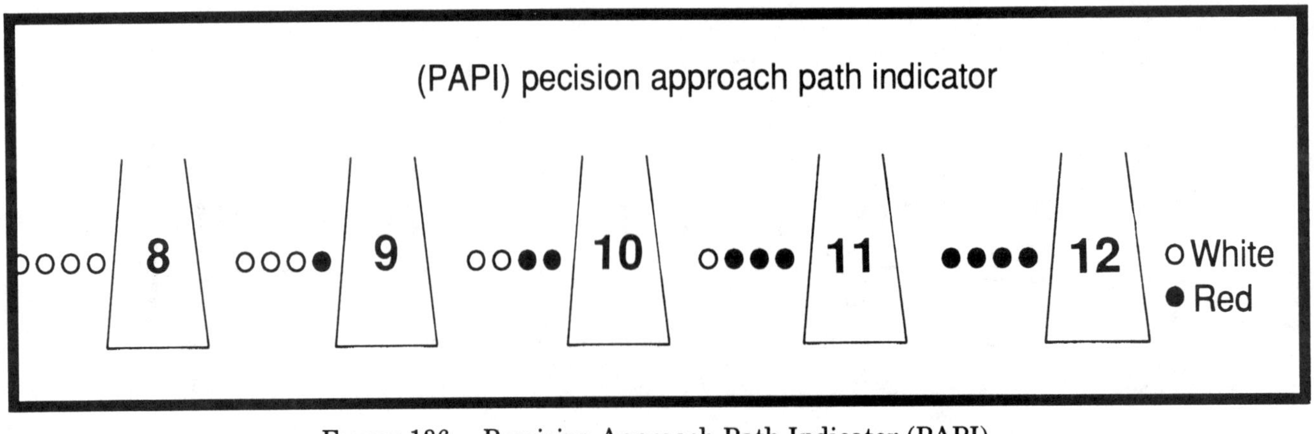

FIGURE 136.—Precision Approach Path Indicator (PAPI).

152

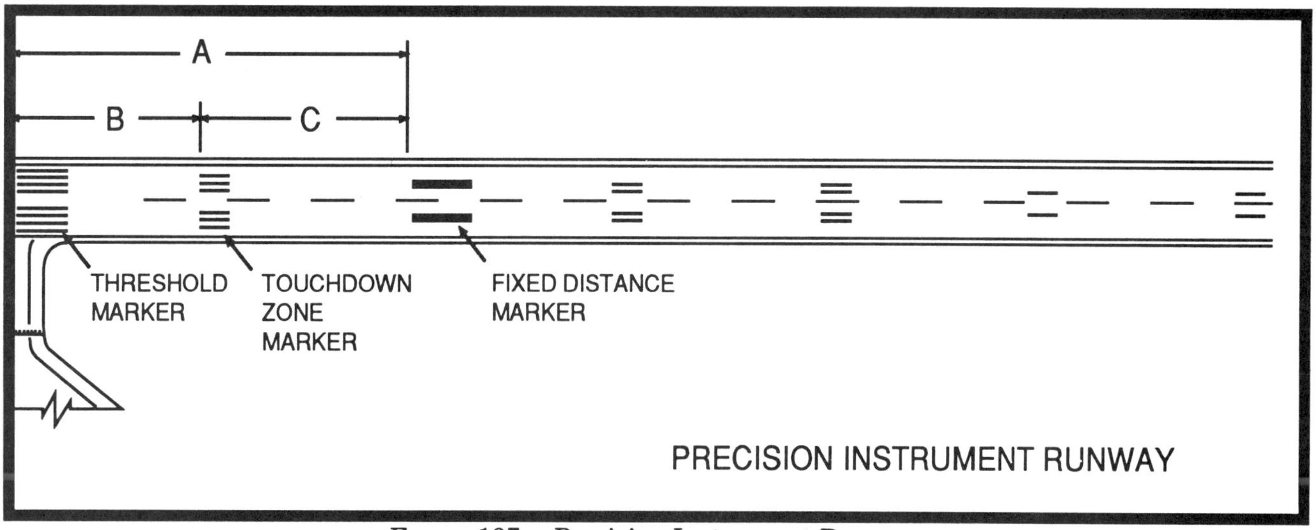

Appendix 3

FIGURE 137.—Precision Instrument Runway.

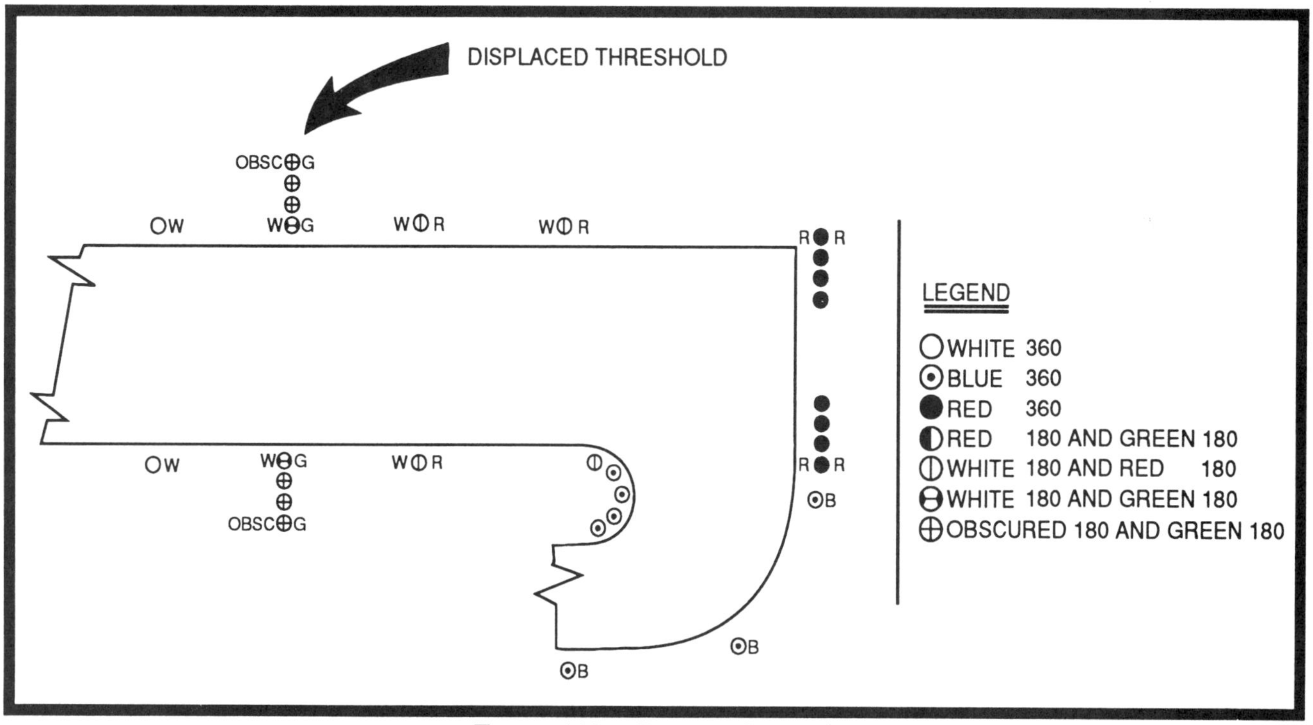

FIGURE 138.—Runway Legend.

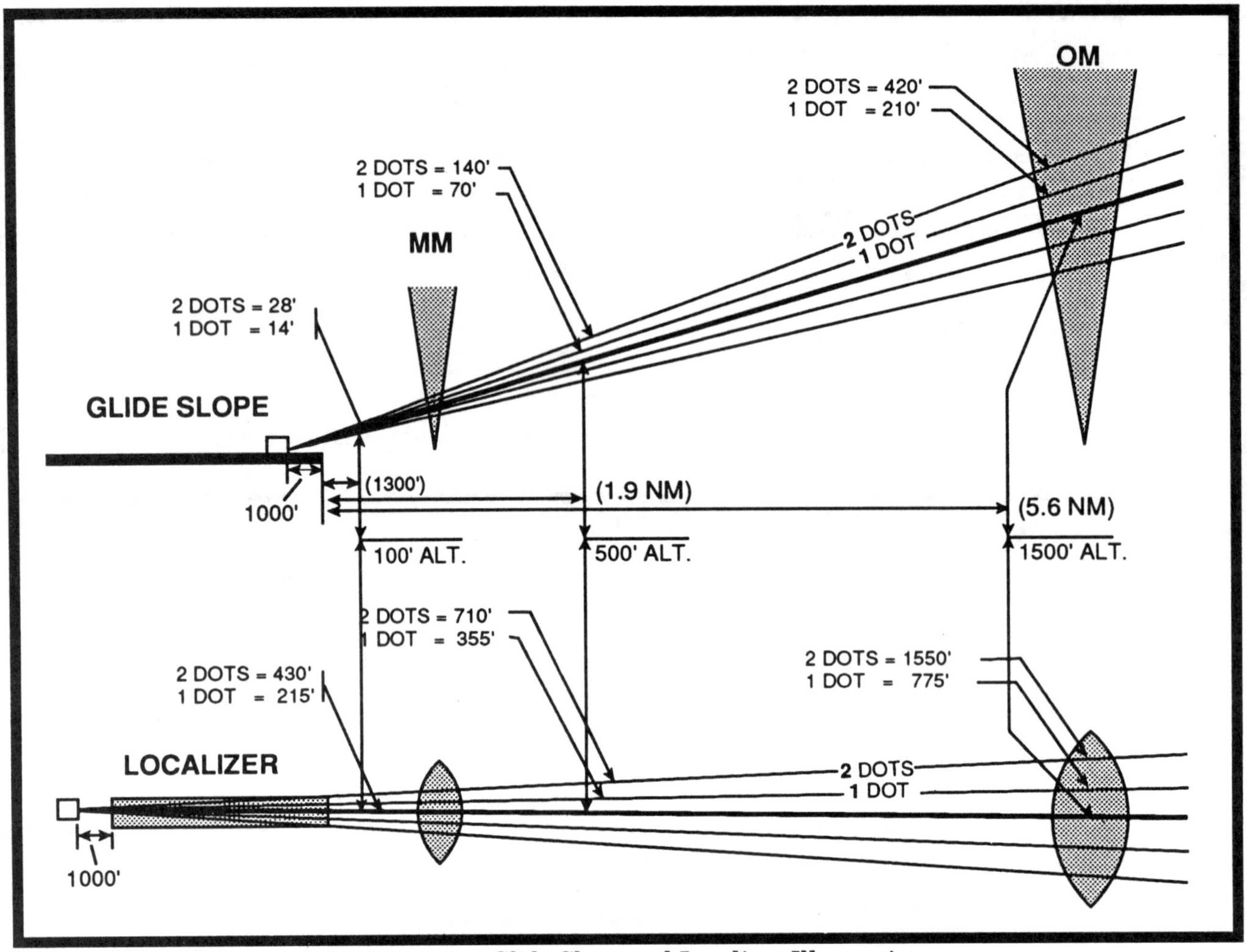

Appendix 3

FIGURE 139.—Glide Slope and Localizer Illustration.

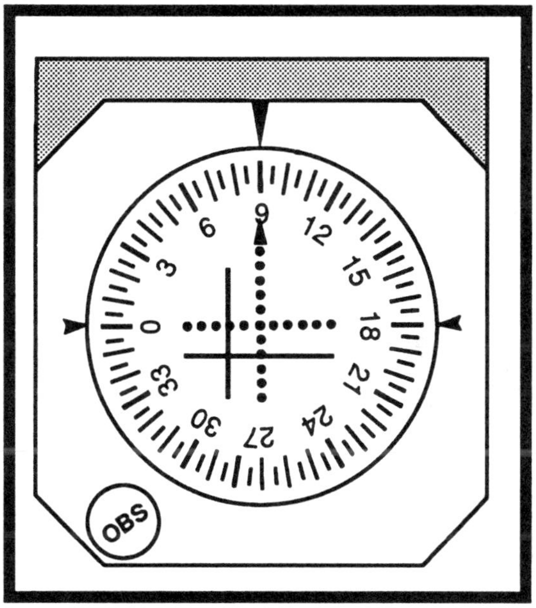

Appendix 3

FIGURE 140.—OBS, ILS, and GS Displacement.

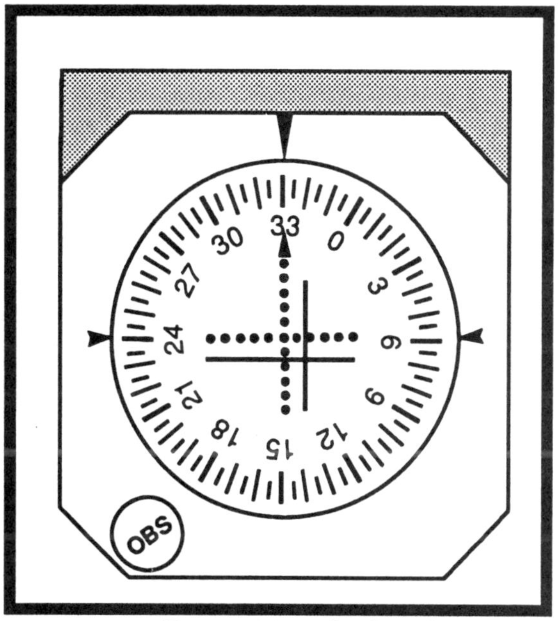

FIGURE 141.—OBS, ILS, and GS Displacement.

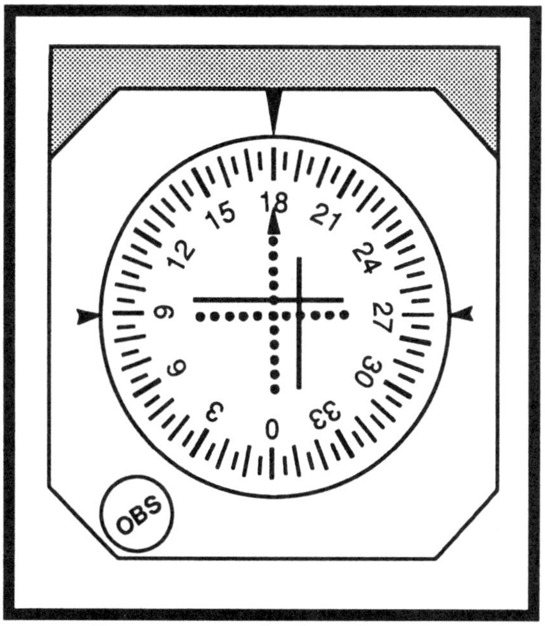

FIGURE 142.—OBS, ILS, and GS Displacement.

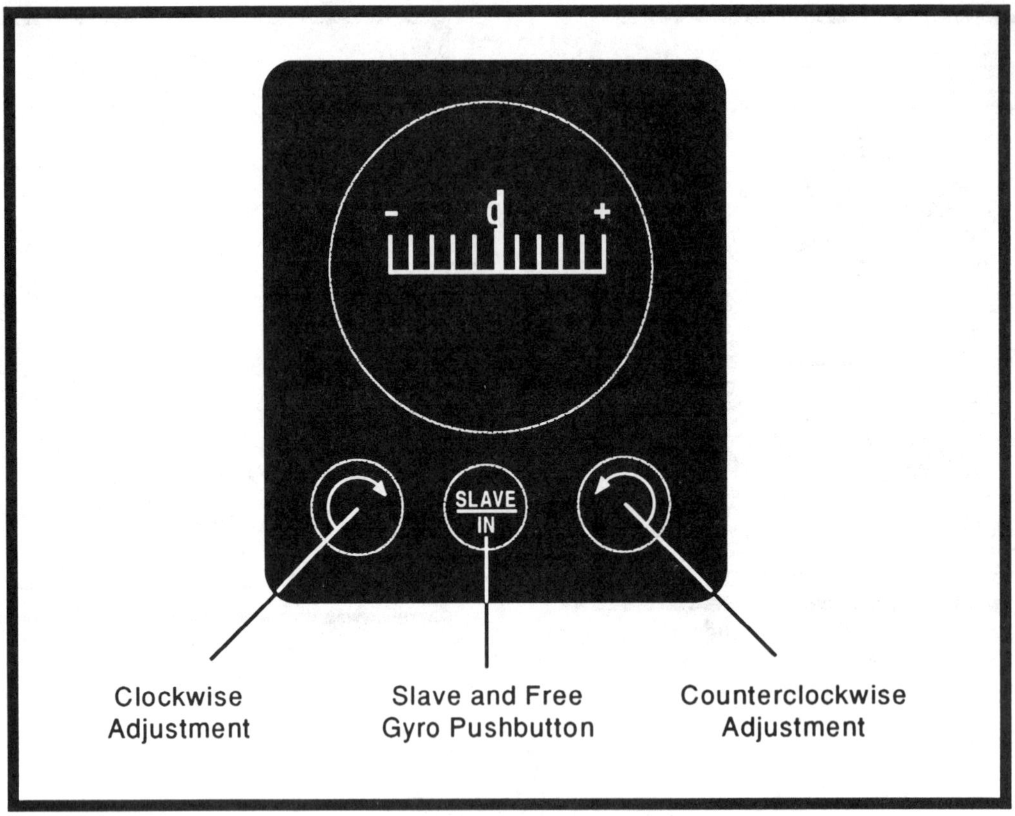

Appendix 3

FIGURE 143.—Slaved Gyro Illustration.

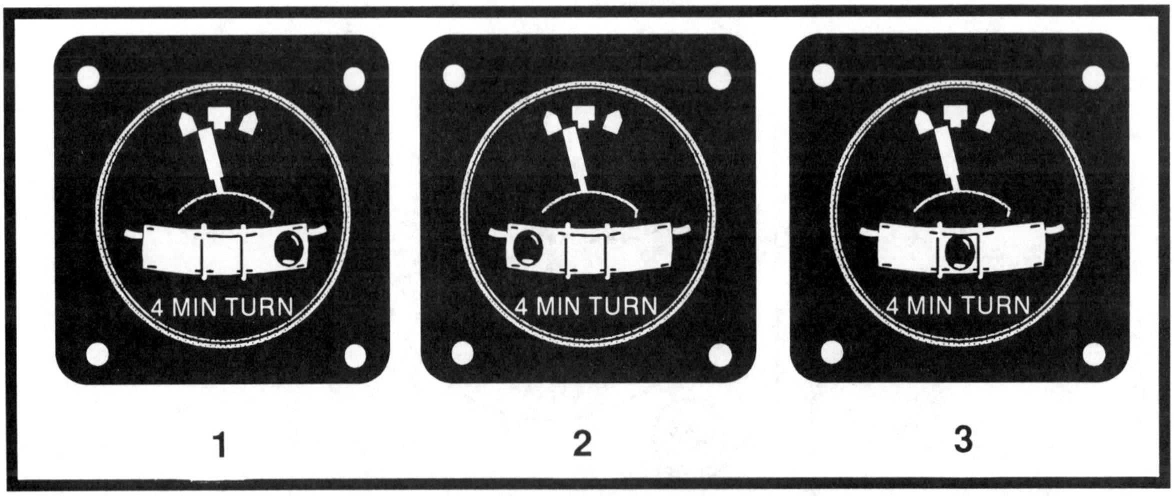

FIGURE 144.—Turn-and-Slip Indicator.

Appendix 3

FIGURE 145.—Instrument Sequence (Unusual Attitude).

Appendix 3

FIGURE 146.—Instrument Sequence (System Failed).

Appendix 3

FIGURE 147.—Instrument Sequence (Unusual Attitude).

Appendix 3

FIGURE 148.—Instrument Interpretation (System Malfunction).

Appendix 3

FIGURE 149.—Instrument Interpretation (System Malfunction).

Appendix 3

FIGURE 150.—Instrument Interpretation (Instrument Malfunction).

Appendix 3

FIGURE 151.—Instrument Interpretation (Instrument Malfunction).

Appendix 3

FIGURE 152.—Instrument Interpretation (System Failed).